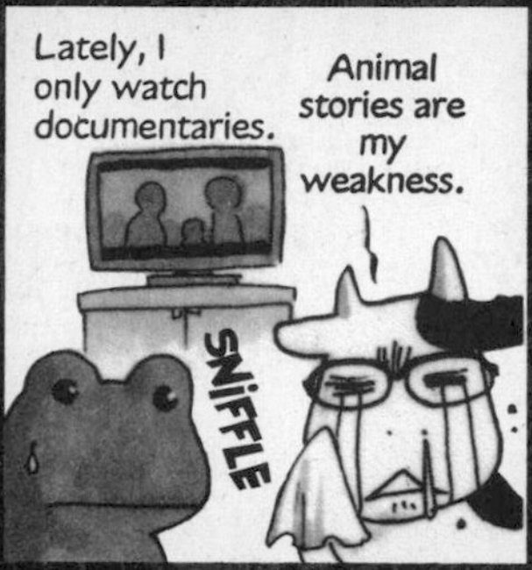
Lately, I only watch documentaries.
Animal stories are my weakness.
SNIFFLE

"Truth is stranger than fiction," as the old saying goes. When I watch a documentary, I can't help crying and then I think to myself, "Fiction can't compete with this." But when I mentioned this to a veteran manga artist friend of mine he said that "fiction brings salvation to characters in stories that would otherwise have no salvation at all." His words strengthened the conviction of my manga spirit.

—Hiromu Arakawa, 2005

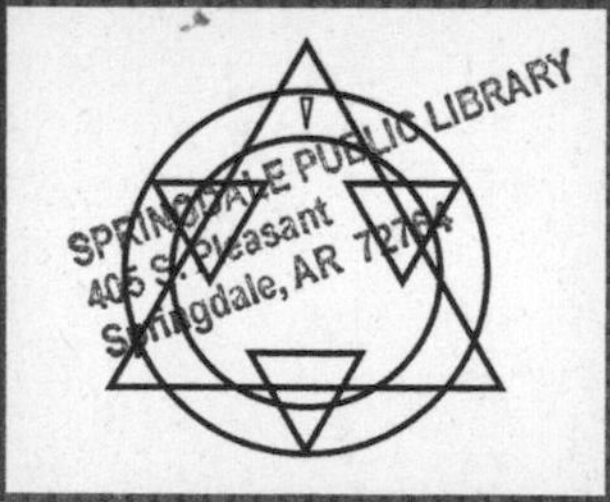
SPRINGDALE PUBLIC LIBRARY
405 S. Pleasant
Springdale, AR 72764

Born in Hokkaido (northern Japan), Hiromu Arakawa first attracted national attention in 1999 with her award-winning manga *Stray Dog*. Her series *Fullmetal Alchemist* debuted in 2001 in Square Enix's monthly manga anthology *Shonen Gangan*.

FULLMETAL ALCHEMIST
VOL. 12

VIZ Media Edition

Story and Art by Hiromu Arakawa

Translation/Akira Watanabe
English Adaptation/Jake Forbes
Touch-up Art & Lettering/Wayne Truman
Design/Amy Martin
Editor/Andy Nakatani

Hagane no RenkinJutsushi vol. 12 © 2005 Hiromu Arakawa/SQUARE
ENIX. First published in Japan in 2005 by SQUARE ENIX CO., LTD.
English translation rights arranged with SQUARE ENIX CO., LTD. and
VIZ Media, LLC.

Printed in the U.S.A.

Published by VIZ Media, LLC
P.O. Box 77010
San Francisco, CA 94107

10 9 8 7 6 5 4
First printing, March 2007
Fourth printing, May 2013

www.viz.com

FULLMETAL ALCHEMIST

鋼の錬金術師

HIROMU ARAKAWA

荒川弘

12

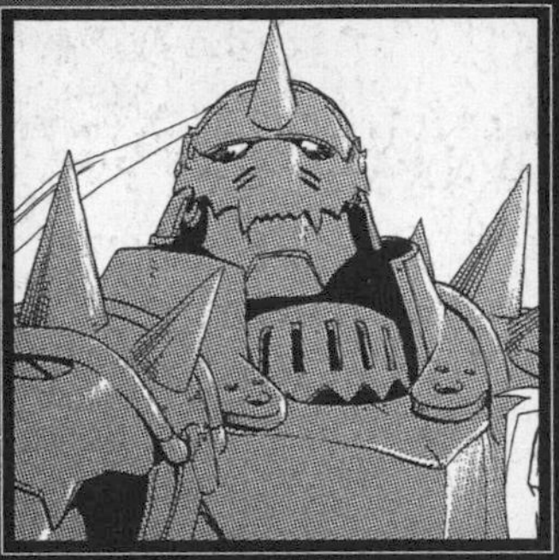

アルフォンス・エルリック

Alphonse Elric

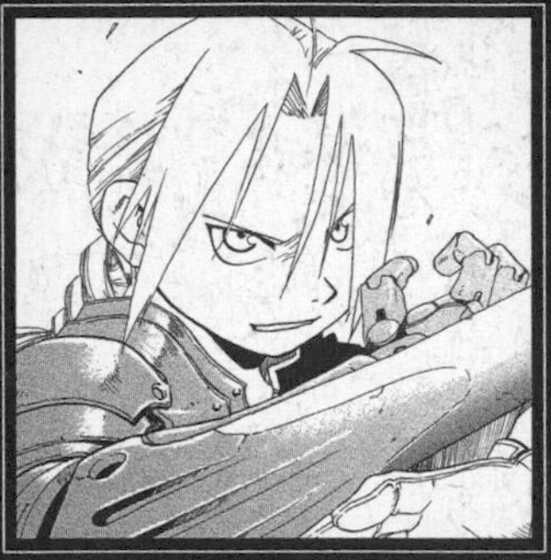

エドワード・エルリック

Edward Elric

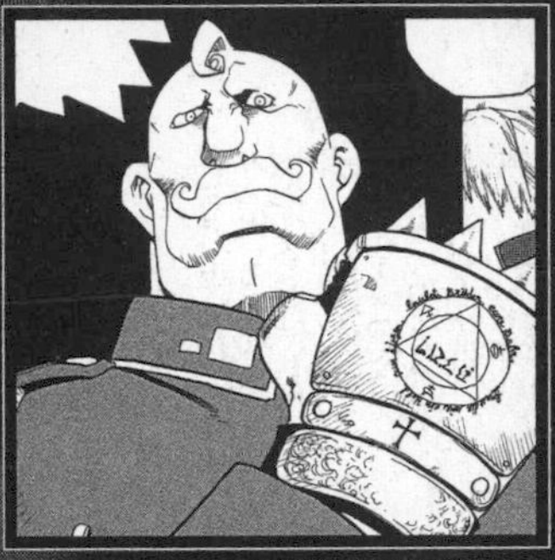

アレックス・ルイ・アームストロング

Alex Louis Armstrong

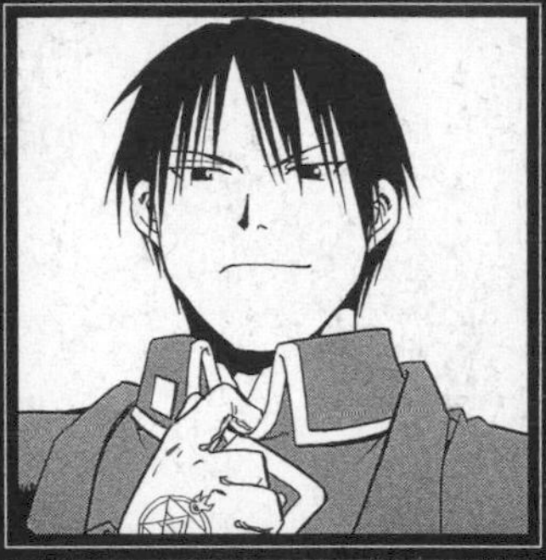

ロイ・マスタング

Roy Mustang

OUTLINE

FULLMETAL ALCHEMIST

Using a forbidden alchemical ritual, the Elric Brothers attempted to bring their dead mother back to life. But the ritual went wrong, consuming Edward Elric's leg and Alphonse Elric's entire body. At the cost of his arm, Edward was able to graft his brother's soul into a suit of armor. Equipped with mechanical "auto-mail" to replace his missing limbs, Edward becomes a state alchemist, serving the military on deadly missions. Now, the two brothers roam the world in search of the Philosopher's Stone, the legendary substance with the power to restore what they have lost…

Scar, the murderous Ishbalan avenger, is on the hunt for State Alchemists, and Ed and Al have put themselves right in his path in order to lure the Homunculi out of hiding. The Elric Brothers, and their allies Colonel Mustang and Prince Lin, all need the homunculi in order to advance their personal causes, but with this bold trap, have they bit off more than they can chew?

鋼の錬金術師
FULLMETAL ALCHEMIST

CHARACTERS
FULLMETAL ALCHEMIST

ウィンリィ・ロックベル

Winry Rockbell

スカー

Scar

グラトニー

Gluttony

キング・ブラッドレイ

King Bradley

リン・ヤオ

Lin Yao

メイ・チャン

May Chang

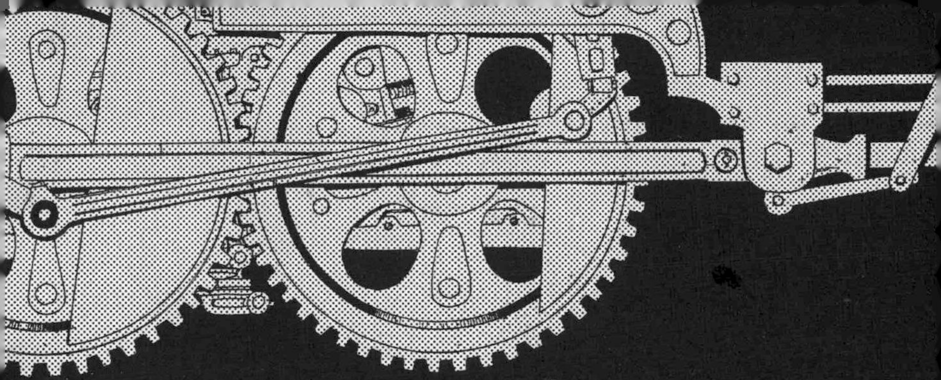

CONTENTS

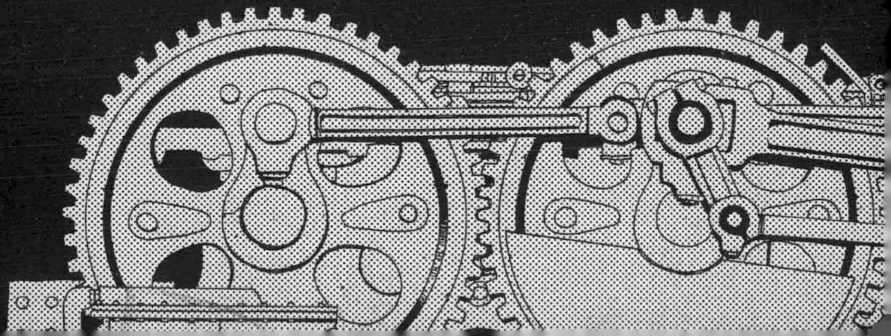

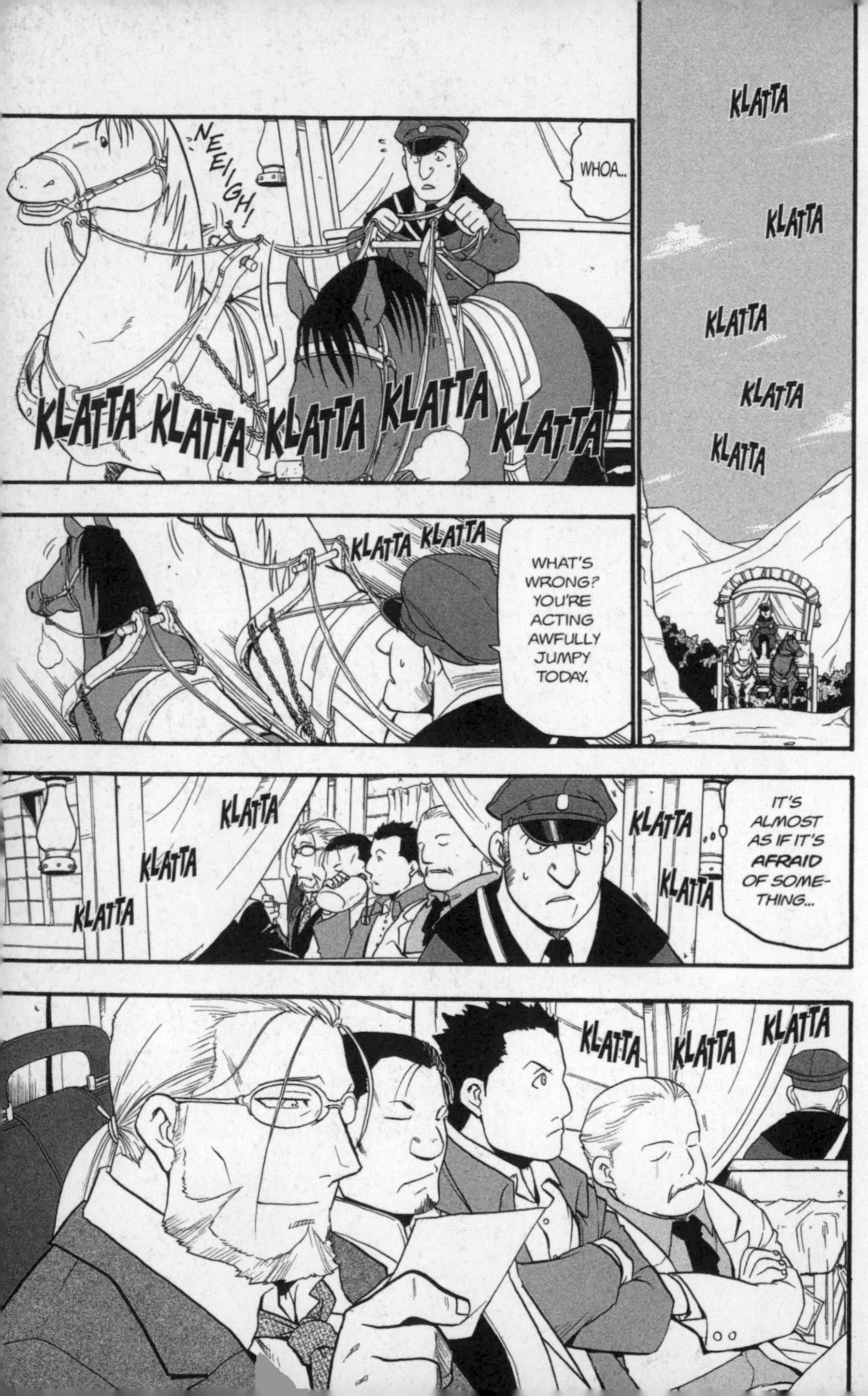
KLATTA
KLATTA
KLATTA
KLATTA
KLATTA
WHOA...
NEEIGH!
KLATTA KLATTA KLATTA KLATTA KLATTA
WHAT'S WRONG? YOU'RE ACTING AWFULLY JUMPY TODAY.
KLATTA KLATTA
IT'S ALMOST AS IF IT'S AFRAID OF SOME-THING...
KLATTA
KLATTA
KLATTA
KLATTA
KLATTA
KLATTA
KLATTA
KLATTA

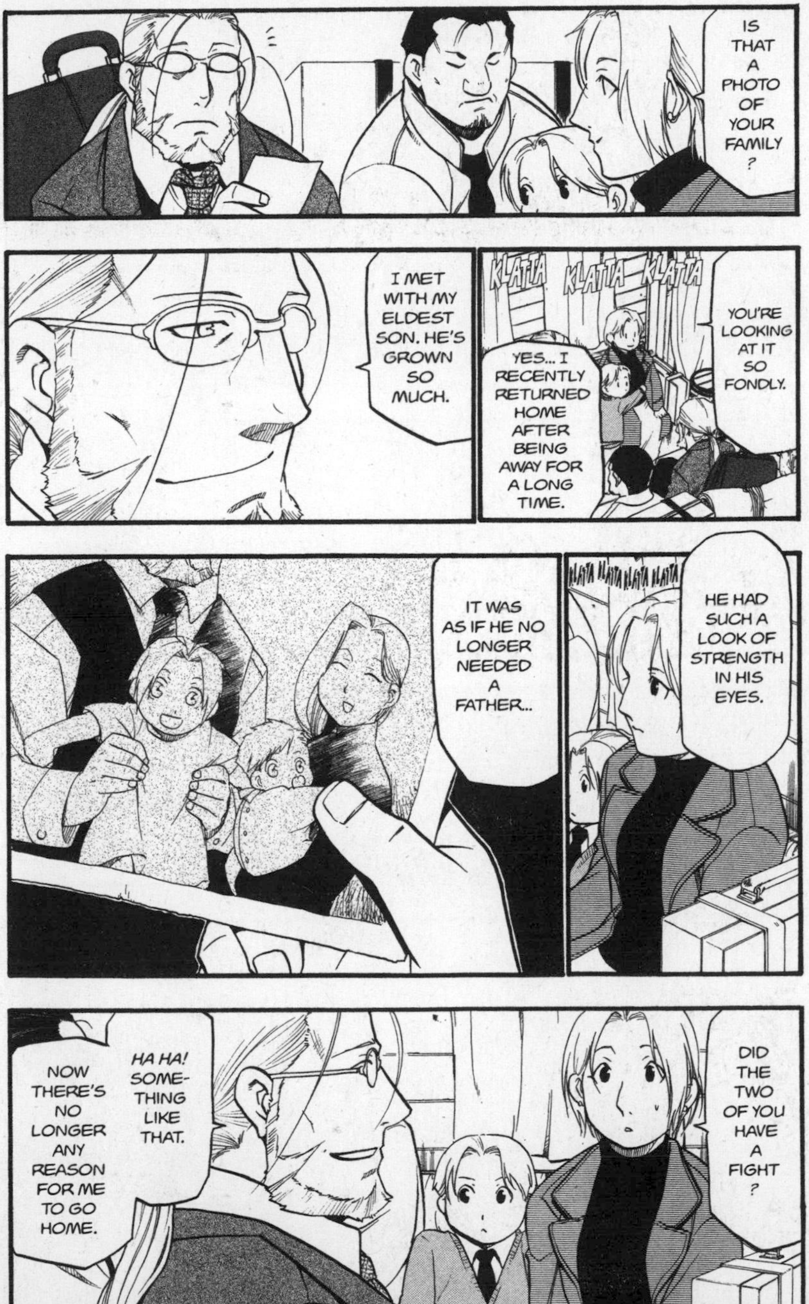
IS THAT A PHOTO OF YOUR FAMILY?
KLATTA KLATTA KLATTA
YOU'RE LOOKING AT IT SO FONDLY.
YES... I RECENTLY RETURNED HOME AFTER BEING AWAY FOR A LONG TIME.
I MET WITH MY ELDEST SON. HE'S GROWN SO MUCH.
KLATTA KLATTA KLATTA KLATTA
HE HAD SUCH A LOOK OF STRENGTH IN HIS EYES.
IT WAS AS IF HE NO LONGER NEEDED A FATHER...
DID THE TWO OF YOU HAVE A FIGHT?
HA HA! SOMETHING LIKE THAT.
NOW THERE'S NO LONGER ANY REASON FOR ME TO GO HOME.

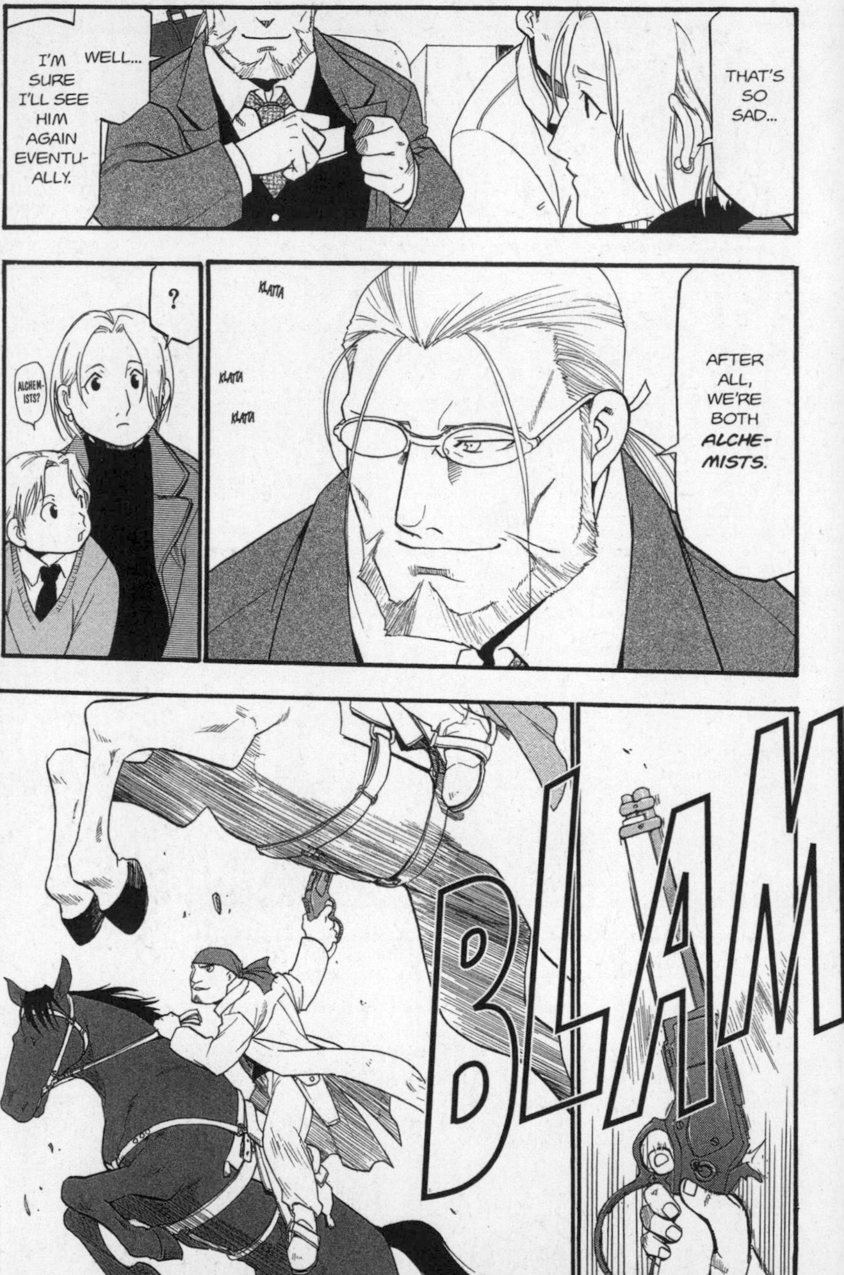
THAT'S SO SAD...
WELL...
I'M SURE I'LL SEE HIM AGAIN EVENTU-ALLY.
AFTER ALL, WE'RE BOTH ALCHE-MISTS.
KLATTA
KLATTA
KLATTA
?
ALCHEM-ISTS?
BLAM

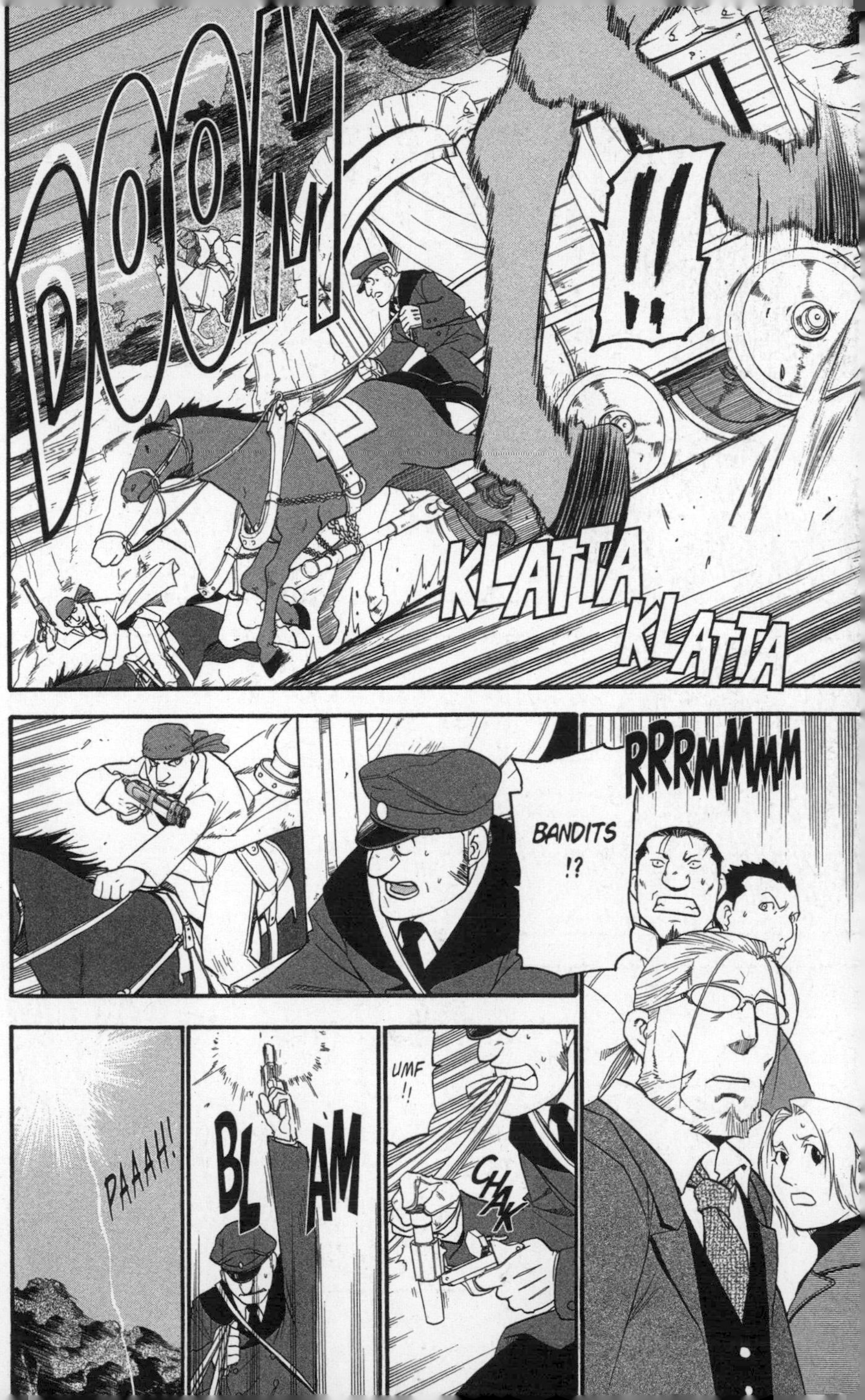

!!
DOOM
KLATTA KLATTA
RRRMMMM
BANDITS !?
UMF !!
CHAK
BLAM
PAAAH!

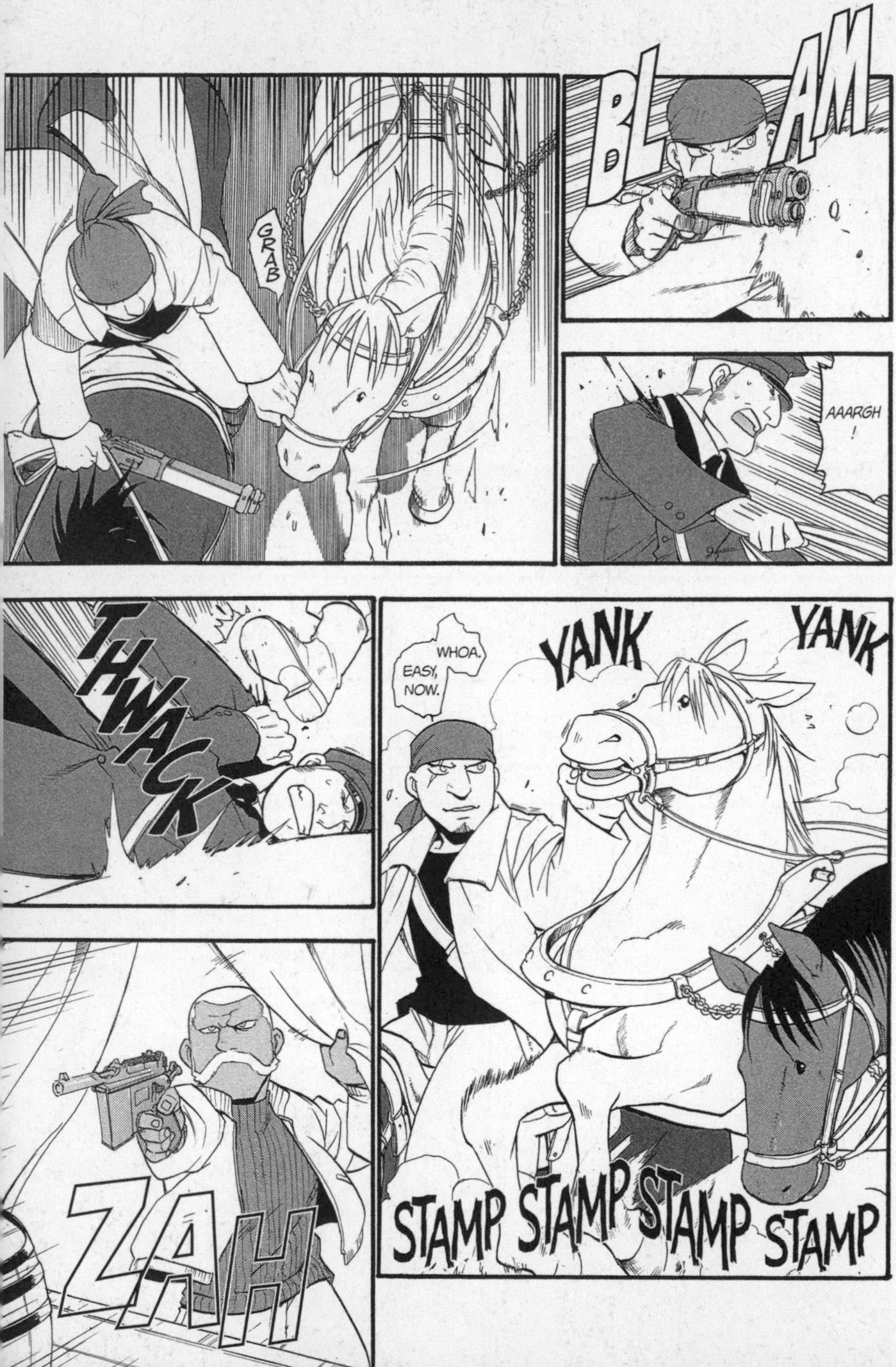
BLAM
AAARGH!
GRAB
YANK
YANK
WHOA. EASY, NOW.
STAMP STAMP STAMP STAMP
THWACK
ZAH

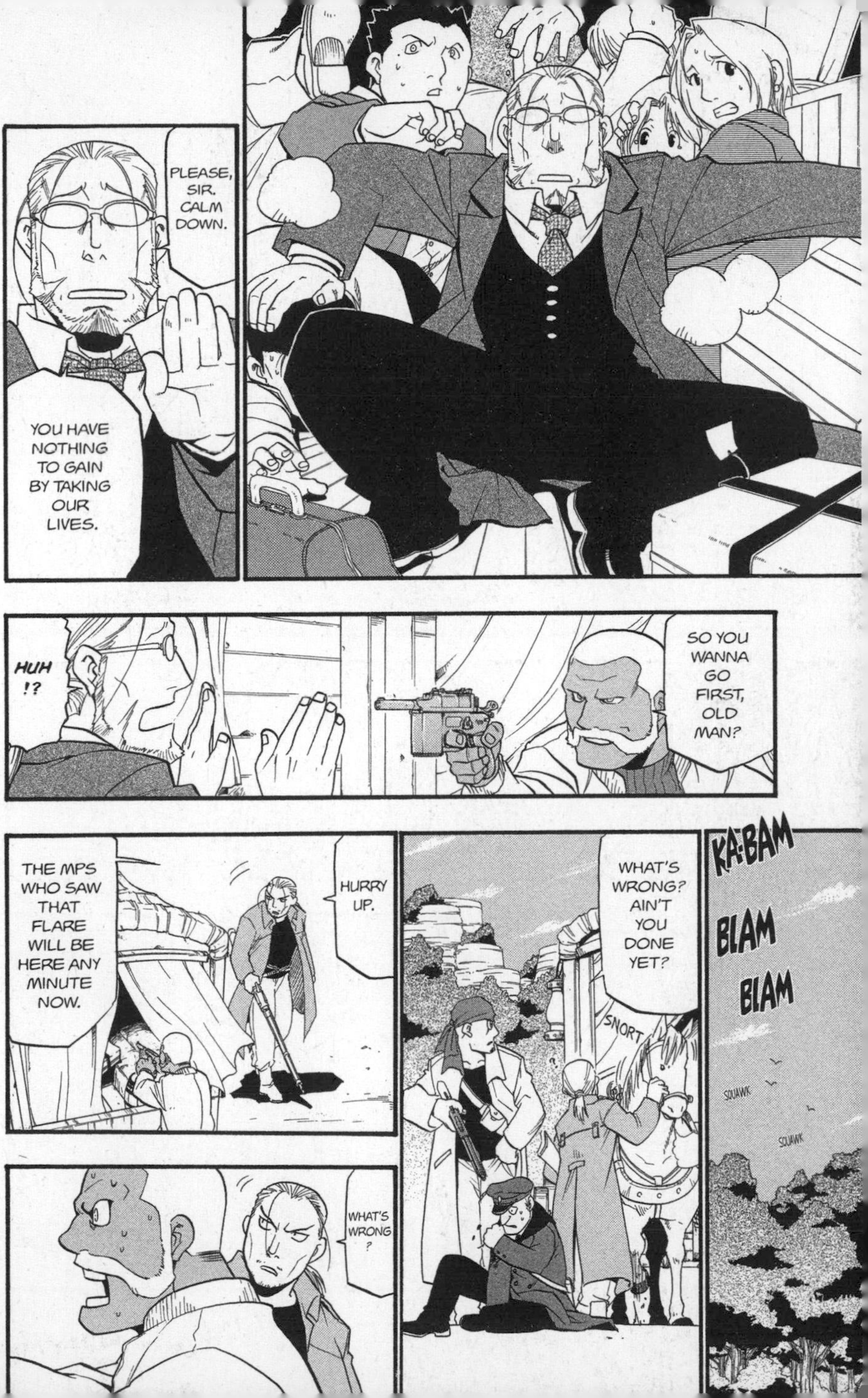
PLEASE, SIR. CALM DOWN.
YOU HAVE NOTHING TO GAIN BY TAKING OUR LIVES.
SO YOU WANNA GO FIRST, OLD MAN?
HUH!?
KA-BAM
BLAM
BLAM
SQUAWK
SQUAWK
WHAT'S WRONG? AIN'T YOU DONE YET?
SNORT
HURRY UP.
THE MPS WHO SAW THAT FLARE WILL BE HERE ANY MINUTE NOW.
WHAT'S WRONG?

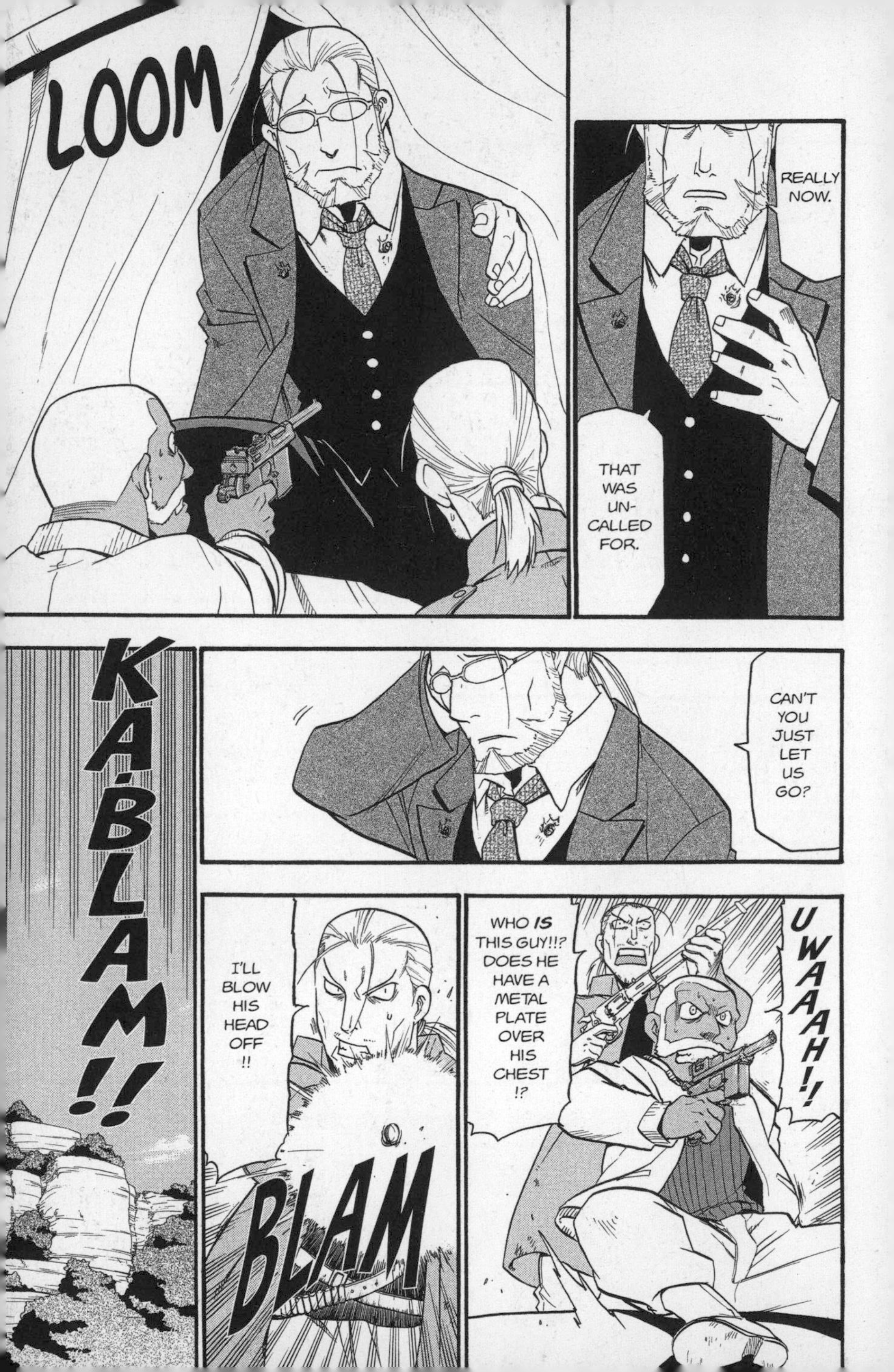
REALLY NOW.
THAT WAS UN-CALLED FOR.
TLOOM
CAN'T YOU JUST LET US GO?
UWAAAH!!
WHO *IS* THIS GUY!!? DOES HE HAVE A METAL PLATE OVER HIS CHEST!?
I'LL BLOW HIS HEAD OFF!!
BLAM
KA-BLAM!!

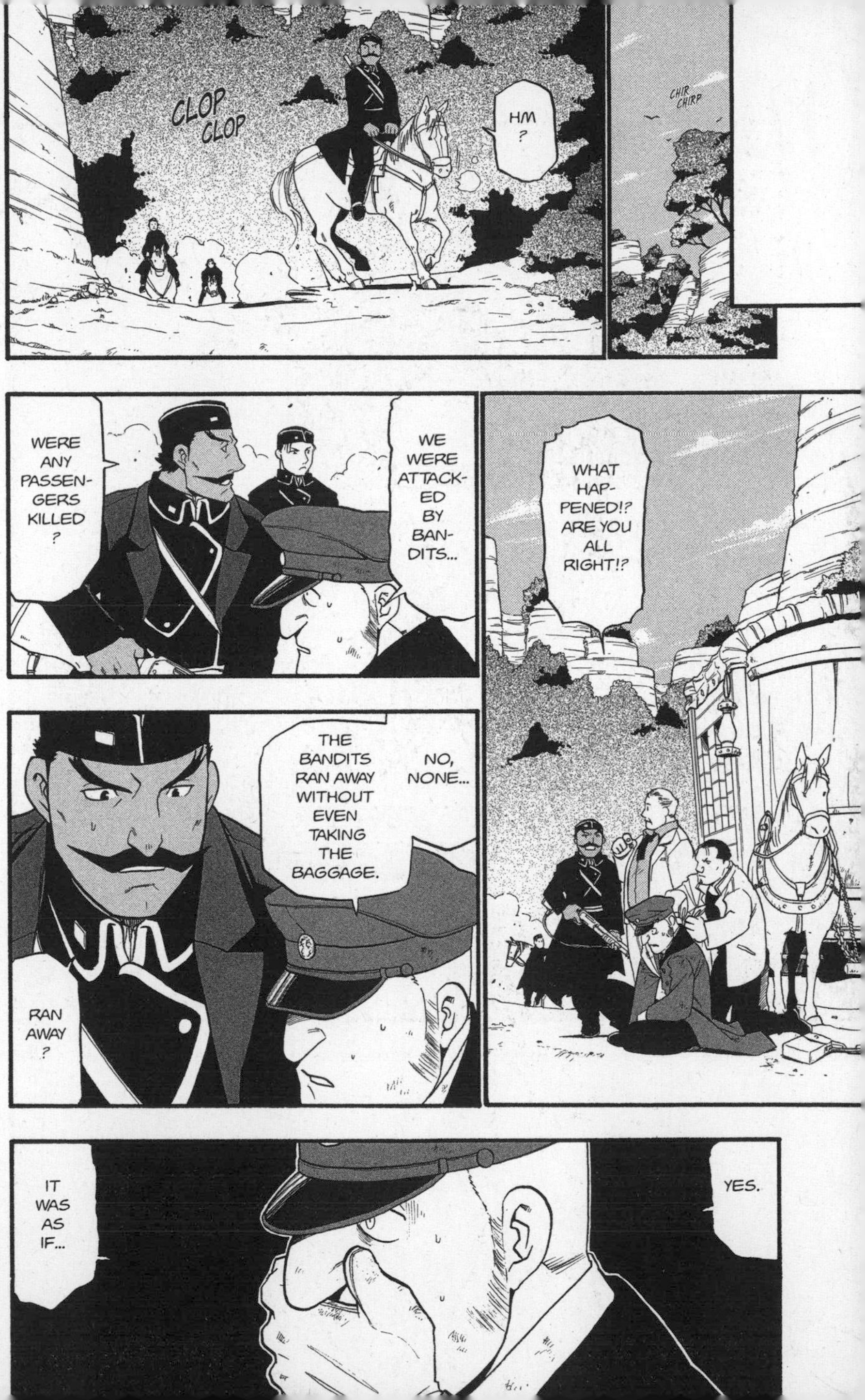
CHIR CHIRP
CLOP CLOP
HM?
WHAT HAPPENED!? ARE YOU ALL RIGHT!?
WE WERE ATTACKED BY BANDITS...
WERE ANY PASSENGERS KILLED?
NO, NONE...
THE BANDITS RAN AWAY WITHOUT EVEN TAKING THE BAGGAGE.
RAN AWAY?
YES.
IT WAS AS IF...

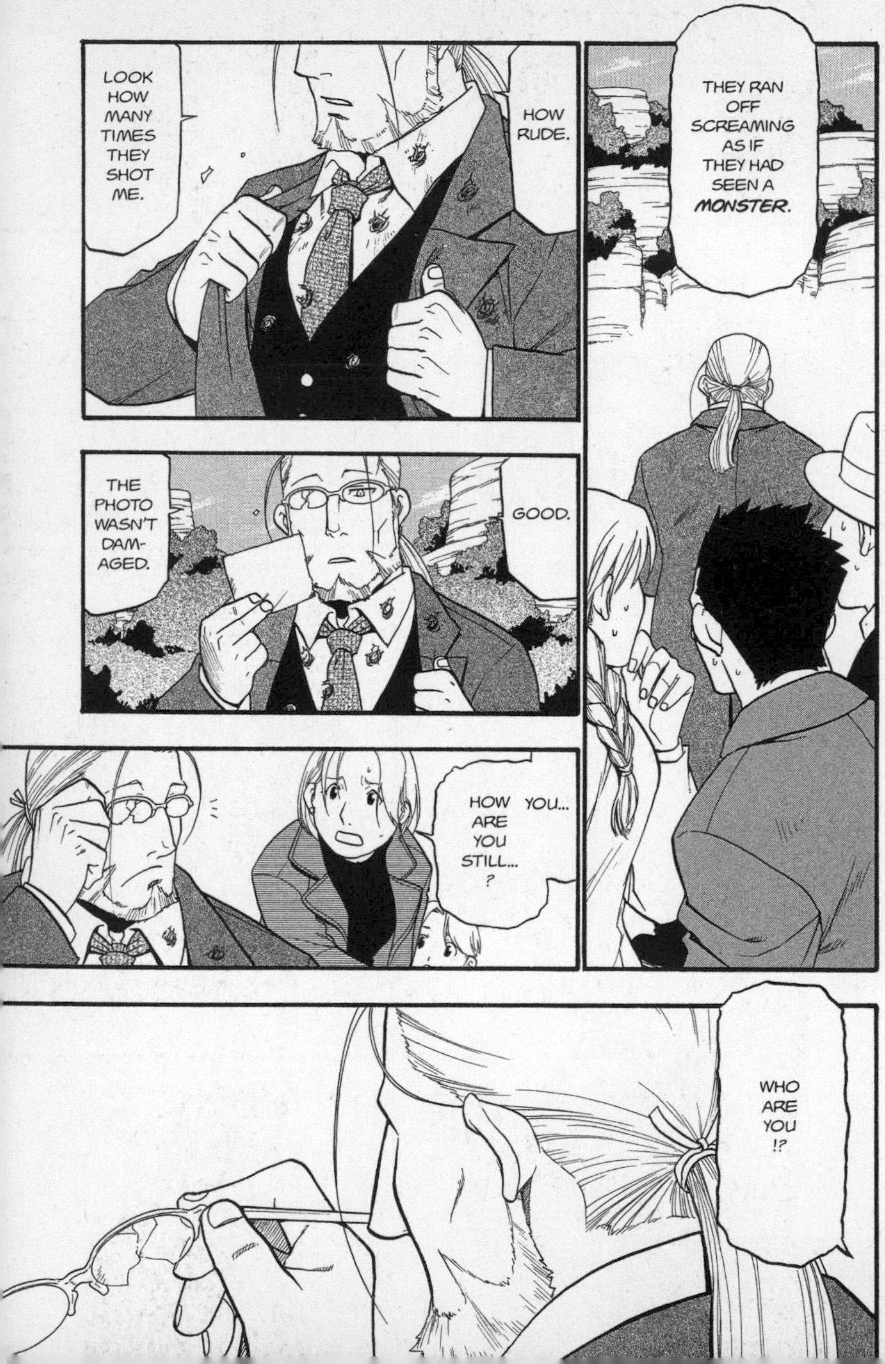
THEY RAN OFF SCREAMING AS IF THEY HAD SEEN A *MONSTER*.
HOW RUDE.
LOOK HOW MANY TIMES THEY SHOT ME.
GOOD.
THE PHOTO WASN'T DAM-AGED.
YOU...
HOW ARE YOU STILL...?
WHO ARE YOU!?

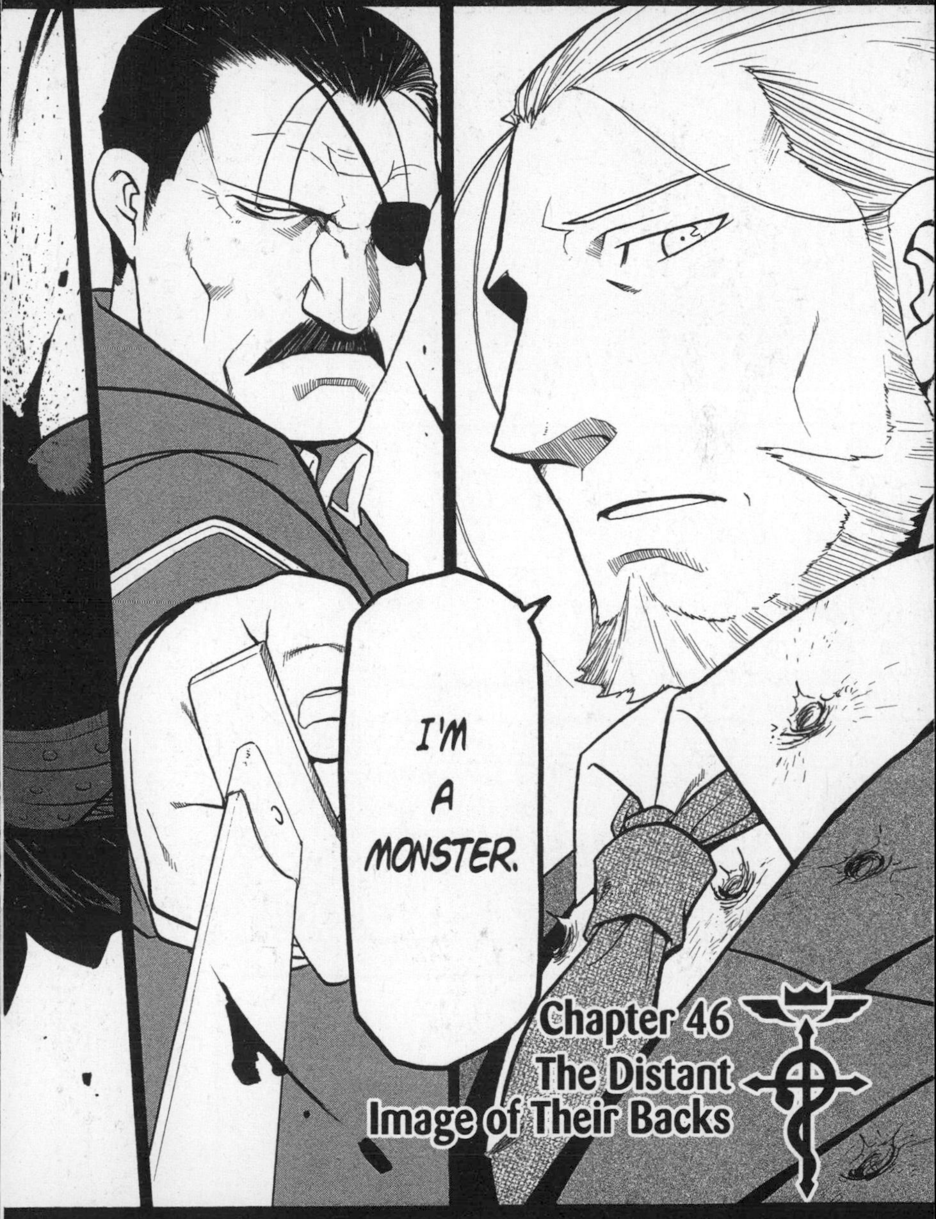
I'M A MONSTER.
Chapter 46 The Distant Image of Their Backs

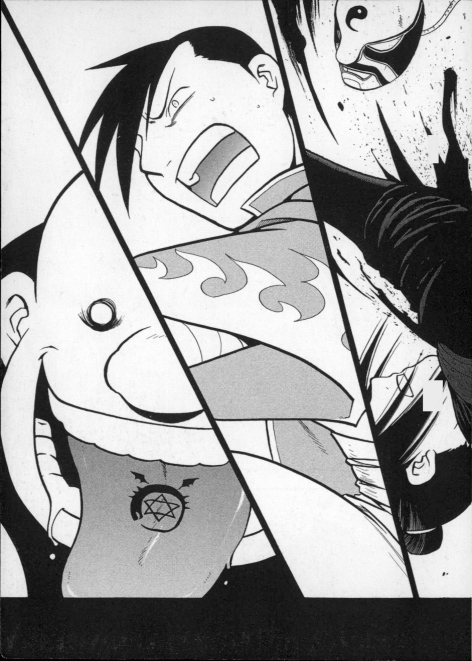

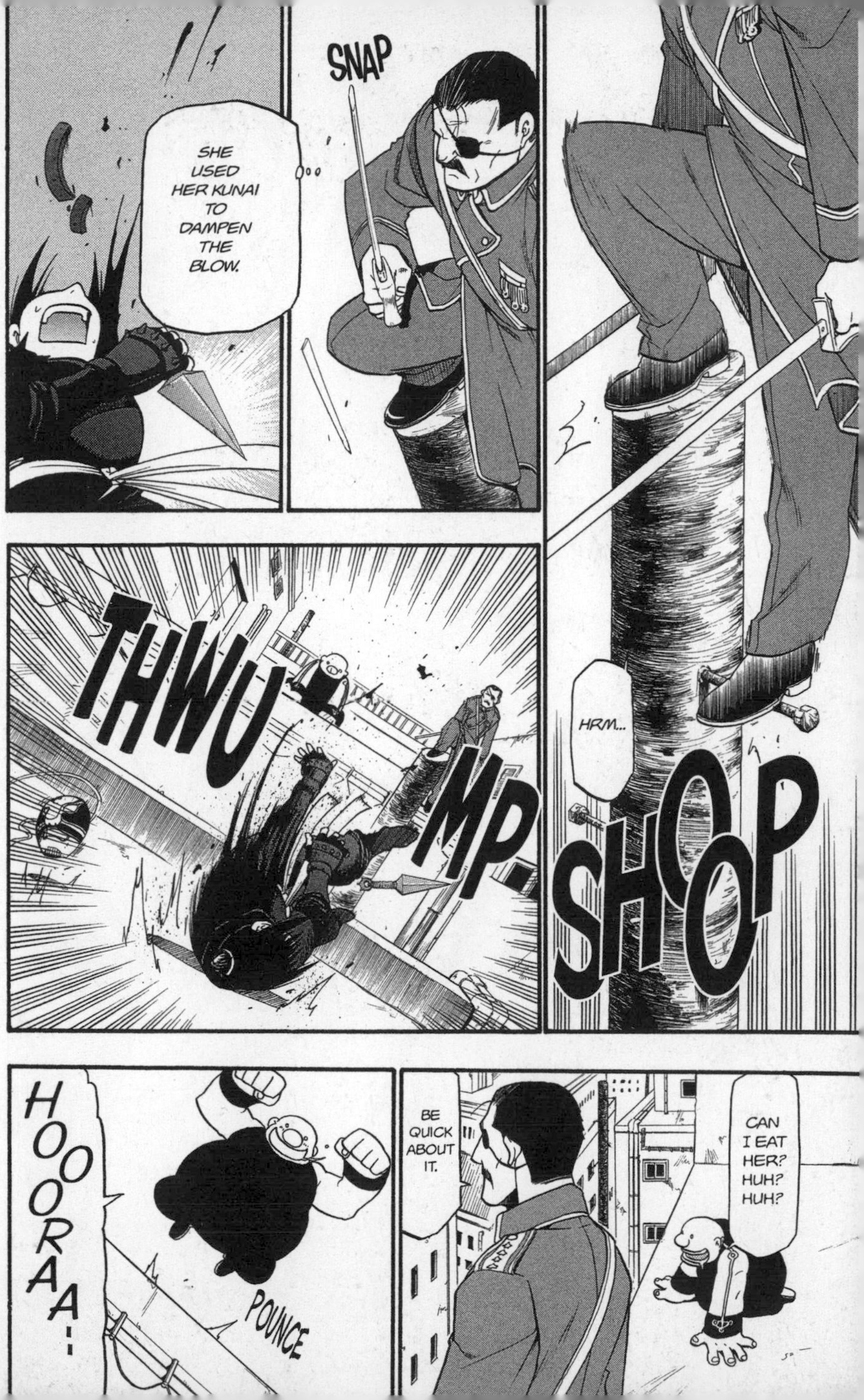
HRM...
SHOOP
SNAP
SHE USED HER KUNAI TO DAMPEN THE BLOW.
THWUMP
CAN I EAT HER? HUH? HUH?
BE QUICK ABOUT IT.
HOOORAA!!
POUNCE

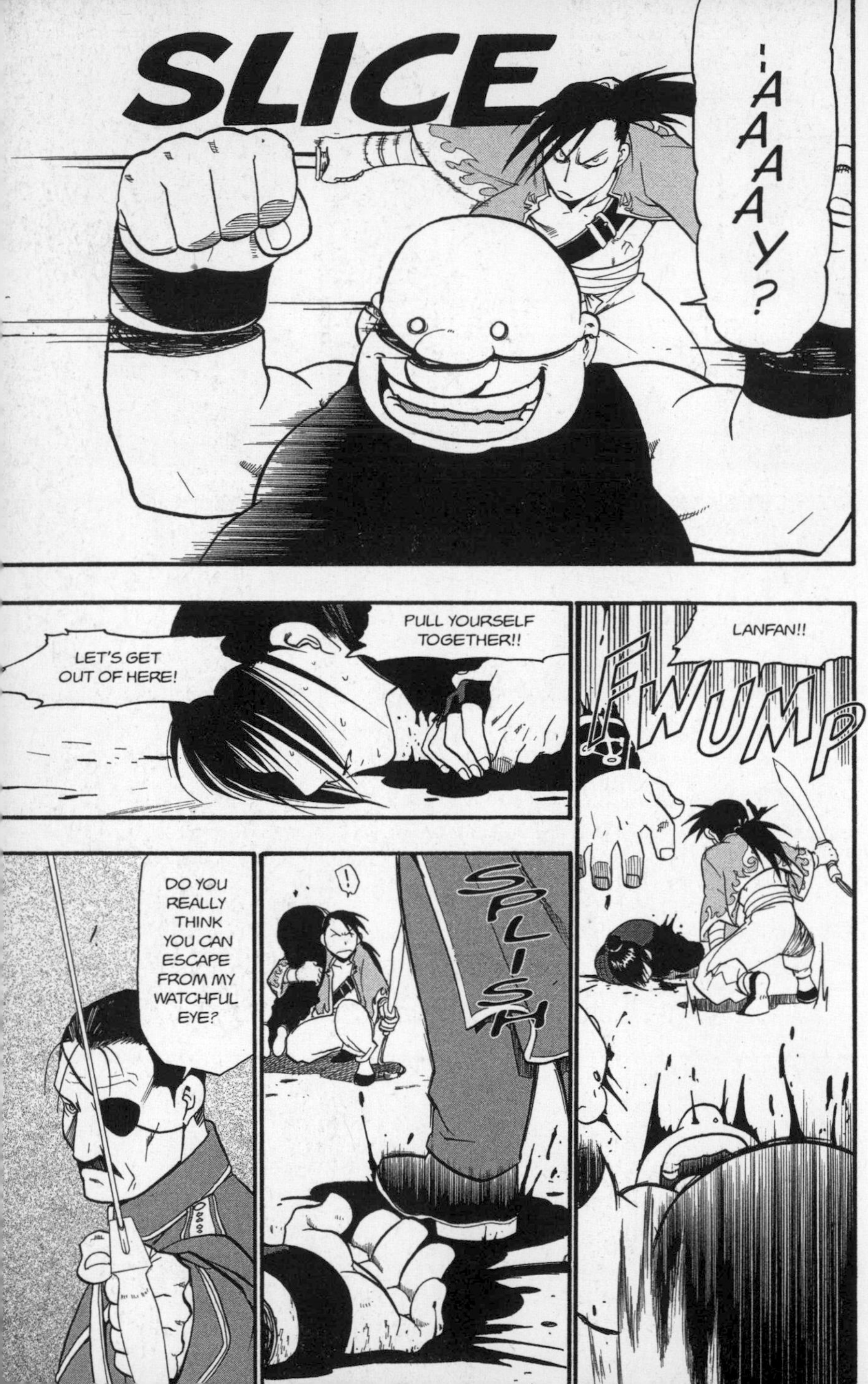
SLICE
!AAAAY?
LANFAN!!
FWUMP
PULL YOURSELF TOGETHER!!
LET'S GET OUT OF HERE!
!
SPLISH
DO YOU REALLY THINK YOU CAN ESCAPE FROM MY WATCHFUL EYE?

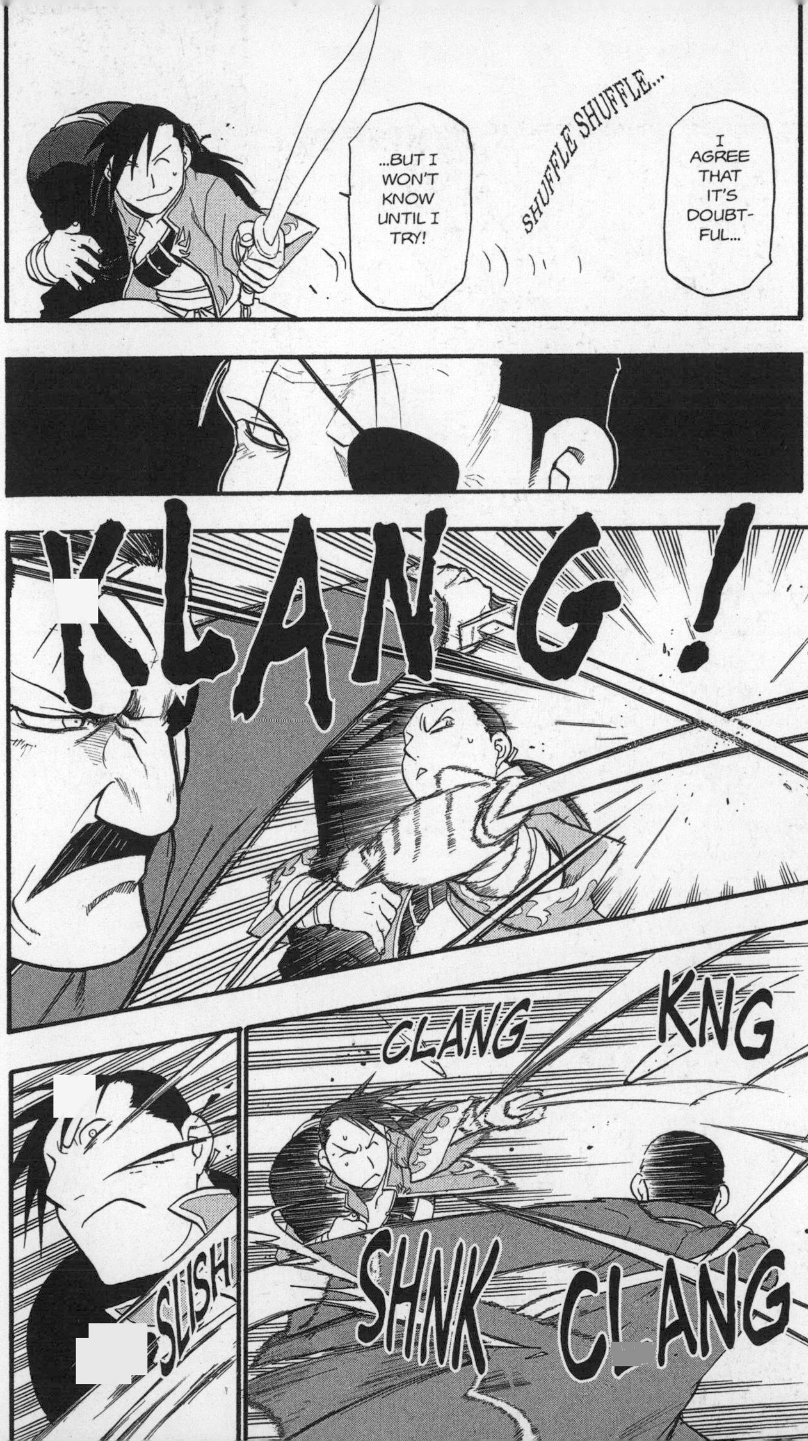
I AGREE THAT IT'S DOUBTFUL...
SHUFFLE SHUFFLE...
...BUT I WON'T KNOW UNTIL I TRY!
KLANG!
KNG
CLANG
CLANG
SHNK
SLISH

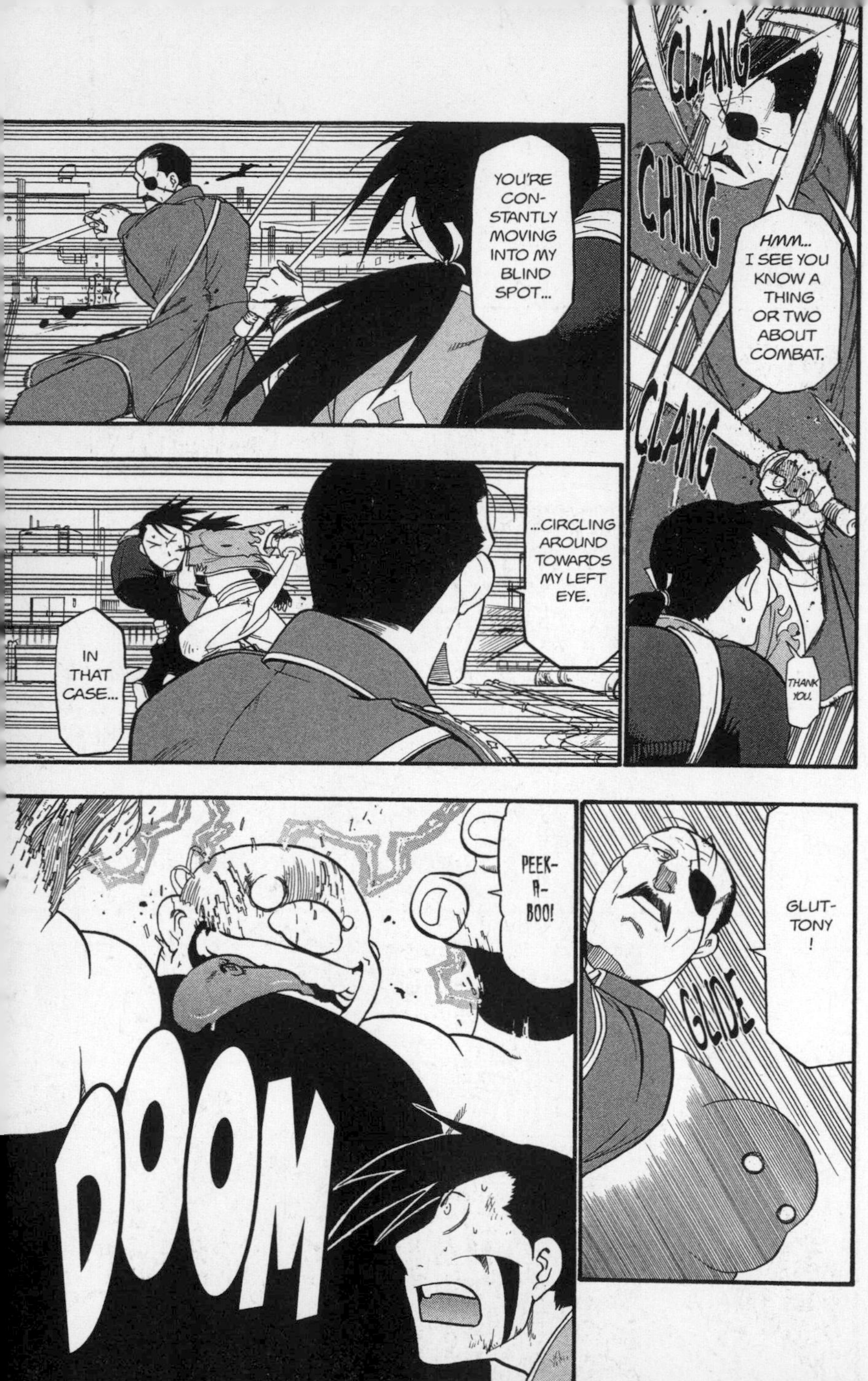
CLANG
CHING
HMM... I SEE YOU KNOW A THING OR TWO ABOUT COMBAT.
CLANG
THANK YOU.
YOU'RE CON-STANTLY MOVING INTO MY BLIND SPOT...
...CIRCLING AROUND TOWARDS MY LEFT EYE.
IN THAT CASE...
GLUT-TONY!
GLIDE
PEEK-A-BOO!
DOOM

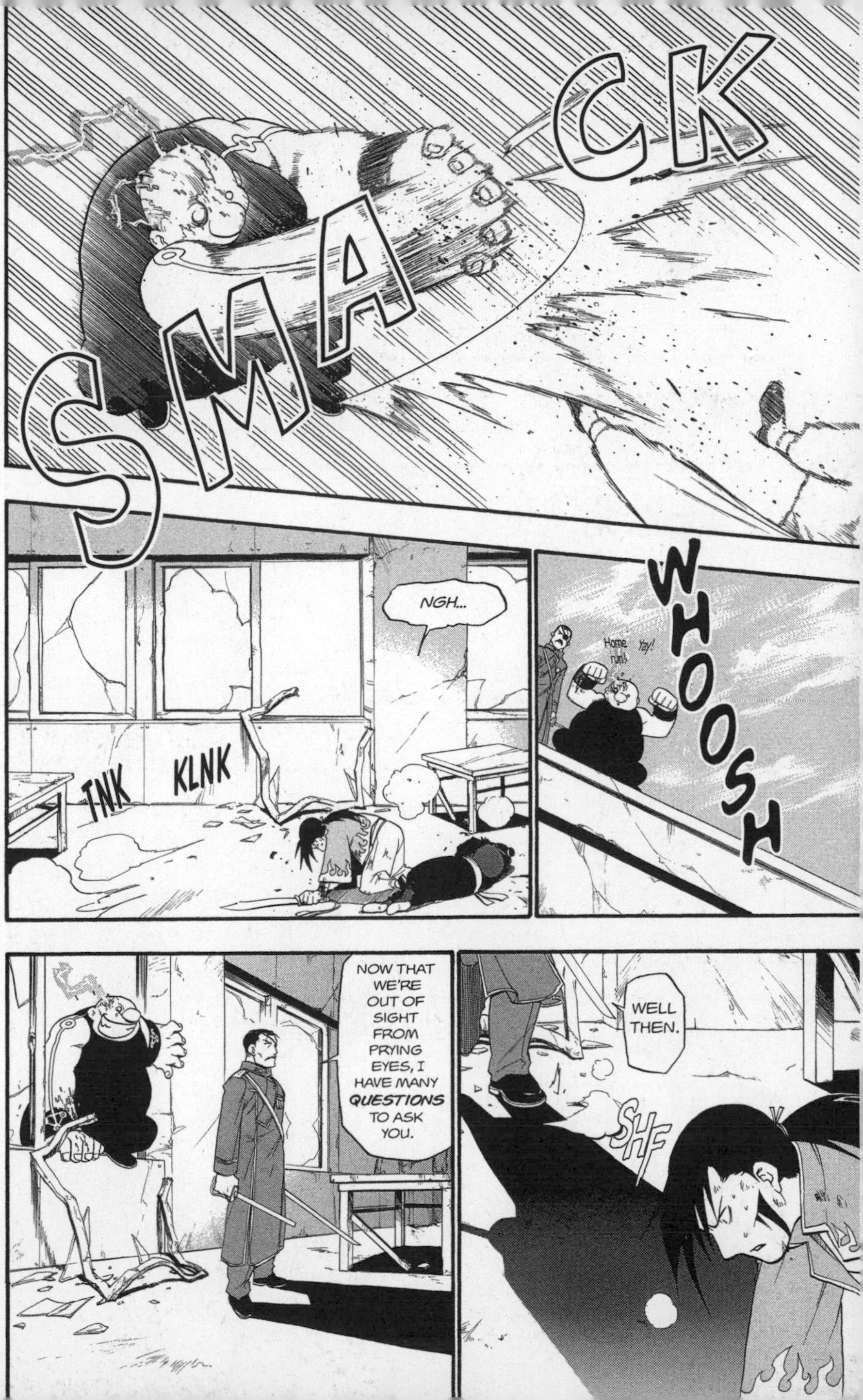
SMACK
WHOOSH
Home run!
Yay!
NGH...
TNK
KLNK
WELL THEN.
SHF
NOW THAT WE'RE OUT OF SIGHT FROM PRYING EYES, I HAVE MANY **QUESTIONS** TO ASK YOU.

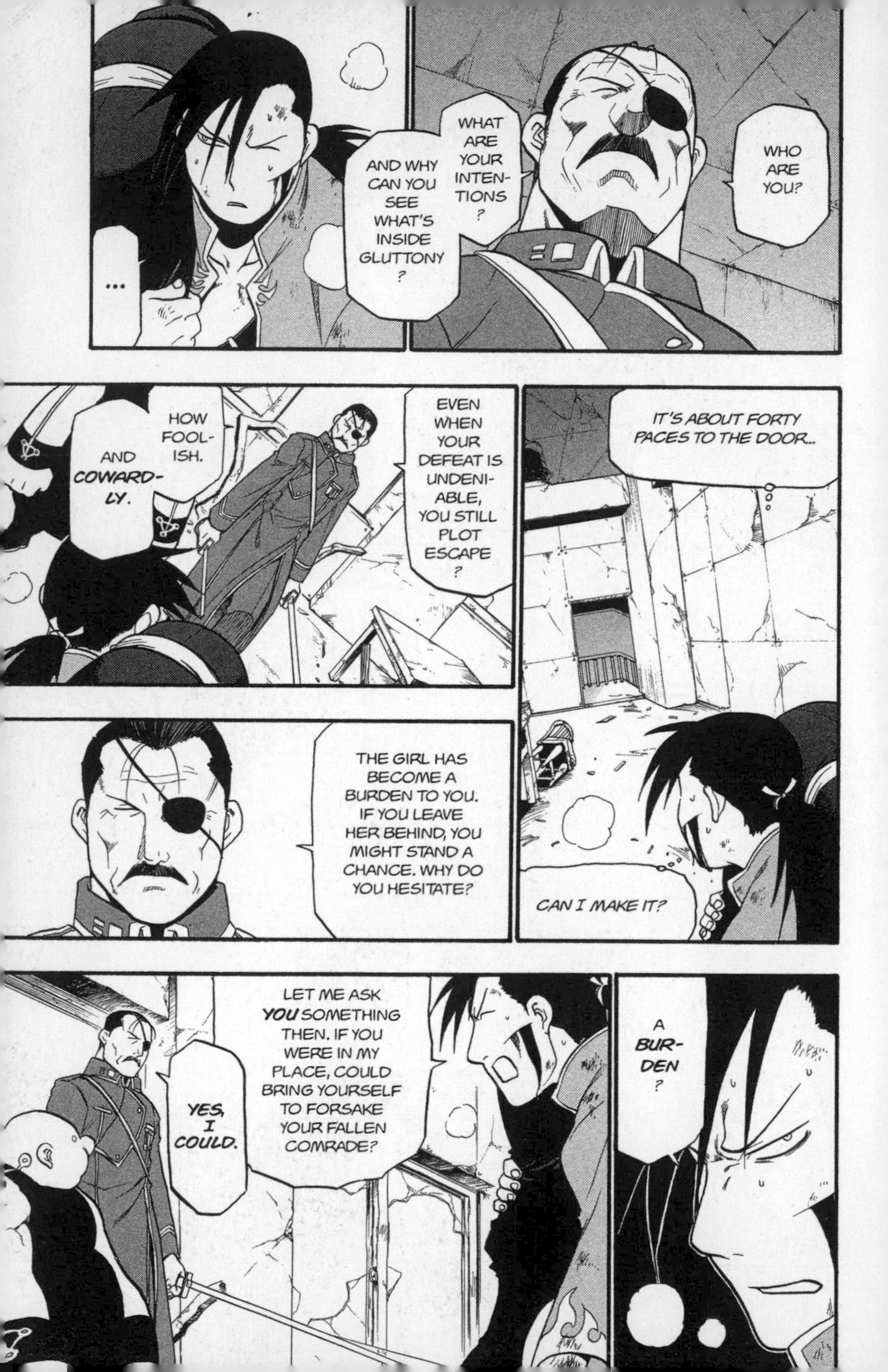
WHO ARE YOU?
WHAT ARE YOUR INTENTIONS?
AND WHY CAN YOU SEE WHAT'S INSIDE GLUTTONY?
...
IT'S ABOUT FORTY PACES TO THE DOOR...
CAN I MAKE IT?
EVEN WHEN YOUR DEFEAT IS UNDENIABLE, YOU STILL PLOT ESCAPE?
HOW FOOLISH.
AND COWARDLY.
THE GIRL HAS BECOME A BURDEN TO YOU. IF YOU LEAVE HER BEHIND, YOU MIGHT STAND A CHANCE. WHY DO YOU HESITATE?
A BURDEN?
LET ME ASK YOU SOMETHING THEN. IF YOU WERE IN MY PLACE, COULD BRING YOURSELF TO FORSAKE YOUR FALLEN COMRADE?
YES, I COULD.

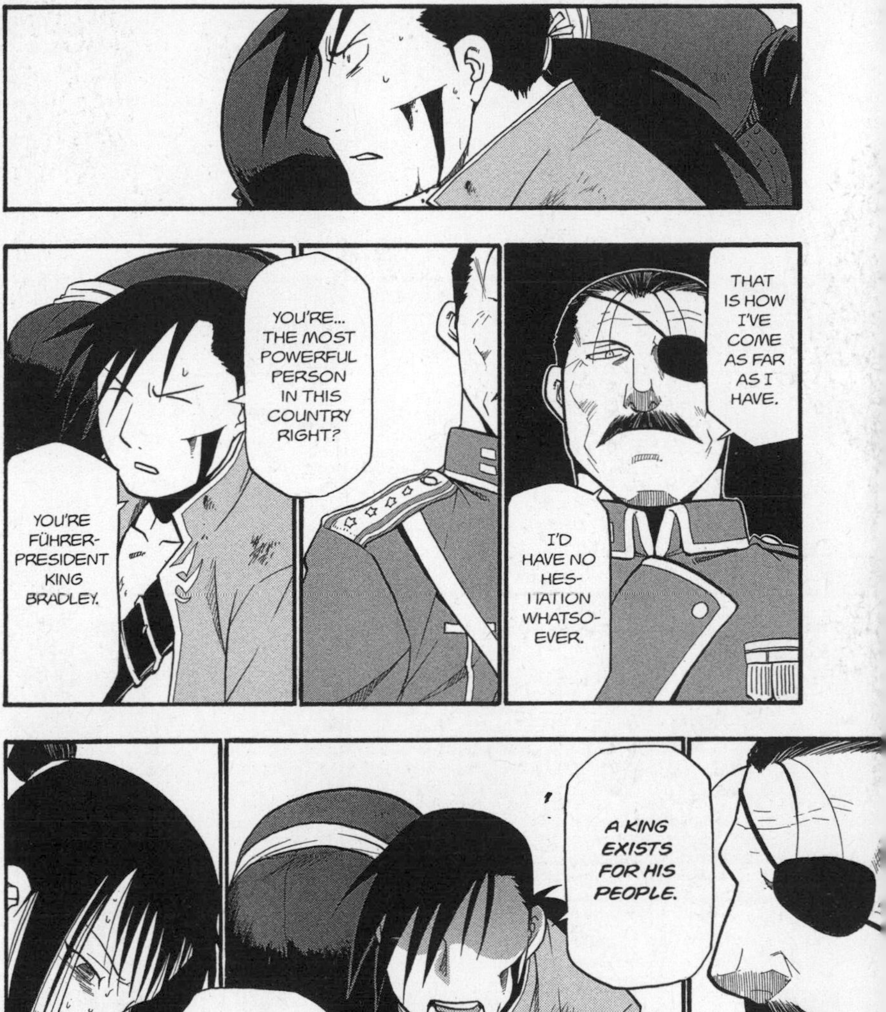
THAT IS HOW I'VE COME AS FAR AS I HAVE.
I'D HAVE NO HES-ITATION WHATSO-EVER.
YOU'RE... THE MOST POWERFUL PERSON IN THIS COUNTRY RIGHT?
YOU'RE FÜHRER-PRESIDENT KING BRADLEY.
A KING EXISTS FOR HIS PEOPLE.
WITHOUT HIS PEOPLE, THERE CAN BE NO KING.

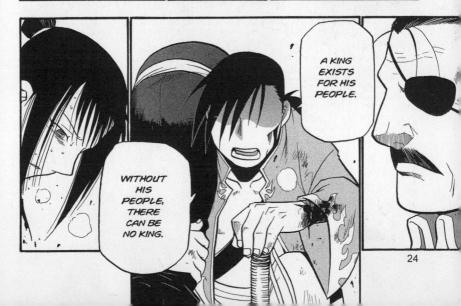

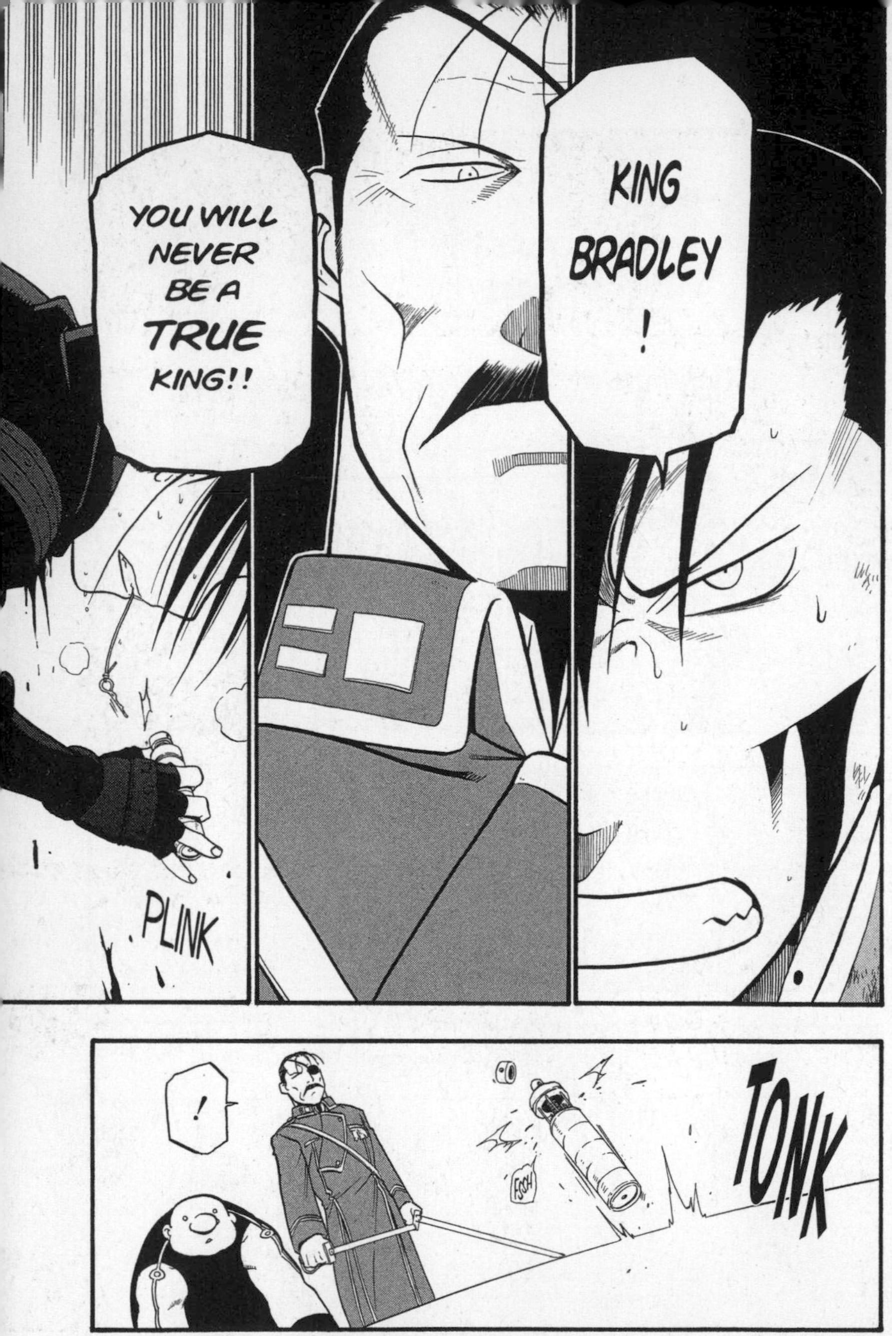
KING BRADLEY
!
YOU WILL NEVER BE A TRUE KING!!
PLINK
TONK
FSSH
!

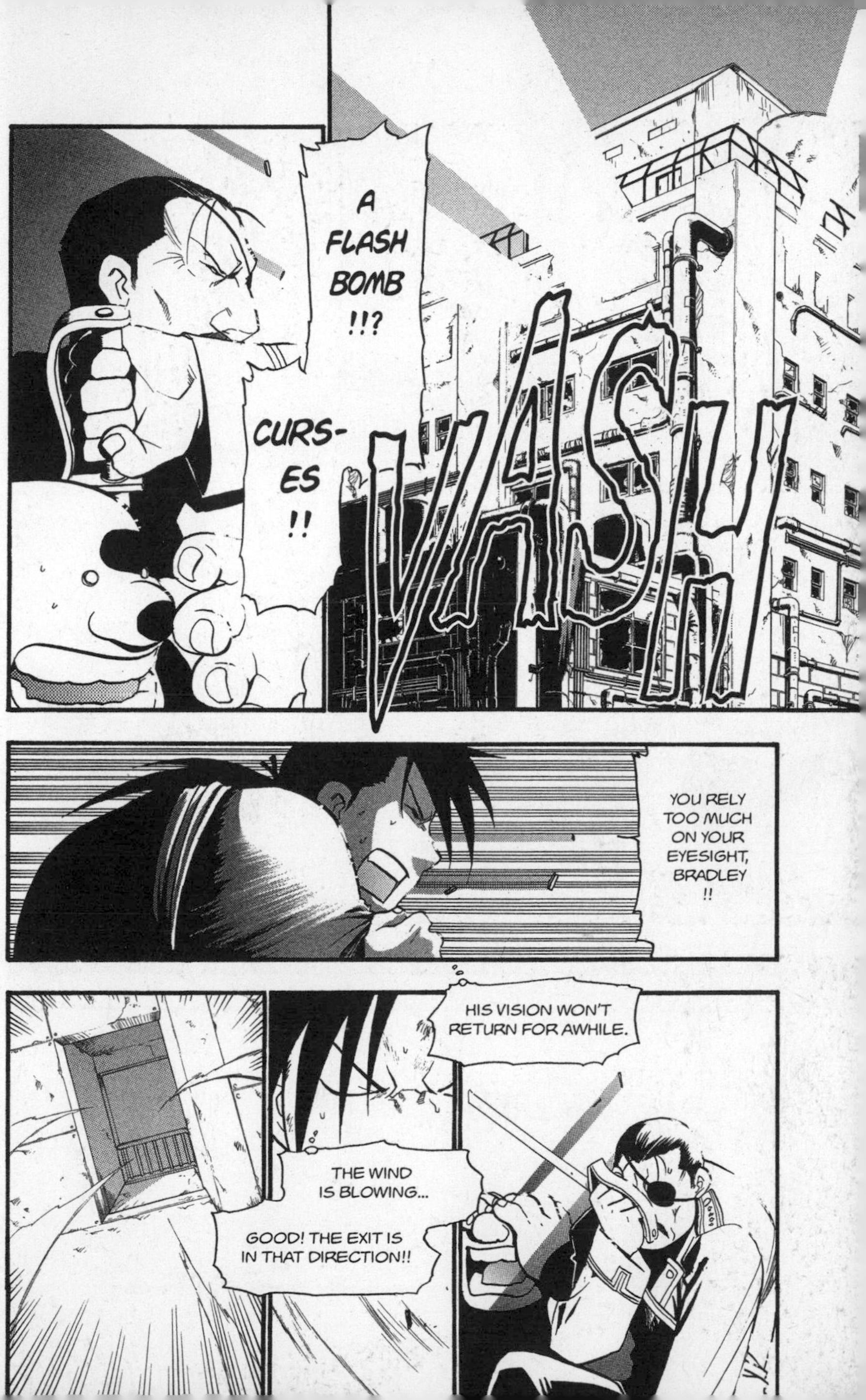
VASH
A FLASH BOMB!!?
CURSES!!
YOU RELY TOO MUCH ON YOUR EYESIGHT, BRADLEY!!
HIS VISION WON'T RETURN FOR AWHILE.
THE WIND IS BLOWING...
GOOD! THE EXIT IS IN THAT DIRECTION!!

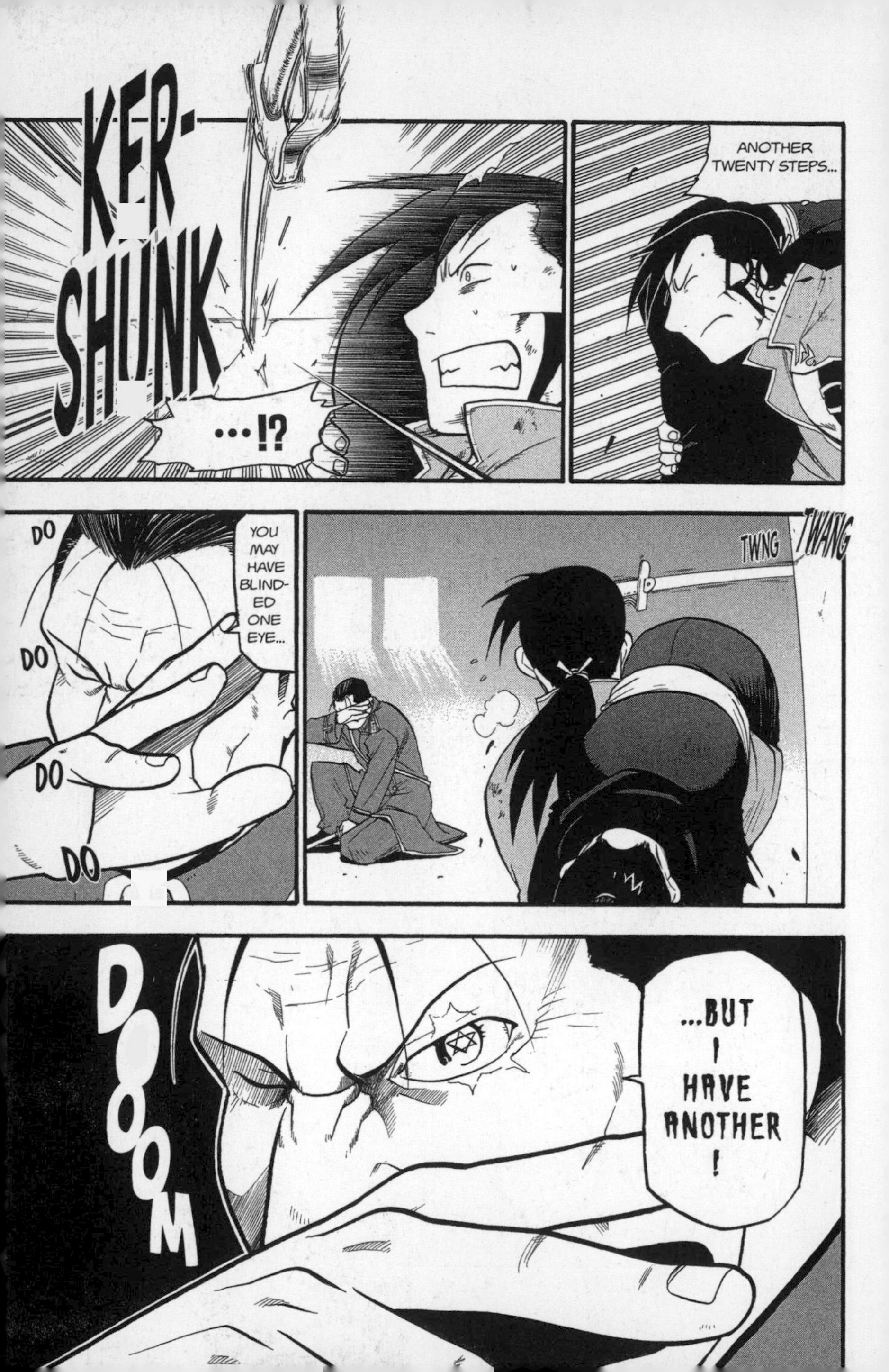
ANOTHER TWENTY STEPS...
KER-SHUNK
...!?
TWNG
TWANG
YOU MAY HAVE BLINDED ONE EYE...
DO DO DO DO
...BUT I HAVE ANOTHER!
DOOOM

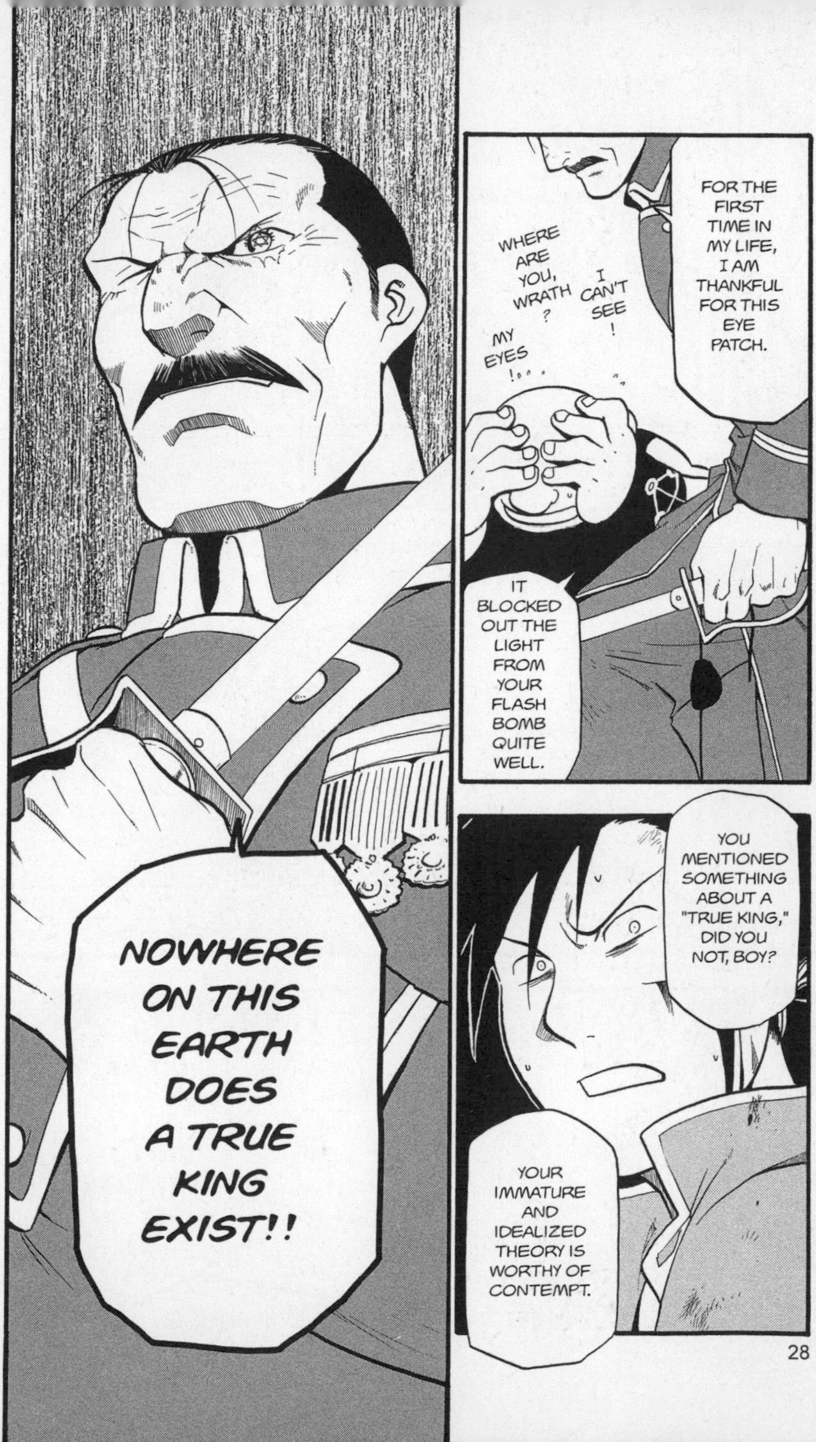
FOR THE FIRST TIME IN MY LIFE, I AM THANKFUL FOR THIS EYE PATCH.
I CAN'T SEE!
WHERE ARE YOU, WRATH?
MY EYES!...
IT BLOCKED OUT THE LIGHT FROM YOUR FLASH BOMB QUITE WELL.
YOU MENTIONED SOMETHING ABOUT A "TRUE KING," DID YOU NOT, BOY?
YOUR IMMATURE AND IDEALIZED THEORY IS WORTHY OF CONTEMPT.
NOWHERE ON THIS EARTH DOES A TRUE KING EXIST!!

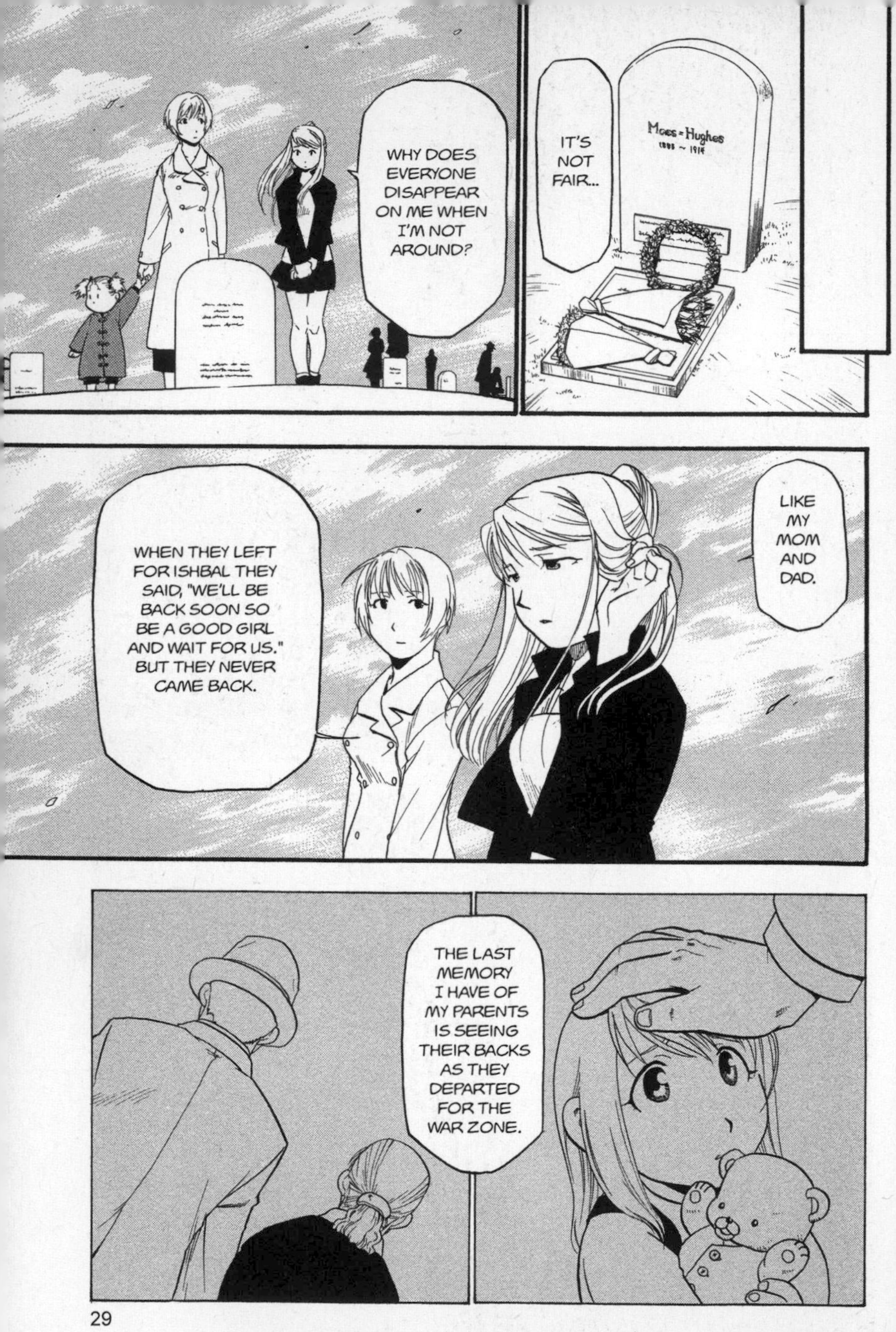
Maes=Hughes
IT'S NOT FAIR...
WHY DOES EVERYONE DISAPPEAR ON ME WHEN I'M NOT AROUND?
LIKE MY MOM AND DAD.
WHEN THEY LEFT FOR ISHBAL THEY SAID, "WE'LL BE BACK SOON SO BE A GOOD GIRL AND WAIT FOR US." BUT THEY NEVER CAME BACK.
THE LAST MEMORY I HAVE OF MY PARENTS IS SEEING THEIR BACKS AS THEY DEPARTED FOR THE WAR ZONE.

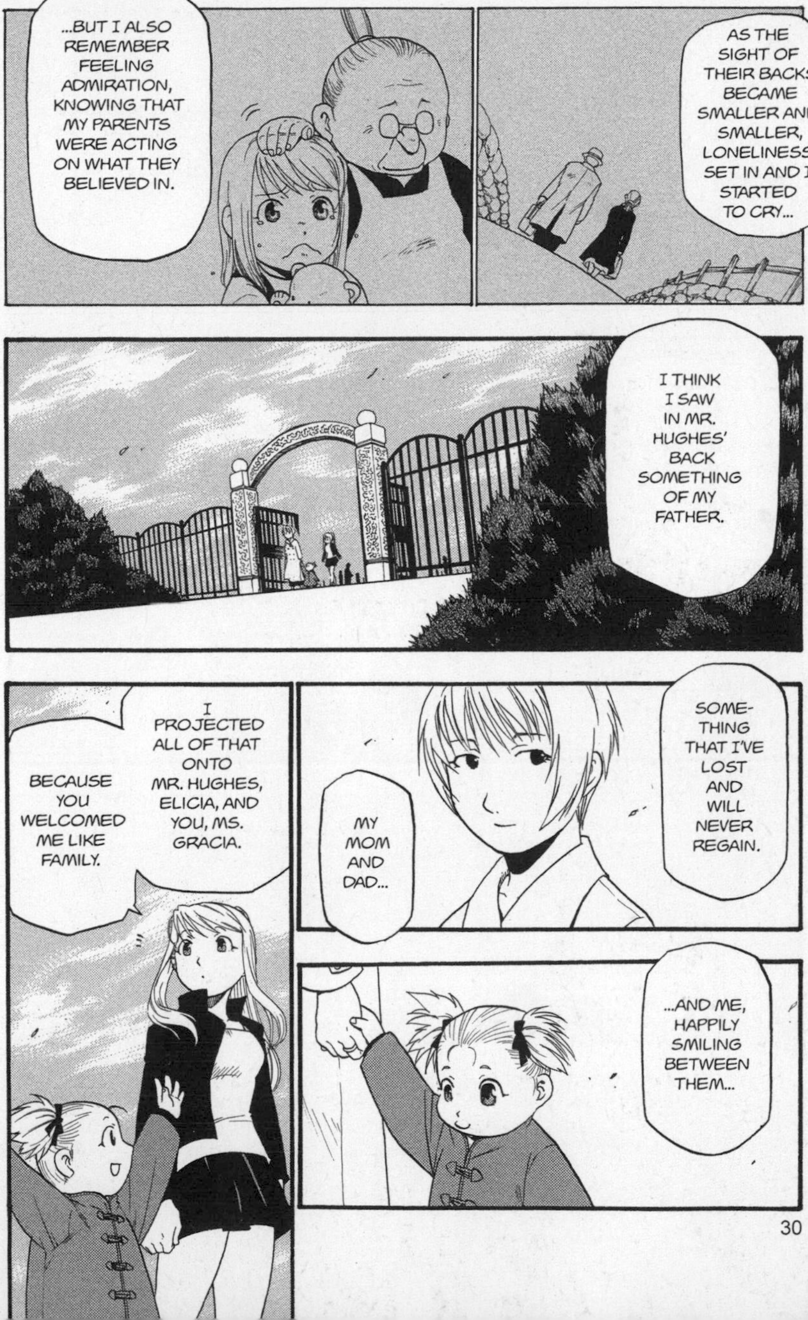
AS THE SIGHT OF THEIR BACKS BECAME SMALLER AND SMALLER, LONELINESS SET IN AND I STARTED TO CRY...
...BUT I ALSO REMEMBER FEELING ADMIRATION, KNOWING THAT MY PARENTS WERE ACTING ON WHAT THEY BELIEVED IN.
I THINK I SAW IN MR. HUGHES' BACK SOMETHING OF MY FATHER.
SOME-THING THAT I'VE LOST AND WILL NEVER REGAIN.
MY MOM AND DAD...
...AND ME, HAPPILY SMILING BETWEEN THEM...
I PROJECTED ALL OF THAT ONTO MR. HUGHES, ELICIA, AND YOU, MS. GRACIA.
BECAUSE YOU WELCOMED ME LIKE FAMILY.

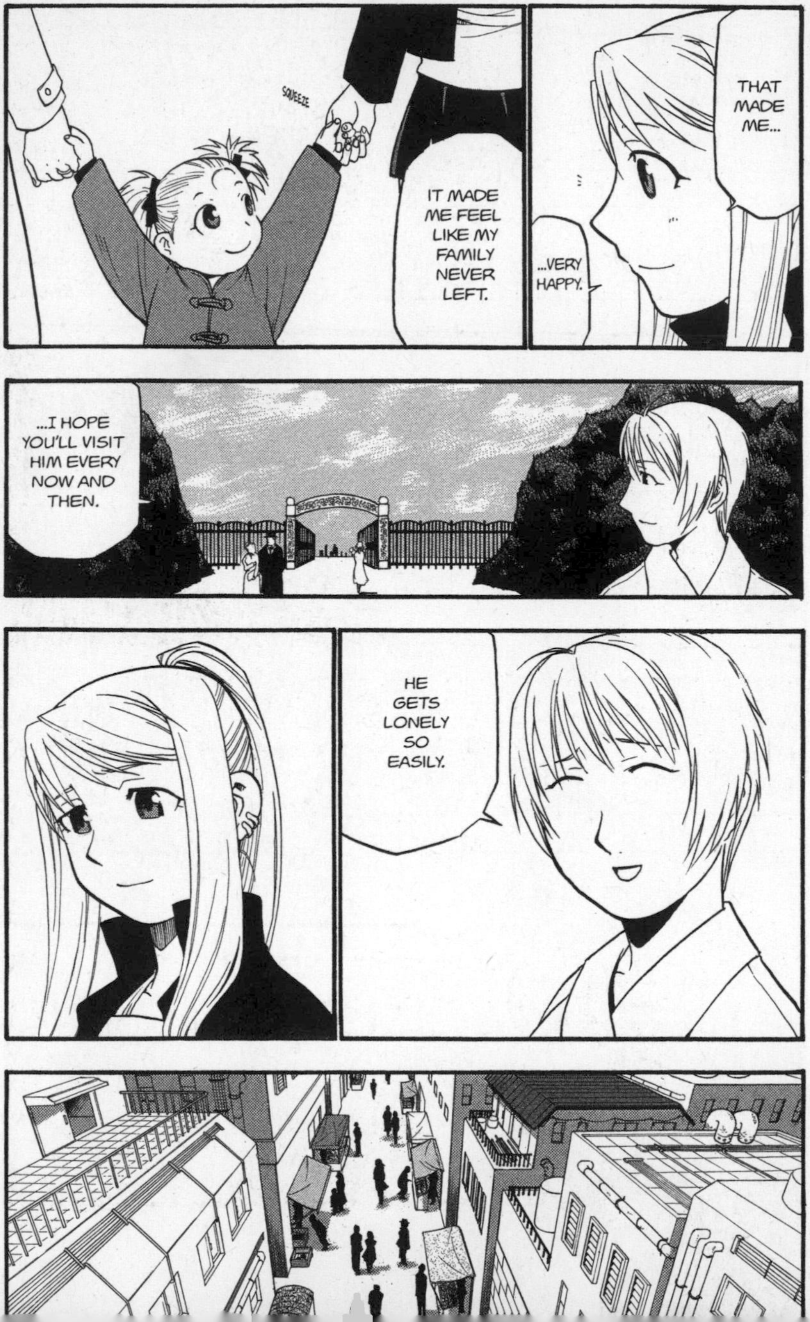
THAT MADE ME...
...VERY HAPPY.
SQUEEZE
IT MADE ME FEEL LIKE MY FAMILY NEVER LEFT.
...I HOPE YOU'LL VISIT HIM EVERY NOW AND THEN.
HE GETS LONELY SO EASILY.

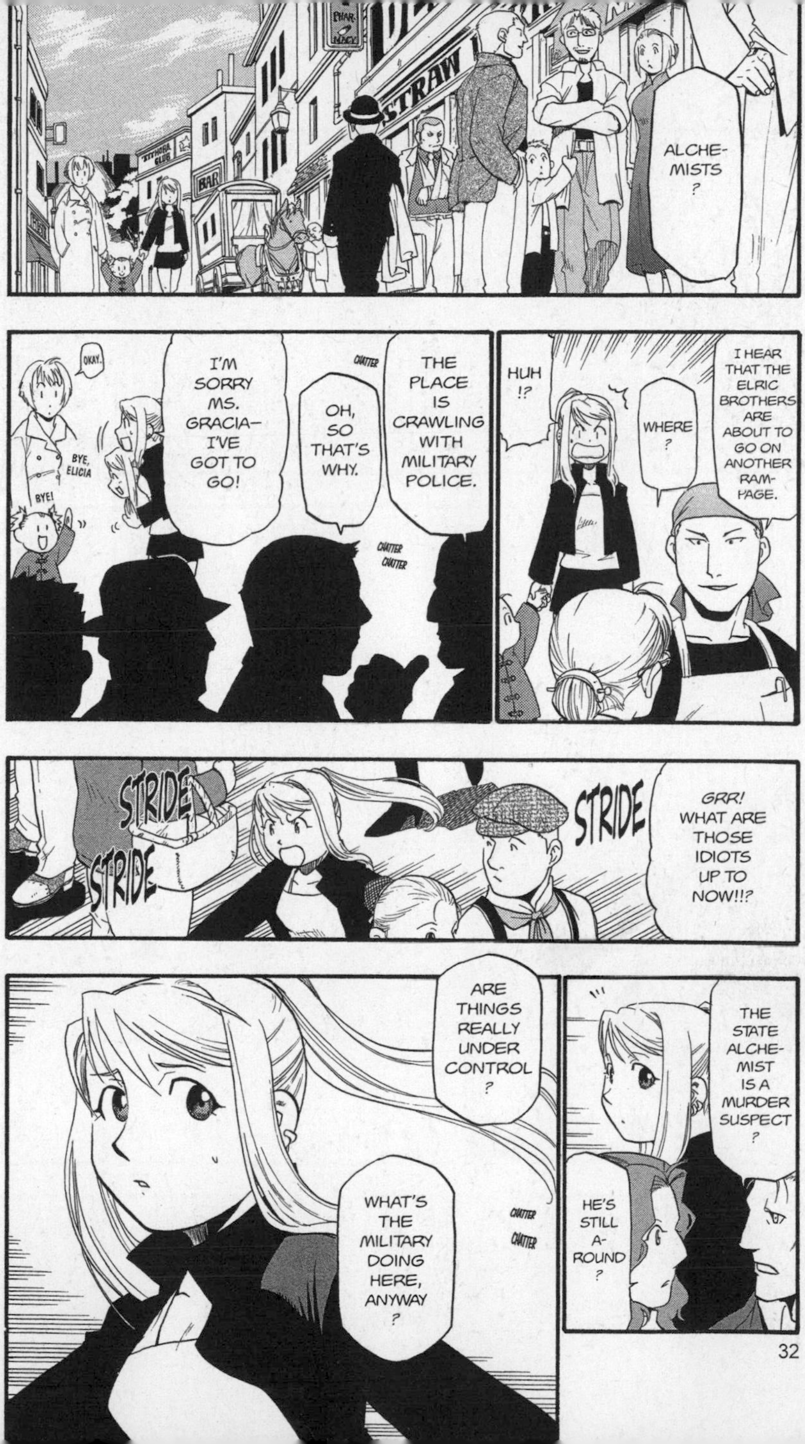
ALCHE-MISTS?
I HEAR THAT THE ELRIC BROTHERS ARE ABOUT TO GO ON ANOTHER RAM-PAGE.
WHERE?
HUH!?
THE PLACE IS CRAWLING WITH MILITARY POLICE.
CHATTER
OH, SO THAT'S WHY.
I'M SORRY MS. GRACIA— I'VE GOT TO GO!
OKAY.
BYE, ELICIA
BYE!
CHATTER CHATTER
GRR! WHAT ARE THOSE IDIOTS UP TO NOW!!?
STRIDE
STRIDE
STRIDE
THE STATE ALCHE-MIST IS A MURDER SUSPECT?
HE'S STILL A-ROUND?
ARE THINGS REALLY UNDER CONTROL?
CHATTER CHATTER
WHAT'S THE MILITARY DOING HERE, ANYWAY?

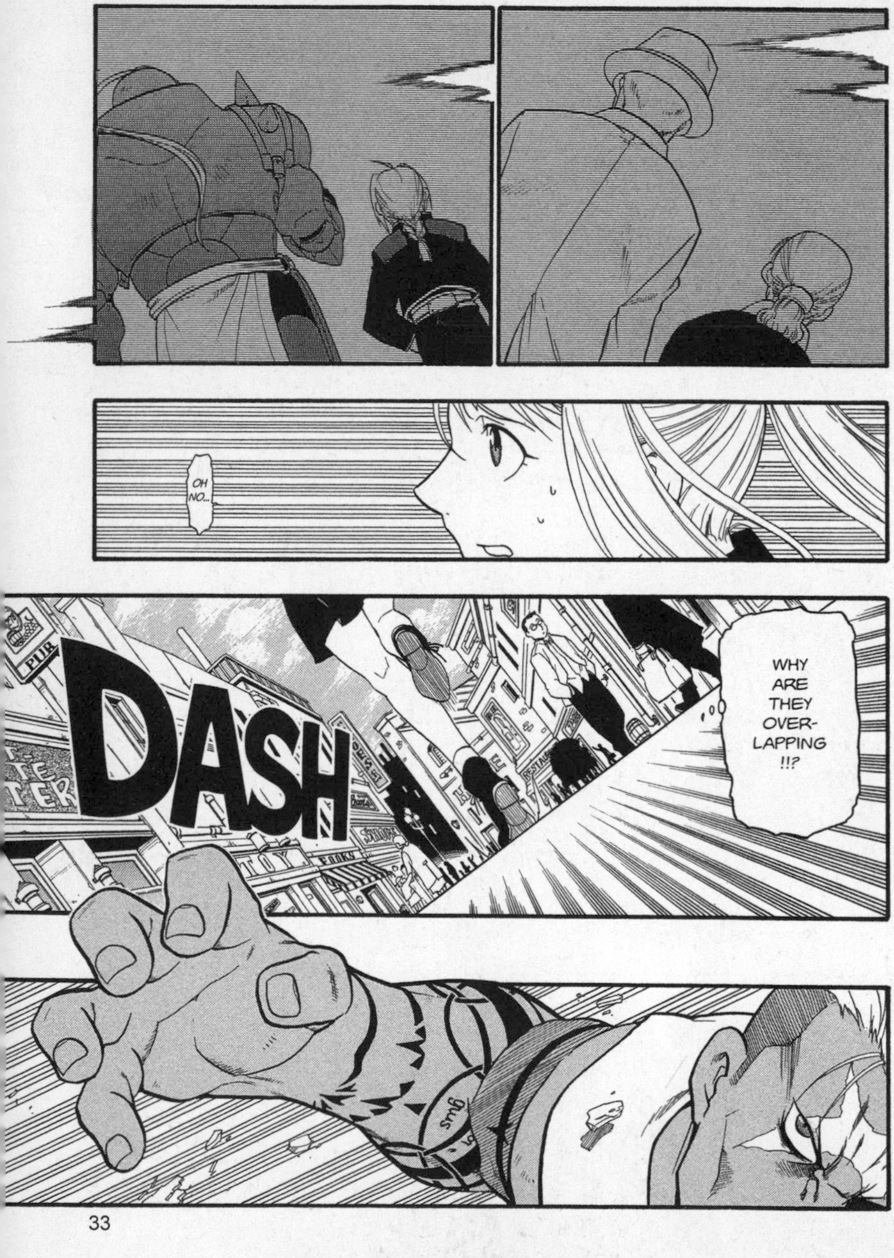
OH NO...
DASH
WHY ARE THEY OVER-LAPPING !!?

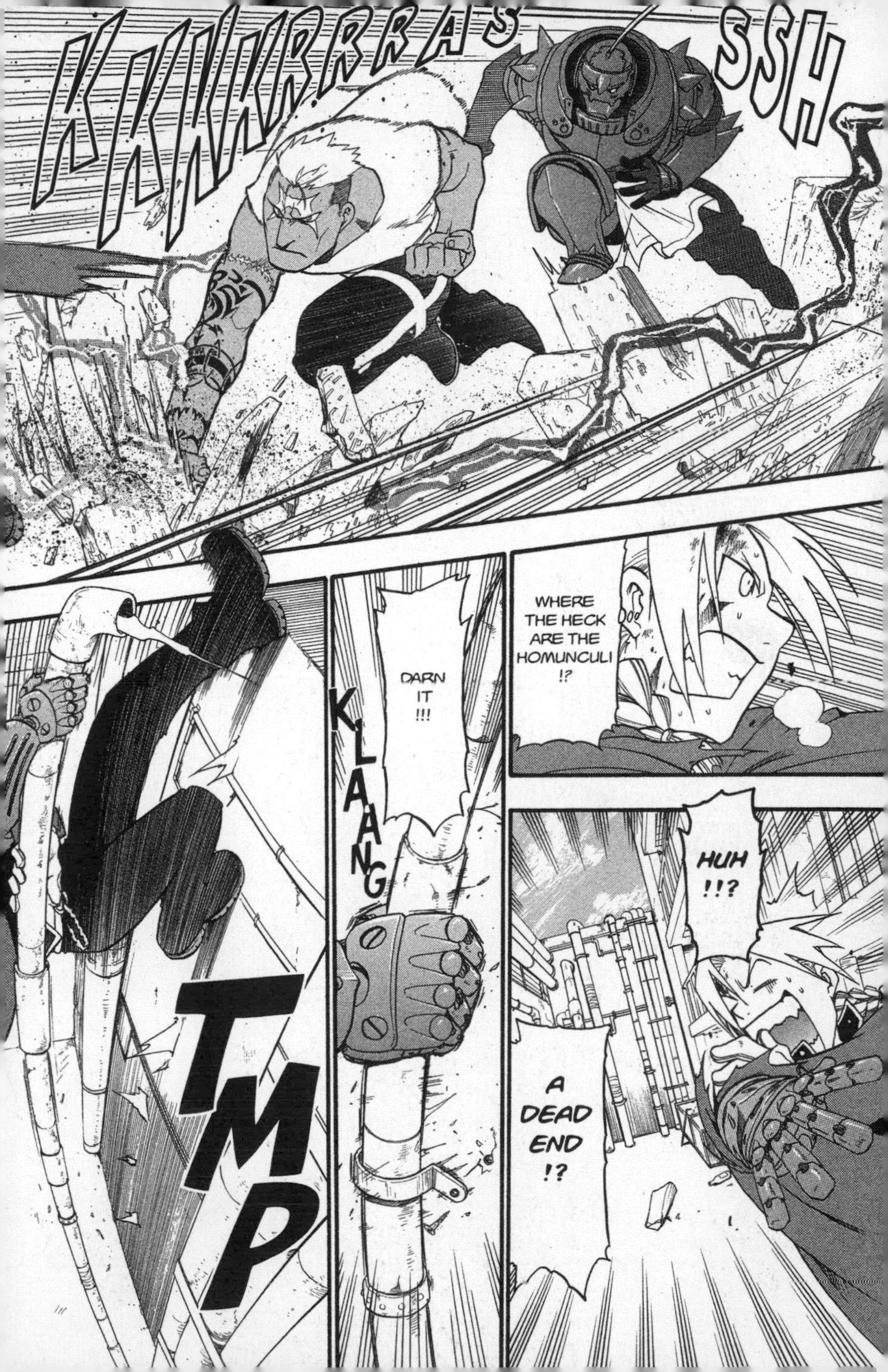
KKWKBRRASSH
WHERE THE HECK ARE THE HOMUNCULI !?
HUH !!?
A DEAD END !?
DARN IT !!!
KLAANG
TMP

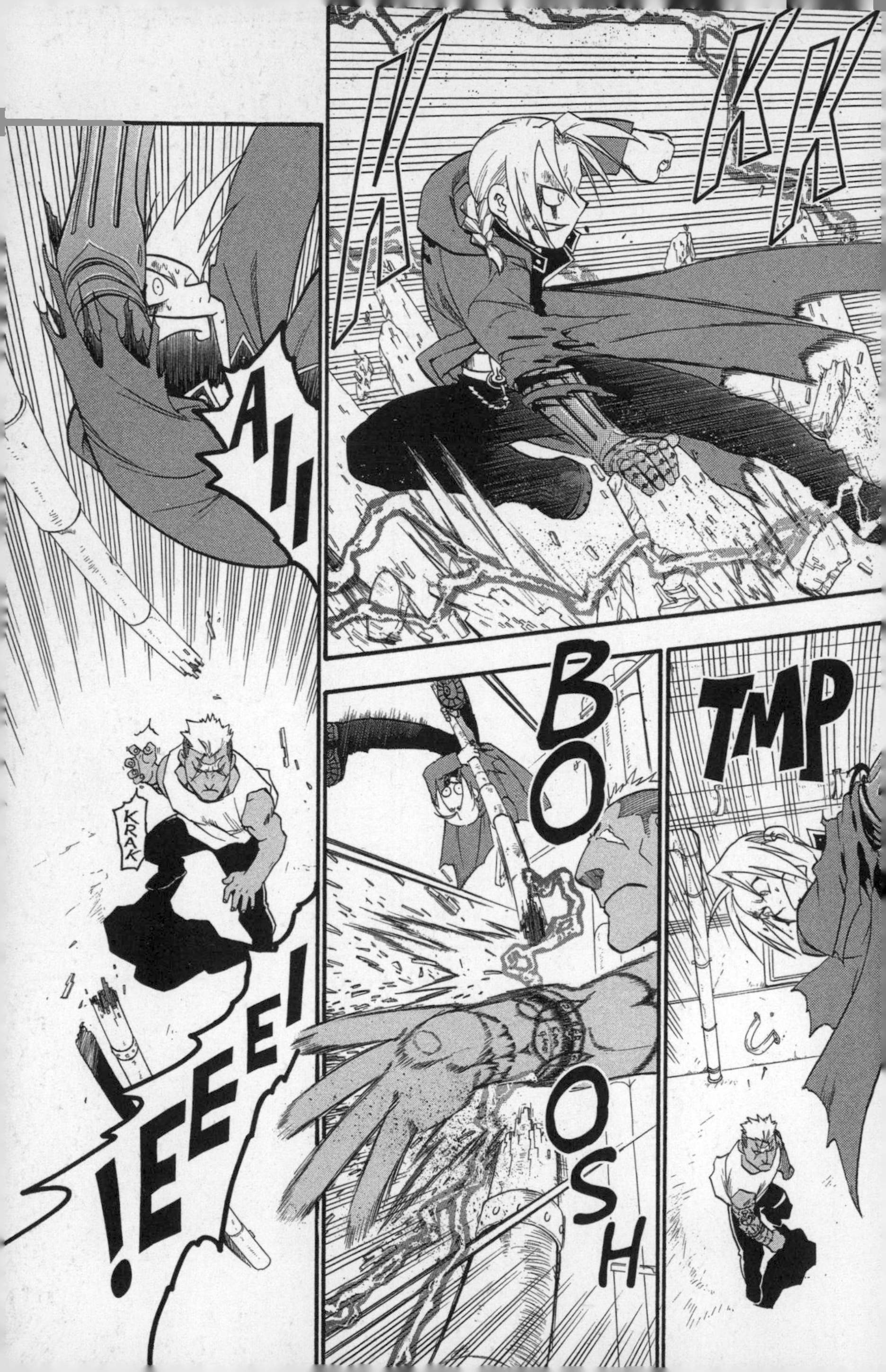
KKK
AIII
!EEEE!
KRAK
TMP
BOOSH

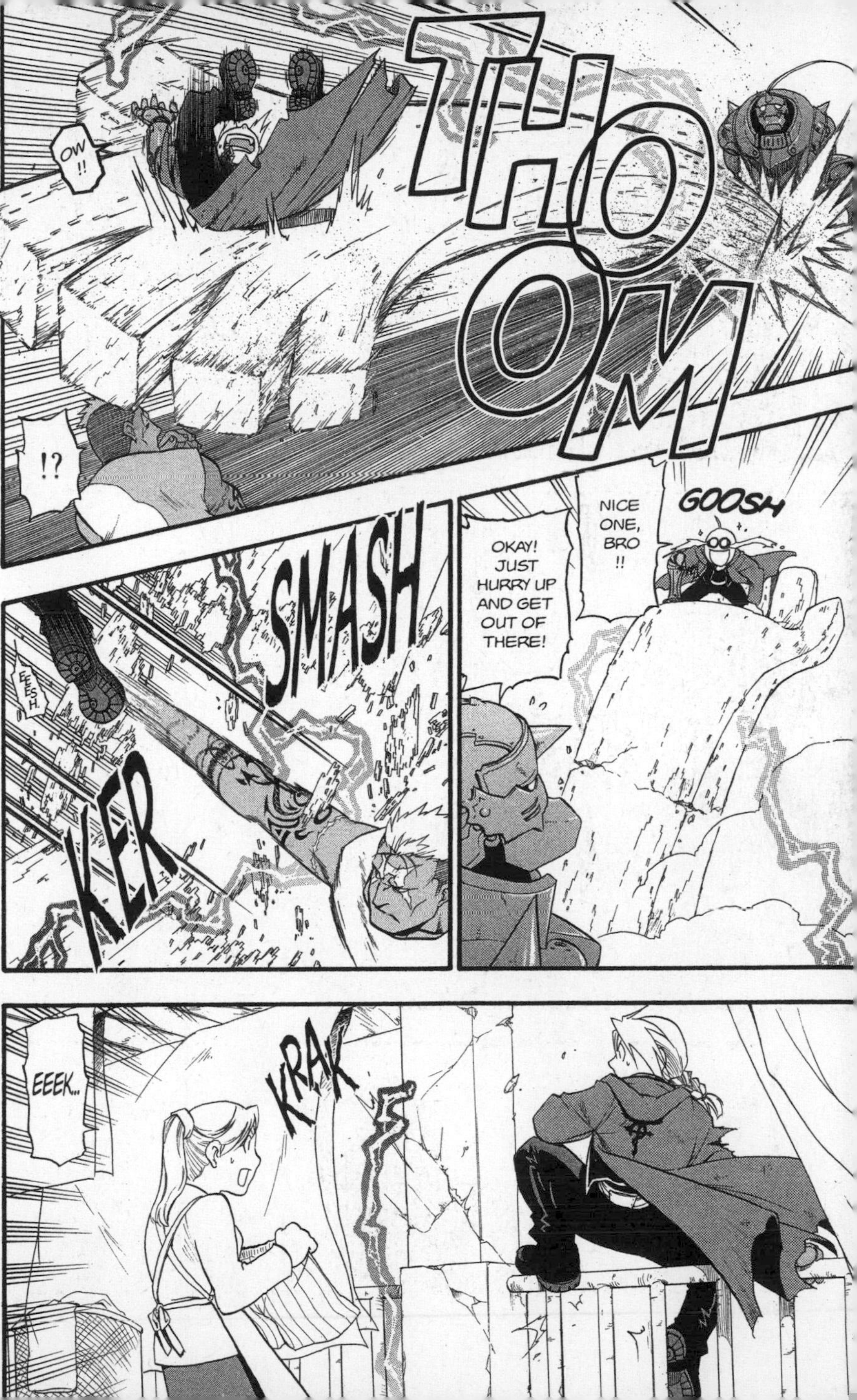
THOOM
OW !!
!?
GOOSH
NICE ONE, BRO !!
OKAY! JUST HURRY UP AND GET OUT OF THERE!
SMASH
EEESH.
KER
KRAK
EEEK...

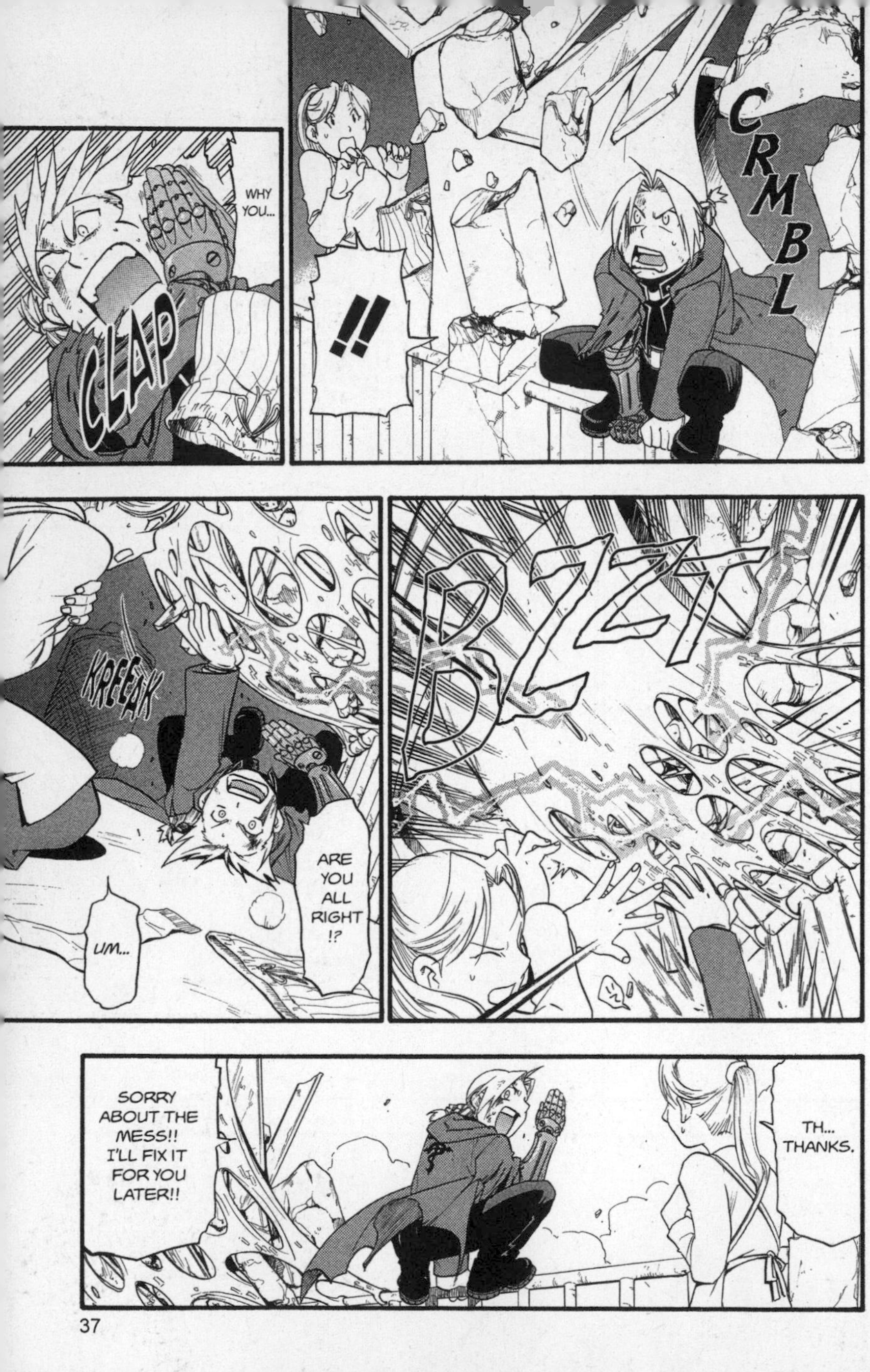
CRMBL
!!
WHY YOU...
CLAP
BZZT
KREEAK
ARE YOU ALL RIGHT !?
UM...
TH... THANKS.
SORRY ABOUT THE MESS!! I'LL FIX IT FOR YOU LATER!!

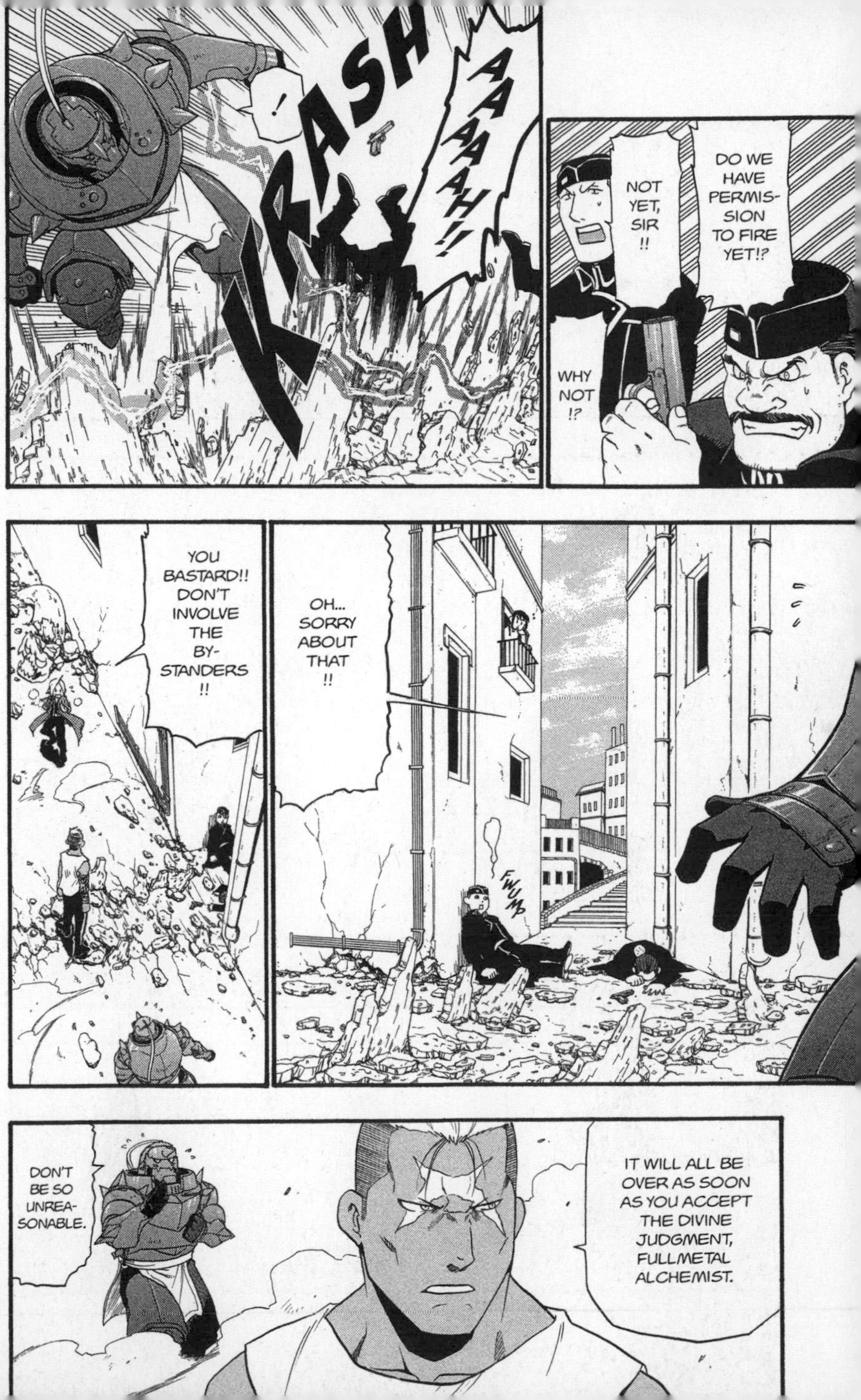
DO WE HAVE PERMISSION TO FIRE YET!?
NOT YET, SIR !!
WHY NOT !?
!
KRASH
AAAAAAH!!
OH... SORRY ABOUT THAT !!
FWUMP
YOU BASTARD!! DON'T INVOLVE THE BY-STANDERS !!
IT WILL ALL BE OVER AS SOON AS YOU ACCEPT THE DIVINE JUDGMENT, FULLMETAL ALCHEMIST.
DON'T BE SO UNREA-SONABLE.

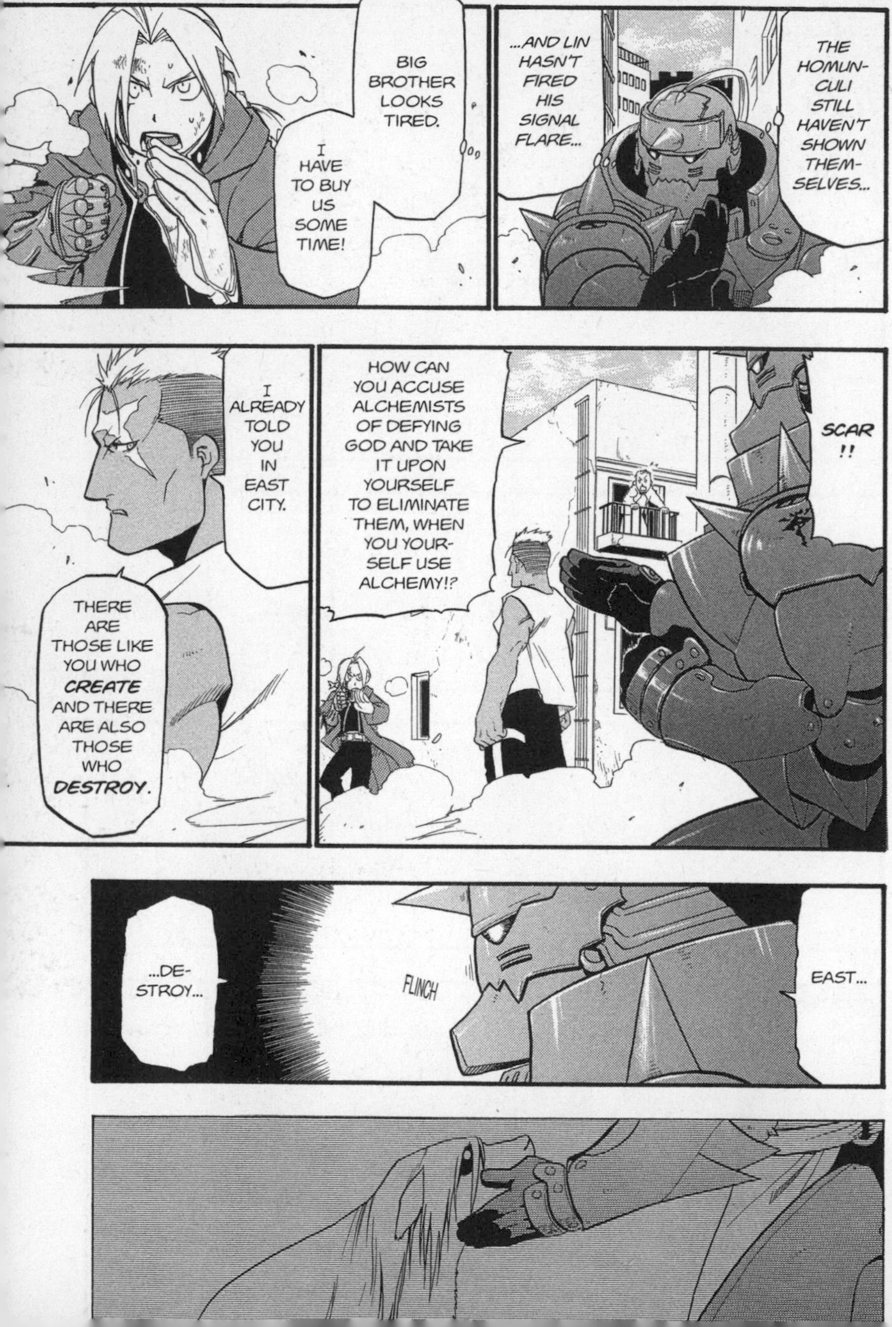
THE HOMUNCULI STILL HAVEN'T SHOWN THEMSELVES...
...AND LIN HASN'T FIRED HIS SIGNAL FLARE...
BIG BROTHER LOOKS TIRED.
I HAVE TO BUY US SOME TIME!
SCAR!!
HOW CAN YOU ACCUSE ALCHEMISTS OF DEFYING GOD AND TAKE IT UPON YOURSELF TO ELIMINATE THEM, WHEN YOU YOURSELF USE ALCHEMY!?
I ALREADY TOLD YOU IN EAST CITY.
THERE ARE THOSE LIKE YOU WHO **CREATE** AND THERE ARE ALSO THOSE WHO **DESTROY**.
EAST...
FLINCH
...DESTROY...

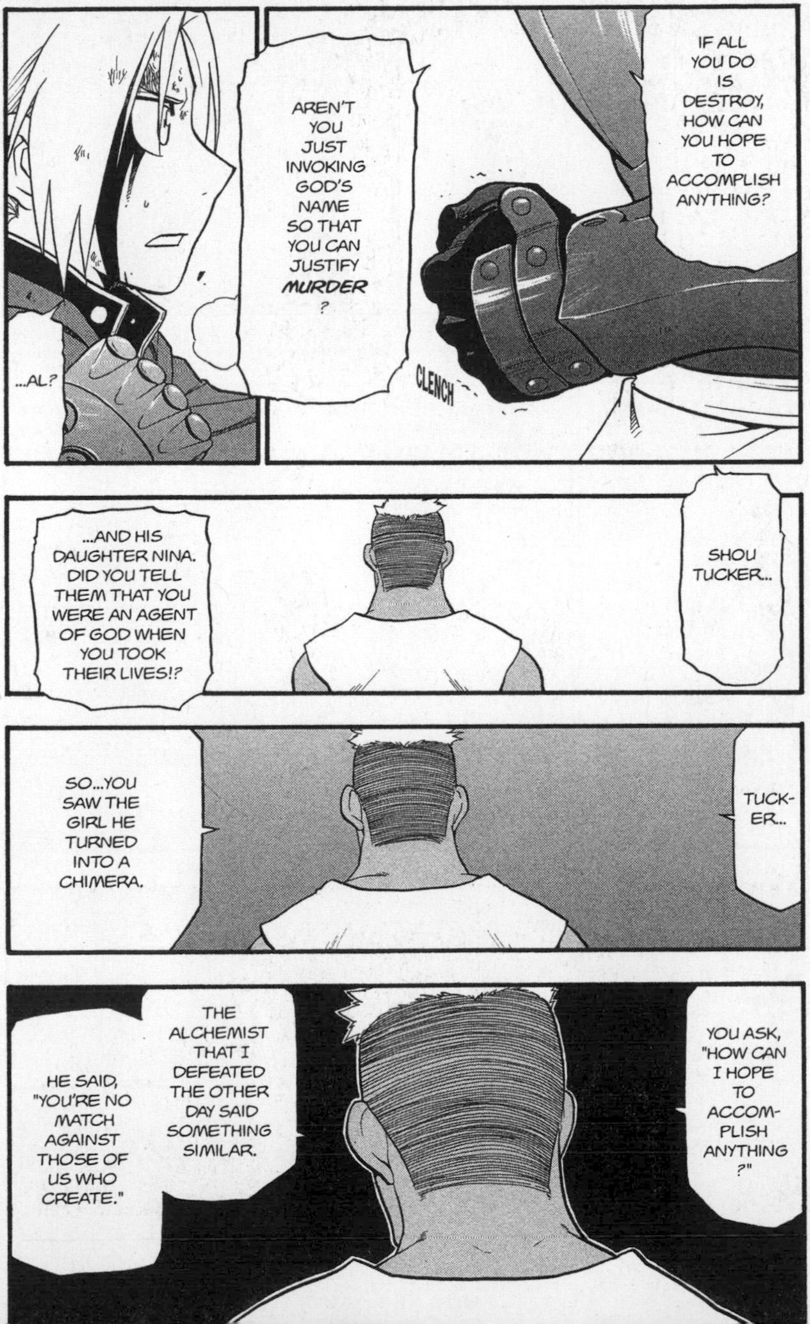
IF ALL YOU DO IS DESTROY, HOW CAN YOU HOPE TO ACCOMPLISH ANYTHING?
AREN'T YOU JUST INVOKING GOD'S NAME SO THAT YOU CAN JUSTIFY *MURDER* ?
CLENCH
...AL?
SHOU TUCKER...
...AND HIS DAUGHTER NINA. DID YOU TELL THEM THAT YOU WERE AN AGENT OF GOD WHEN YOU TOOK THEIR LIVES!?
TUCK-ER...
SO...YOU SAW THE GIRL HE TURNED INTO A CHIMERA.
YOU ASK, "HOW CAN I HOPE TO ACCOM-PLISH ANYTHING ?"
THE ALCHEMIST THAT I DEFEATED THE OTHER DAY SAID SOMETHING SIMILAR.
HE SAID, "YOU'RE NO MATCH AGAINST THOSE OF US WHO CREATE."

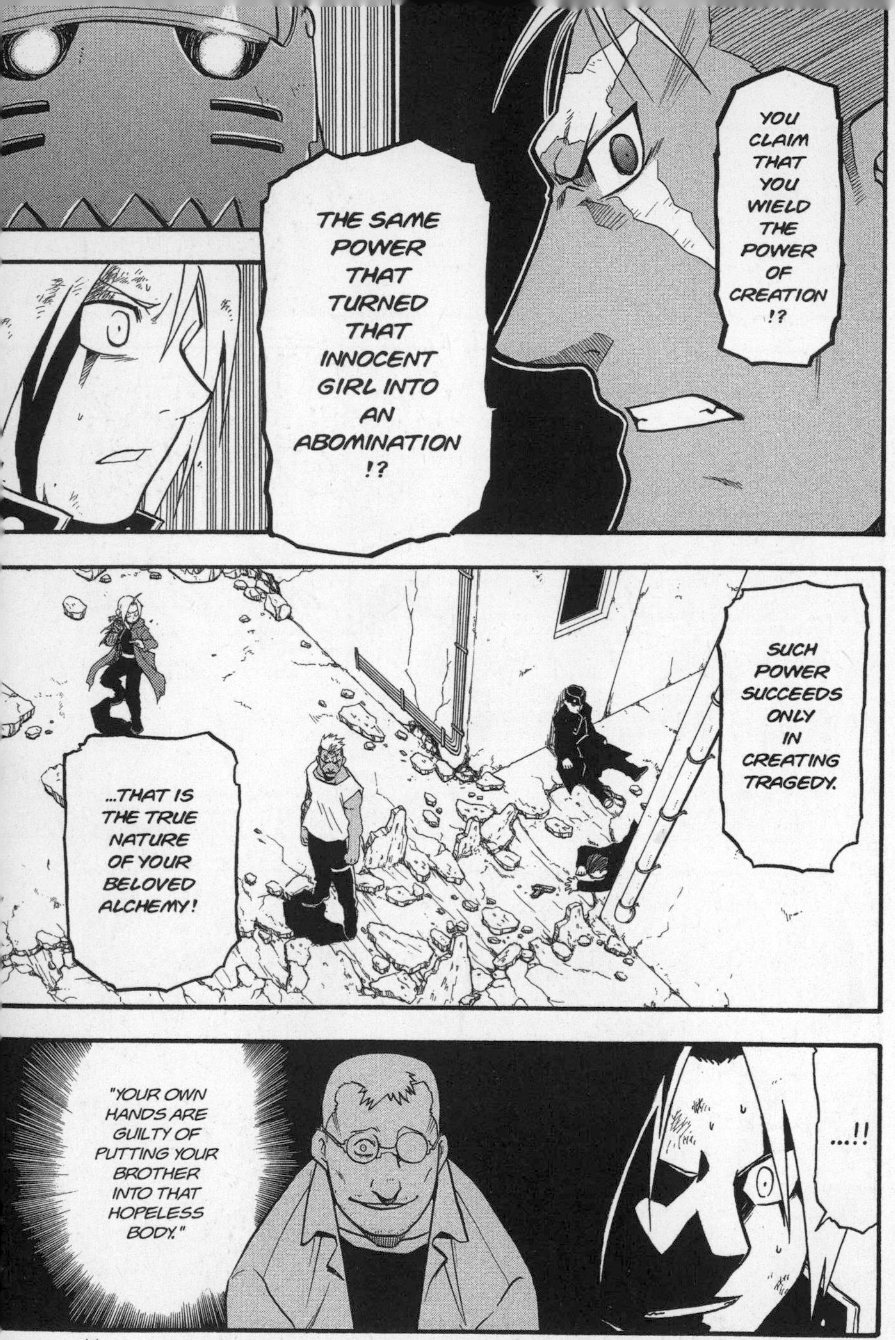
YOU CLAIM THAT YOU WIELD THE POWER OF CREATION !?
THE SAME POWER THAT TURNED THAT INNOCENT GIRL INTO AN ABOMINATION !?
SUCH POWER SUCCEEDS ONLY IN CREATING TRAGEDY.
...THAT IS THE TRUE NATURE OF YOUR BELOVED ALCHEMY!
...!!
"YOUR OWN HANDS ARE GUILTY OF PUTTING YOUR BROTHER INTO THAT HOPELESS BODY."

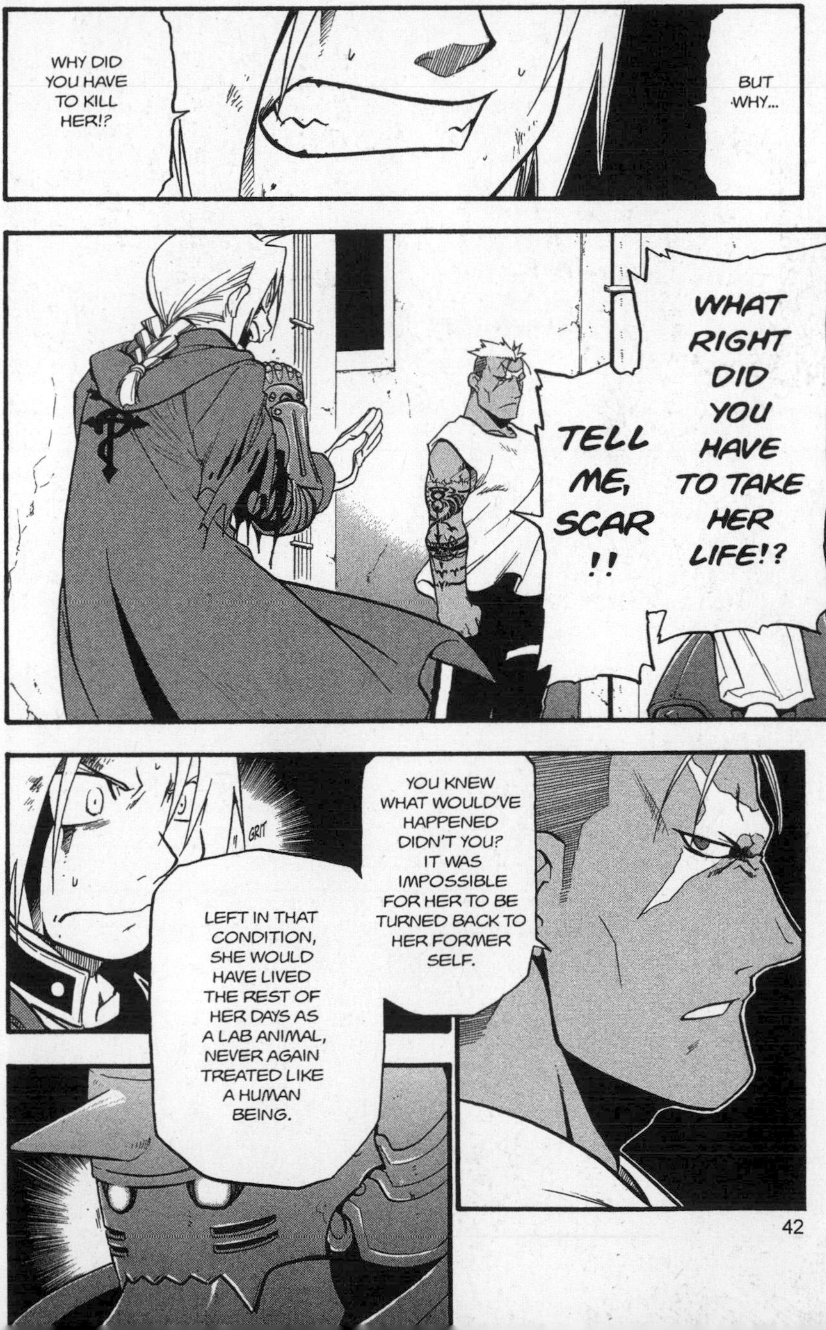
BUT WHY...
WHY DID YOU HAVE TO KILL HER!?
WHAT RIGHT DID YOU HAVE TO TAKE HER LIFE!?
TELL ME, SCAR!!
YOU KNEW WHAT WOULD'VE HAPPENED DIDN'T YOU? IT WAS IMPOSSIBLE FOR HER TO BE TURNED BACK TO HER FORMER SELF.
GRIT
LEFT IN THAT CONDITION, SHE WOULD HAVE LIVED THE REST OF HER DAYS AS A LAB ANIMAL, NEVER AGAIN TREATED LIKE A HUMAN BEING.

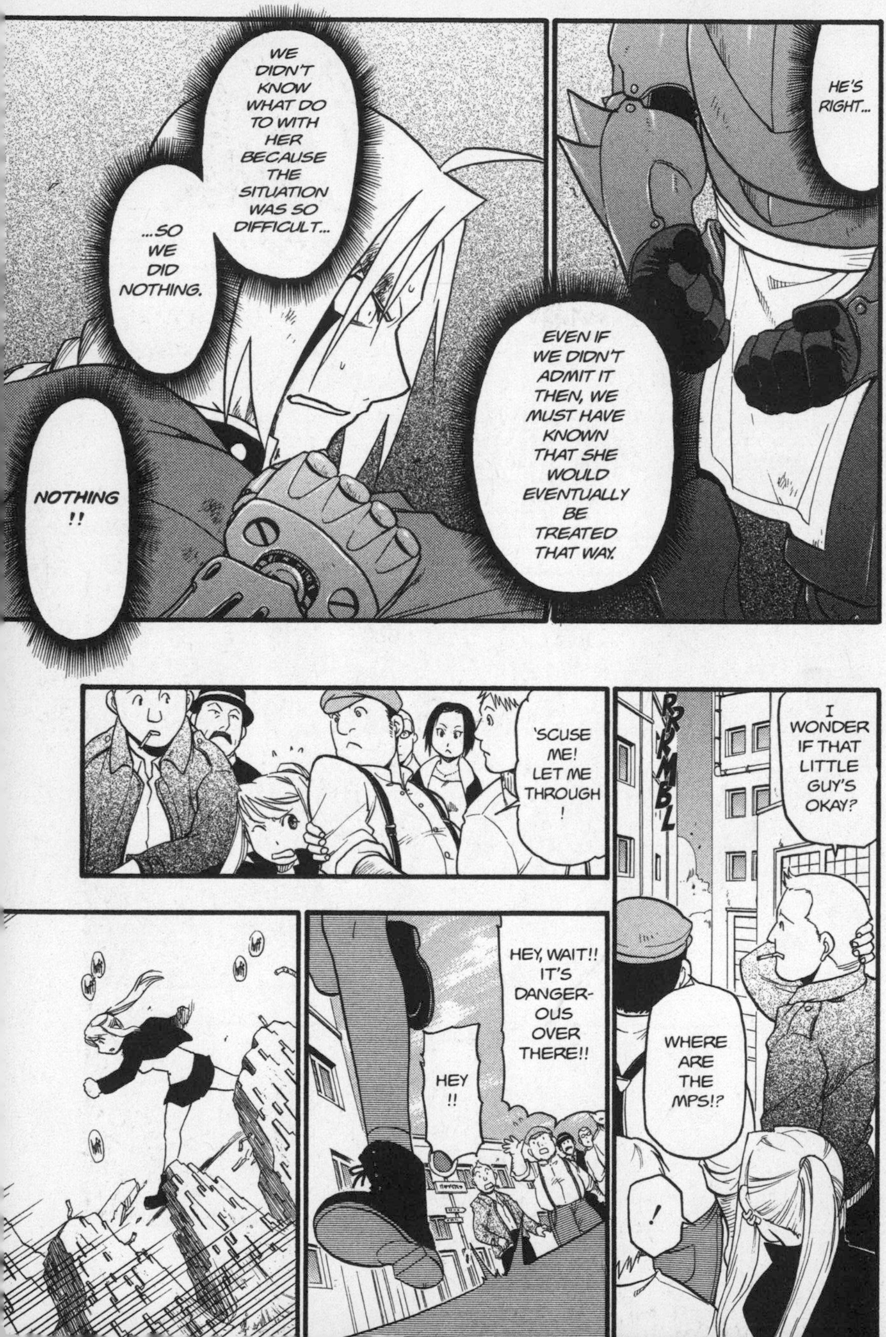
HE'S RIGHT...
EVEN IF WE DIDN'T ADMIT IT THEN, WE MUST HAVE KNOWN THAT SHE WOULD EVENTUALLY BE TREATED THAT WAY.
WE DIDN'T KNOW WHAT DO TO WITH HER BECAUSE THE SITUATION WAS SO DIFFICULT...
...SO WE DID NOTHING.
NOTHING!!
I WONDER IF THAT LITTLE GUY'S OKAY?
RRRMBL
WHERE ARE THE MPS!?
!
'SCUSE ME! LET ME THROUGH!
HEY, WAIT!! IT'S DANGER-OUS OVER THERE!!
HEY!!

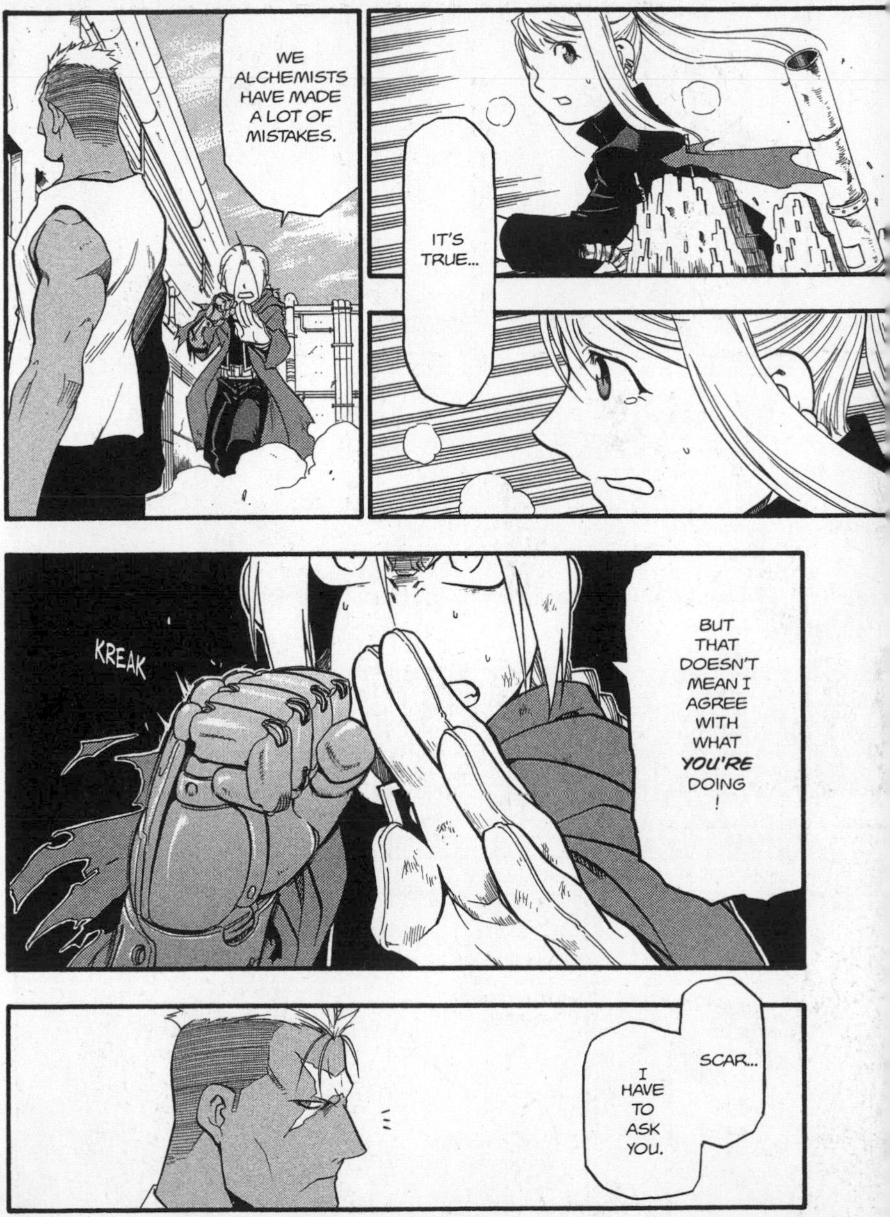
IT'S TRUE...
WE ALCHEMISTS HAVE MADE A LOT OF MISTAKES.
BUT THAT DOESN'T MEAN I AGREE WITH WHAT *YOU'RE* DOING!
KREAK
SCAR...
I HAVE TO ASK YOU.

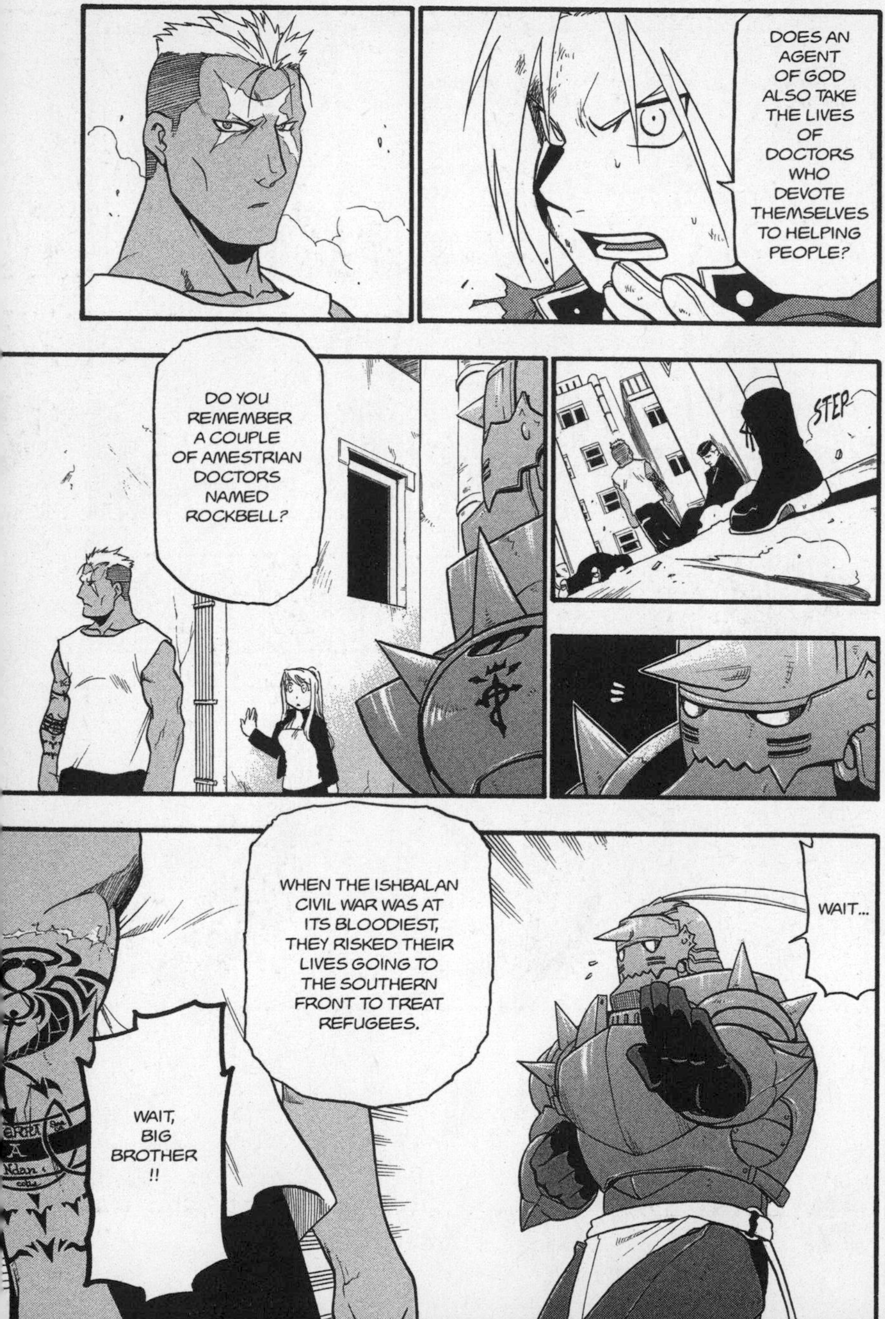
DOES AN AGENT OF GOD ALSO TAKE THE LIVES OF DOCTORS WHO DEVOTE THEMSELVES TO HELPING PEOPLE?
STEP
DO YOU REMEMBER A COUPLE OF AMESTRIAN DOCTORS NAMED ROCKBELL?
WAIT...
WHEN THE ISHBALAN CIVIL WAR WAS AT ITS BLOODIEST, THEY RISKED THEIR LIVES GOING TO THE SOUTHERN FRONT TO TREAT REFUGEES.
WAIT, BIG BROTHER !!

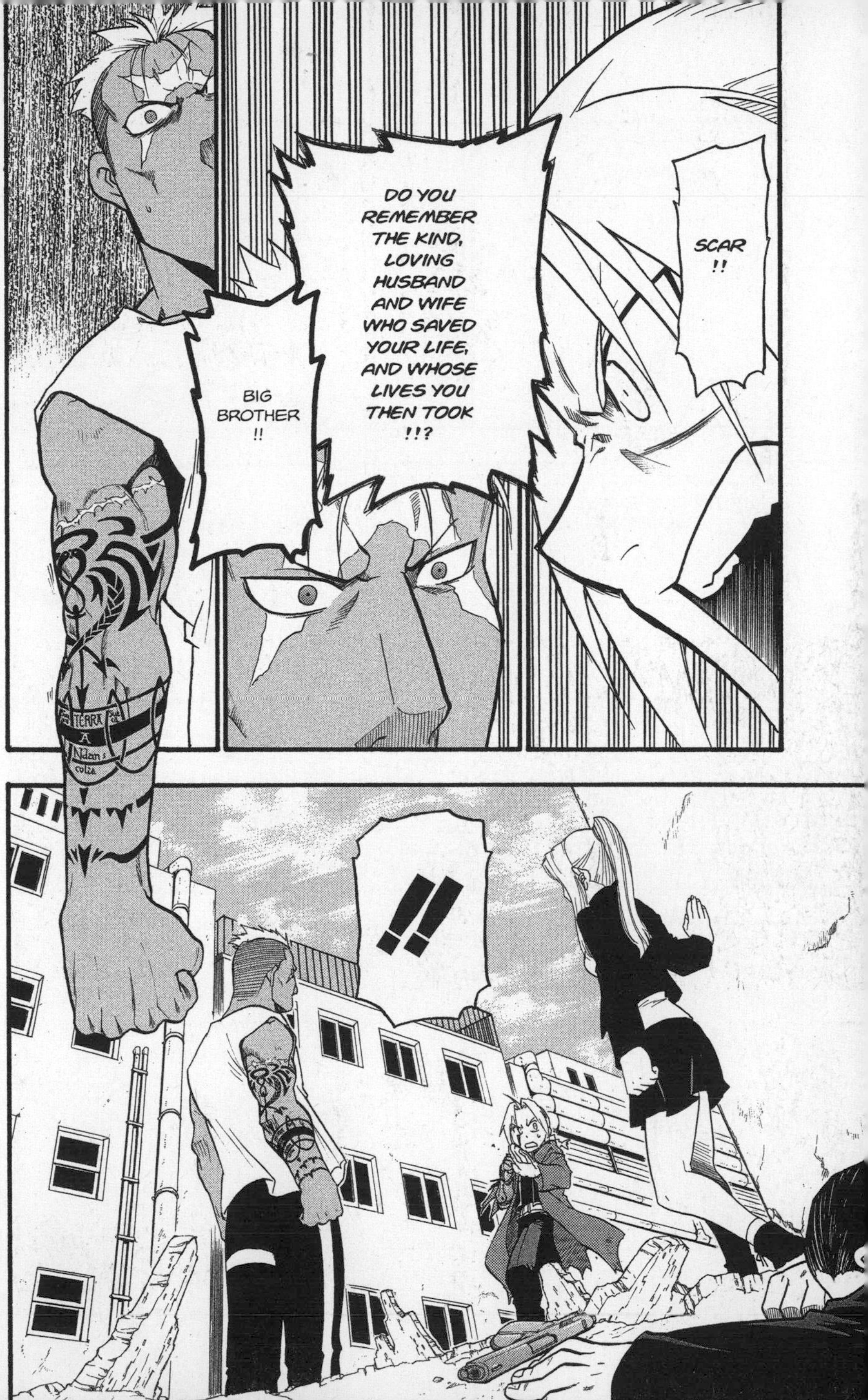
SCAR !!
DO YOU REMEMBER THE KIND, LOVING HUSBAND AND WIFE WHO SAVED YOUR LIFE, AND WHOSE LIVES YOU THEN TOOK !!?
BIG BROTHER !!
!!

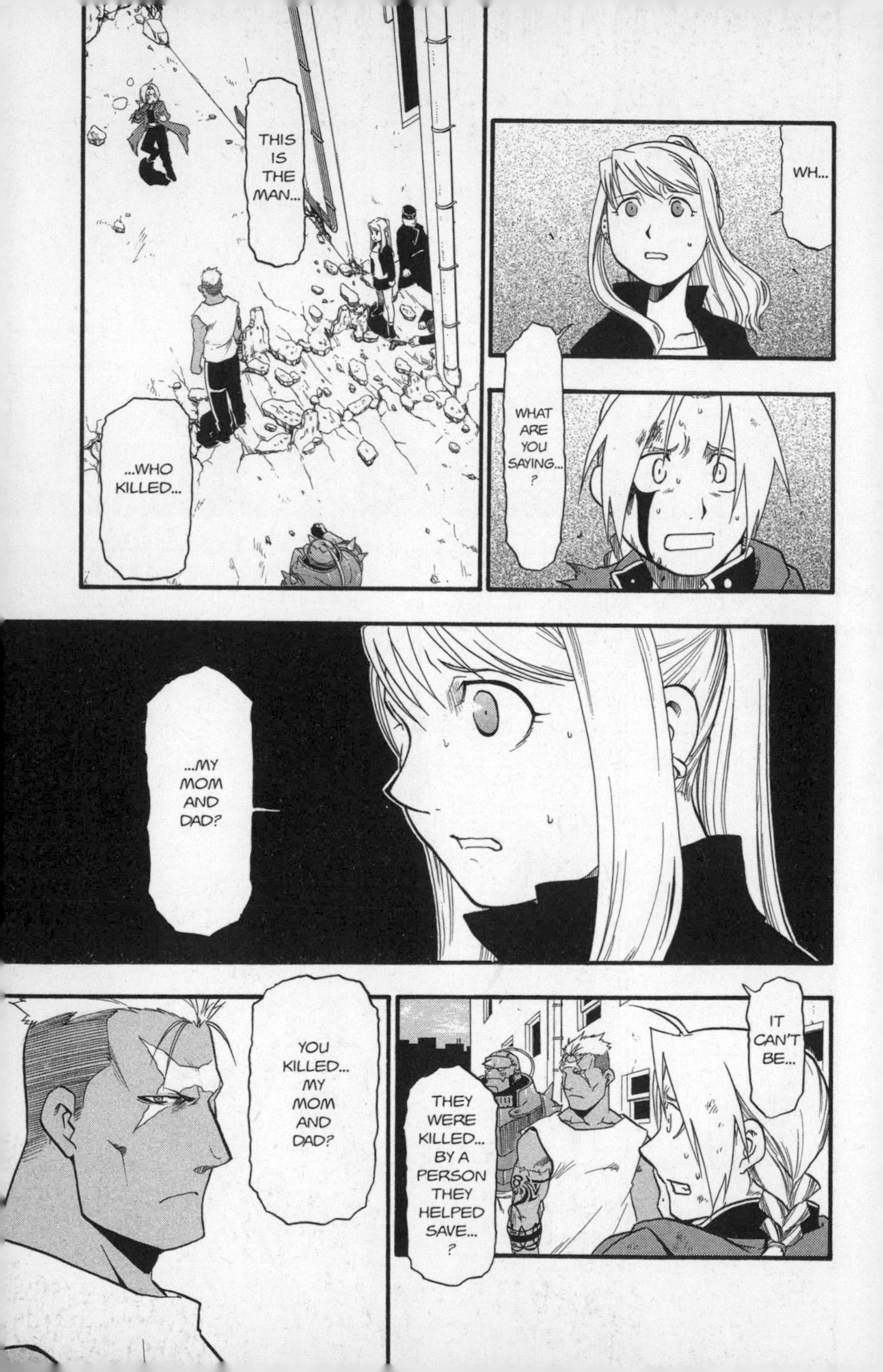
WH...
WHAT ARE YOU SAYING...?
THIS IS THE MAN...
...WHO KILLED...
...MY MOM AND DAD?
IT CAN'T BE...
THEY WERE KILLED... BY A PERSON THEY HELPED SAVE...?
YOU KILLED... MY MOM AND DAD?

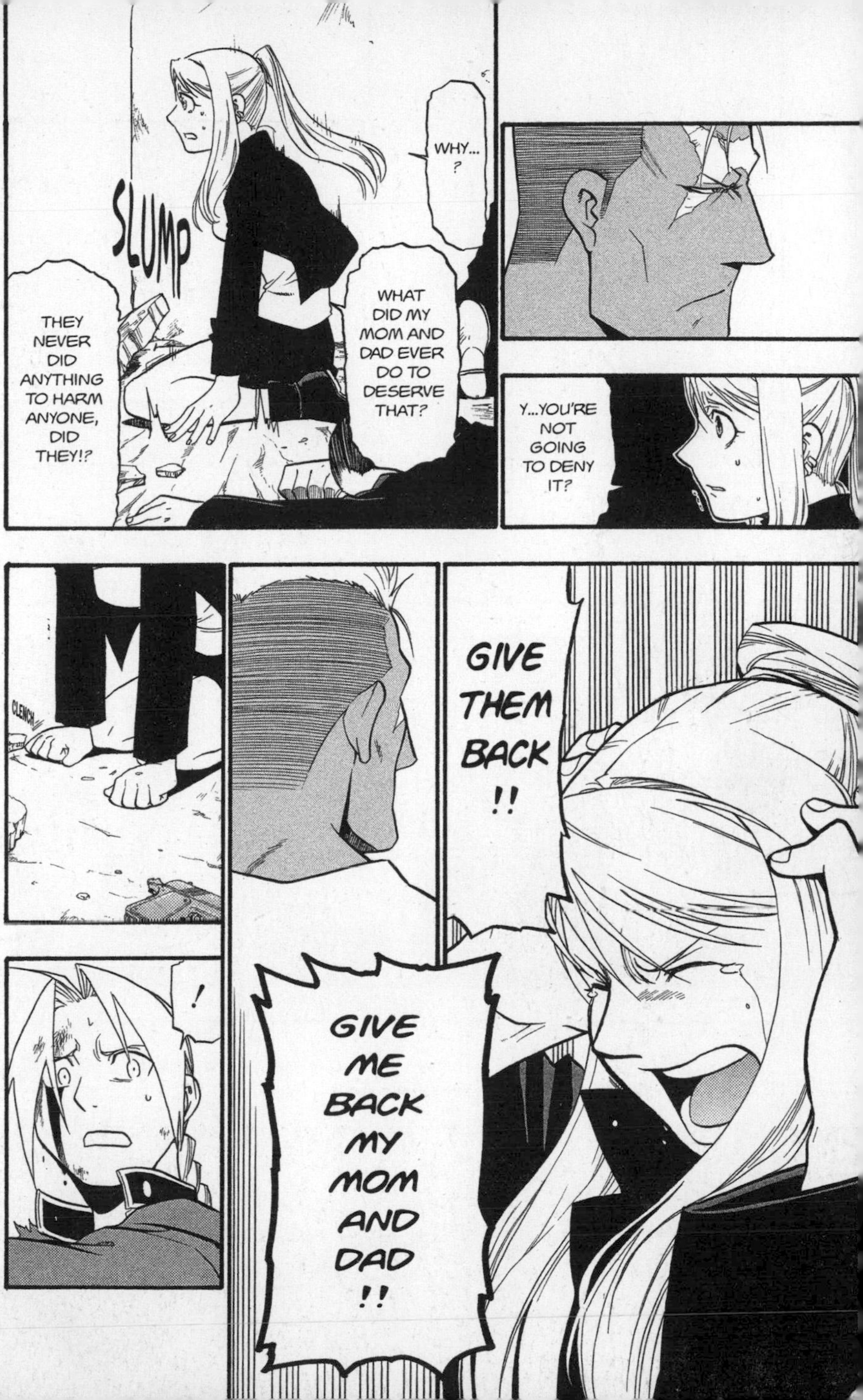
Y...YOU'RE NOT GOING TO DENY IT?
WHY...?
SLUMP
WHAT DID MY MOM AND DAD EVER DO TO DESERVE THAT?
THEY NEVER DID ANYTHING TO HARM ANYONE, DID THEY!?
GIVE THEM BACK!!
GIVE ME BACK MY MOM AND DAD!!
CLENCH
!

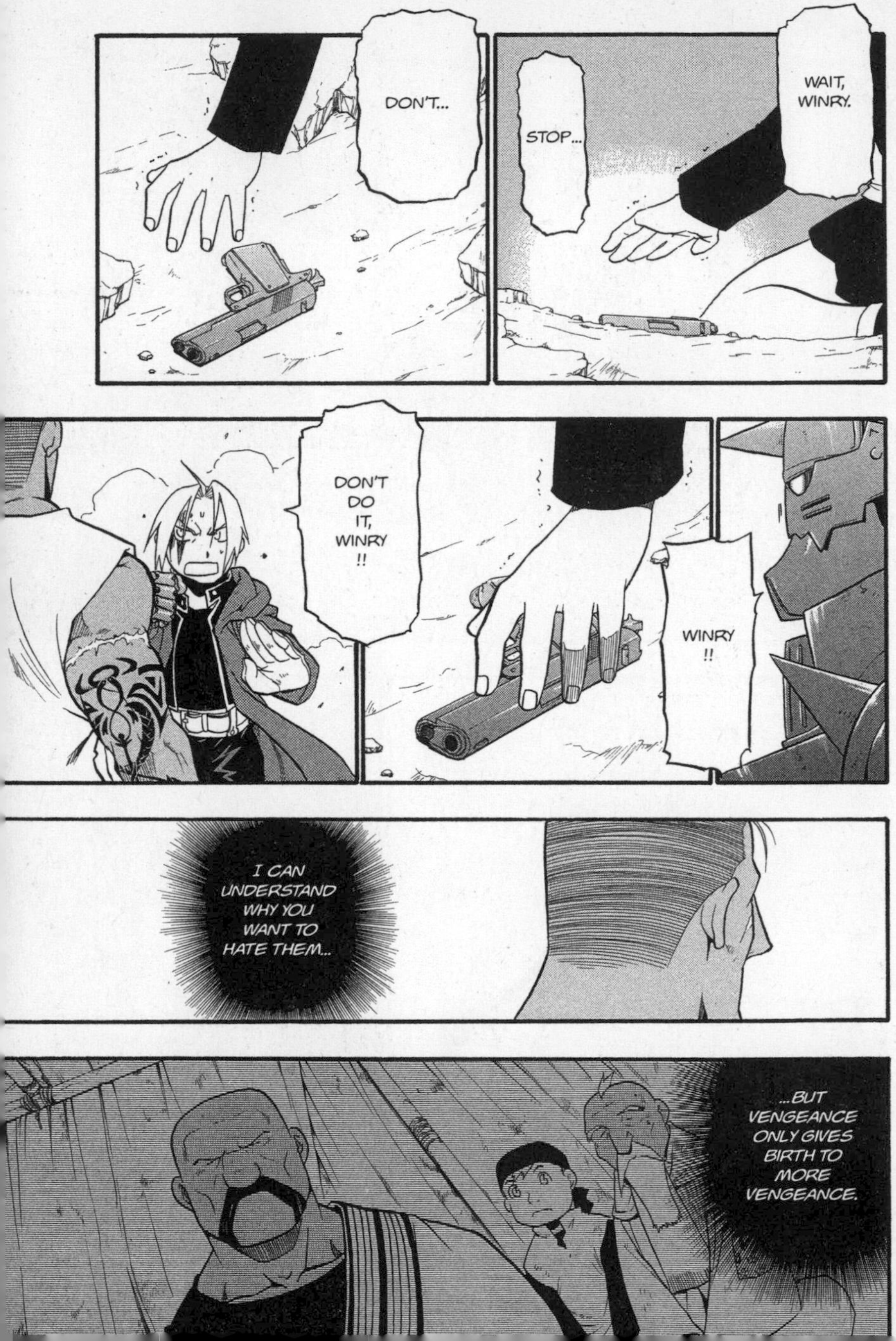
WAIT, WINRY.
STOP...
DON'T...
WINRY!!
DON'T DO IT, WINRY!!
I CAN UNDERSTAND WHY YOU WANT TO HATE THEM...
...BUT VENGEANCE ONLY GIVES BIRTH TO MORE VENGEANCE.

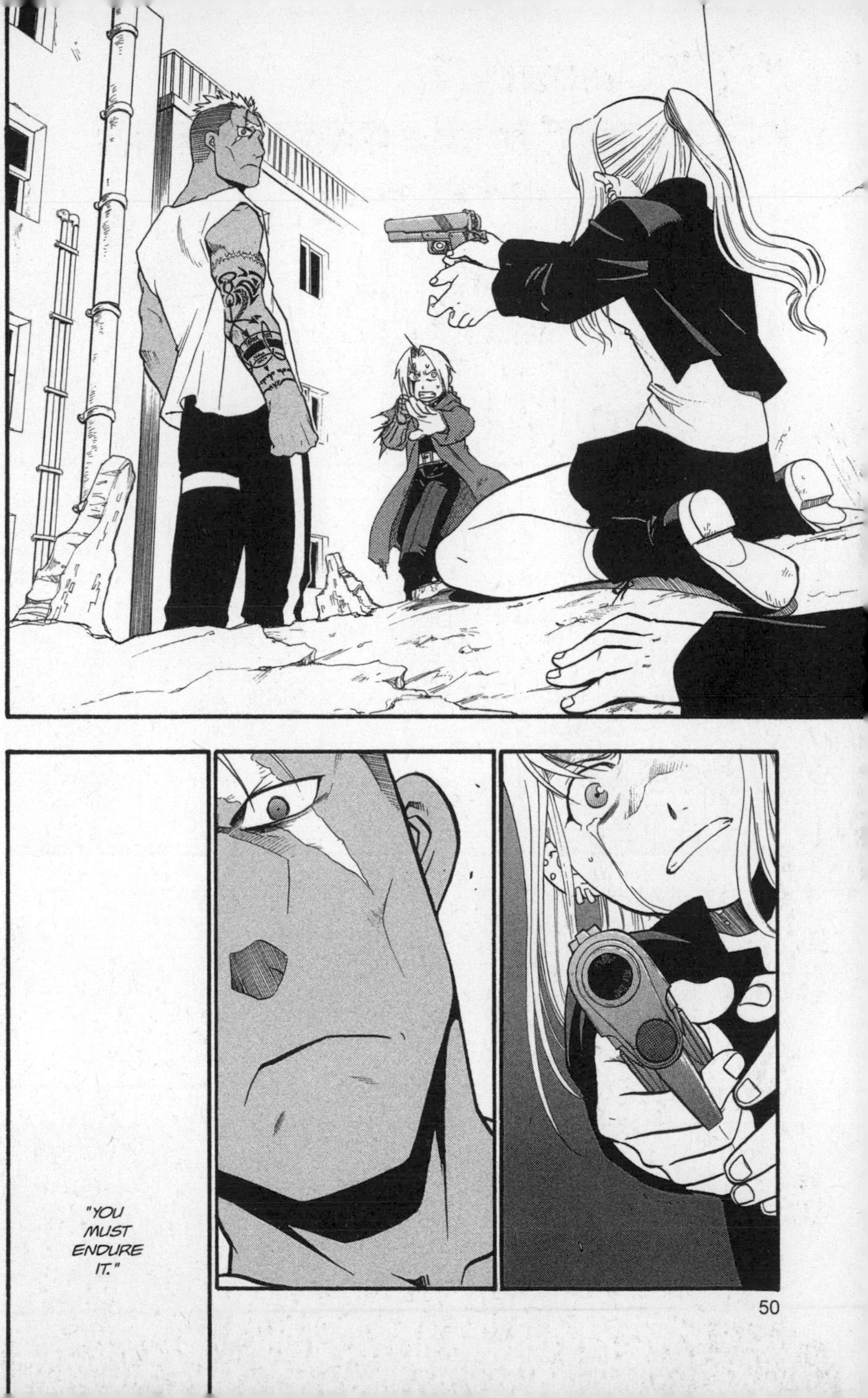
"YOU MUST ENDURE IT."

Chapter 47
A Girl in the Grip of Battles Past and Present

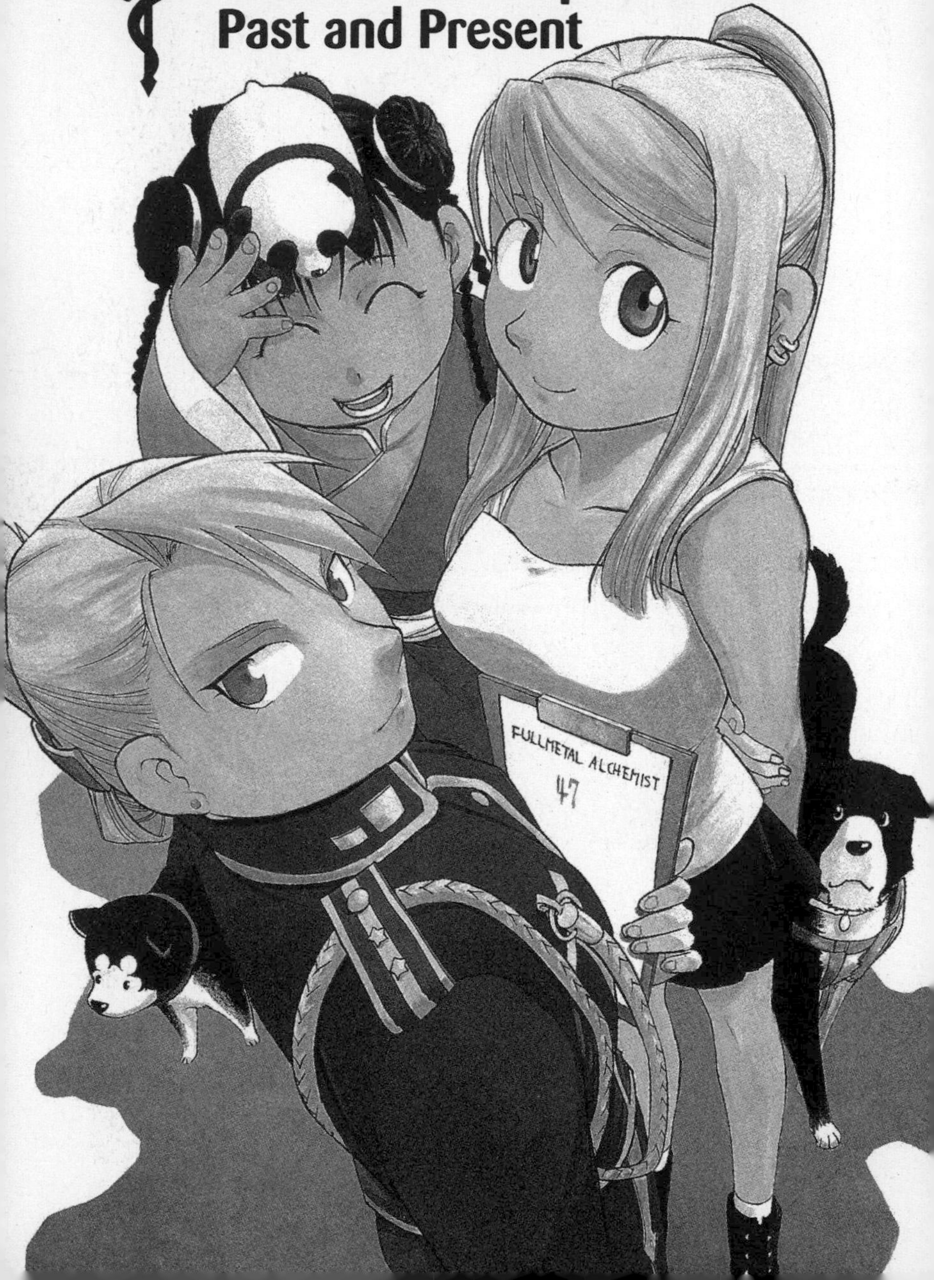
FULLMETAL ALCHEMIST
47

FULLMETAL
ALCHEMIST

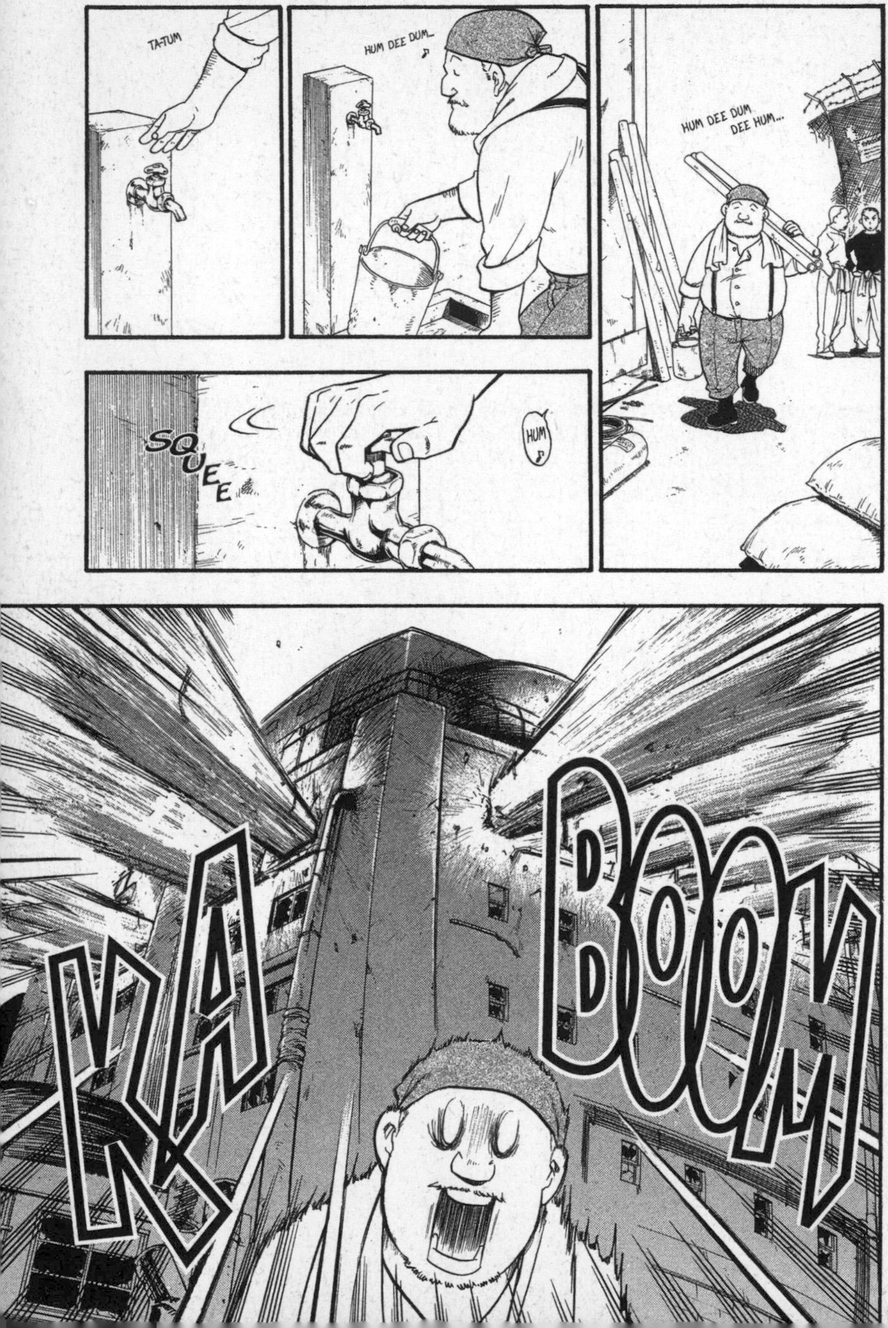
HUM DEE DUM DEE HUM...
HUM DEE DUM...
TA-TUM
HUM
SQUEE
KA BOOM

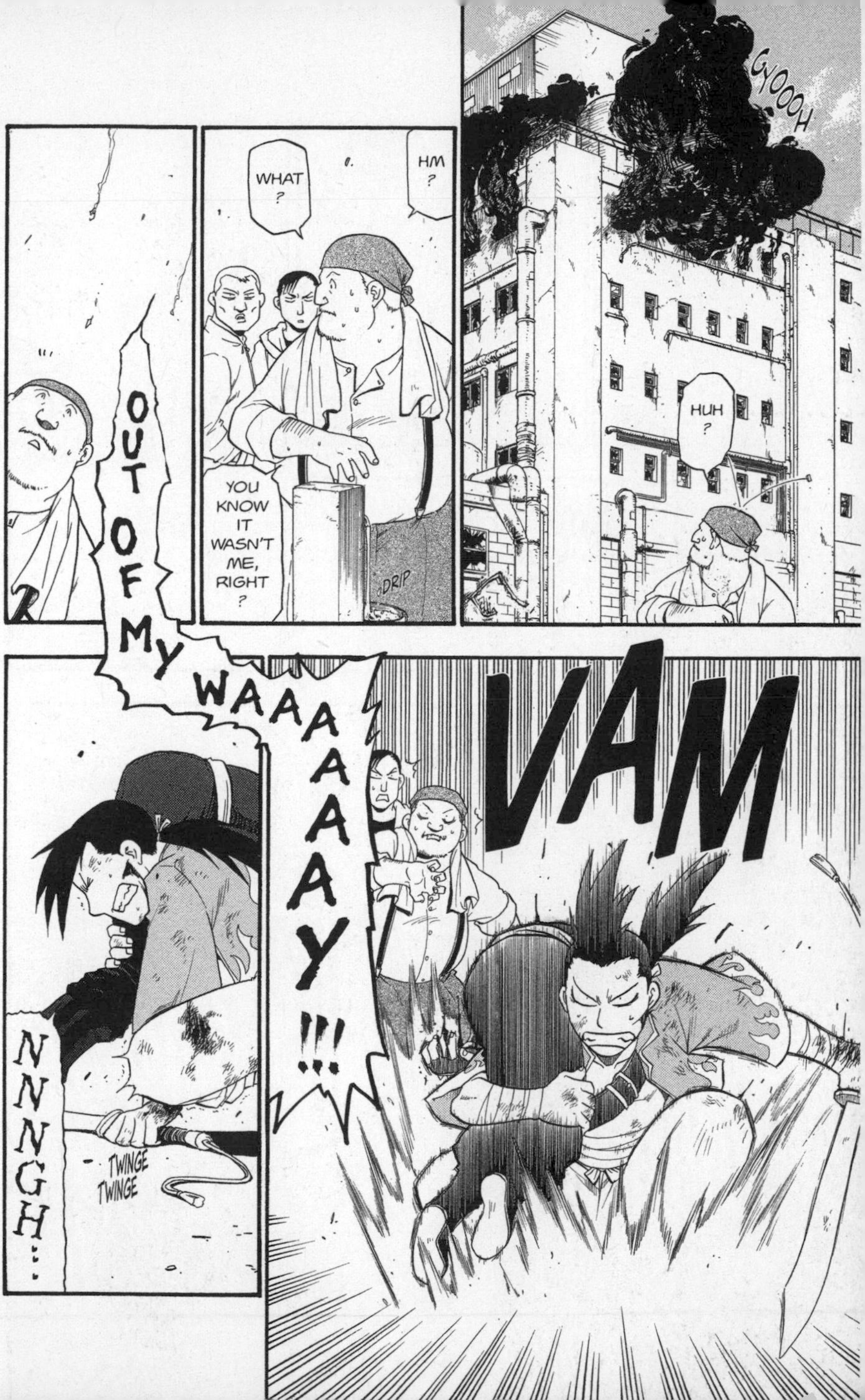
GYOOOH
HUH ?
HM ?
WHAT ?
YOU KNOW IT WASN'T ME, RIGHT ?
DRIP
...
OUT OF MY WAAAAAAAY!!!
VAM
NNNGH...
TWINGE TWINGE

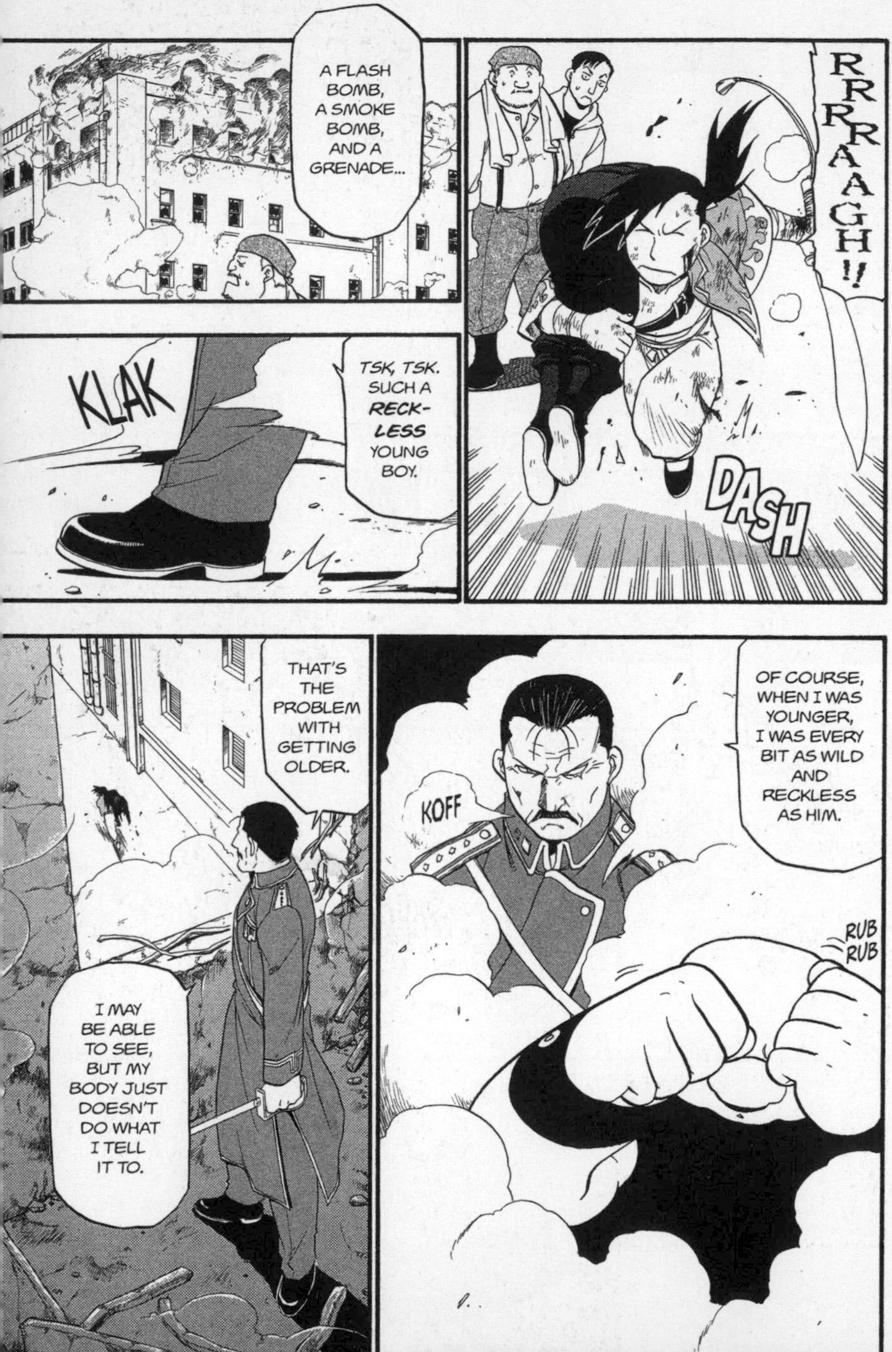
RRRAAGH!!
DASH
A FLASH BOMB, A SMOKE BOMB, AND A GRENADE...
TSK, TSK. SUCH A **RECK-LESS** YOUNG BOY.
KLAK
OF COURSE, WHEN I WAS YOUNGER, I WAS EVERY BIT AS WILD AND RECKLESS AS HIM.
KOFF
RUB RUB
THAT'S THE PROBLEM WITH GETTING OLDER.
I MAY BE ABLE TO SEE, BUT MY BODY JUST DOESN'T DO WHAT I TELL IT TO.

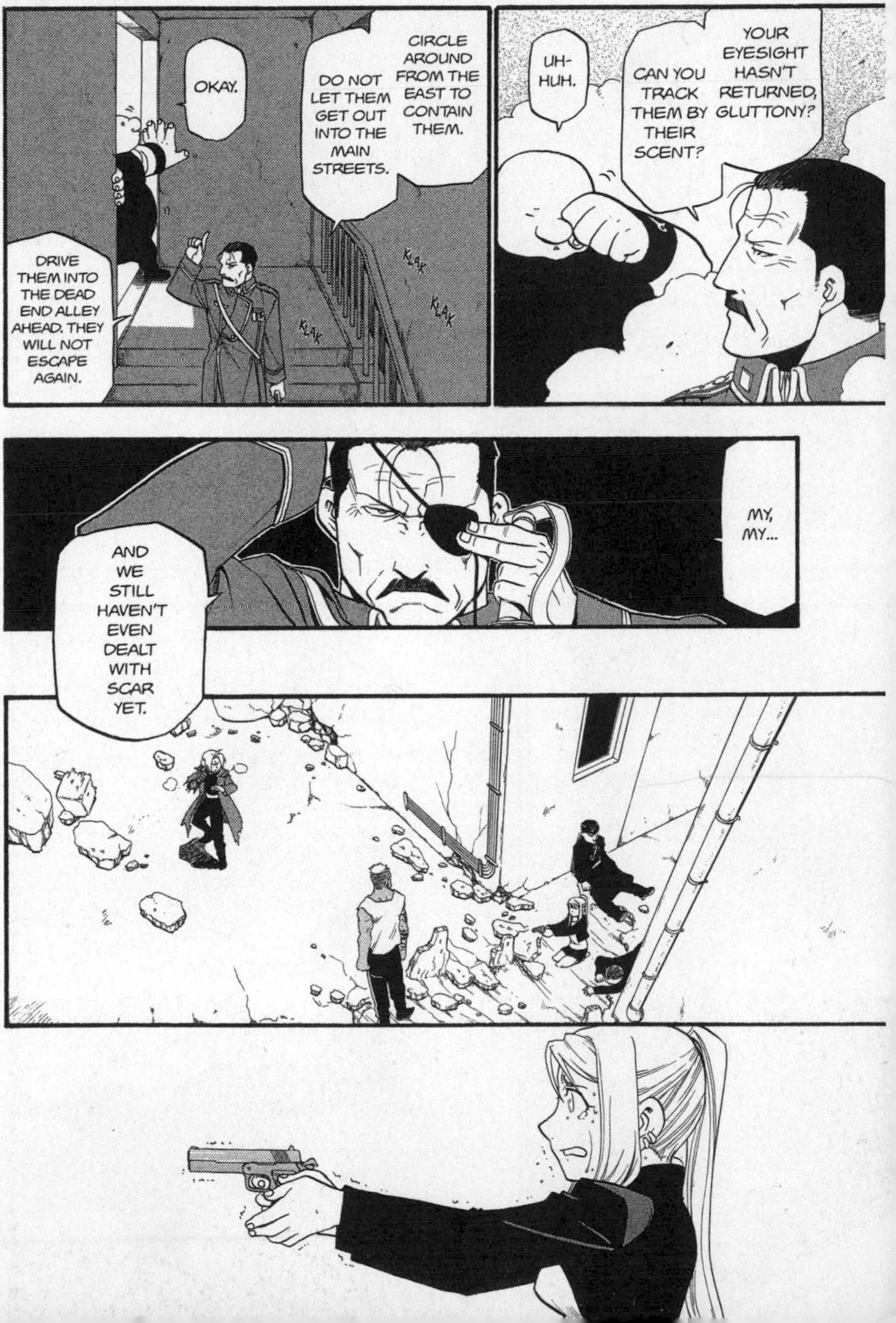
YOUR EYESIGHT HASN'T RETURNED, GLUTTONY?
CAN YOU TRACK THEM BY THEIR SCENT?
UH-HUH.
CIRCLE AROUND FROM THE EAST TO CONTAIN THEM.
DO NOT LET THEM GET OUT INTO THE MAIN STREETS.
OKAY.
KLAK
KLAK
KLAK
DRIVE THEM INTO THE DEAD END ALLEY AHEAD. THEY WILL NOT ESCAPE AGAIN.
MY, MY...
AND WE STILL HAVEN'T EVEN DEALT WITH SCAR YET.

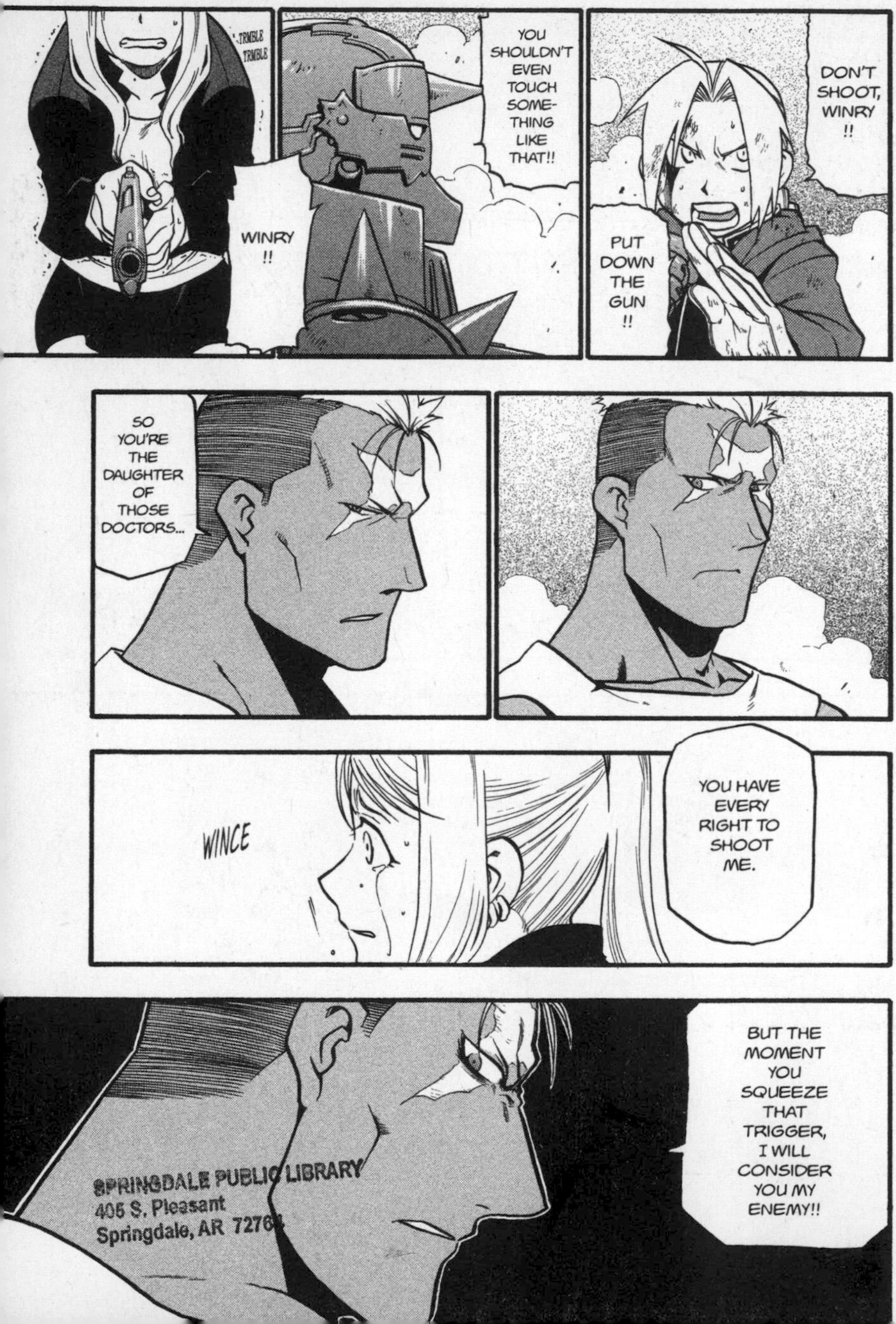
DON'T SHOOT, WINRY !!
PUT DOWN THE GUN !!
YOU SHOULDN'T EVEN TOUCH SOME-THING LIKE THAT!!
WINRY !!
TRMBLE TRMBLE
SO YOU'RE THE DAUGHTER OF THOSE DOCTORS...
YOU HAVE EVERY RIGHT TO SHOOT ME.
WINCE
BUT THE MOMENT YOU SQUEEZE THAT TRIGGER, I WILL CONSIDER YOU MY ENEMY!!

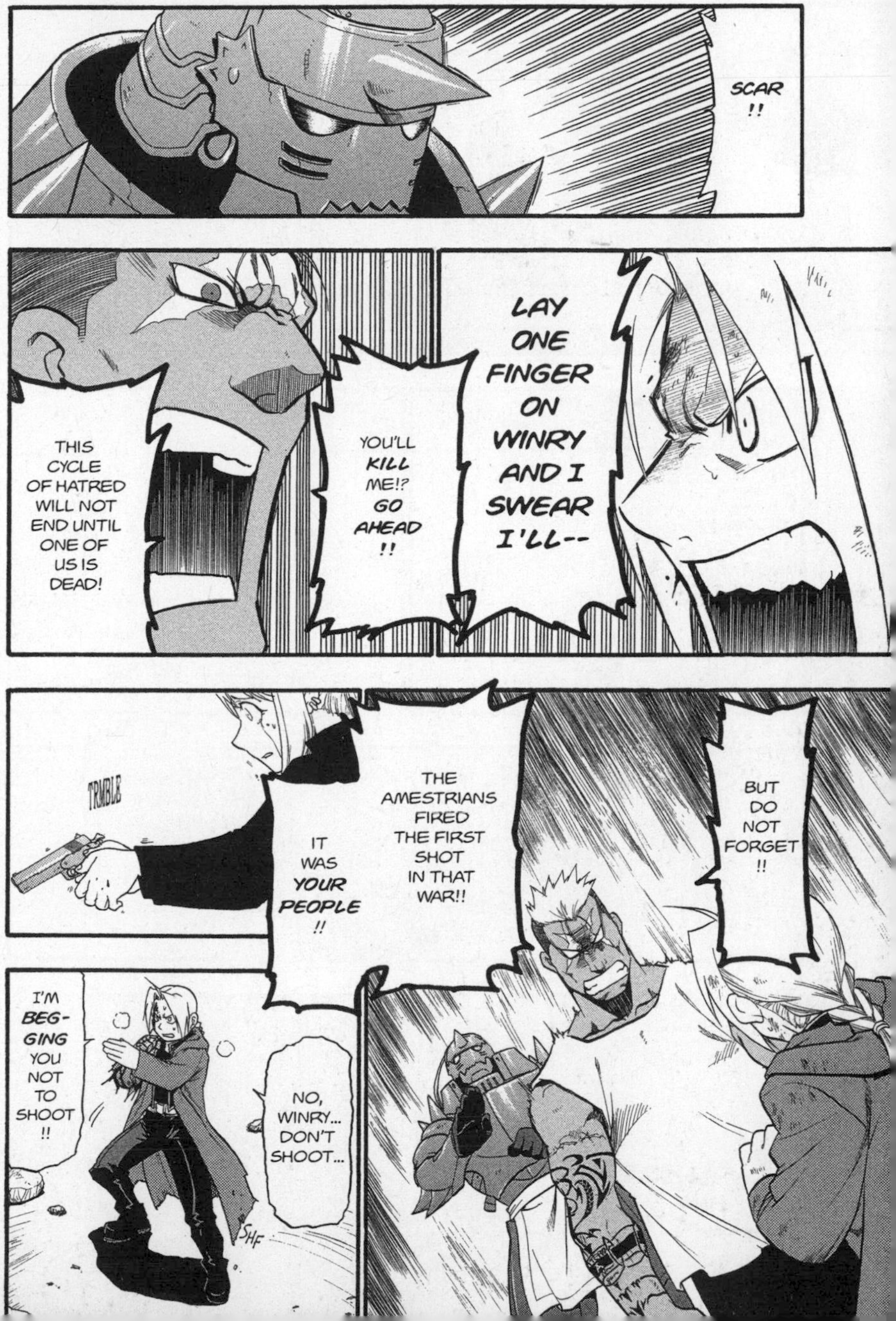
SCAR!!
LAY ONE FINGER ON WINRY AND I SWEAR I'LL--
YOU'LL KILL ME!? GO AHEAD!!
THIS CYCLE OF HATRED WILL NOT END UNTIL ONE OF US IS DEAD!
BUT DO NOT FORGET!!
THE AMESTRIANS FIRED THE FIRST SHOT IN THAT WAR!!
IT WAS YOUR PEOPLE!!
TRMBLE
NO, WINRY... DON'T SHOOT...
I'M BEGGING YOU NOT TO SHOOT!!
SHF

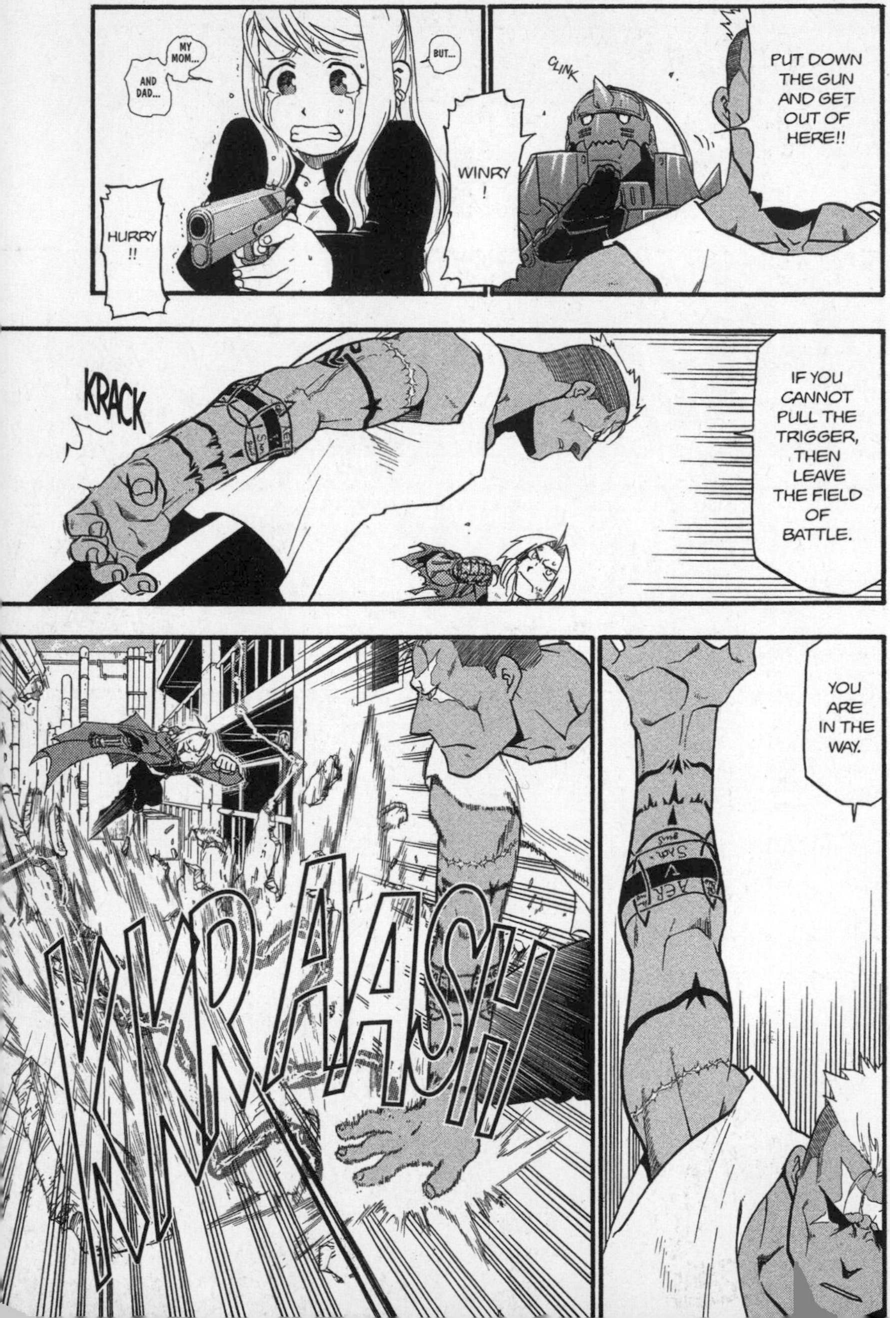
PUT DOWN THE GUN AND GET OUT OF HERE!!
CLINK
WINRY!
BUT...
MY MOM...
AND DAD...
HURRY!!
IF YOU CANNOT PULL THE TRIGGER, THEN LEAVE THE FIELD OF BATTLE.
KRACK
YOU ARE IN THE WAY.
KRAASH

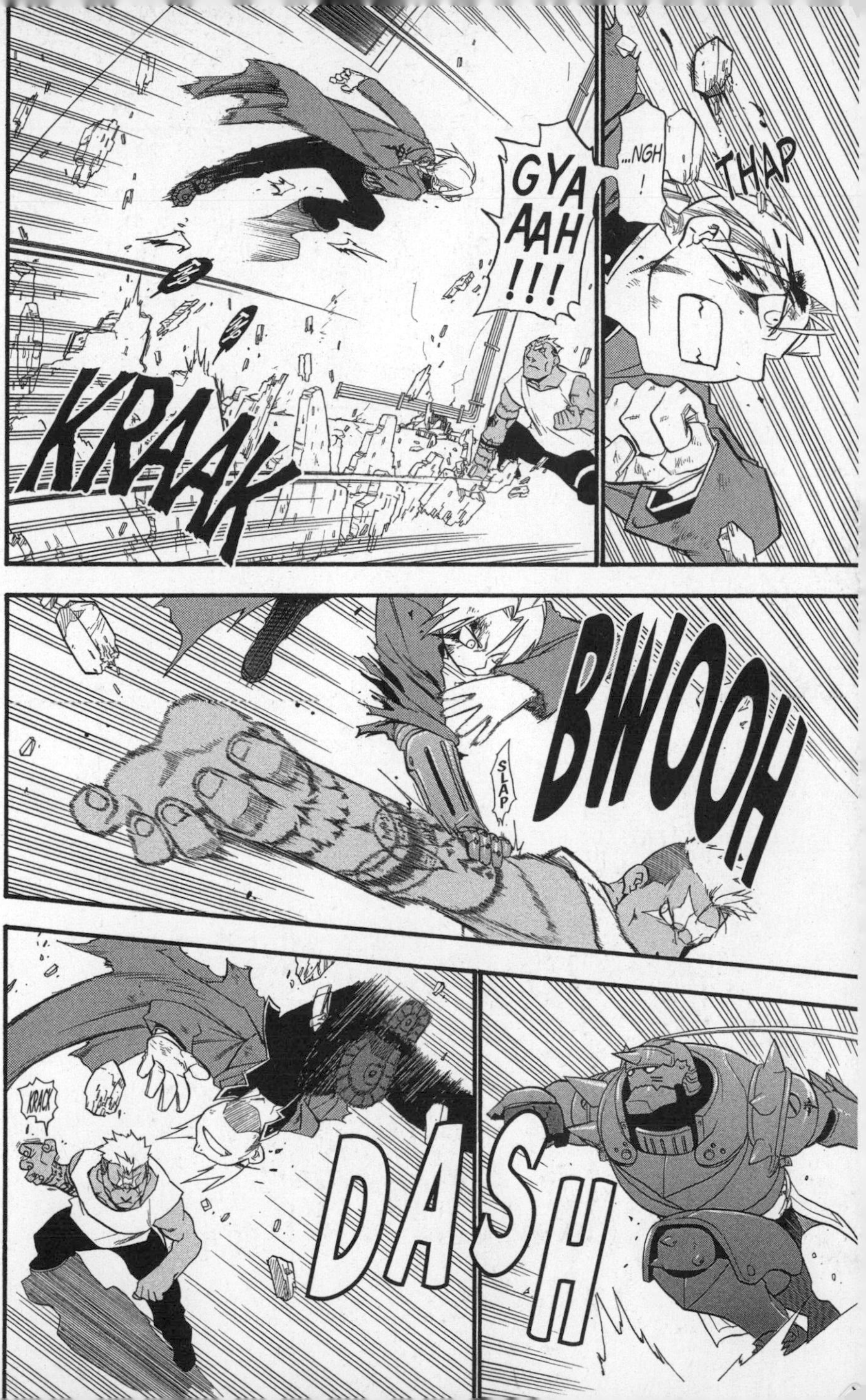
...NGH!
THAP
GYAAAH!!!
THP
THP
KRAAK
BWOOH
SLAP
DASH
KRACK

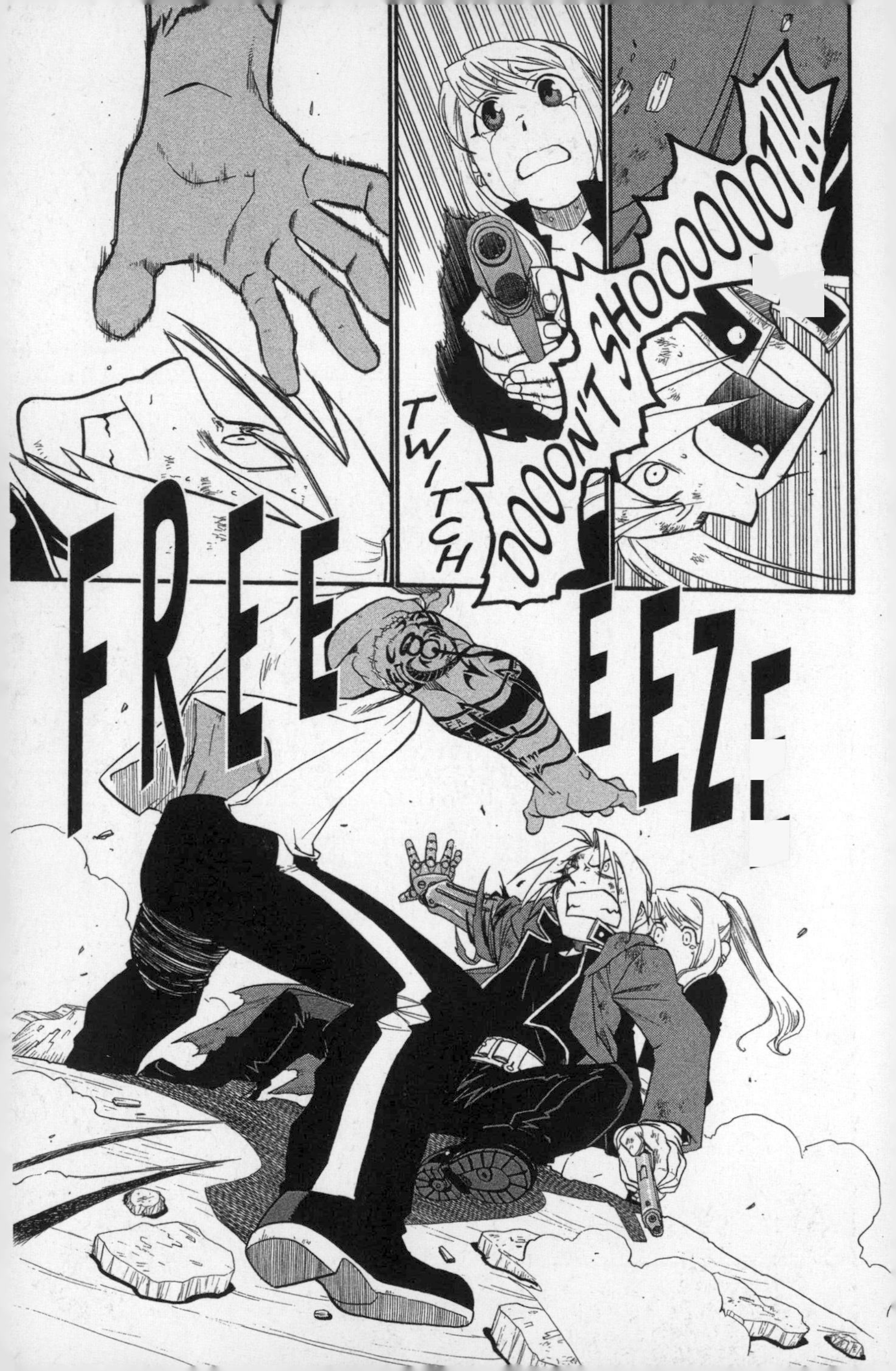
DOOOON'T SHOOOOOOT!!!
TWITCH
FREEEEZE

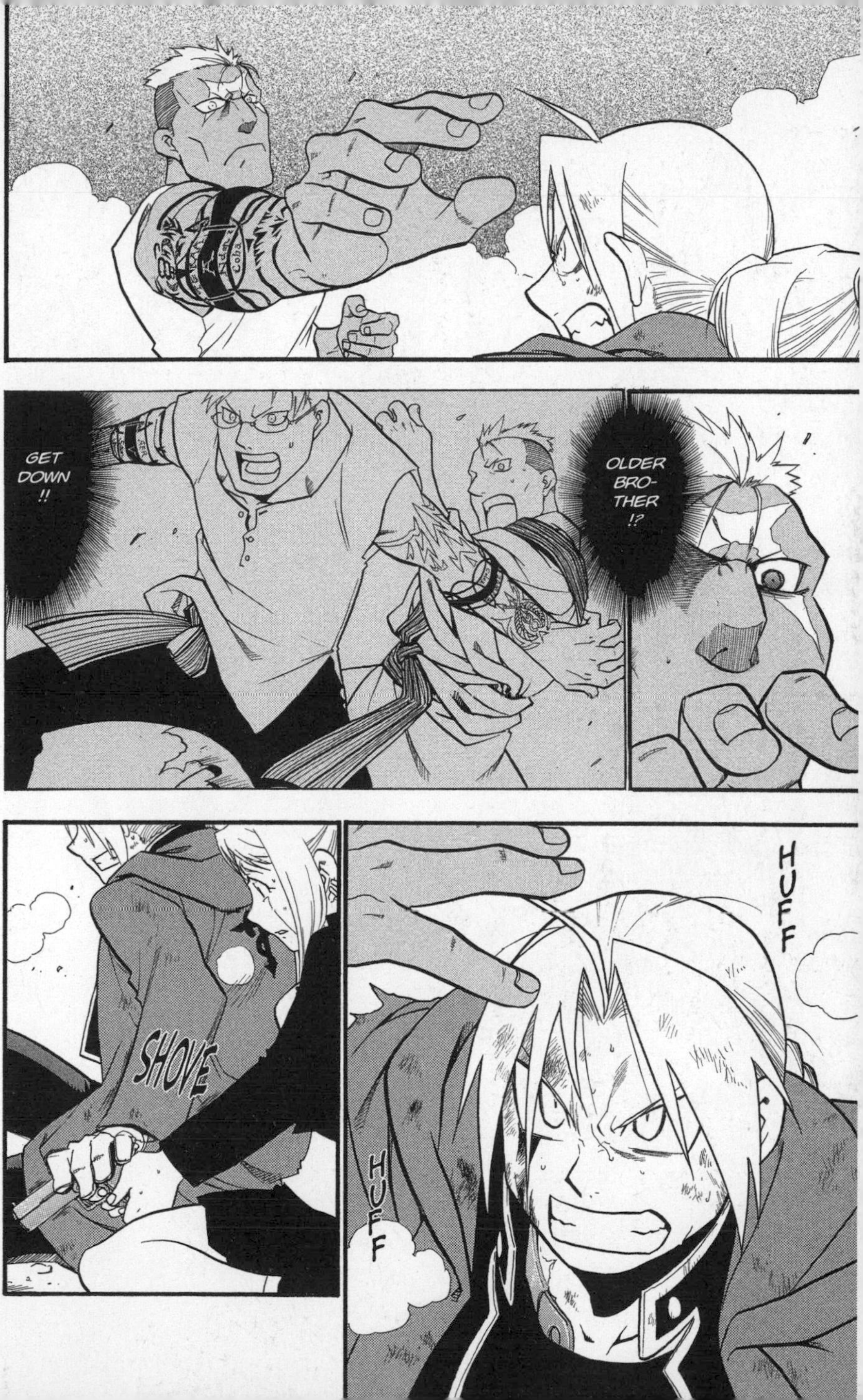
OLDER BROTHER!?
GET DOWN!!
HUFF
HUFF
SHOVE

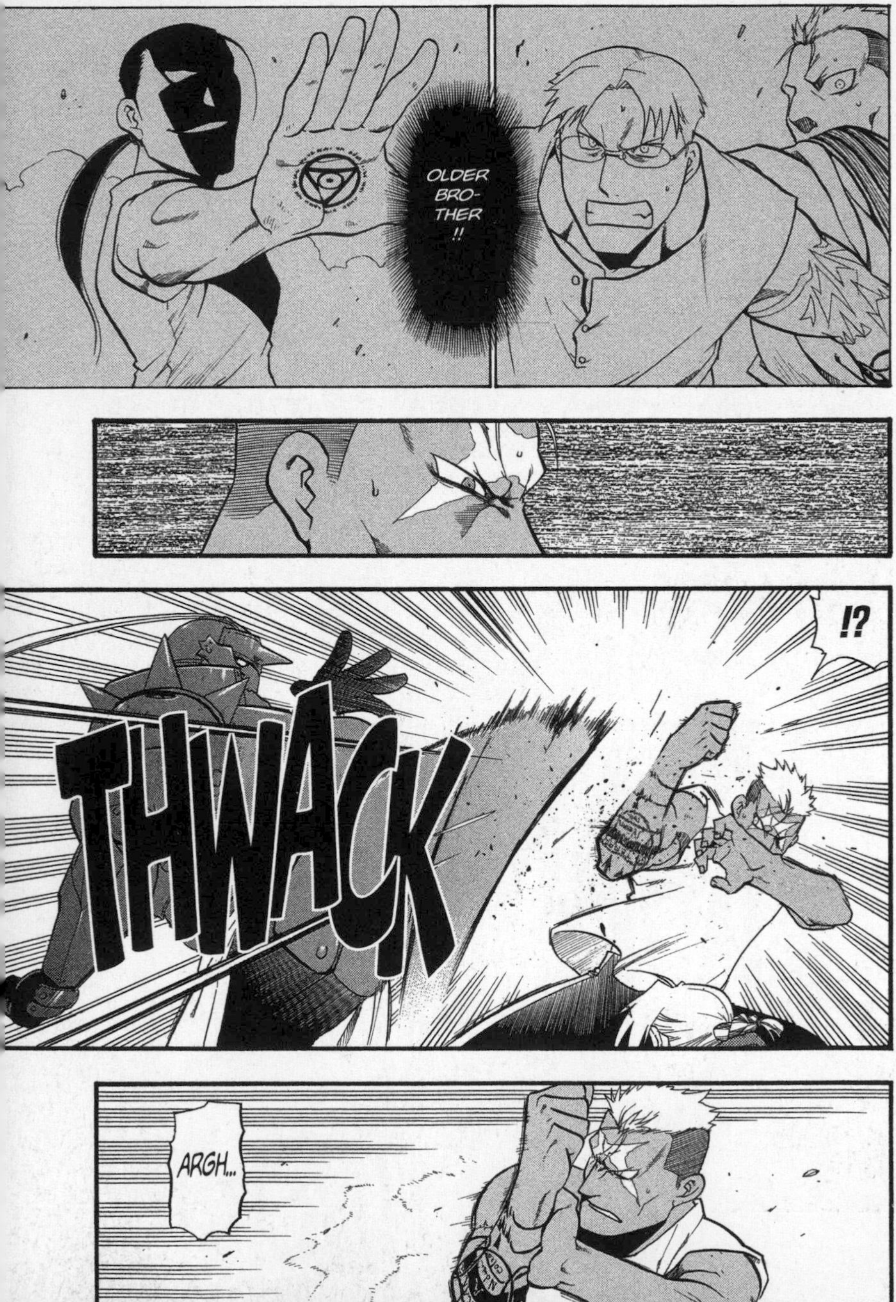

OLDER
BRO-
THER
!!
!?
THWACK
ARGH...

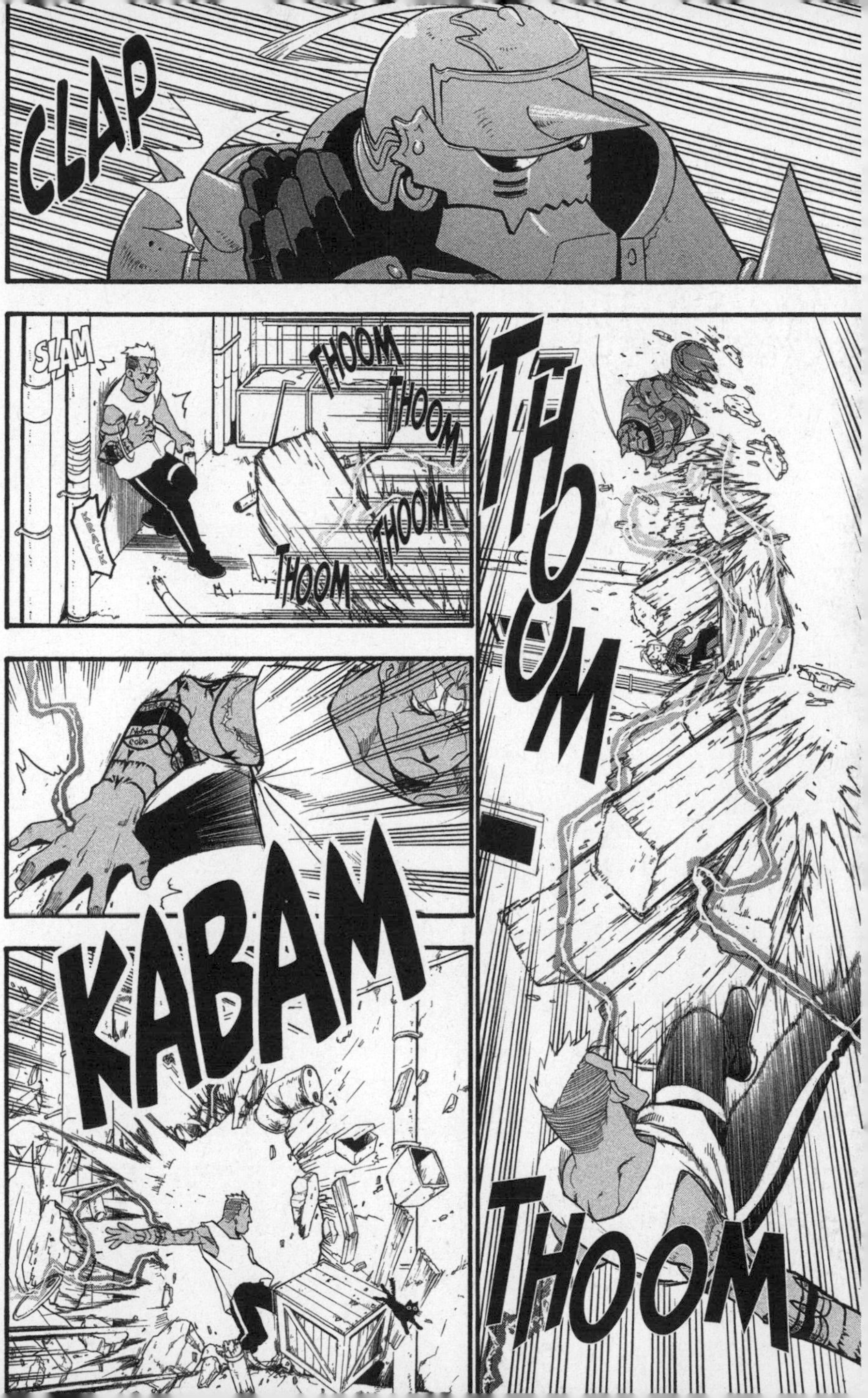
CLAP
THOOM
THOOM
SLAM
THOOM
THOOM
THOOM
THOOM
KRACK
KABAM

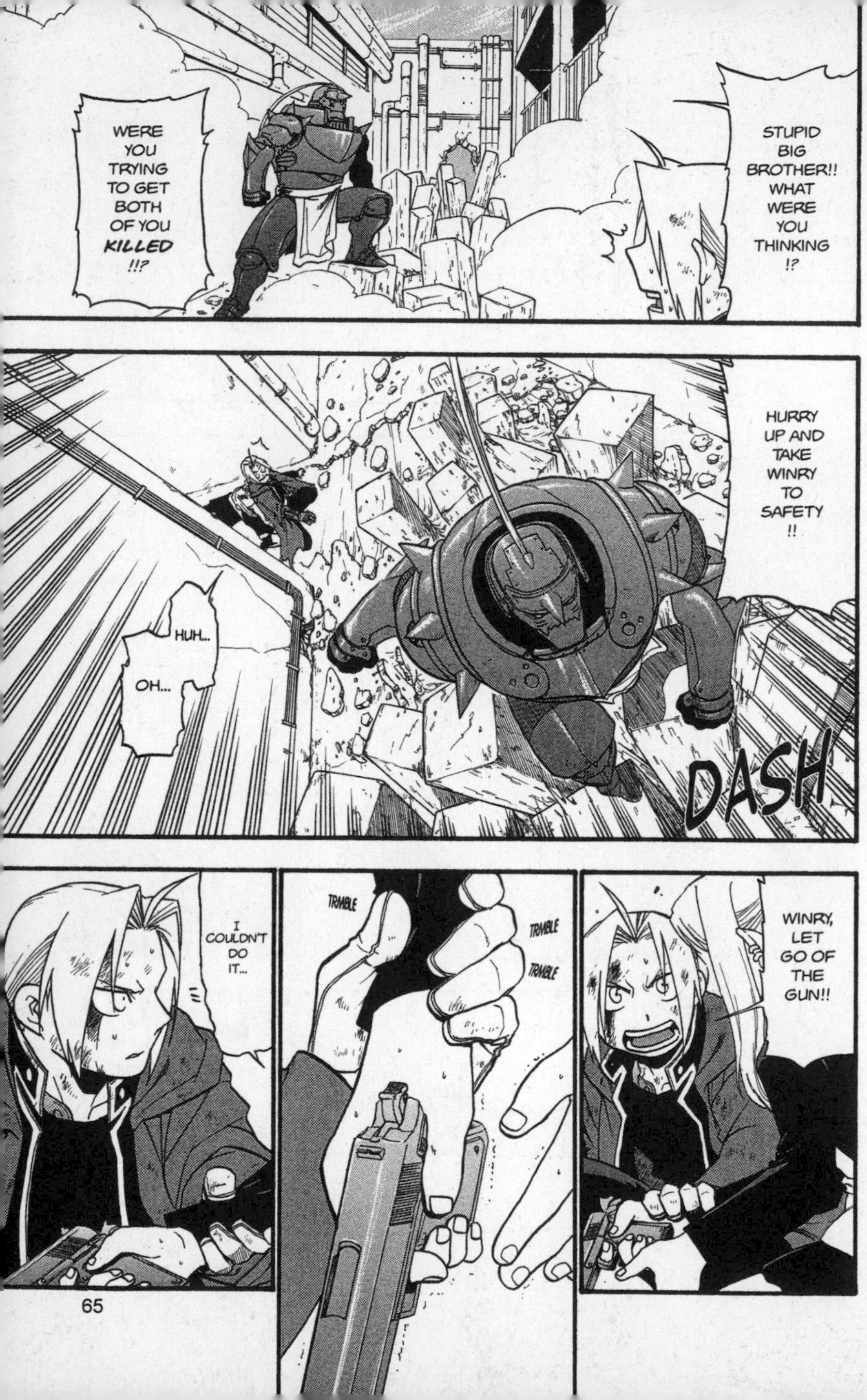
STUPID BIG BROTHER!! WHAT WERE YOU THINKING !?
WERE YOU TRYING TO GET BOTH OF YOU **KILLED** !!?
HURRY UP AND TAKE WINRY TO SAFETY !!
HUH...
OH...
DASH
WINRY, LET GO OF THE GUN!!
TRMBLE
TRMBLE
TRMBLE
I COULDN'T DO IT...

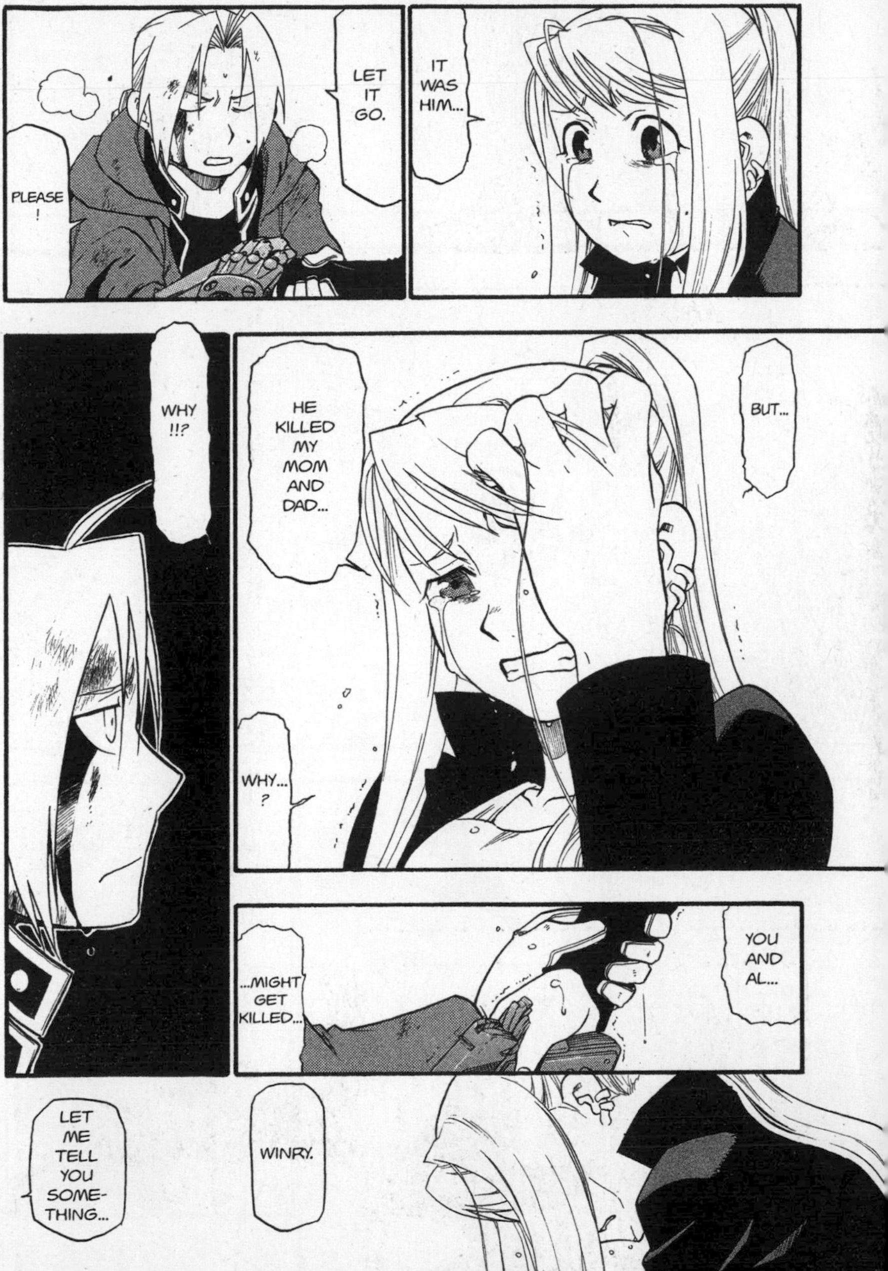
IT WAS HIM...
LET IT GO.
PLEASE!
BUT...
HE KILLED MY MOM AND DAD...
WHY...?
YOU AND AL...
...MIGHT GET KILLED...
WHY!!?
WINRY.
LET ME TELL YOU SOMETHING...

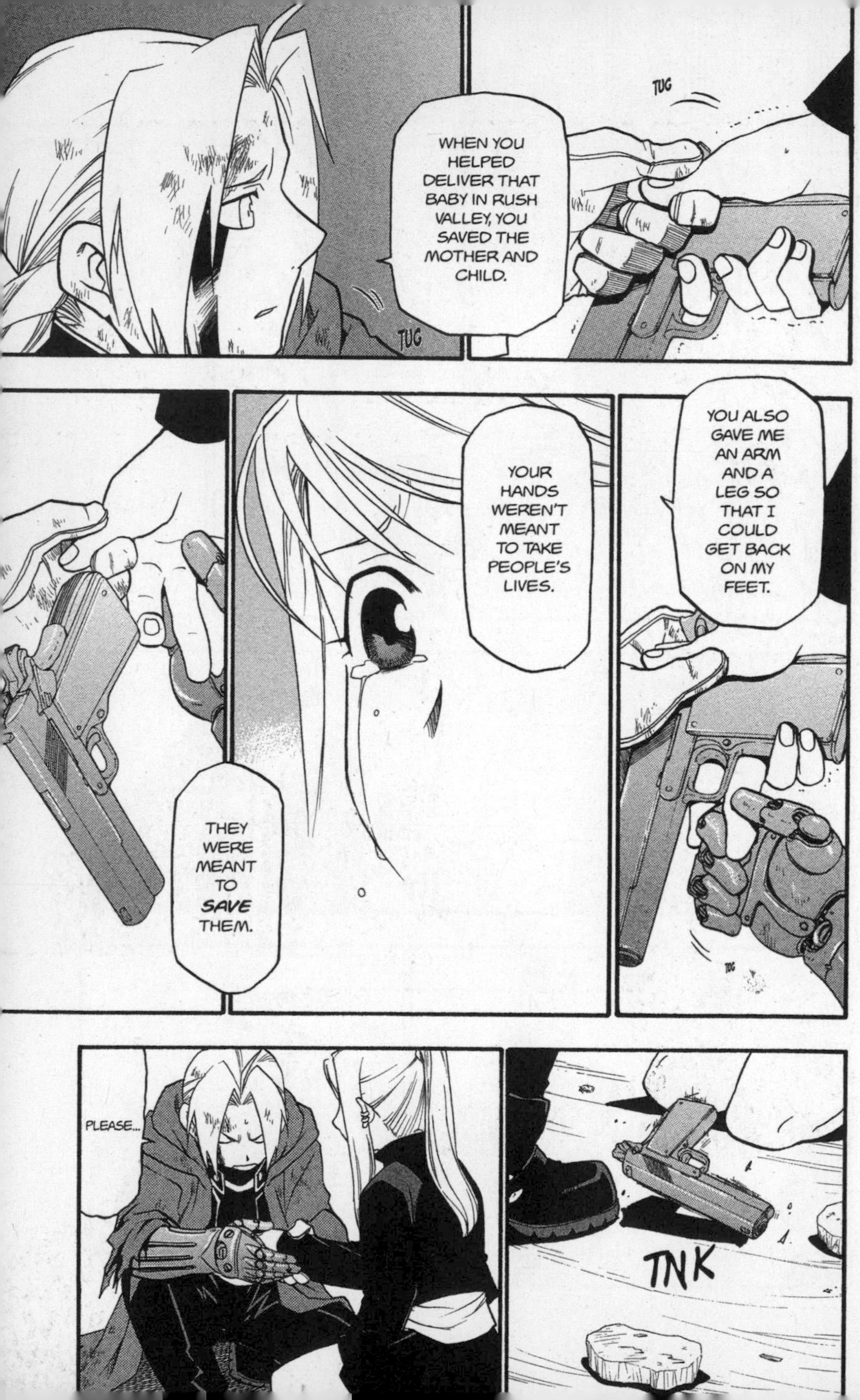
TUG
WHEN YOU HELPED DELIVER THAT BABY IN RUSH VALLEY, YOU SAVED THE MOTHER AND CHILD.
TUG
YOU ALSO GAVE ME AN ARM AND A LEG SO THAT I COULD GET BACK ON MY FEET.
TUG
YOUR HANDS WEREN'T MEANT TO TAKE PEOPLE'S LIVES.
THEY WERE MEANT TO *SAVE* THEM.
TNK
PLEASE...

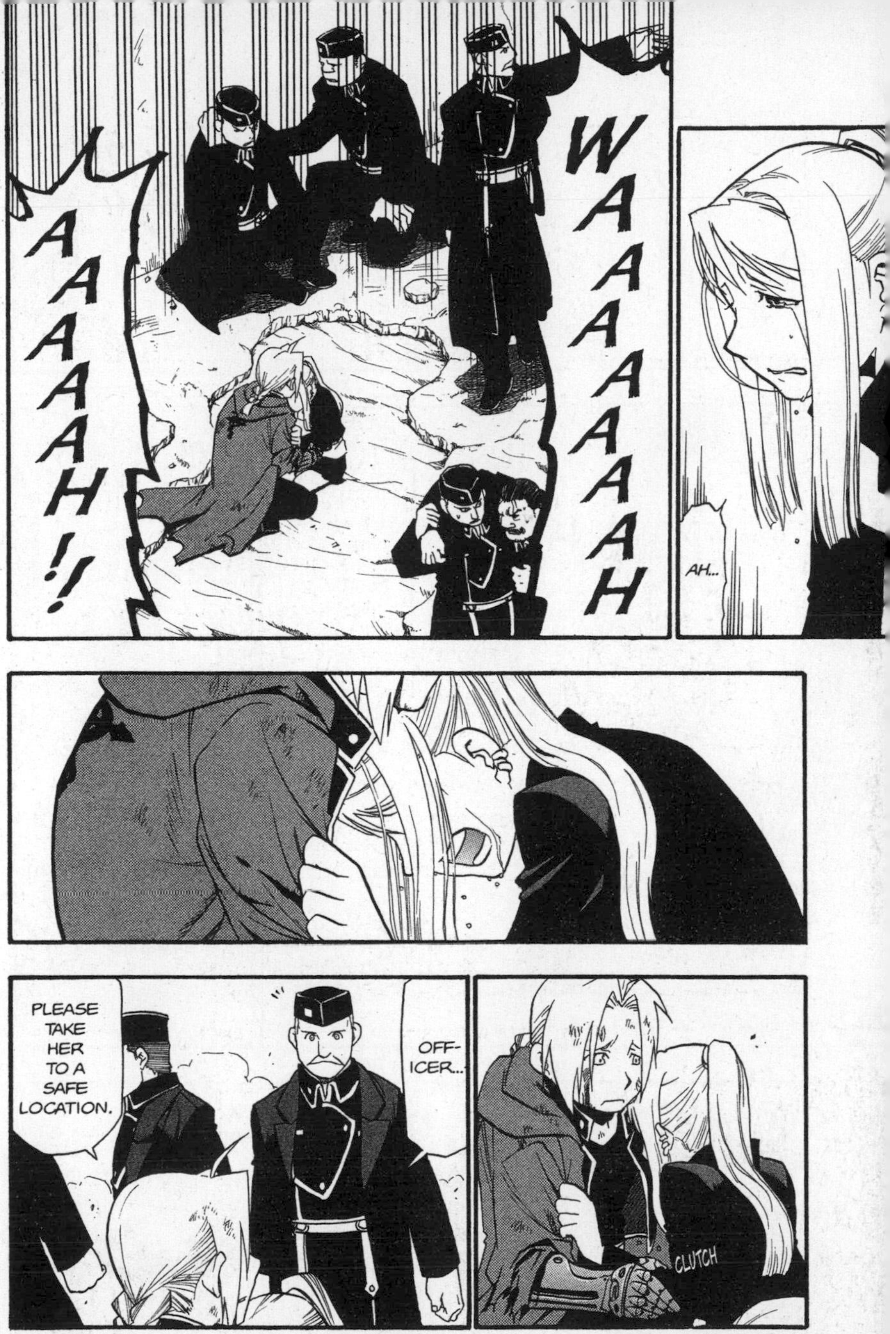
AH...
WAAAAAAAAH
AAAAAH!!
CLUTCH
OFF-ICER...
PLEASE TAKE HER TO A SAFE LOCATION.

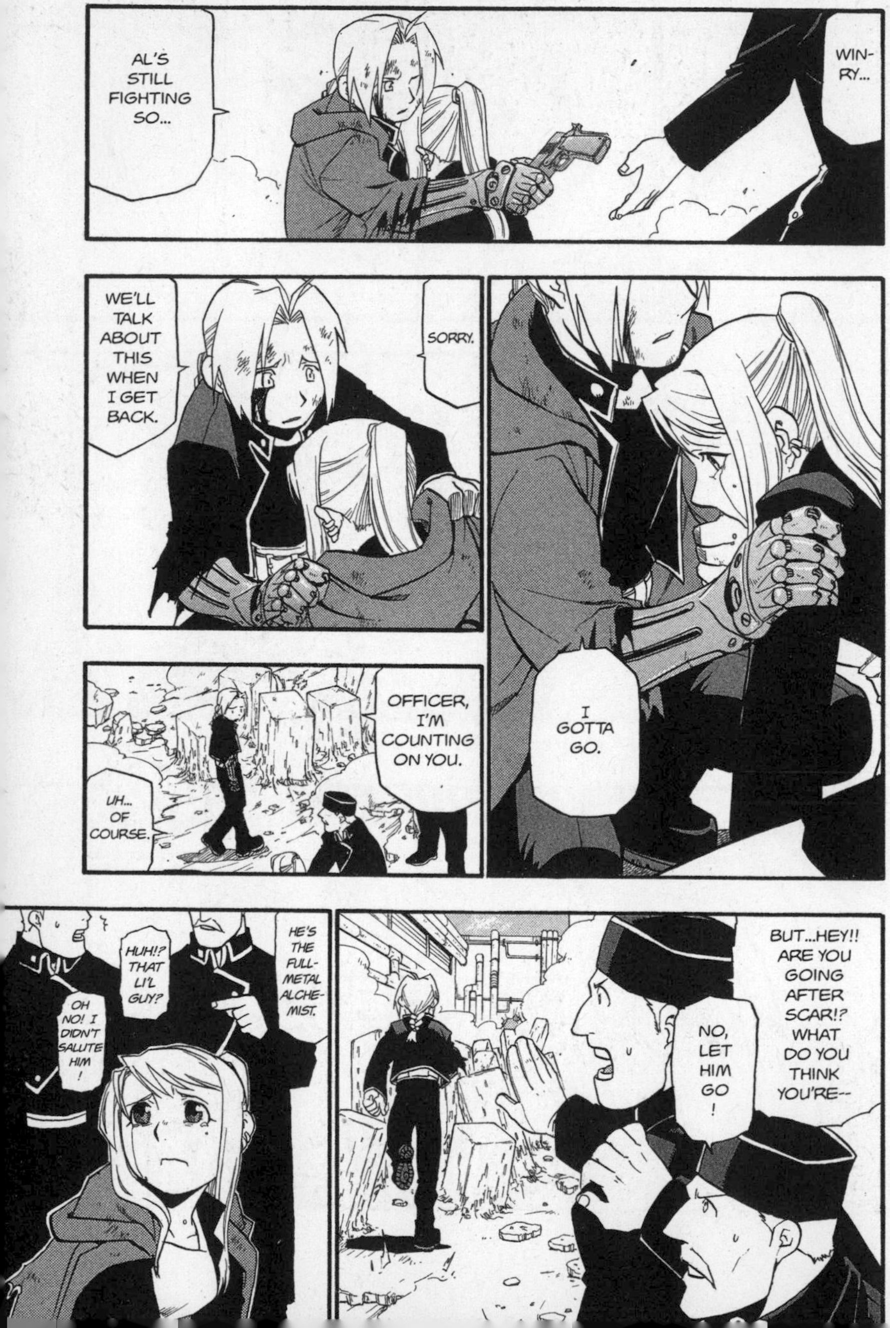
WIN-RY...
AL'S STILL FIGHTING SO...
I GOTTA GO.
SORRY.
WE'LL TALK ABOUT THIS WHEN I GET BACK.
OFFICER, I'M COUNTING ON YOU.
UH... OF COURSE.
BUT...HEY!! ARE YOU GOING AFTER SCAR!? WHAT DO YOU THINK YOU'RE--
NO, LET HIM GO!
HE'S THE FULL-METAL ALCHE-MIST.
HUH!? THAT LI'L GUY?
OH NO! I DIDN'T SALUTE HIM!

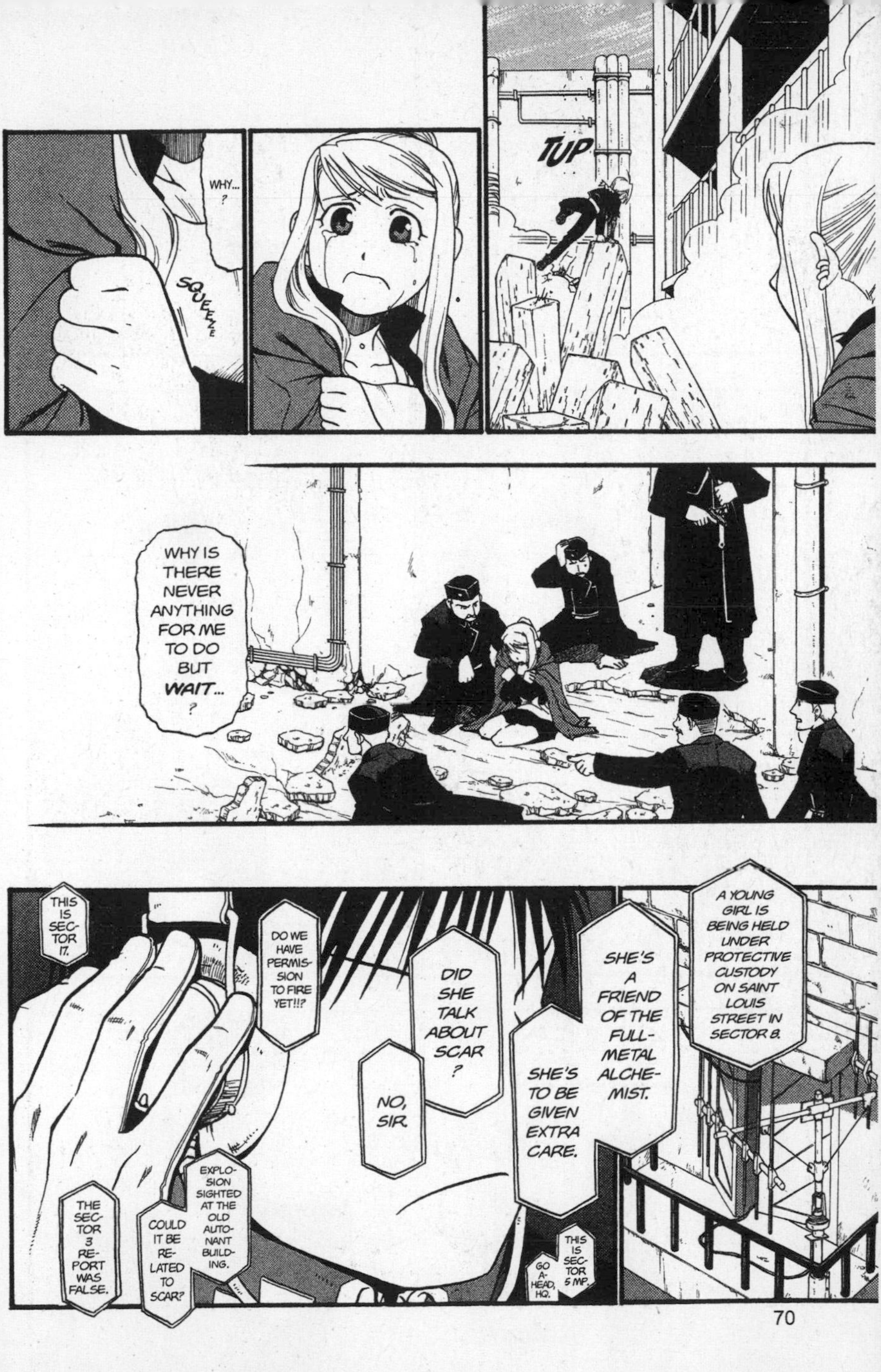
TUP
WHY... ?
SQUEEZE
WHY IS THERE NEVER ANYTHING FOR ME TO DO BUT WAIT...?
A YOUNG GIRL IS BEING HELD UNDER PROTECTIVE CUSTODY ON SAINT LOUIS STREET IN SECTOR 8.
SHE'S A FRIEND OF THE FULL-METAL ALCHE-MIST.
SHE'S TO BE GIVEN EXTRA CARE.
THIS IS SEC-TOR 5 MP.
GO A-HEAD, HQ.
DID SHE TALK ABOUT SCAR?
NO, SIR.
DO WE HAVE PERMIS-SION TO FIRE YET!!?
THIS IS SEC-TOR 17.
EXPLO-SION SIGHTED AT THE OLD AUTO-NANT BUILD-ING.
COULD IT BE RE-LATED TO SCAR?
THE SEC-TOR 3 RE-PORT WAS FALSE.

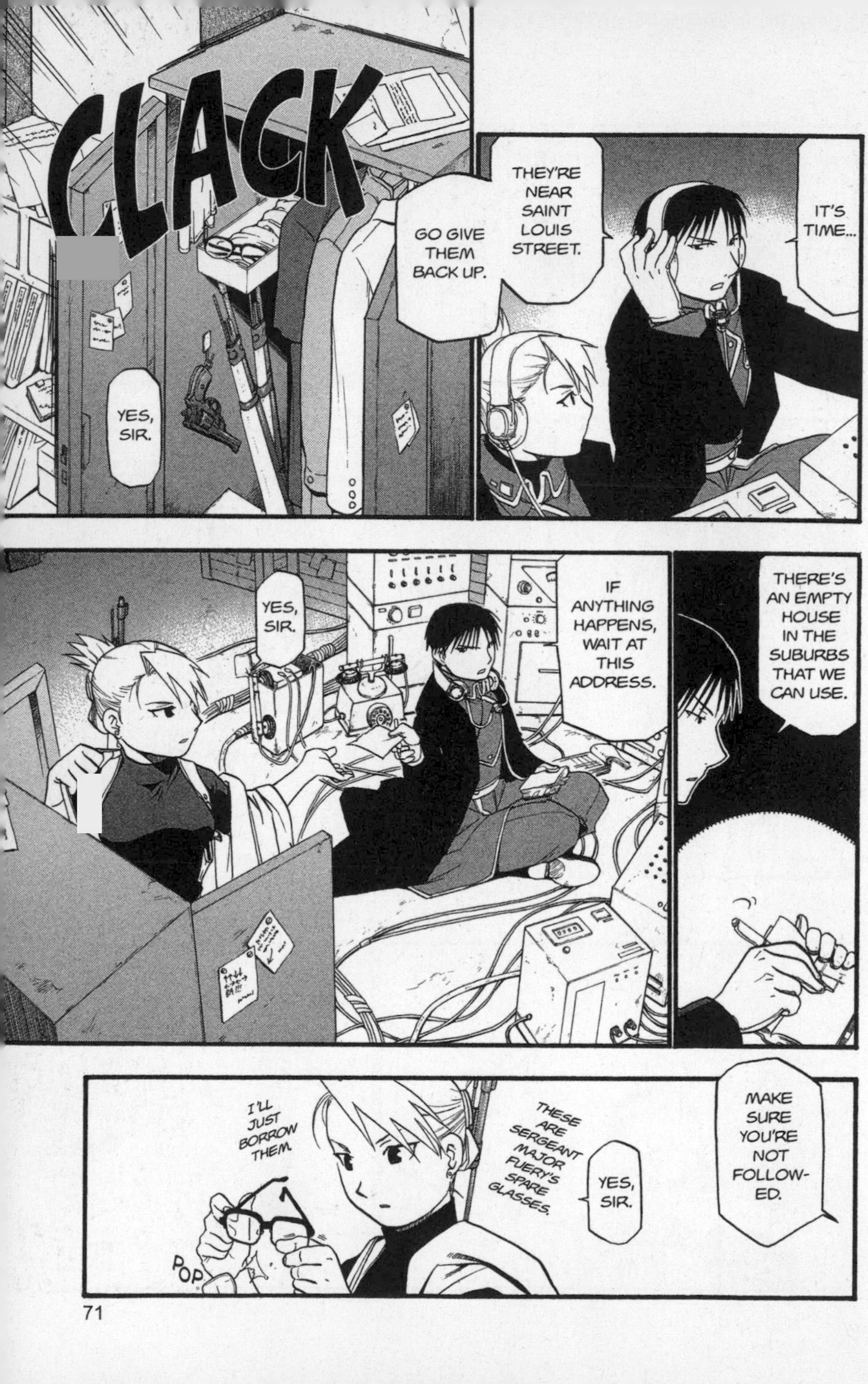
IT'S TIME...
THEY'RE NEAR SAINT LOUIS STREET.
GO GIVE THEM BACK UP.
CLACK
YES, SIR.
THERE'S AN EMPTY HOUSE IN THE SUBURBS THAT WE CAN USE.
IF ANYTHING HAPPENS, WAIT AT THIS ADDRESS.
YES, SIR.
MAKE SURE YOU'RE NOT FOLLOW-ED.
YES, SIR.
THESE ARE SERGEANT MAJOR FUERY'S SPARE GLASSES.
I'LL JUST BORROW THEM.
POP

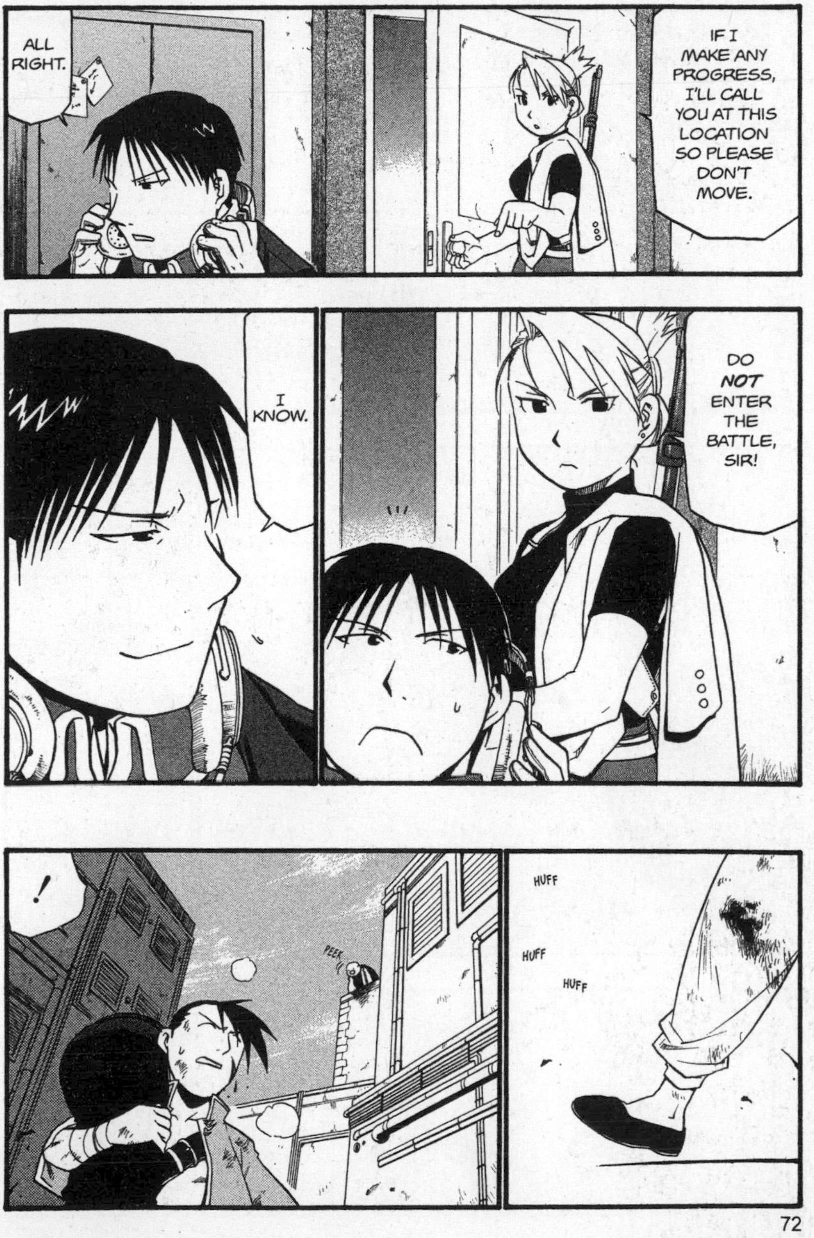
IF I MAKE ANY PROGRESS, I'LL CALL YOU AT THIS LOCATION SO PLEASE DON'T MOVE.
ALL RIGHT.
DO **NOT** ENTER THE BATTLE, SIR!
I KNOW.
HUFF
HUFF
HUFF
!
PEEK

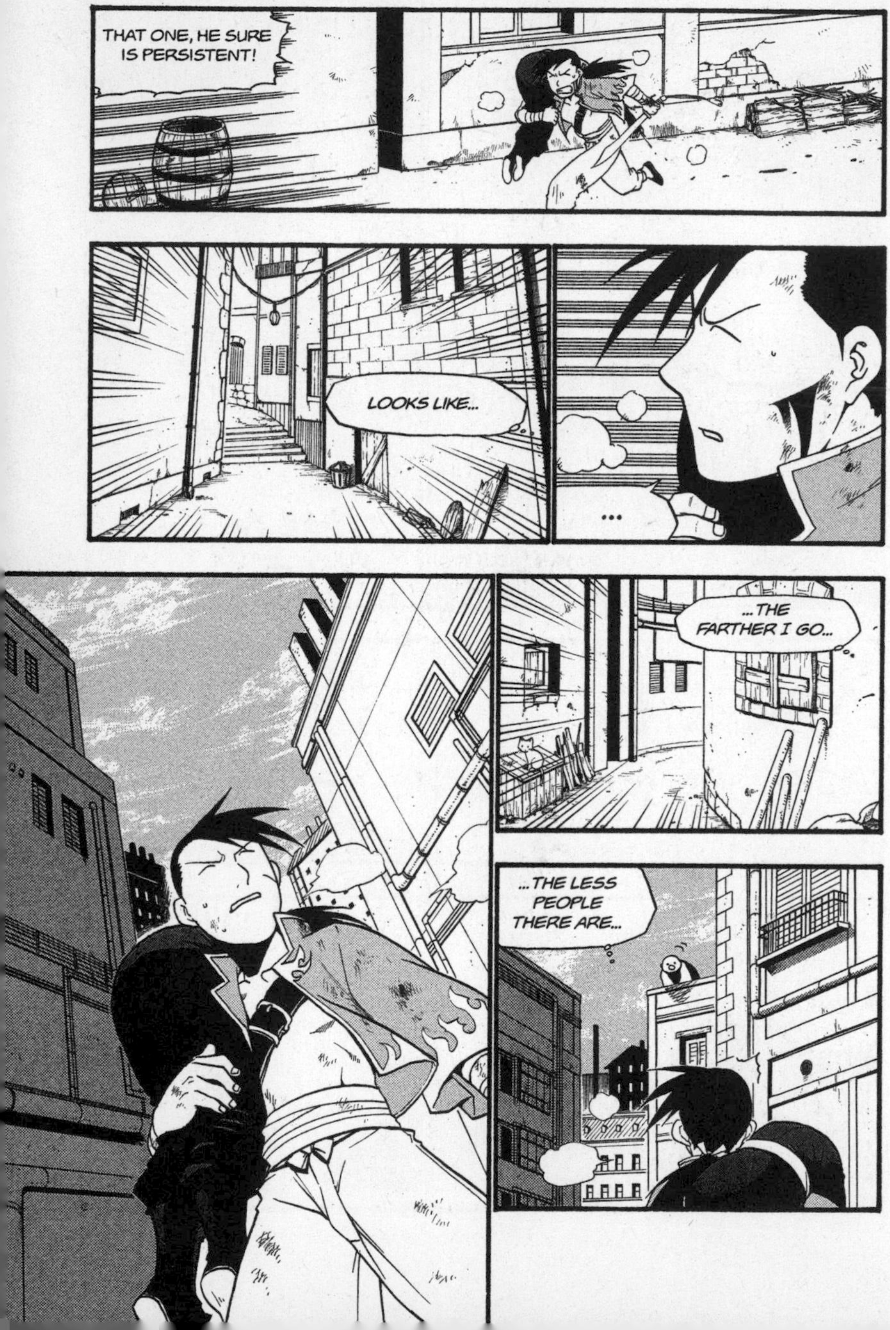
THAT ONE, HE SURE IS PERSISTENT!
...
LOOKS LIKE...
...THE FARTHER I GO...
...THE LESS PEOPLE THERE ARE...

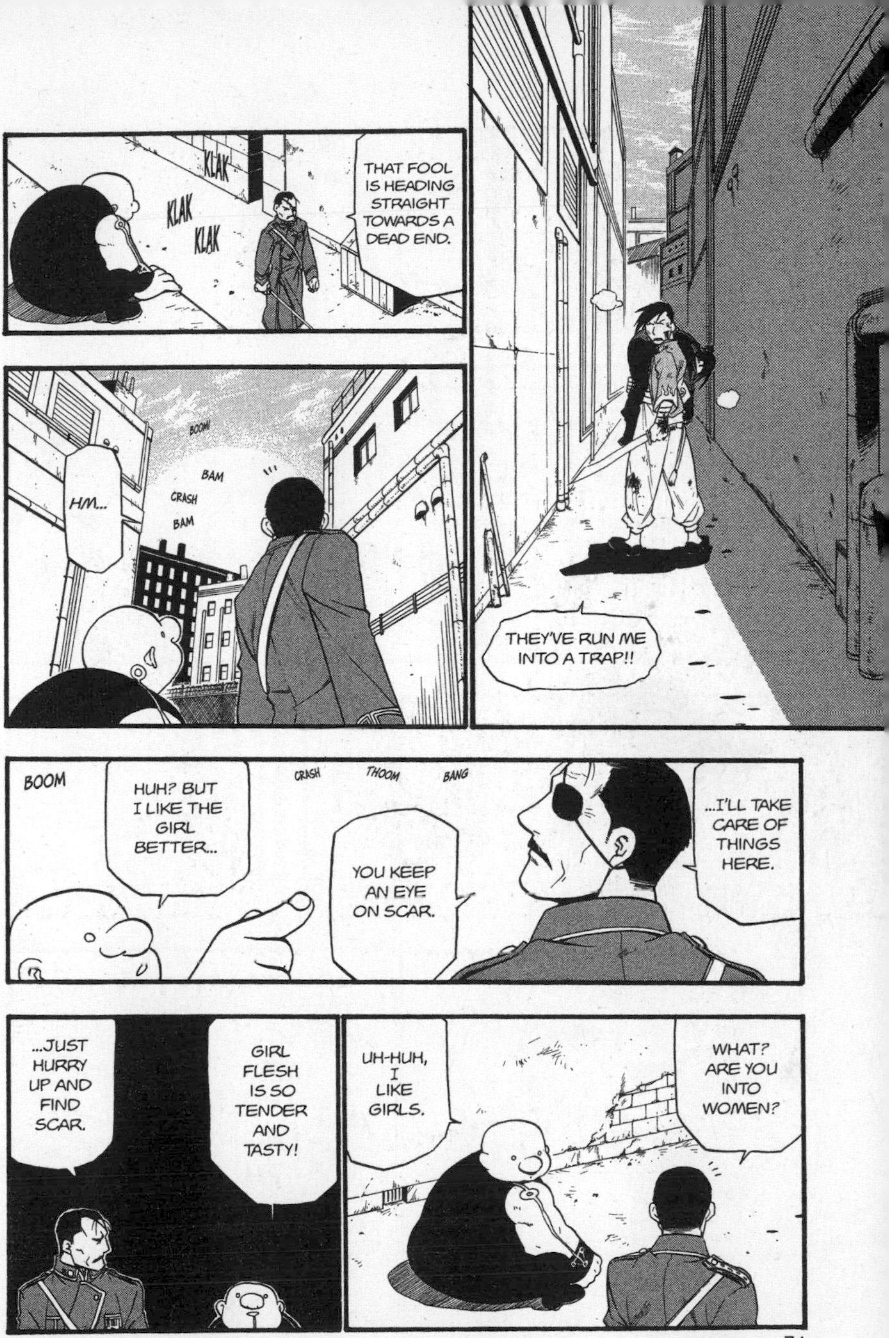
THEY'VE RUN ME INTO A TRAP!!
THAT FOOL IS HEADING STRAIGHT TOWARDS A DEAD END.
KLAK
KLAK
KLAK
BOOM!
BAM
CRASH
BAM
HM...
...I'LL TAKE CARE OF THINGS HERE.
YOU KEEP AN EYE ON SCAR.
BANG
THOOM
CRASH
HUH? BUT I LIKE THE GIRL BETTER...
BOOM
WHAT? ARE YOU INTO WOMEN?
UH-HUH, I LIKE GIRLS.
GIRL FLESH IS SO TENDER AND TASTY!
...JUST HURRY UP AND FIND SCAR.

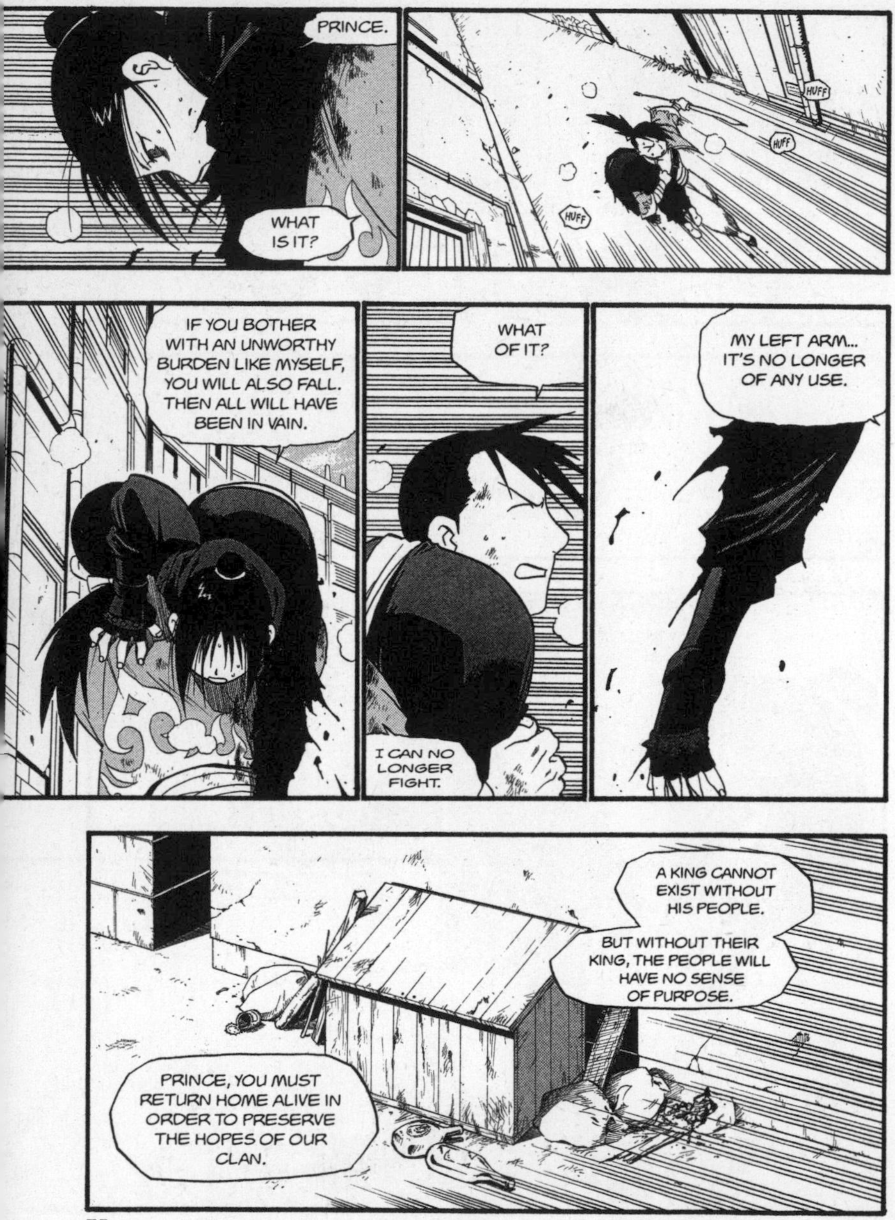
HUFF
HUFF
HUFF
PRINCE.
WHAT IS IT?
MY LEFT ARM... IT'S NO LONGER OF ANY USE.
WHAT OF IT?
I CAN NO LONGER FIGHT.
IF YOU BOTHER WITH AN UNWORTHY BURDEN LIKE MYSELF, YOU WILL ALSO FALL. THEN ALL WILL HAVE BEEN IN VAIN.
A KING CANNOT EXIST WITHOUT HIS PEOPLE.
BUT WITHOUT THEIR KING, THE PEOPLE WILL HAVE NO SENSE OF PURPOSE.
PRINCE, YOU MUST RETURN HOME ALIVE IN ORDER TO PRESERVE THE HOPES OF OUR CLAN.

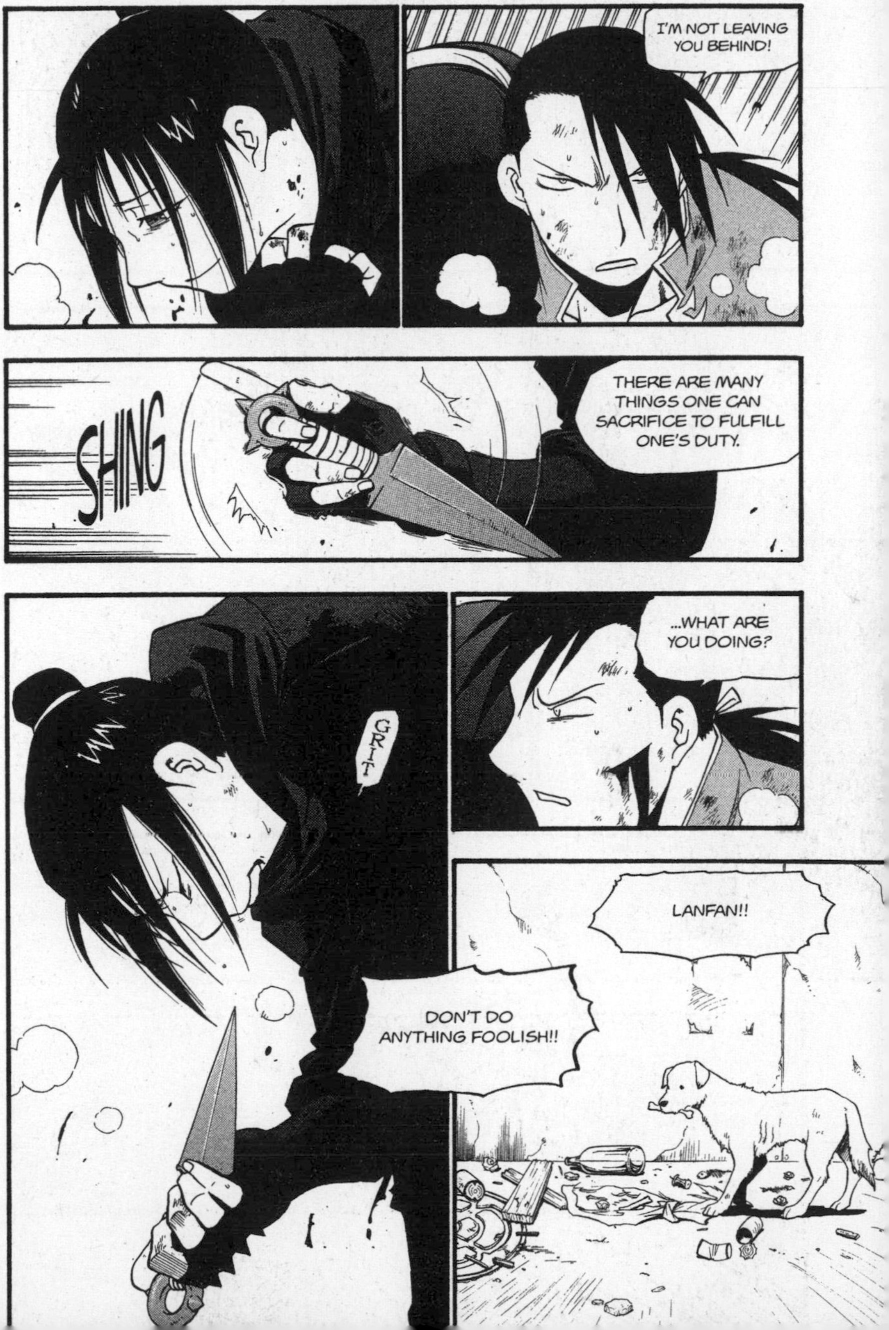
I'M NOT LEAVING YOU BEHIND!
THERE ARE MANY THINGS ONE CAN SACRIFICE TO FULFILL ONE'S DUTY.
SHING
...WHAT ARE YOU DOING?
LANFAN!!
DON'T DO ANYTHING FOOLISH!!
GRIT

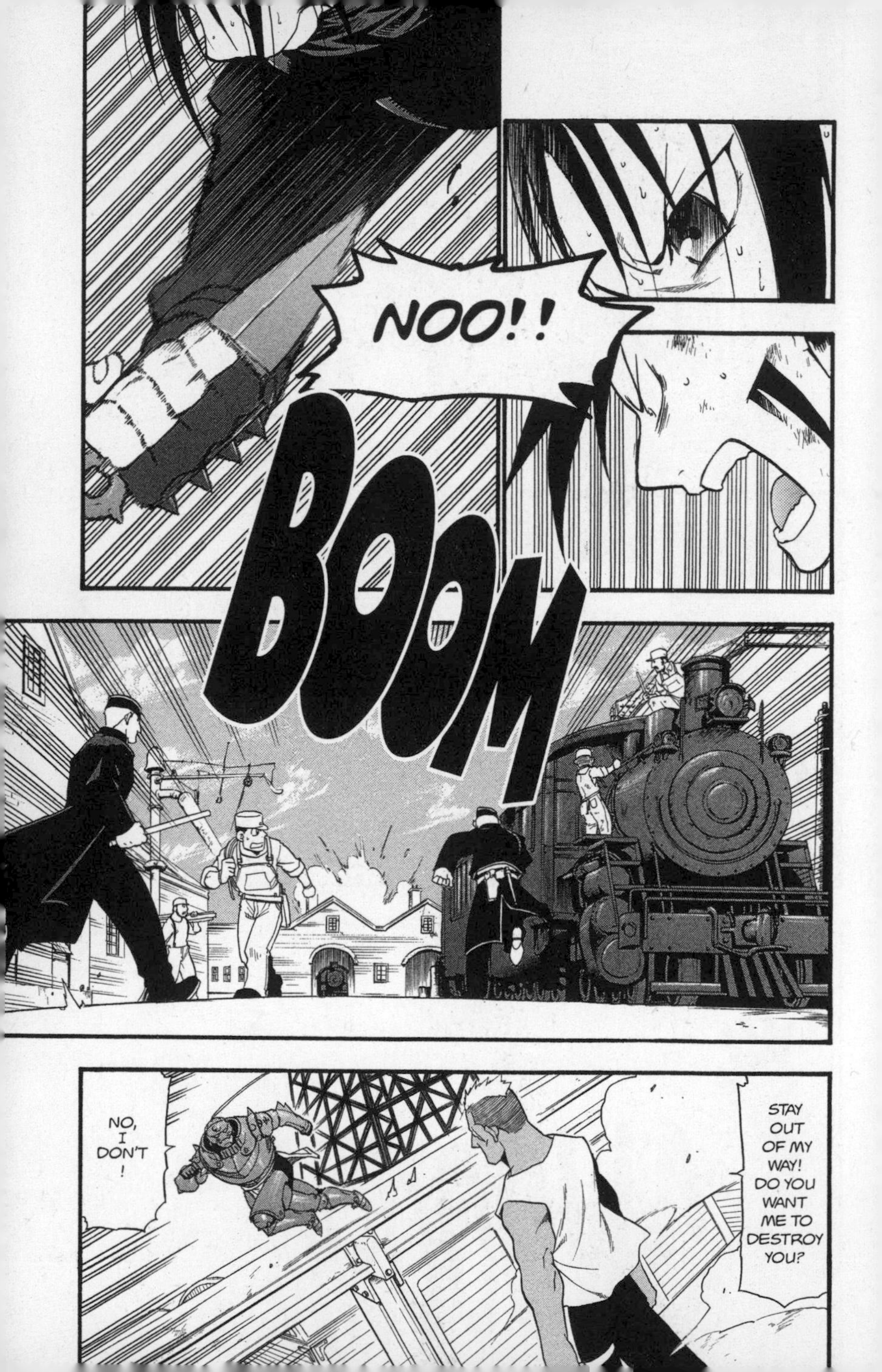
NOO!!
BOOM
STAY OUT OF MY WAY! DO YOU WANT ME TO DESTROY YOU?
NO, I DON'T!

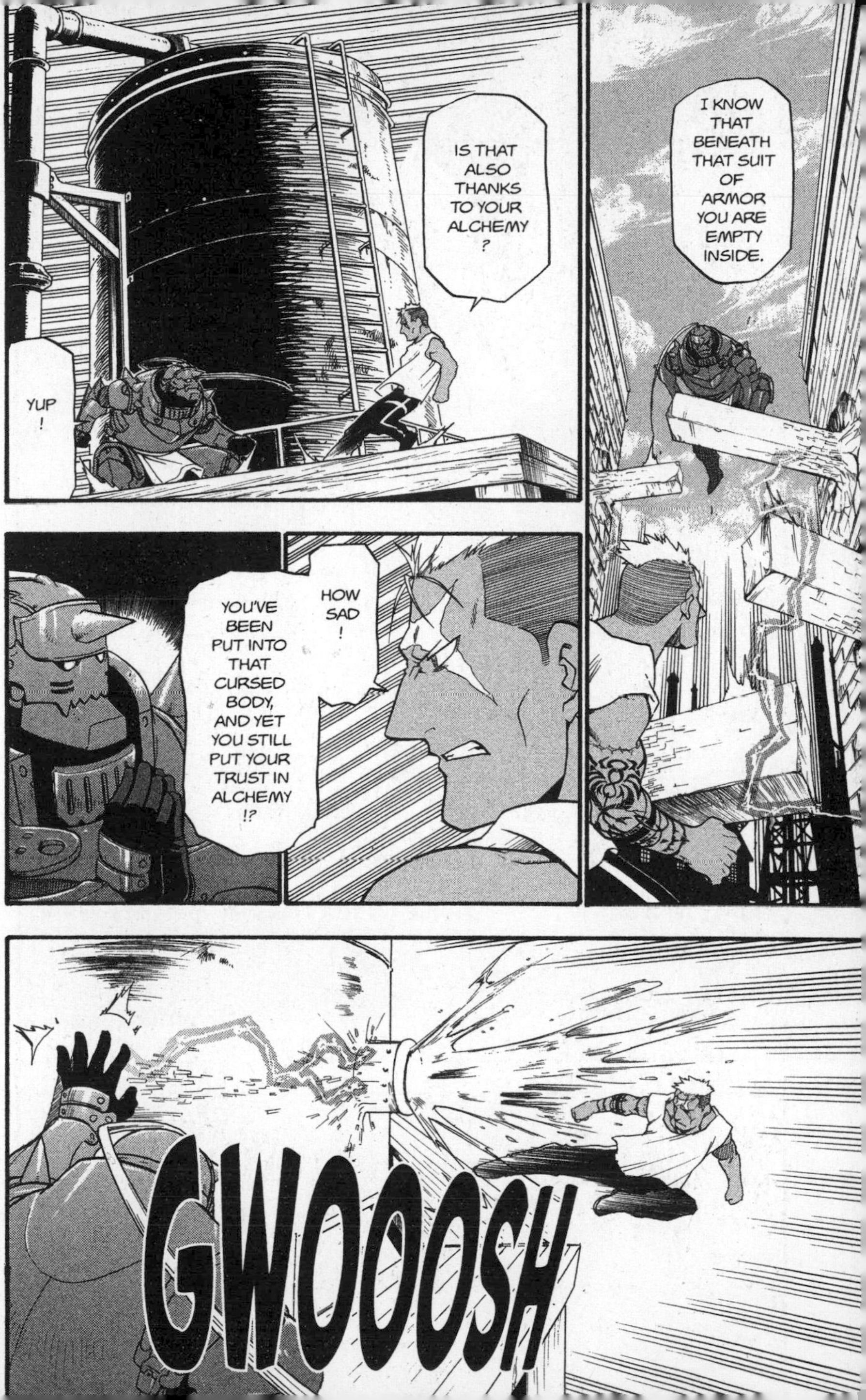
I KNOW THAT BENEATH THAT SUIT OF ARMOR YOU ARE EMPTY INSIDE.
IS THAT ALSO THANKS TO YOUR ALCHEMY?
YUP!
HOW SAD!
YOU'VE BEEN PUT INTO THAT CURSED BODY, AND YET YOU STILL PUT YOUR TRUST IN ALCHEMY!?
GWOOOSH

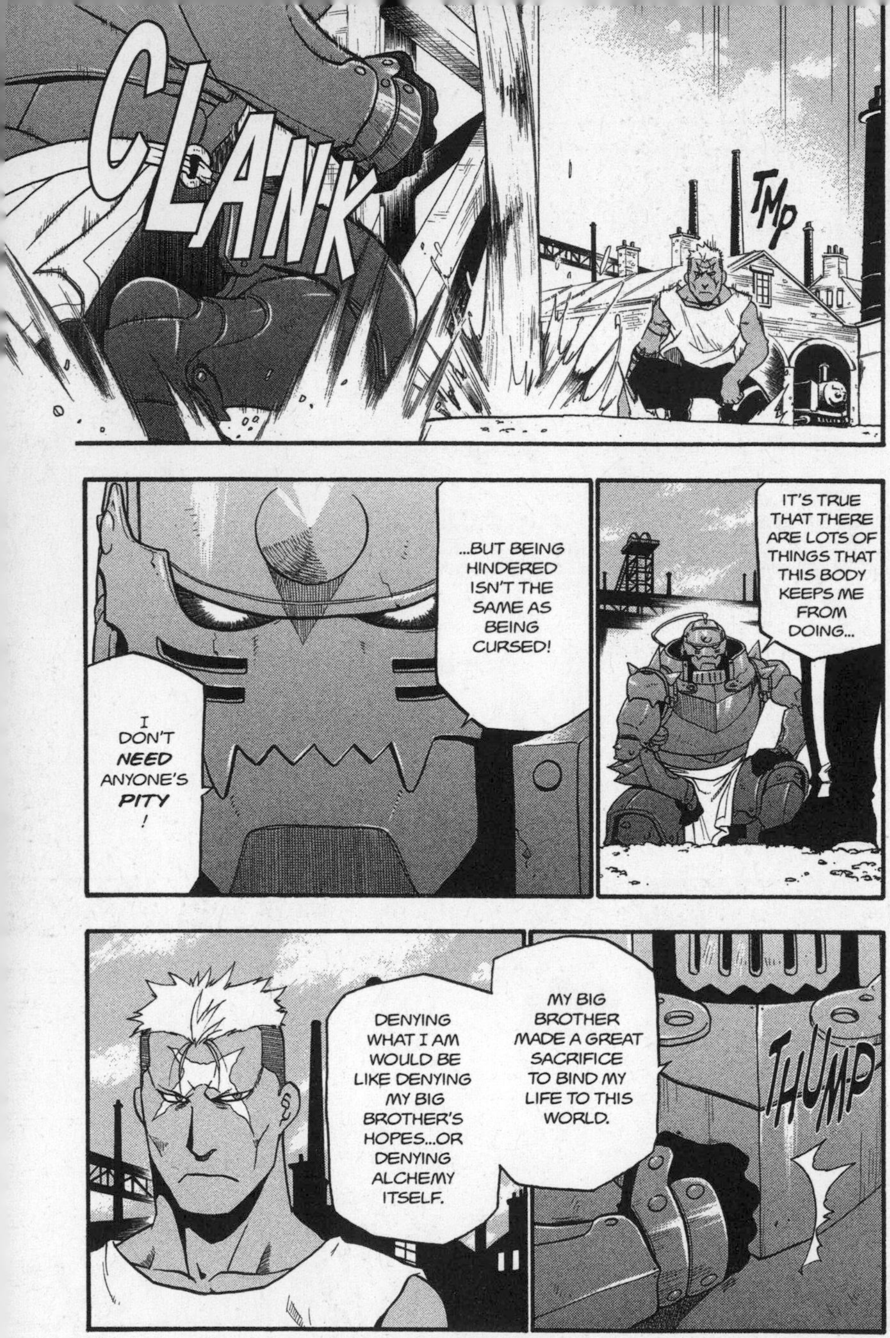
TMP
CLANK
IT'S TRUE THAT THERE ARE LOTS OF THINGS THAT THIS BODY KEEPS ME FROM DOING...
...BUT BEING HINDERED ISN'T THE SAME AS BEING CURSED!
I DON'T **NEED** ANYONE'S **PITY**!
MY BIG BROTHER MADE A GREAT SACRIFICE TO BIND MY LIFE TO THIS WORLD.
THUMP
DENYING WHAT I AM WOULD BE LIKE DENYING MY BIG BROTHER'S HOPES...OR DENYING ALCHEMY ITSELF.

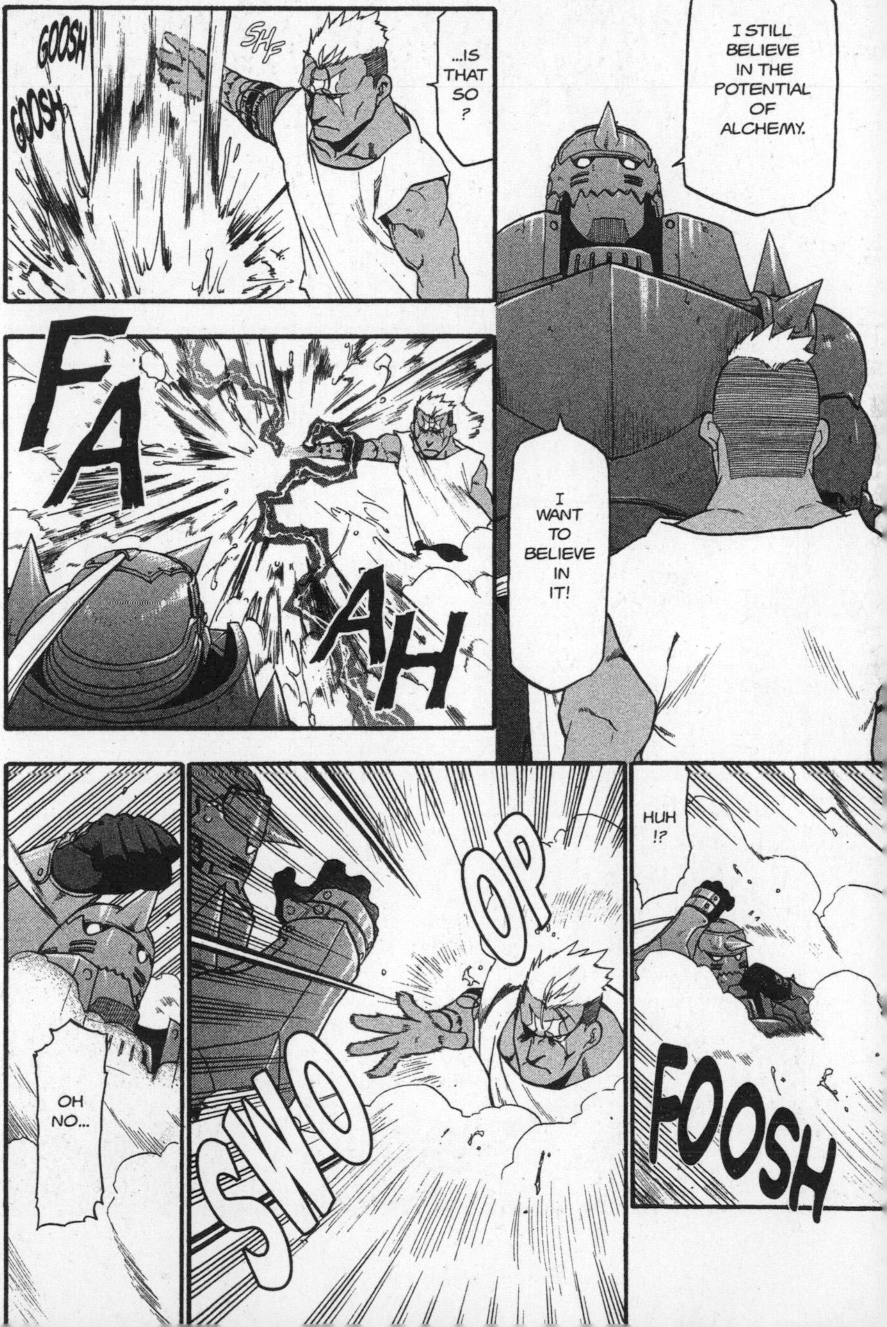
I STILL BELIEVE IN THE POTENTIAL OF ALCHEMY.
I WANT TO BELIEVE IN IT!
...IS THAT SO?
SHF
GOOSH
GOOSH
FA
AH
HUH!?
FOOSH
SWO
OP
OH NO...

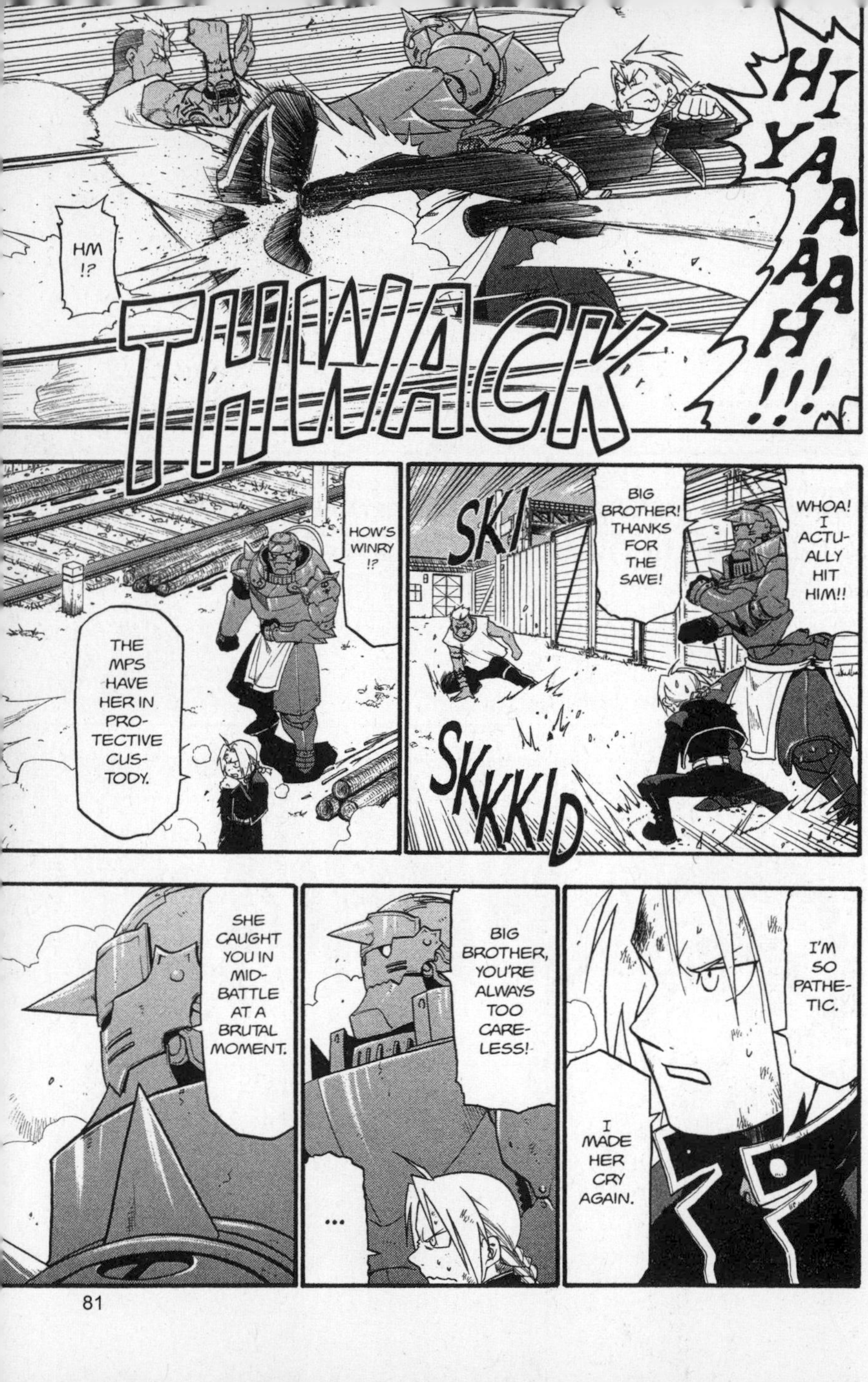
HIYAAAAH!!!
THWACK
HM!?
WHOA! I ACTUALLY HIT HIM!!
BIG BROTHER! THANKS FOR THE SAVE!
SKI
SKKKID
HOW'S WINRY!?
THE MPS HAVE HER IN PROTECTIVE CUSTODY.
I'M SO PATHETIC.
I MADE HER CRY AGAIN.
BIG BROTHER, YOU'RE ALWAYS TOO CARELESS!
...
SHE CAUGHT YOU IN MID-BATTLE AT A BRUTAL MOMENT.

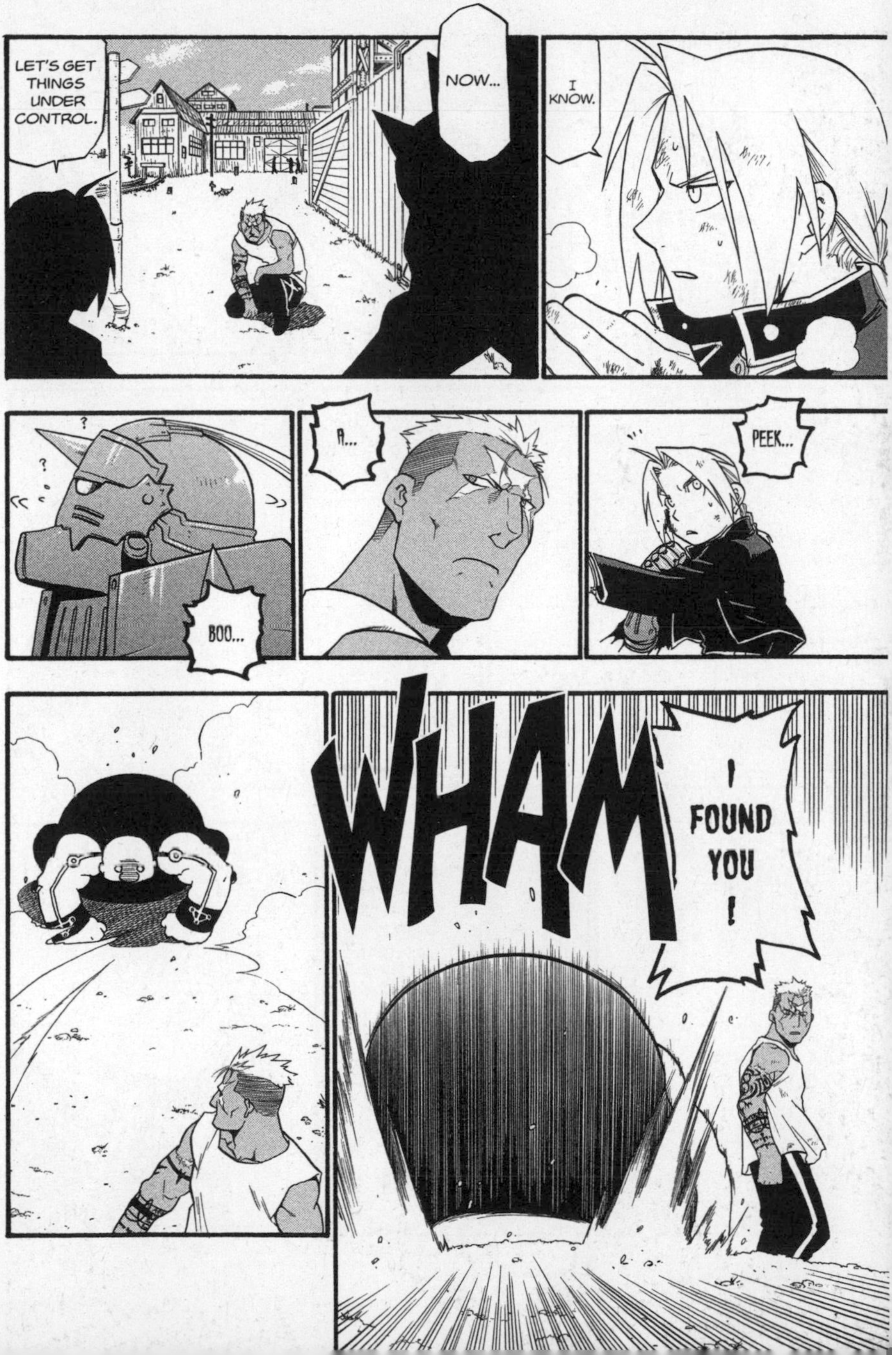
I KNOW.
NOW...
LET'S GET THINGS UNDER CONTROL.
PEEK...
A...
BOO...
WHAM
I FOUND YOU!

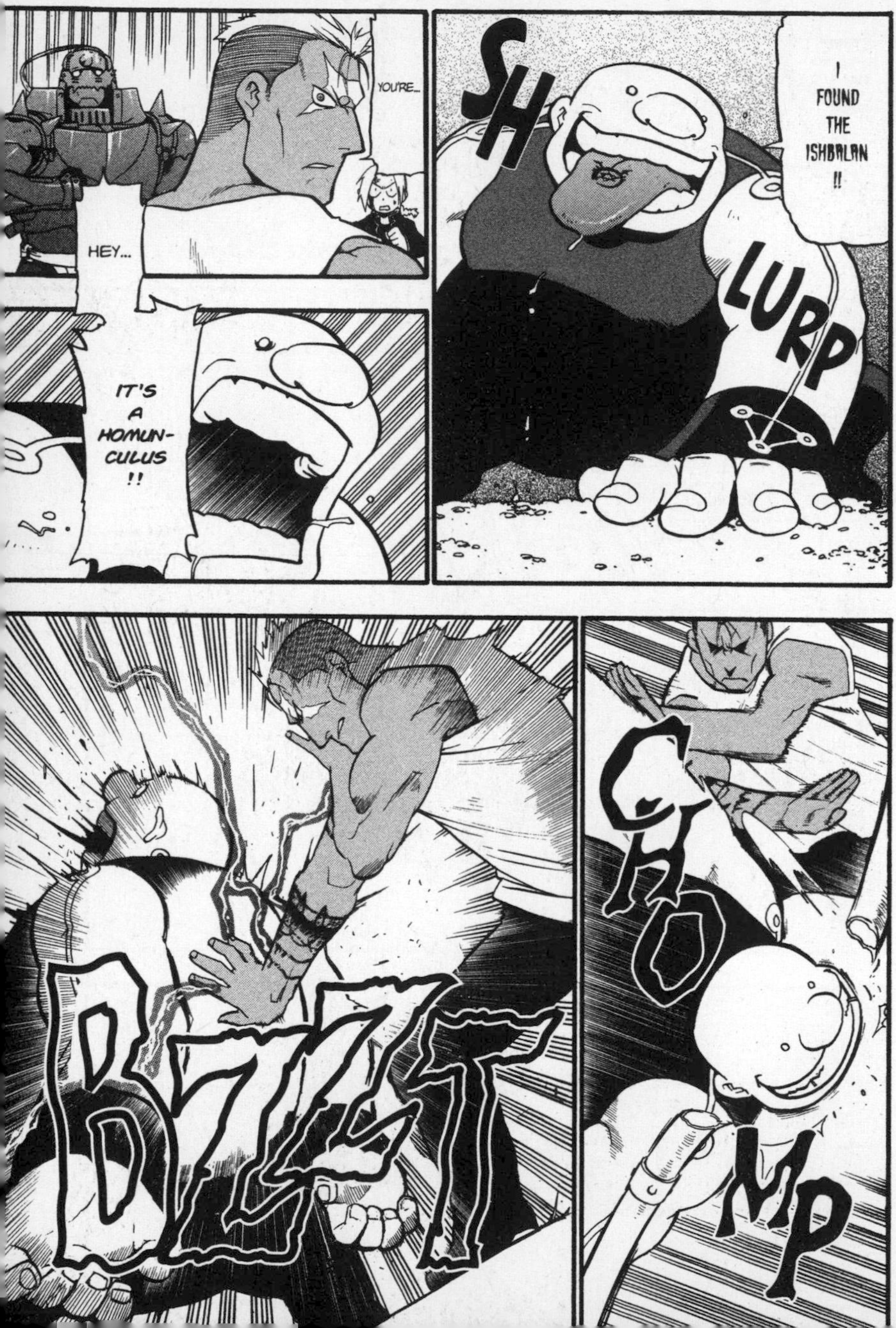
I FOUND THE ISHBALAN!!
SHLURP
YOU'RE...
HEY...
IT'S A HOMUNCULUS!!
CHOMP

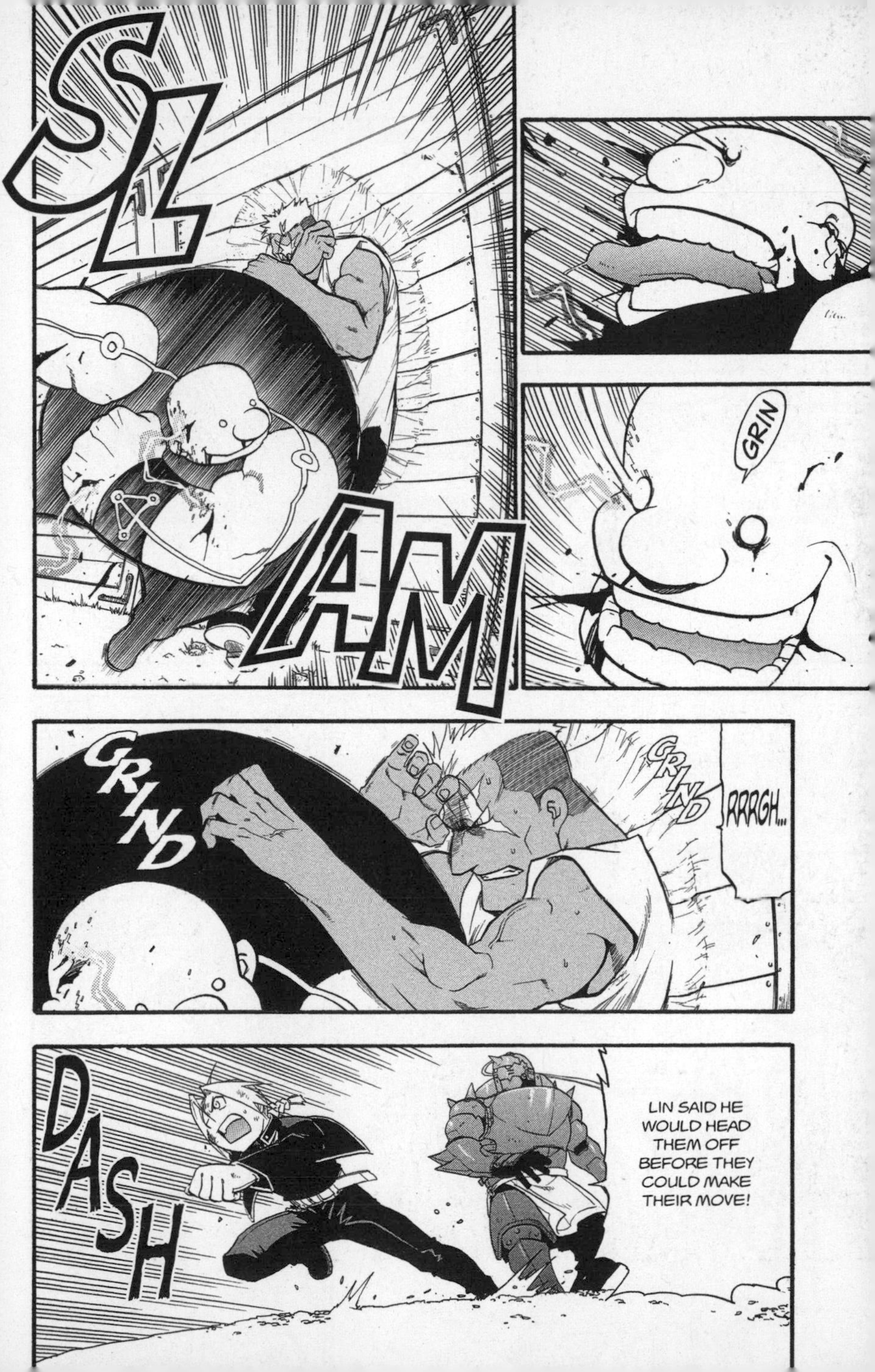
GRIN
SLAM
GRIND
RRRGH...
GRIND
LIN SAID HE WOULD HEAD THEM OFF BEFORE THEY COULD MAKE THEIR MOVE!
DASH

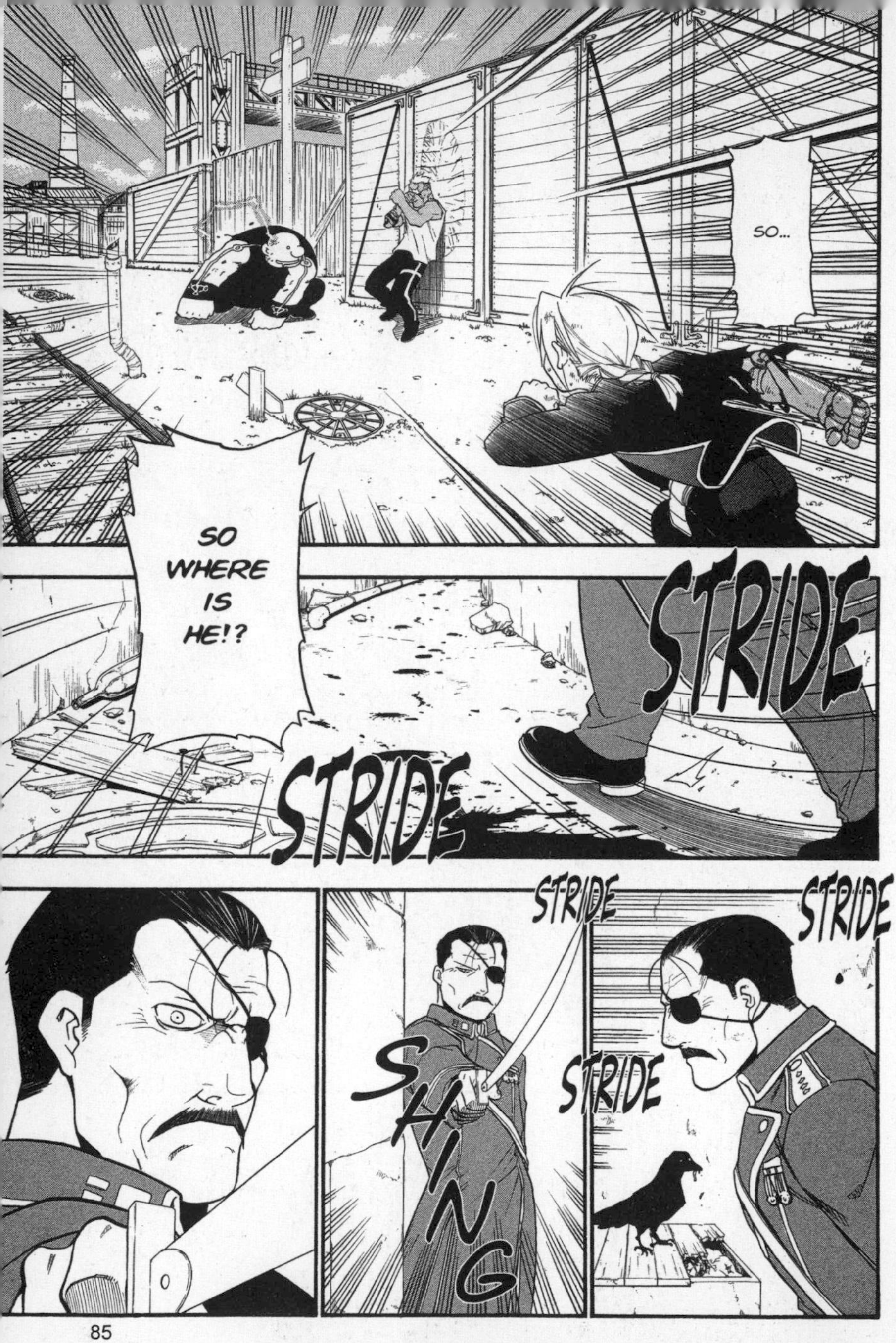
SO...
SO WHERE IS HE!?
STRIDE
STRIDE
STRIDE
STRIDE
STRIDE
SHING

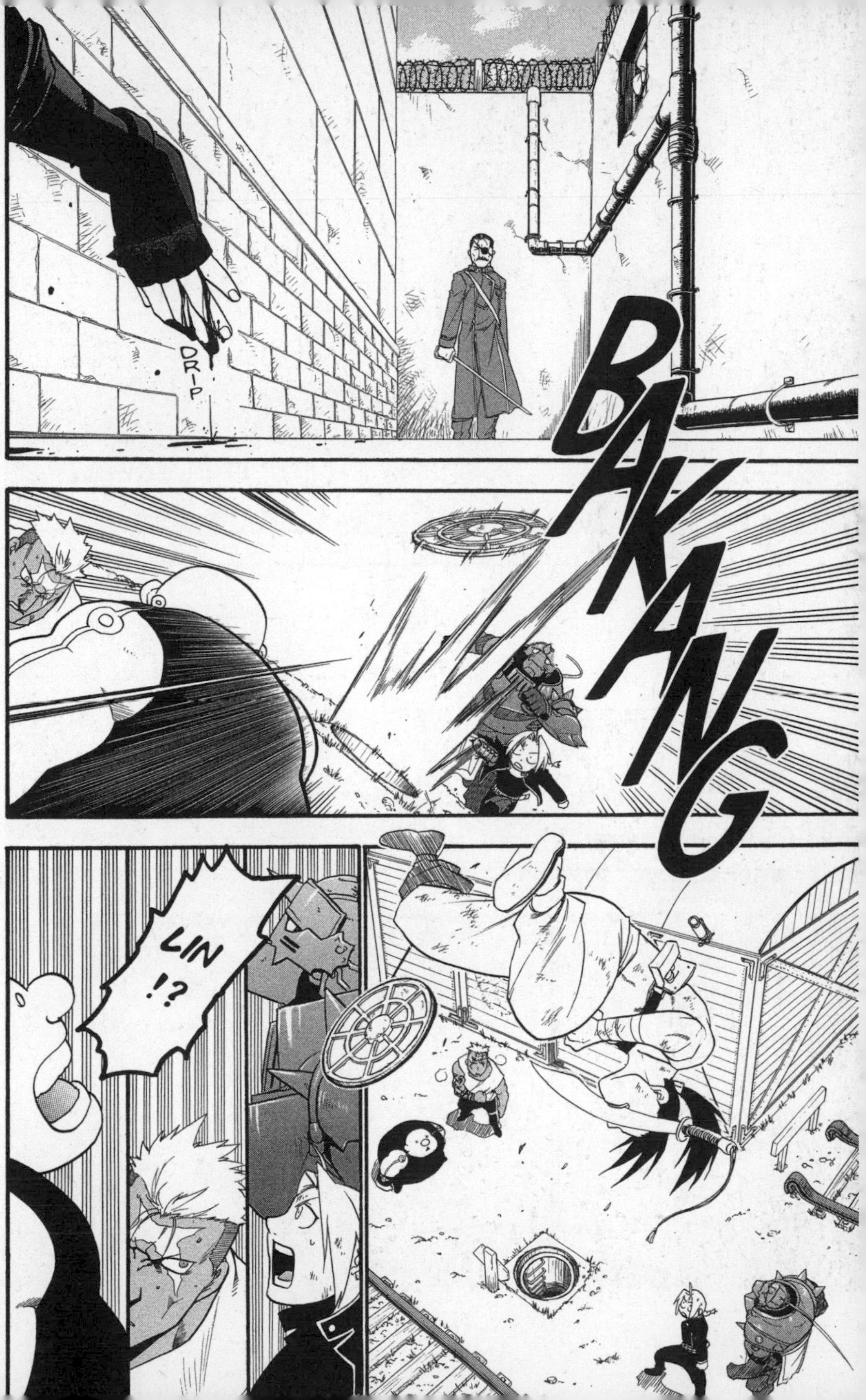
DRIP
BAKANG
LIN !?

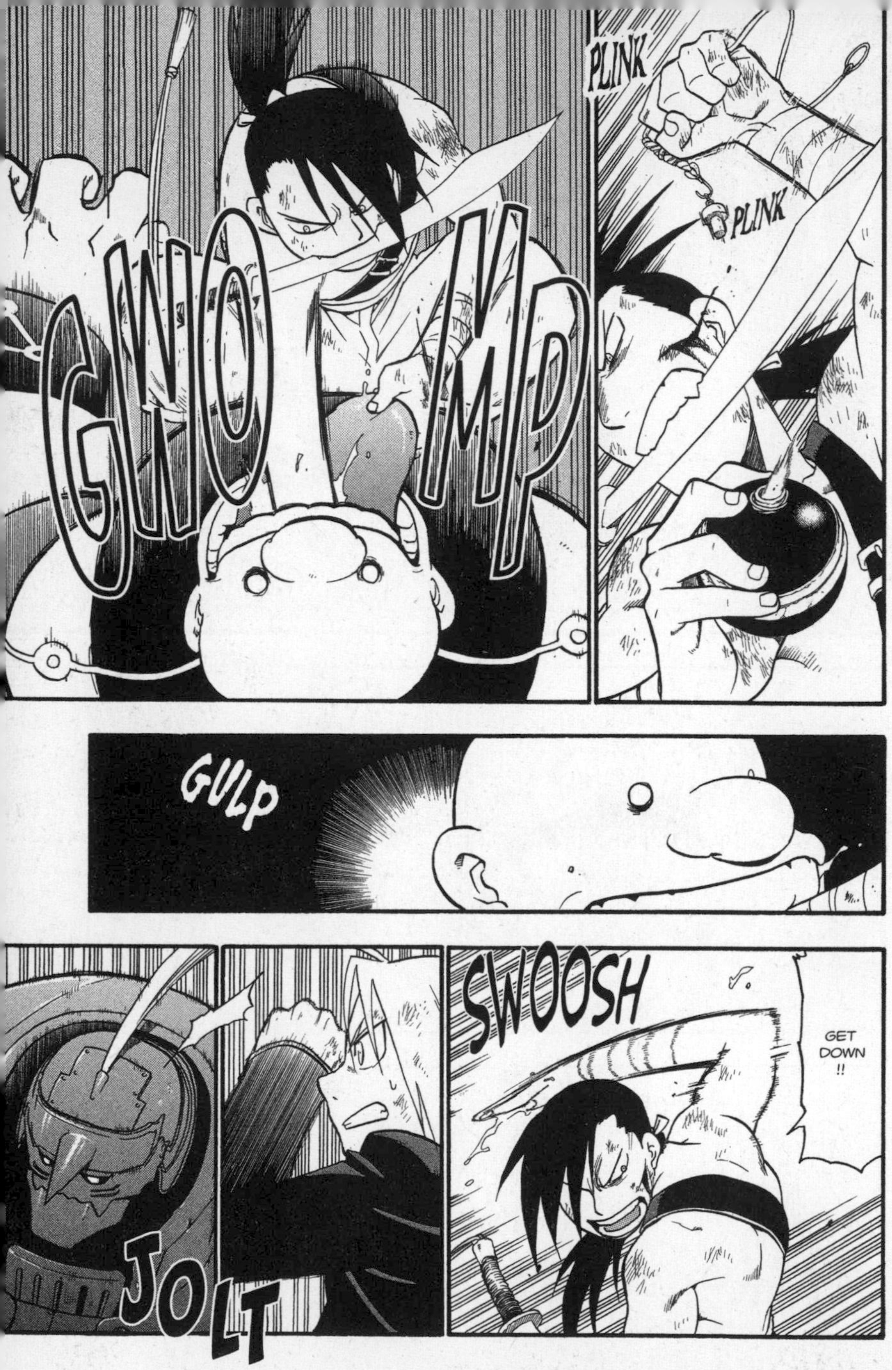
PLINK
PLINK
GNOMP
GULP
SWOOSH
GET DOWN!!
JOLT

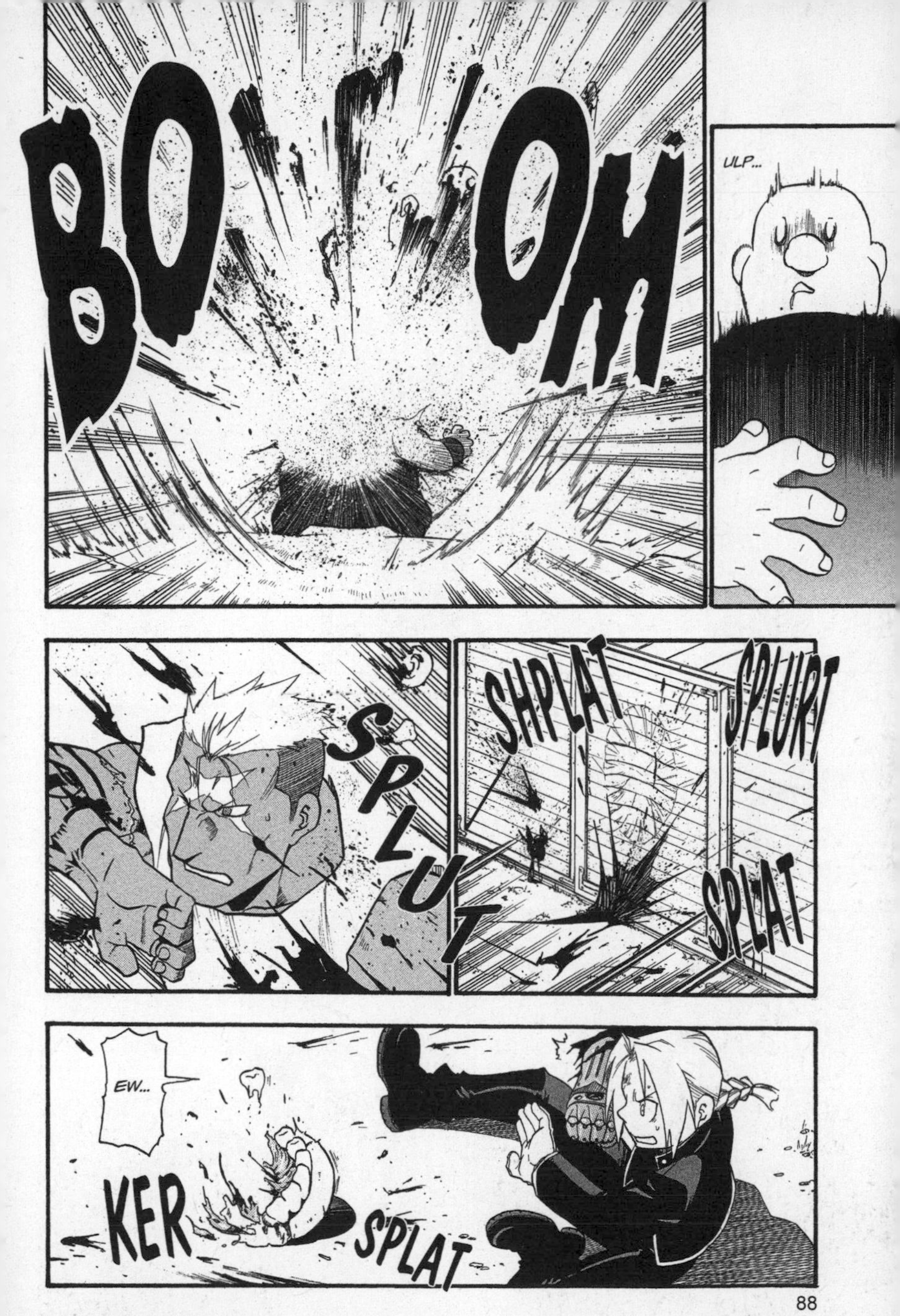
ULP...
BOOM
SPLURT
SHPLAT
SPLAT
SPLUT
EW...
KER
SPLAT

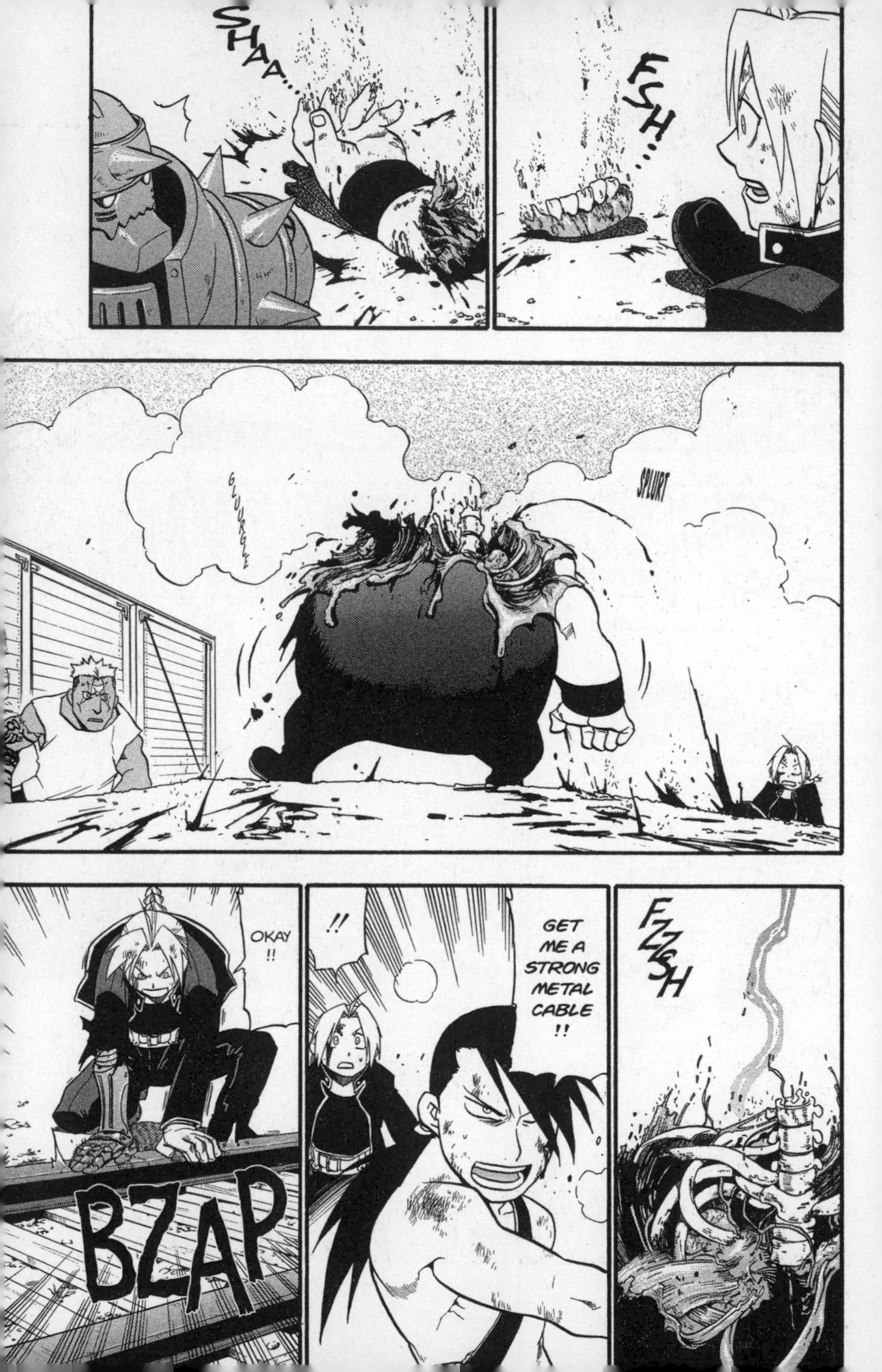
FSH...
SHAA...
SPLURT
GLUURGLE
FZZSH
GET ME A STRONG METAL CABLE !!
!!
OKAY !!
BZAP

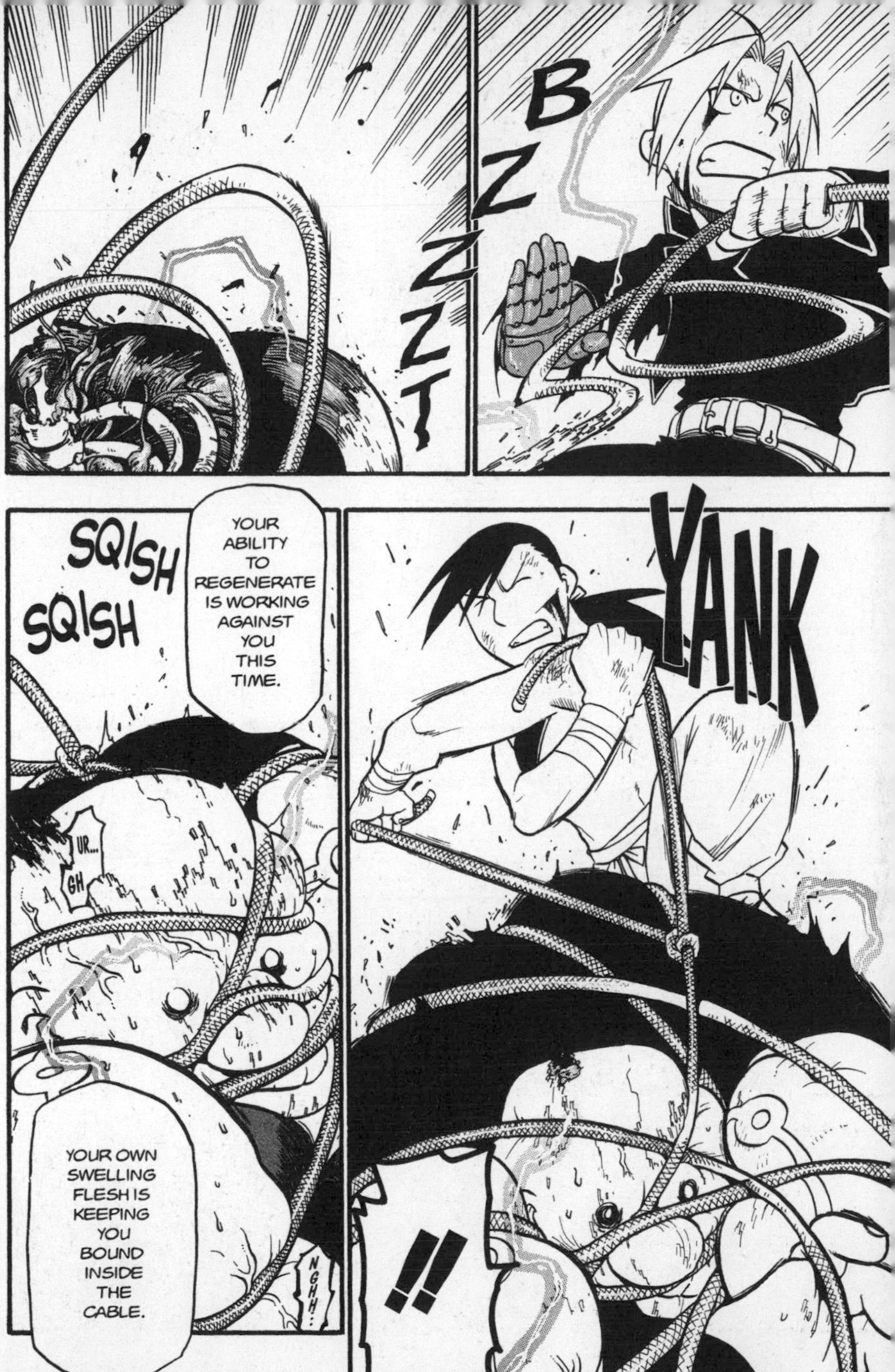
BZZZZT
YANK
!!
SQISH
SQISH
YOUR ABILITY TO REGENERATE IS WORKING AGAINST YOU THIS TIME.
UR... GH
YOUR OWN SWELLING FLESH IS KEEPING YOU BOUND INSIDE THE CABLE.
NGHH...

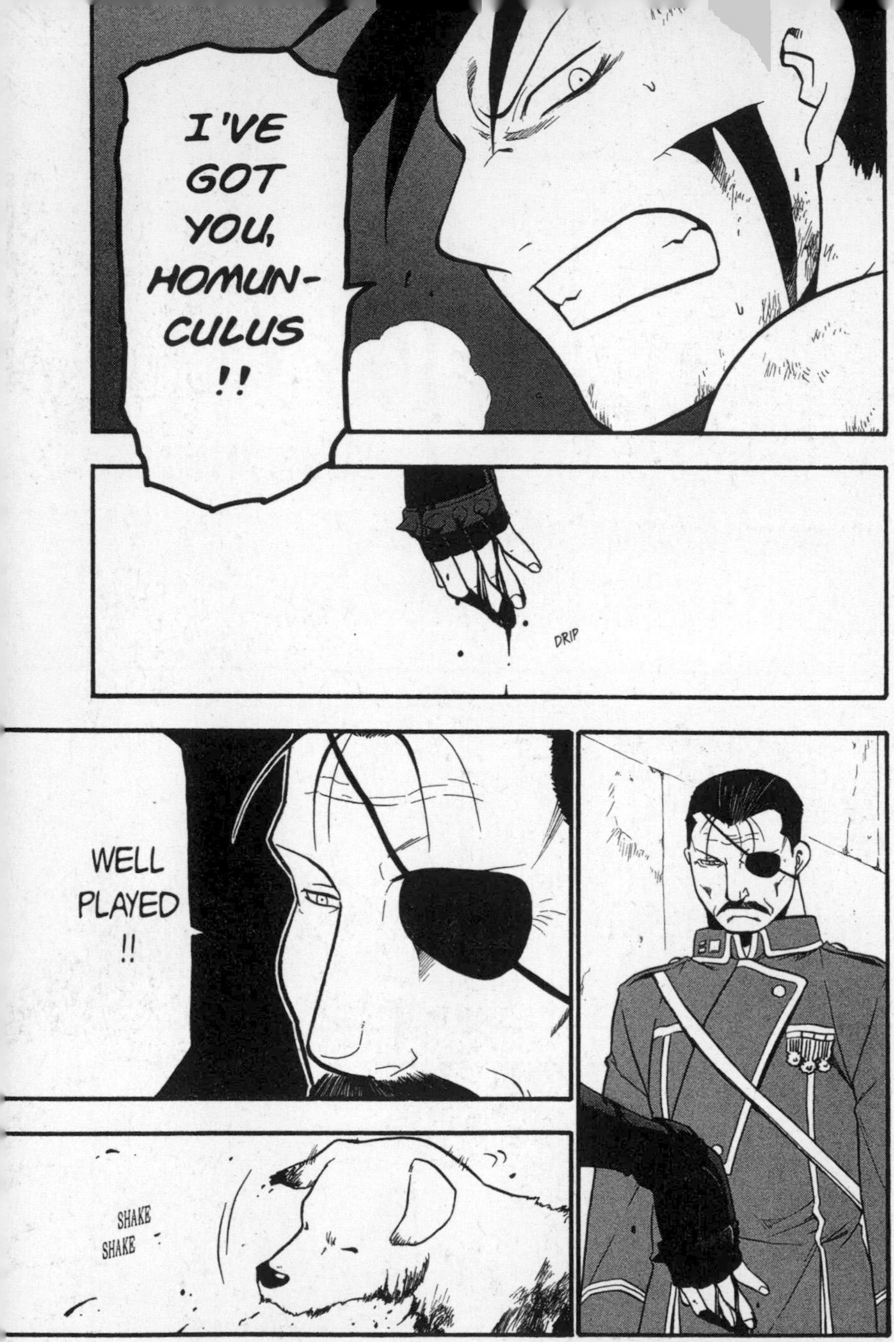
I'VE GOT YOU, HOMUNCULUS!!
DRIP
WELL PLAYED!!
SHAKE SHAKE

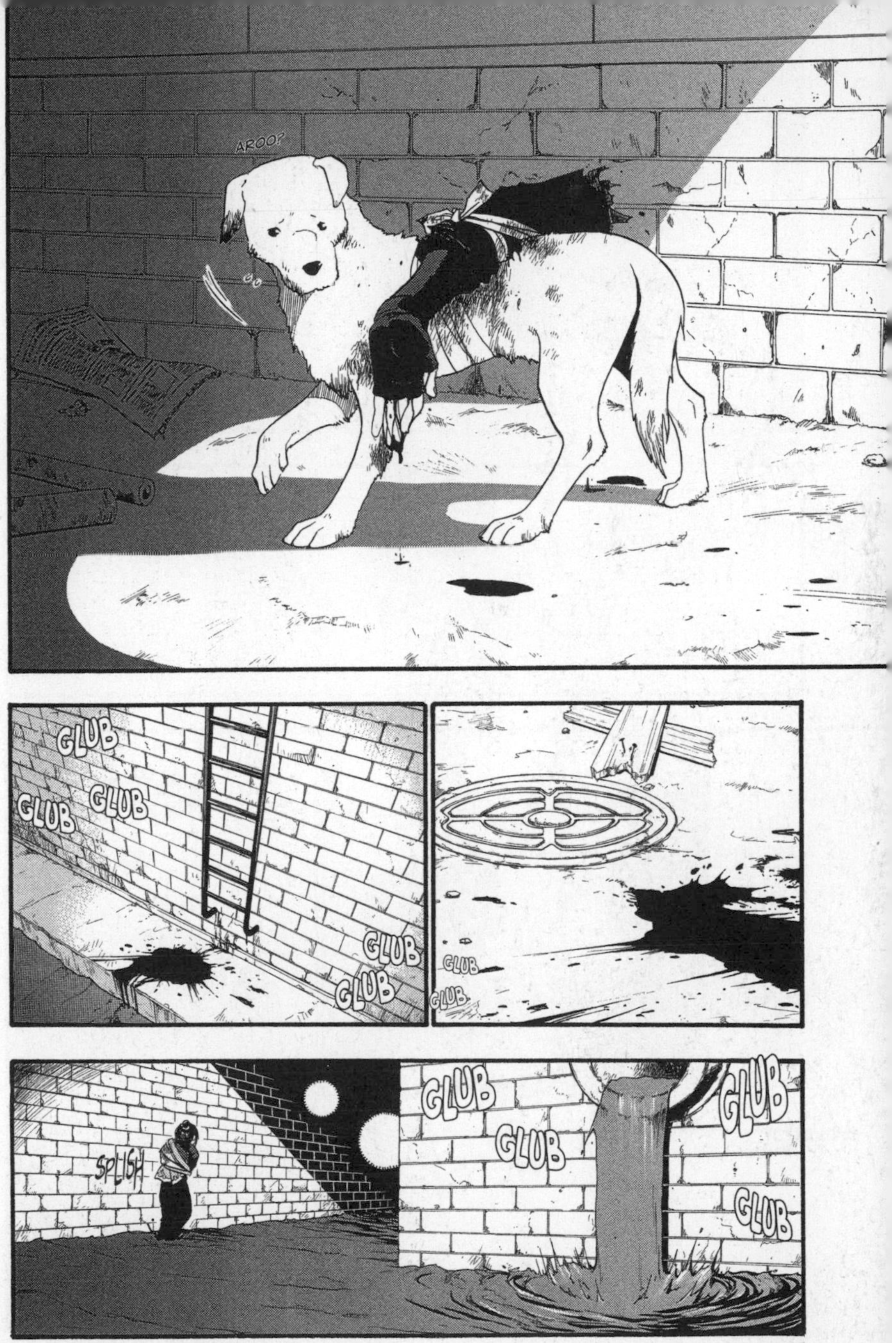
AROOP
GLUB
GLUB
GLUB
GLUB
GLUB
GLUB
GLUB
GLUB
GLUB
GLUB
GLUB
GLUB
SPLISH

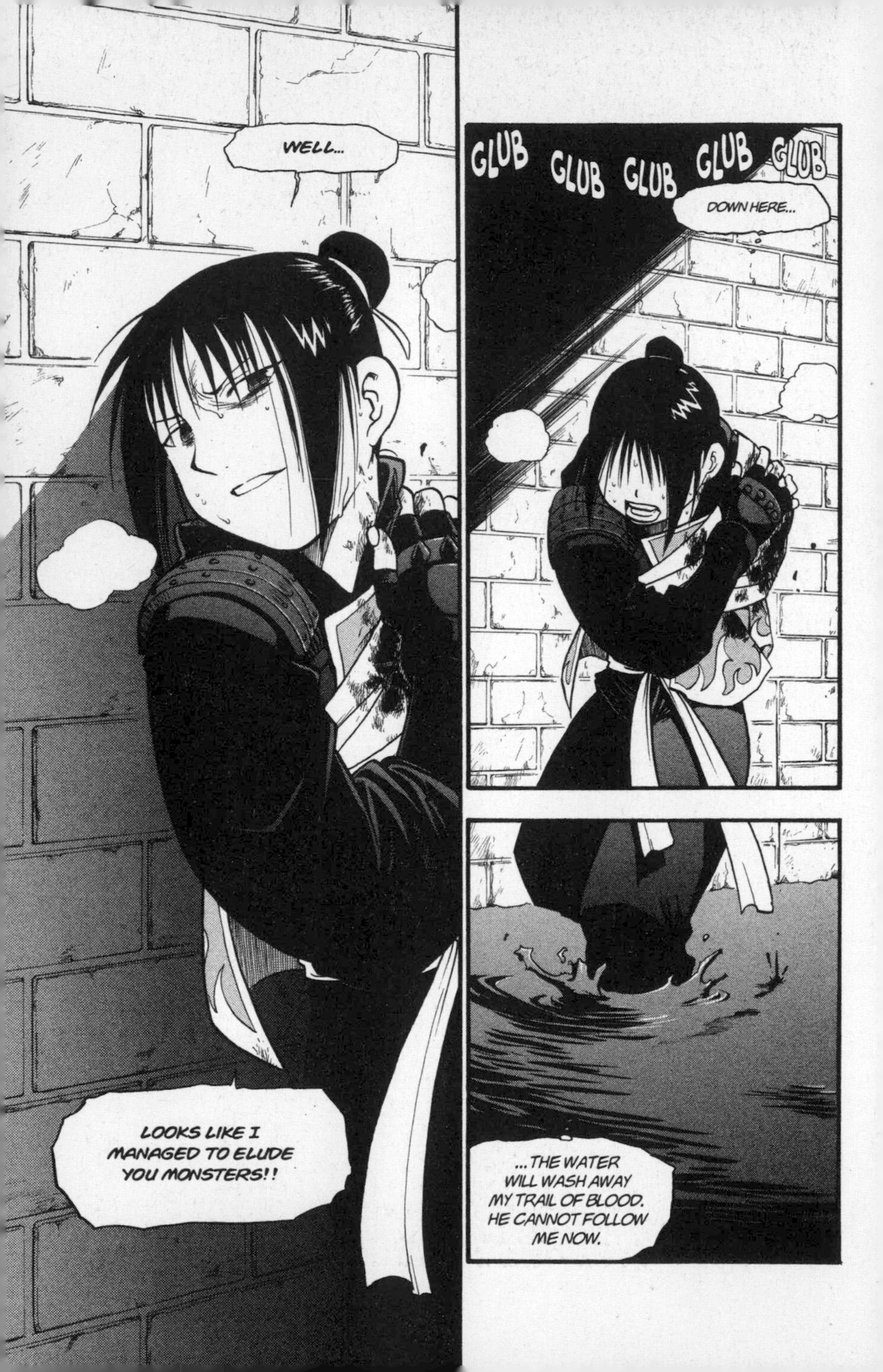
GLUB GLUB GLUB GLUB GLUB
DOWN HERE...
...THE WATER WILL WASH AWAY MY TRAIL OF BLOOD. HE CANNOT FOLLOW ME NOW.
WELL...
LOOKS LIKE I MANAGED TO ELUDE YOU MONSTERS!!

FULLMETAL
ALCHEMIST

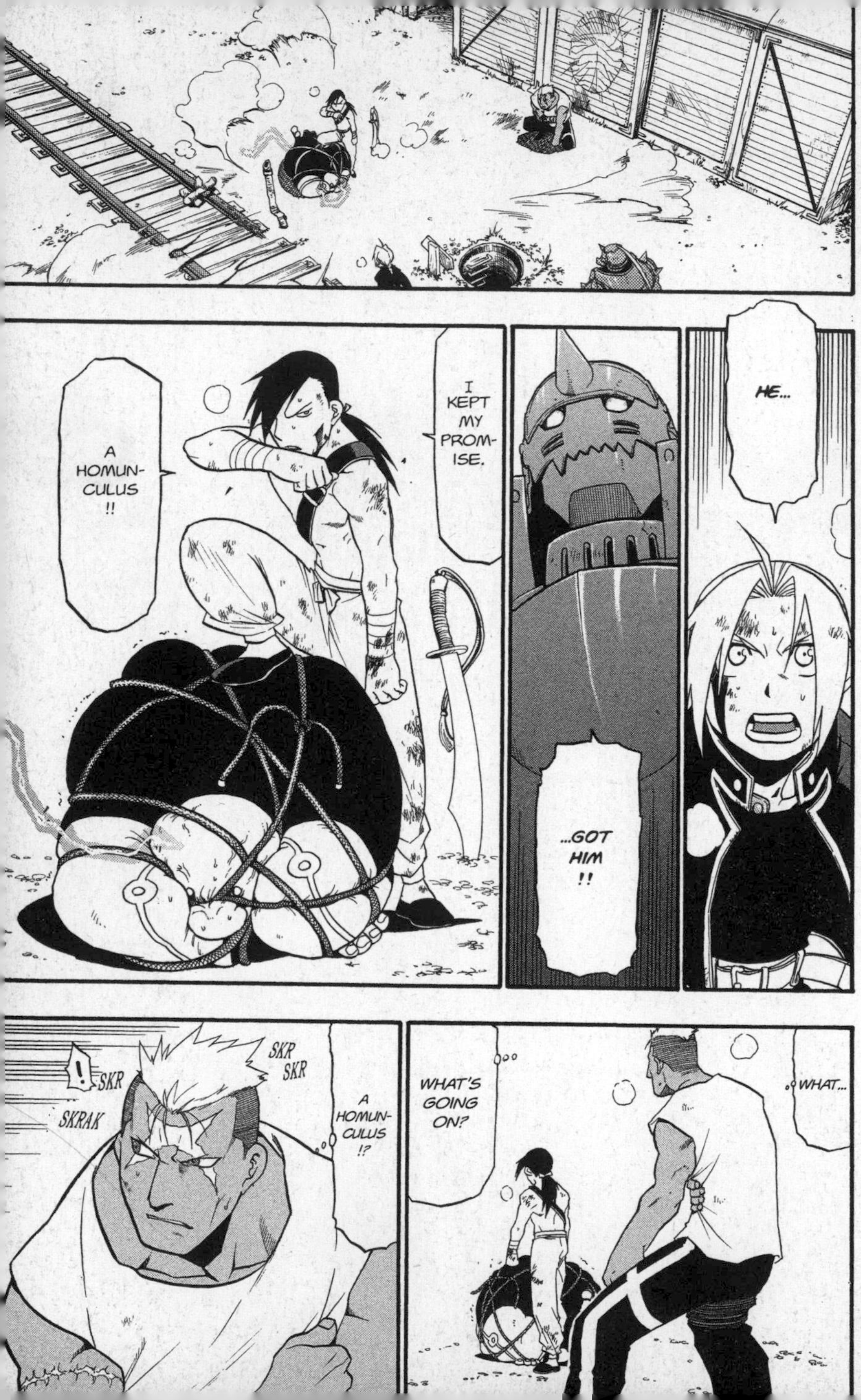
HE...
...GOT HIM !!
I KEPT MY PROMISE.
A HOMUNCULUS !!
WHAT...
WHAT'S GOING ON?
A HOMUNCULUS !?
SKR SKR
!
SKR
SKRAK

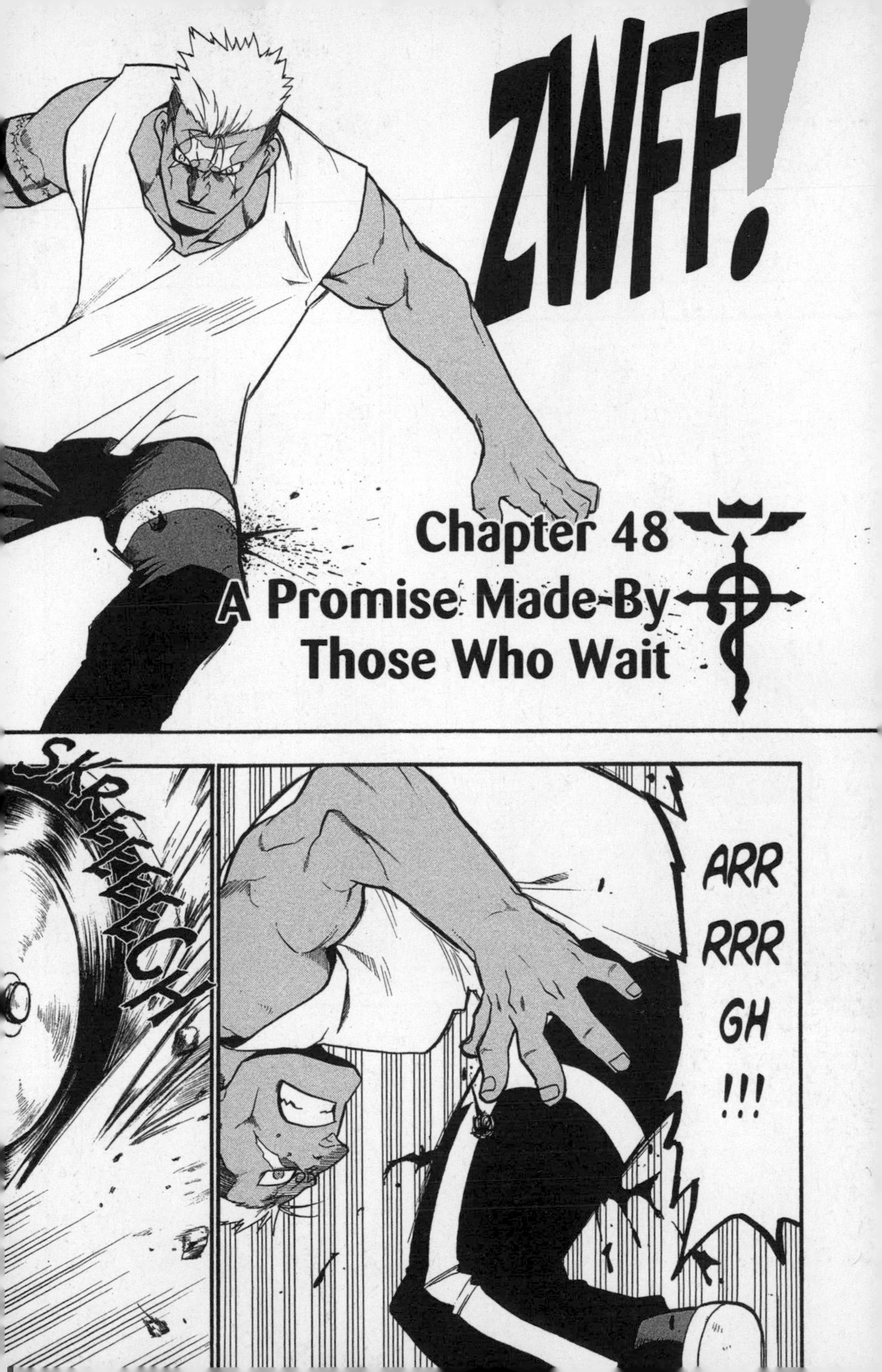
ZWFF!
Chapter 48
A Promise Made By
Those Who Wait
ARRRRRGH!!!
SKREEEECH

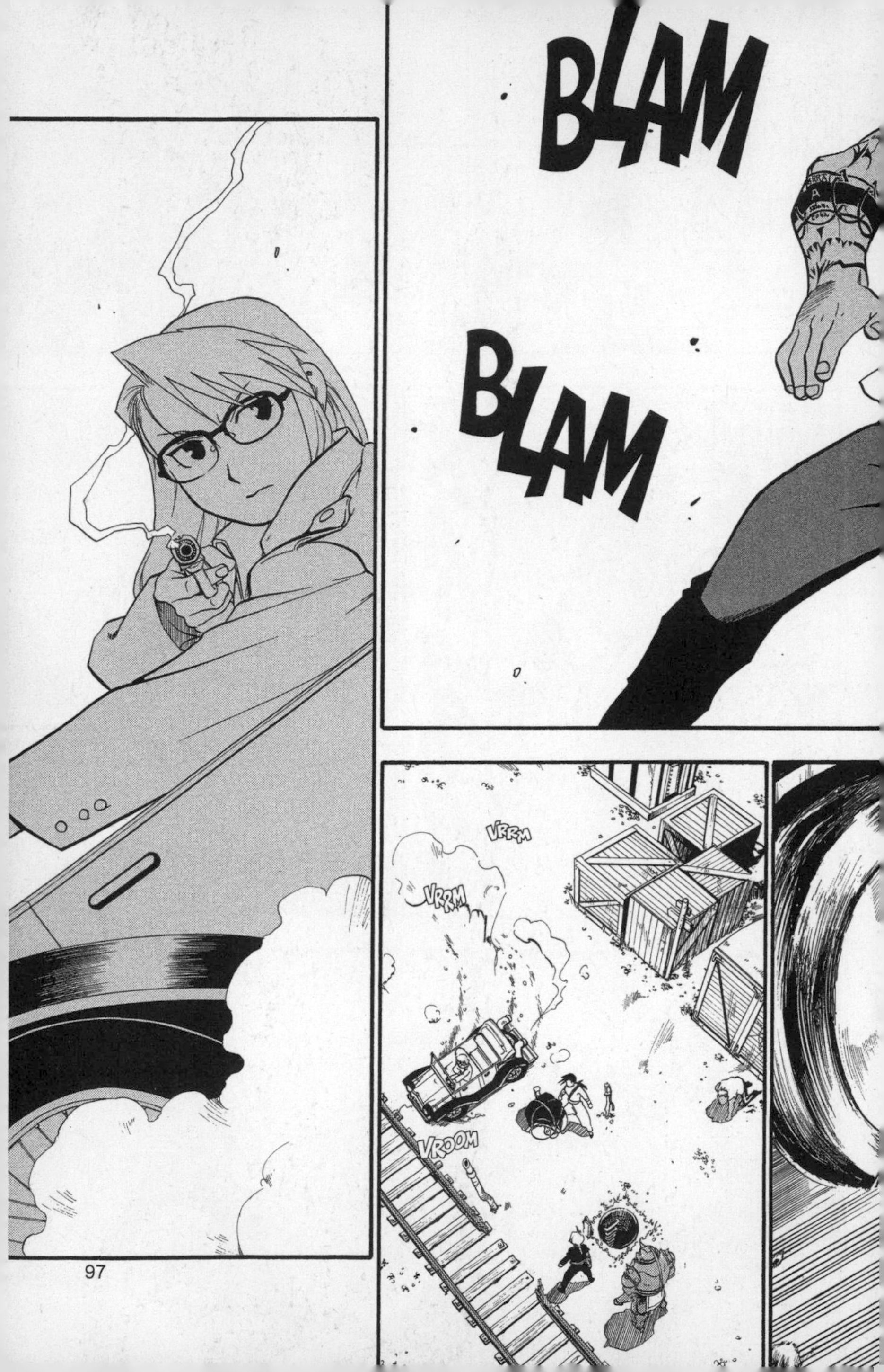
BLAM
BLAM
VRRM
VRRM
VROOM

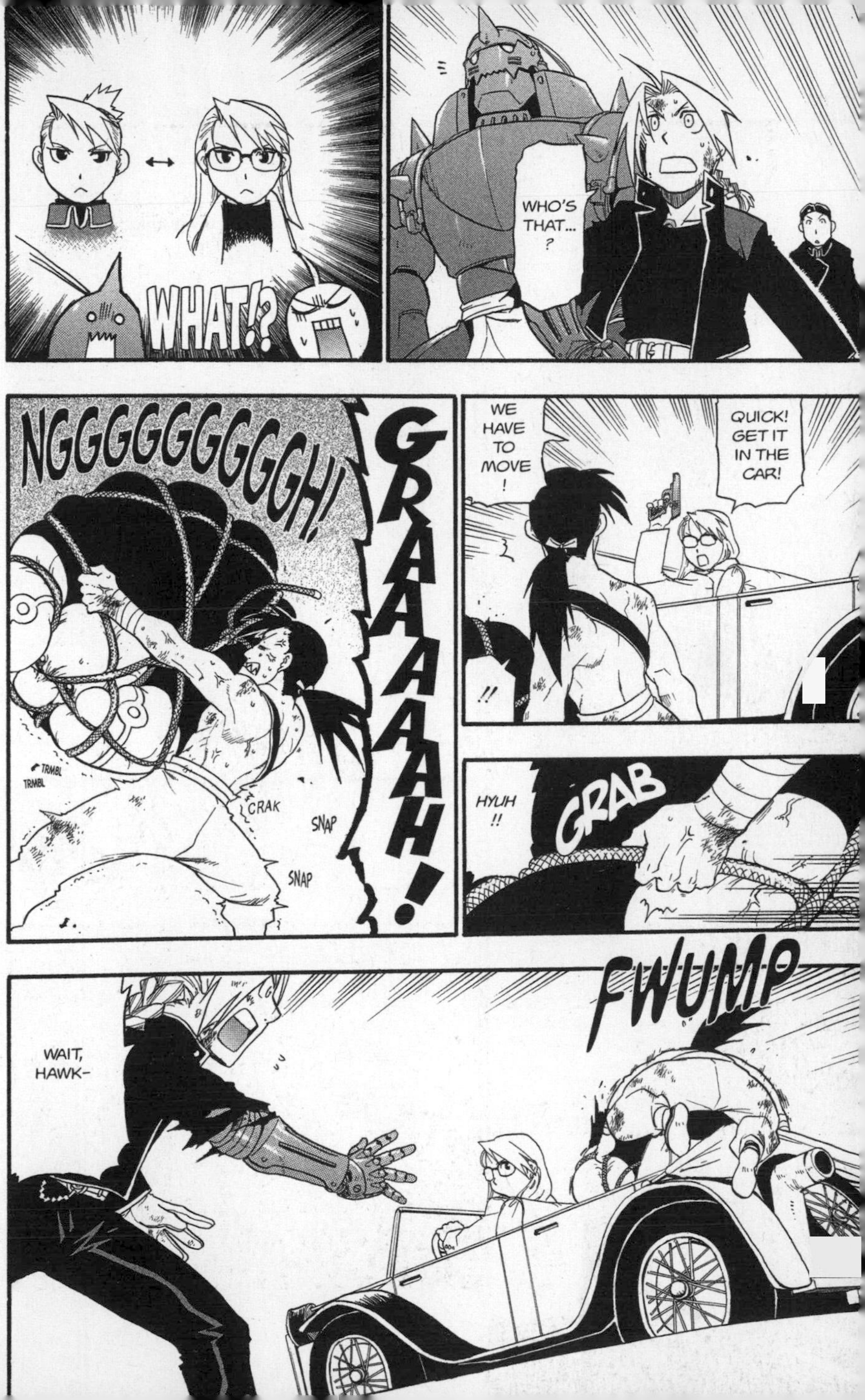
WHO'S THAT... ?
WHAT!?
QUICK! GET IT IN THE CAR!
WE HAVE TO MOVE !
!!
GRAB
HYUH !!
GRAAAAH!
NGGGGGGGGH!
TRMBL TRMBL
CRAK
SNAP
SNAP
FWUMP
WAIT, HAWK-

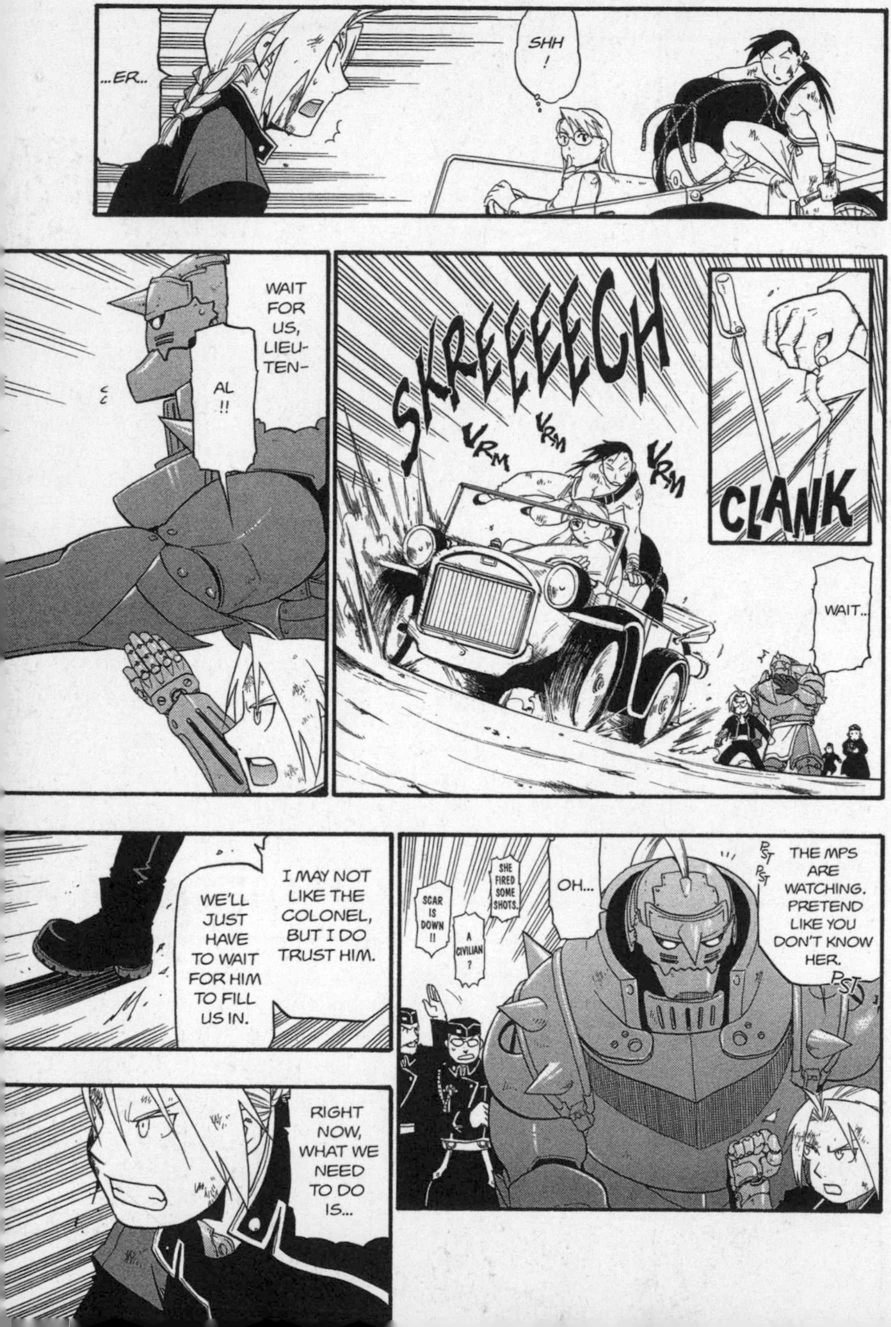
SHH !
...ER...
CLANK
SKREEEECH
VRM
VRM
VRM
WAIT...
WAIT FOR US, LIEU-TEN-
AL !!
PST PST
THE MPS ARE WATCHING. PRETEND LIKE YOU DON'T KNOW HER.
PST
OH...
SHE FIRED SOME SHOTS.
SCAR IS DOWN !!
A CIVILIAN ?
I MAY NOT LIKE THE COLONEL, BUT I DO TRUST HIM.
WE'LL JUST HAVE TO WAIT FOR HIM TO FILL US IN.
RIGHT NOW, WHAT WE NEED TO DO IS...

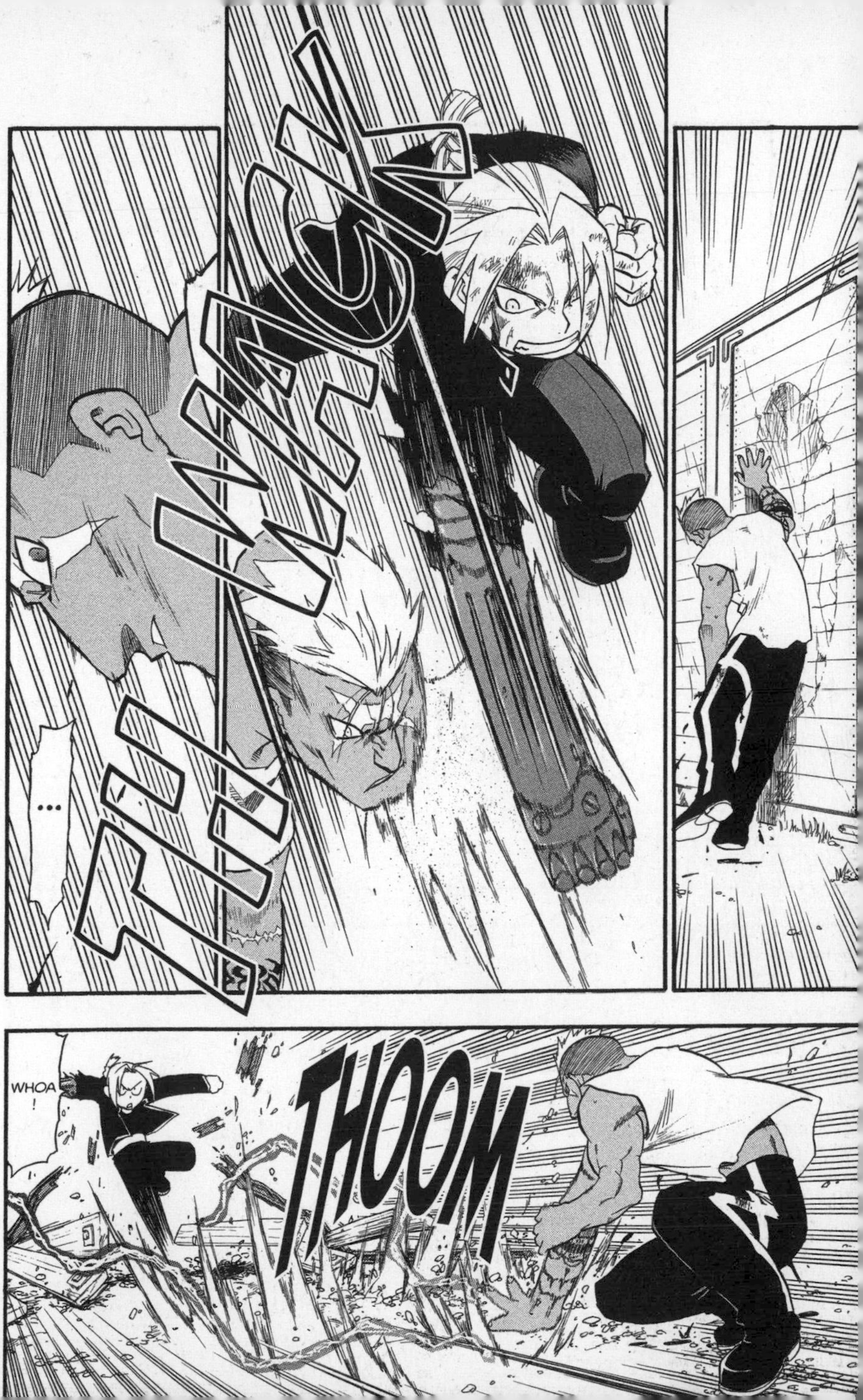
THWACK
...
THOOM
WHOA!

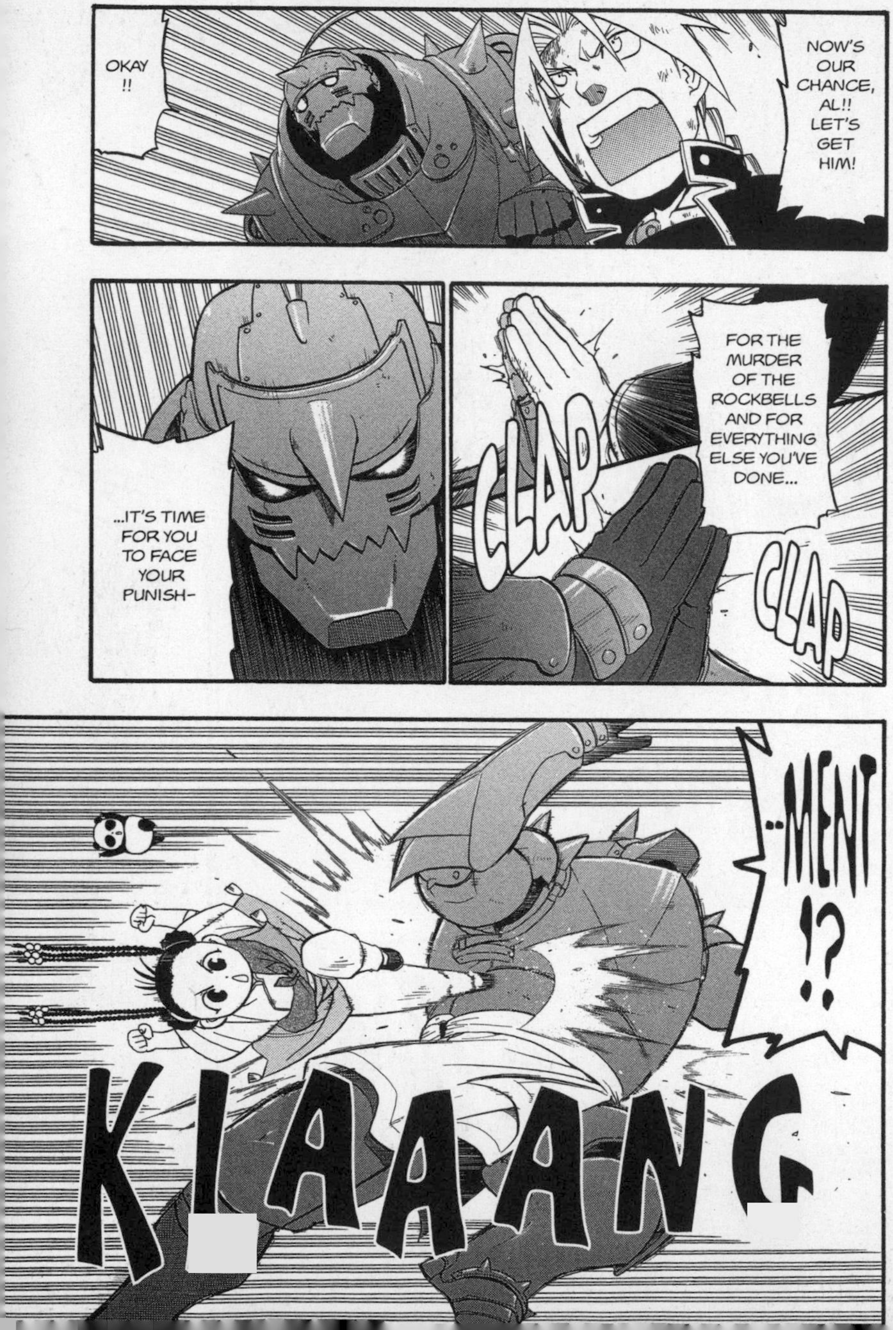
NOW'S OUR CHANCE, AL!! LET'S GET HIM!
OKAY !!
FOR THE MURDER OF THE ROCKBELLS AND FOR EVERYTHING ELSE YOU'VE DONE...
CLAP
CLAP
...IT'S TIME FOR YOU TO FACE YOUR PUNISH-
...MENT !?
KIAANG

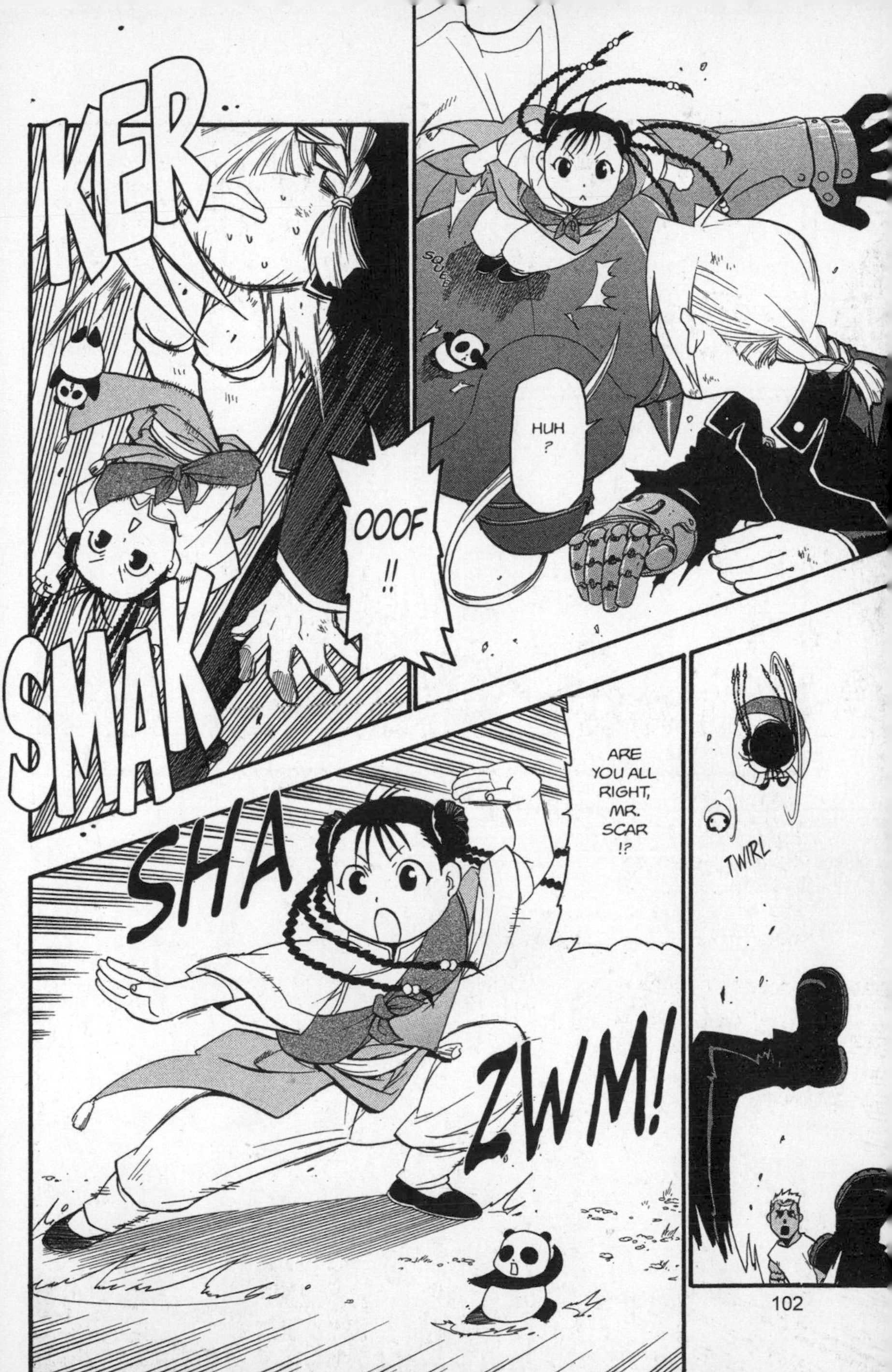
HUH ?
KER
SMAK
OOOF !!
TWIRL
ARE YOU ALL RIGHT, MR. SCAR !?
SHA
ZWM!

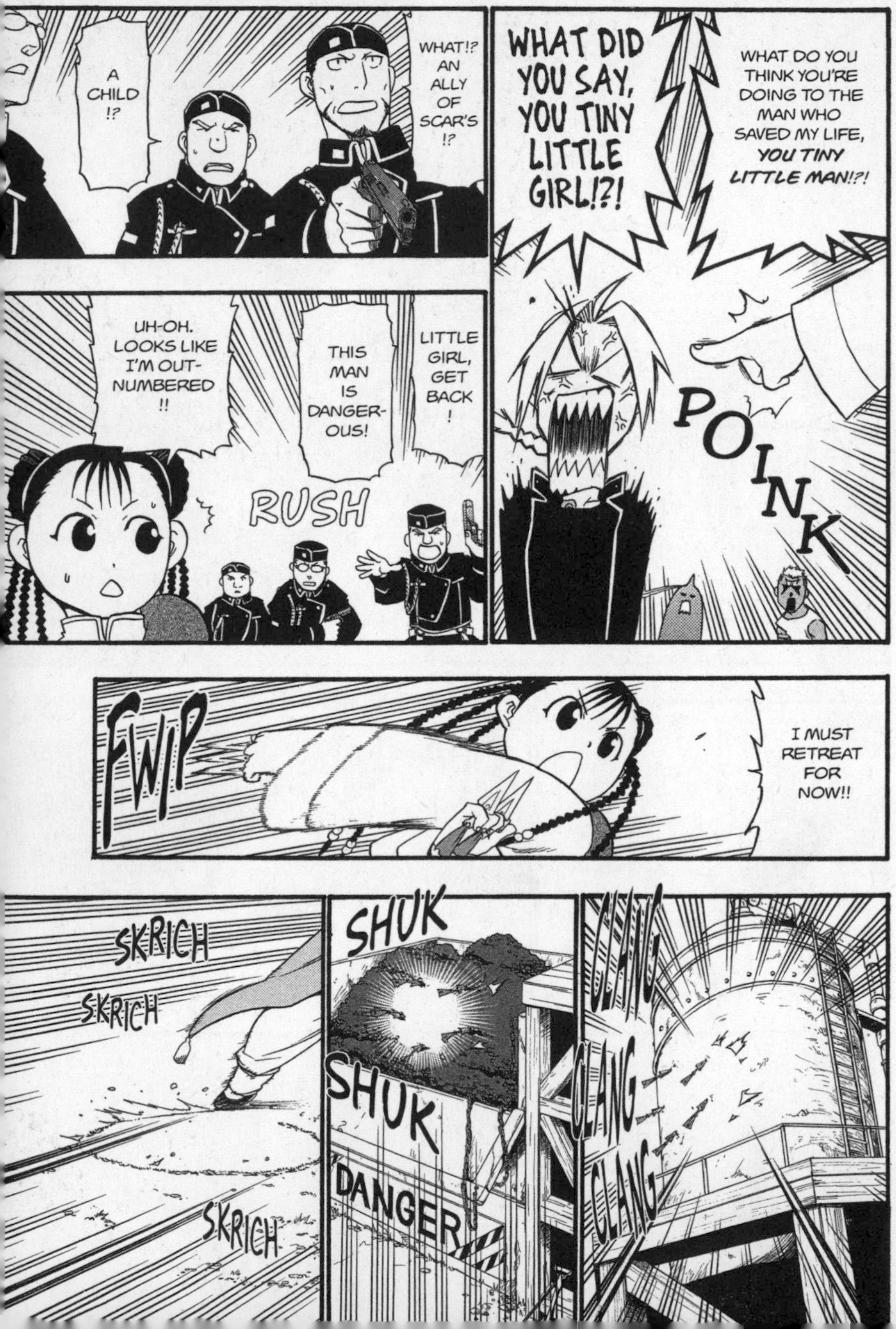
WHAT DO YOU THINK YOU'RE DOING TO THE MAN WHO SAVED MY LIFE, *YOU TINY LITTLE MAN!?!*
WHAT DID YOU SAY, YOU TINY LITTLE GIRL!?!
POINK
WHAT!? AN ALLY OF SCAR'S !?
A CHILD !?
LITTLE GIRL, GET BACK !
THIS MAN IS DANGER-OUS!
UH-OH. LOOKS LIKE I'M OUT-NUMBERED !!
RUSH
I MUST RETREAT FOR NOW!!
FWIP
CLANG
CLANG
CLANG
CLANG
SHUK
SHUK
DANGER
SKRICH
SKRICH
SKRICH

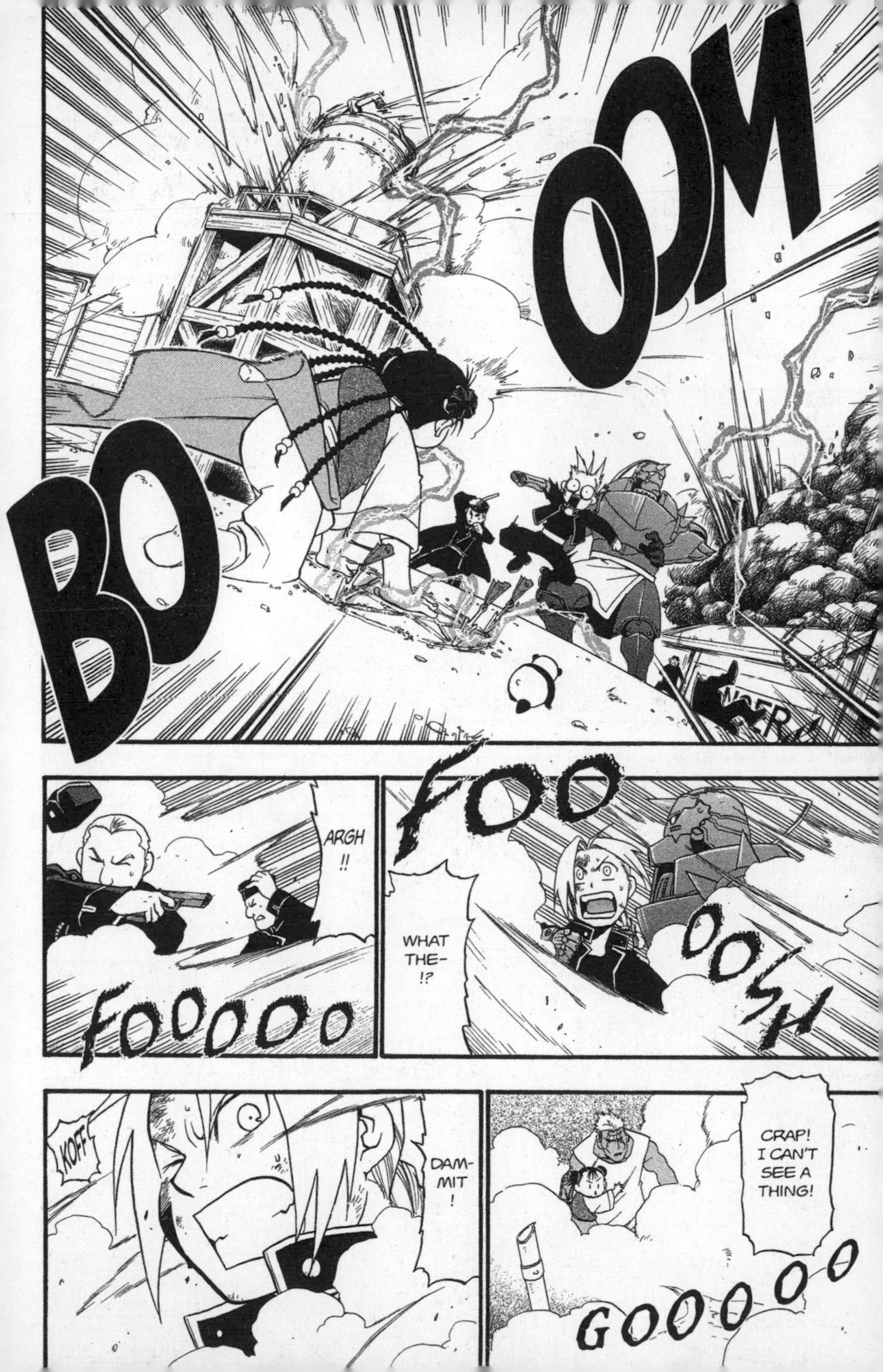
BO
OOM
FOO
OOSH
WHAT THE-!?
ARGH!!
FOOOOO
CRAP! I CAN'T SEE A THING!
GOOOOOO
KOFF
DAM-MIT!

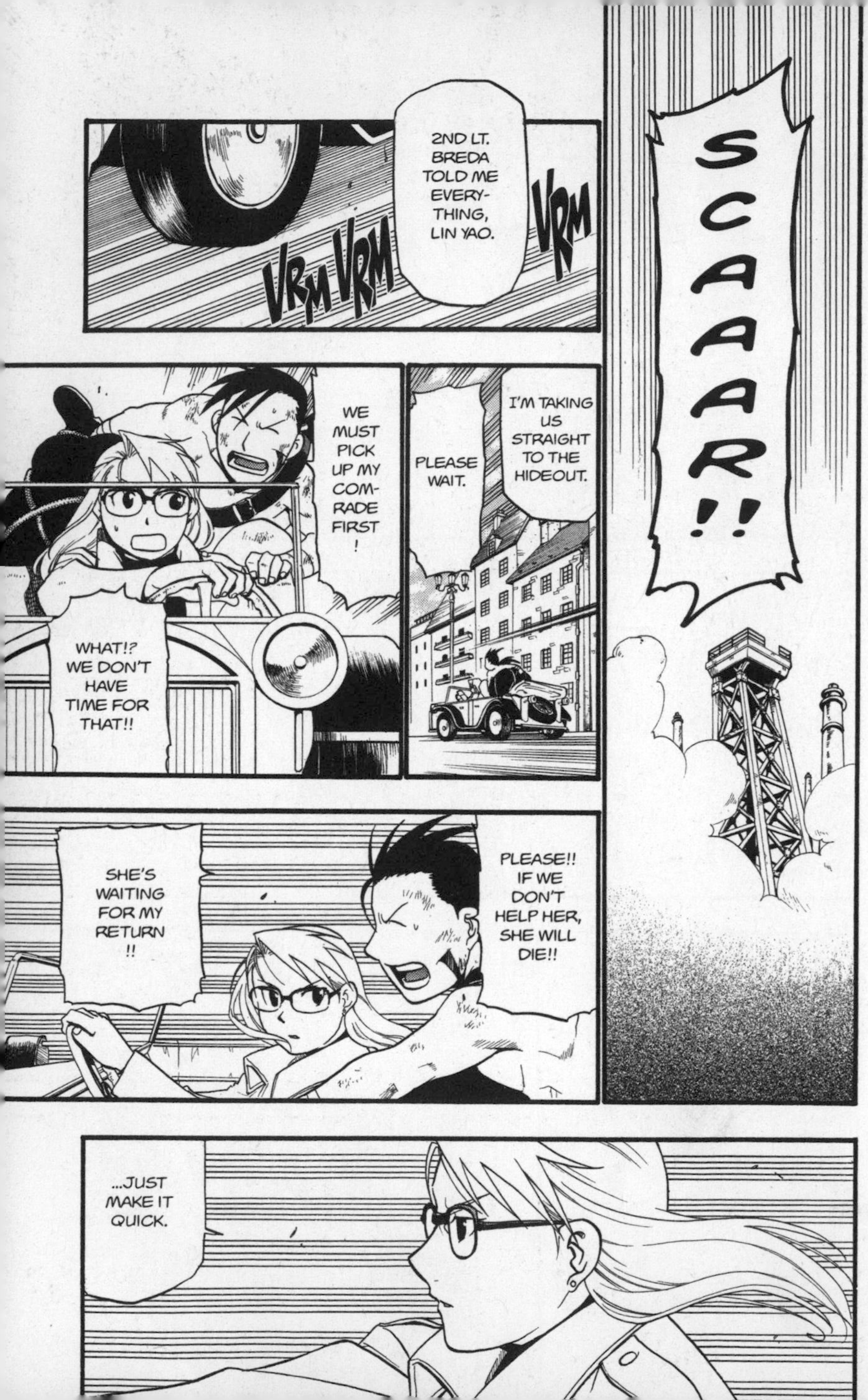
SCAAAR!!
VRM VRM VRM
2ND LT. BREDA TOLD ME EVERY-THING, LIN YAO.
I'M TAKING US STRAIGHT TO THE HIDEOUT.
PLEASE WAIT.
WE MUST PICK UP MY COM-RADE FIRST!
WHAT!? WE DON'T HAVE TIME FOR THAT!!
PLEASE!! IF WE DON'T HELP HER, SHE WILL DIE!!
SHE'S WAITING FOR MY RETURN!!
...JUST MAKE IT QUICK.

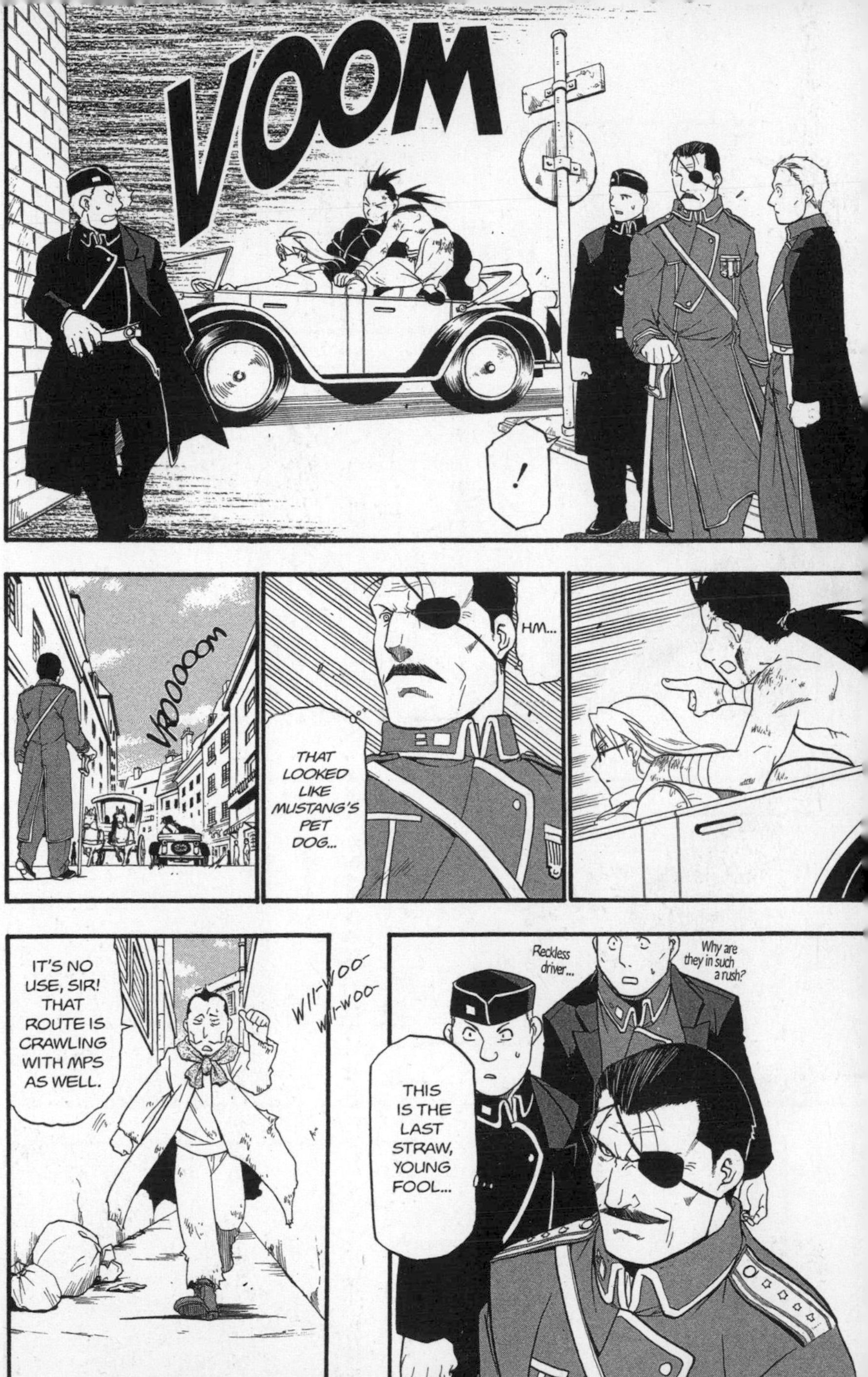
VOOM
!
HM...
THAT LOOKED LIKE MUSTANG'S PET DOG...
VROOOOOOM
Why are they in such a rush?
Reckless driver...
THIS IS THE LAST STRAW, YOUNG FOOL...
IT'S NO USE, SIR! THAT ROUTE IS CRAWLING WITH MPS AS WELL.
WII-WOO
WII-WOO

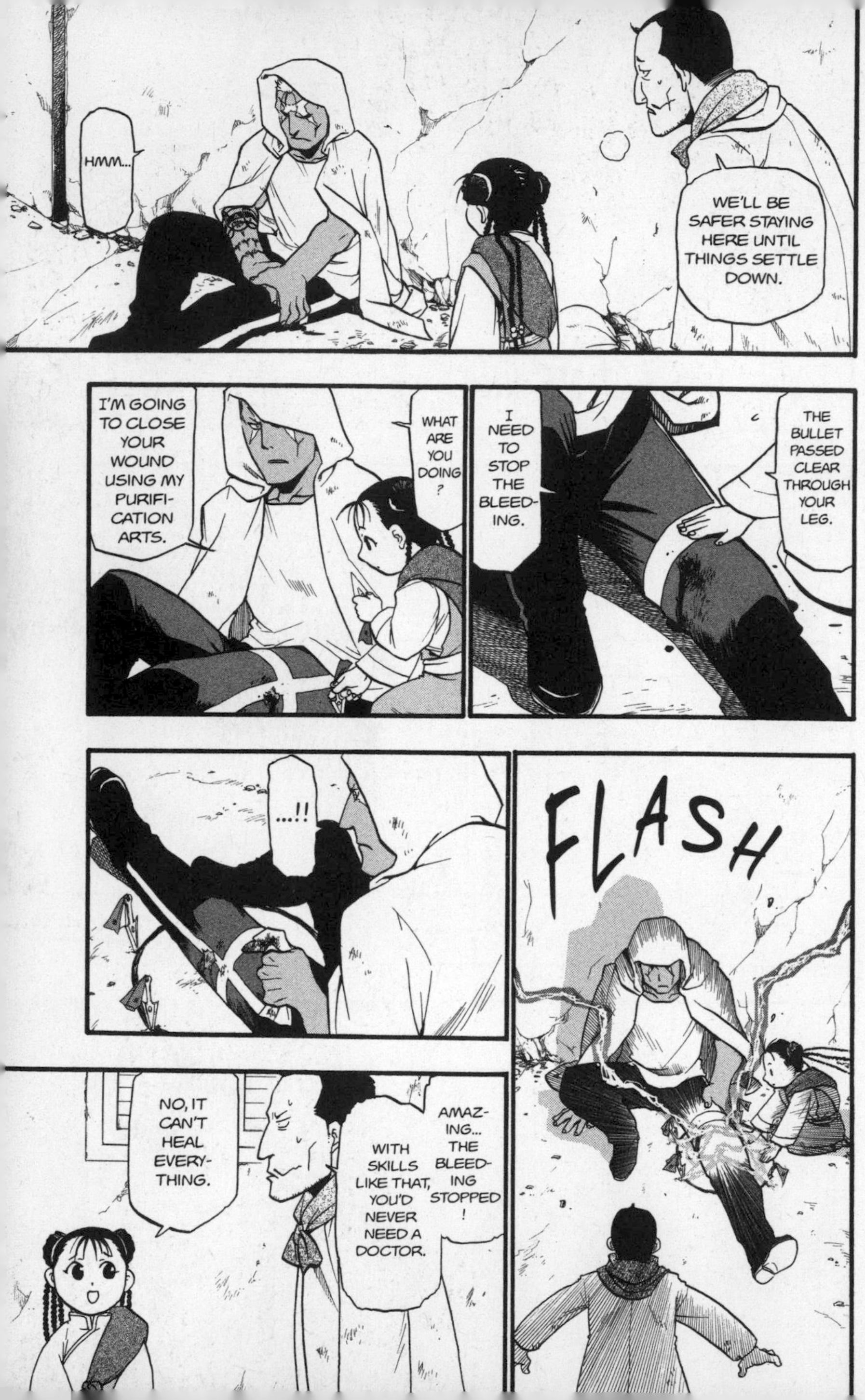
WE'LL BE SAFER STAYING HERE UNTIL THINGS SETTLE DOWN.
HMM...
THE BULLET PASSED CLEAR THROUGH YOUR LEG.
I NEED TO STOP THE BLEEDING.
WHAT ARE YOU DOING?
I'M GOING TO CLOSE YOUR WOUND USING MY PURIFICATION ARTS.
FLASH
...!!
AMAZING... THE BLEEDING STOPPED!
WITH SKILLS LIKE THAT, YOU'D NEVER NEED A DOCTOR.
NO, IT CAN'T HEAL EVERYTHING.

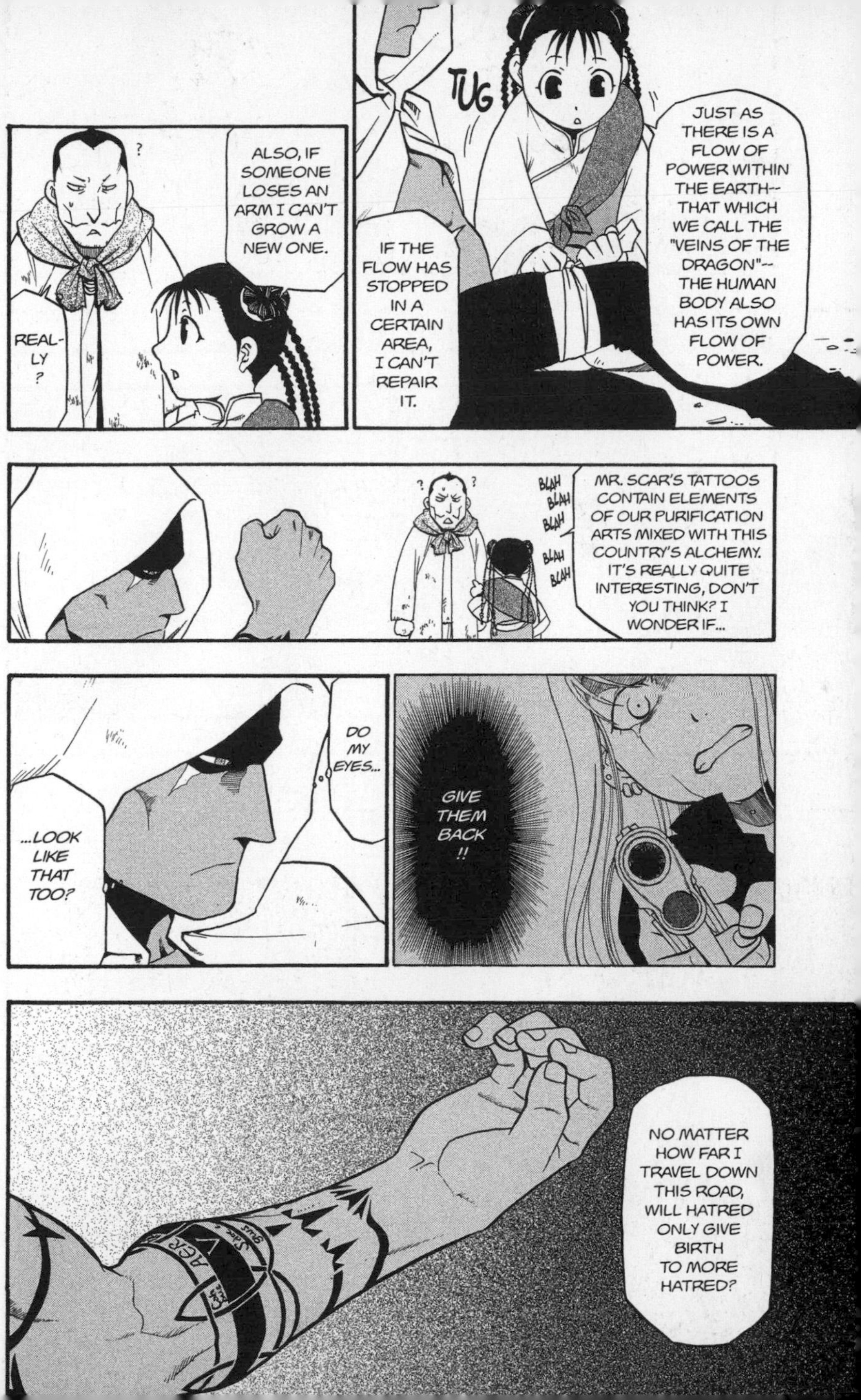
TUG
JUST AS THERE IS A FLOW OF POWER WITHIN THE EARTH--THAT WHICH WE CALL THE "VEINS OF THE DRAGON"--THE HUMAN BODY ALSO HAS ITS OWN FLOW OF POWER.
IF THE FLOW HAS STOPPED IN A CERTAIN AREA, I CAN'T REPAIR IT.
ALSO, IF SOMEONE LOSES AN ARM I CAN'T GROW A NEW ONE.
?
REAL-LY?
MR. SCAR'S TATTOOS CONTAIN ELEMENTS OF OUR PURIFICATION ARTS MIXED WITH THIS COUNTRY'S ALCHEMY. IT'S REALLY QUITE INTERESTING, DON'T YOU THINK? I WONDER IF...
BLAH BLAH BLAH BLAH BLAH
? ?
GIVE THEM BACK!!
DO MY EYES...
...LOOK LIKE THAT TOO?
NO MATTER HOW FAR I TRAVEL DOWN THIS ROAD, WILL HATRED ONLY GIVE BIRTH TO MORE HATRED?

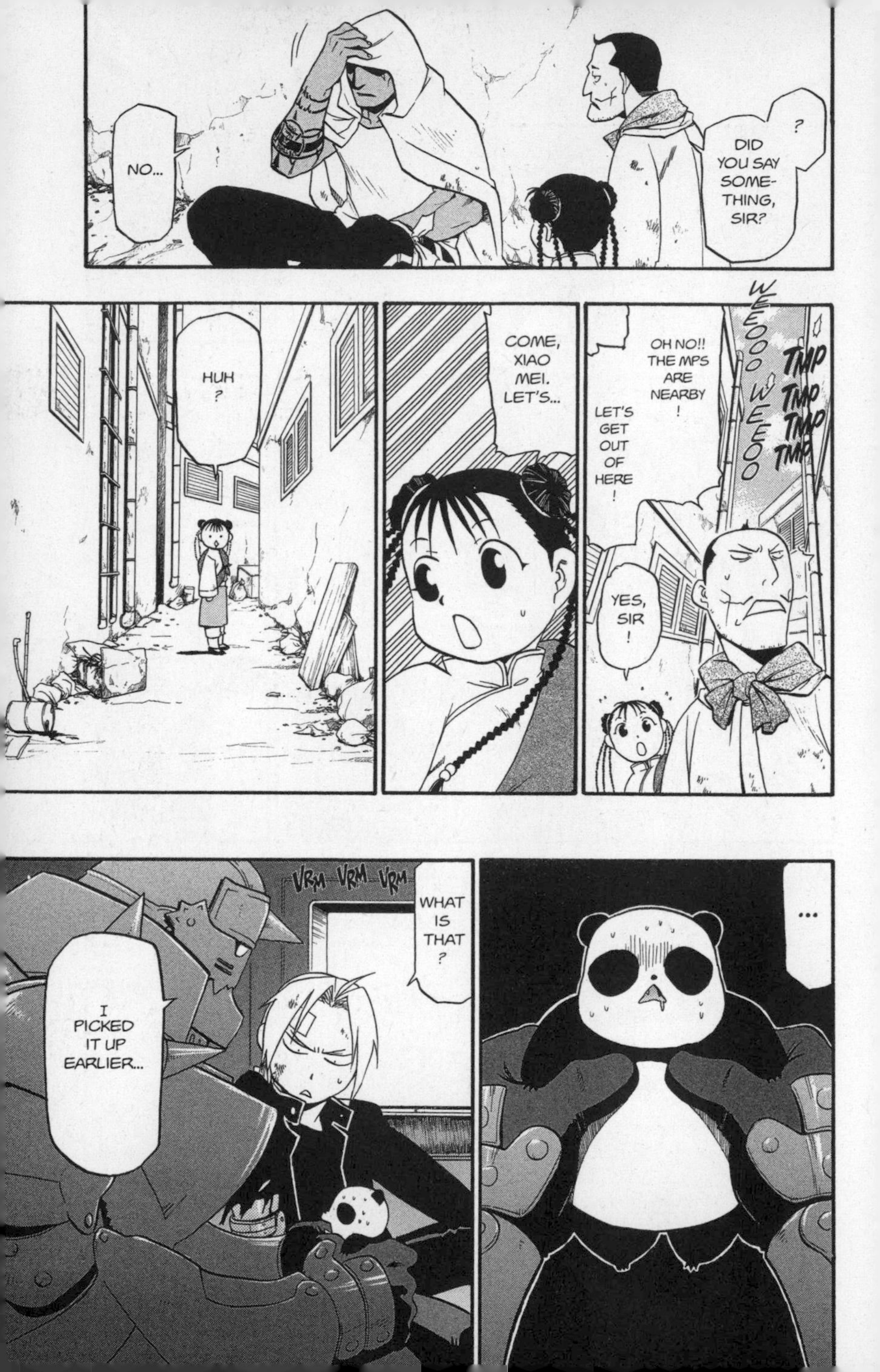
?
DID YOU SAY SOMETHING, SIR?
NO...
WEEOOO WEEOOO
TMP TMP TMP TMP
OH NO!! THE MPS ARE NEARBY!
LET'S GET OUT OF HERE!
YES, SIR!
COME, XIAO MEI. LET'S...
HUH?
...
VRM VRM VRM
WHAT IS THAT?
I PICKED IT UP EARLIER...

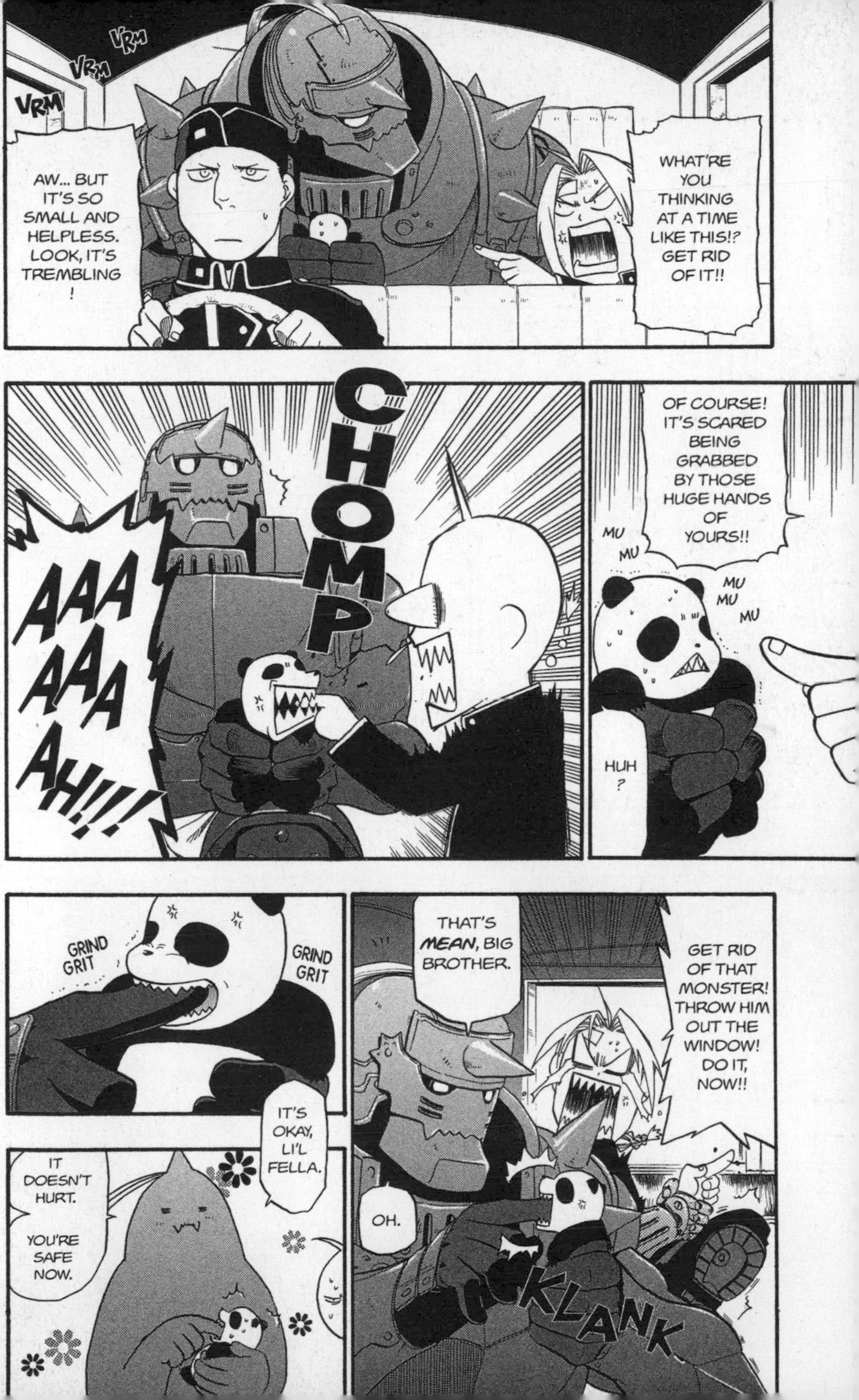
WHAT'RE YOU THINKING AT A TIME LIKE THIS!? GET RID OF IT!!
VRM
VRM
VRM
AW... BUT IT'S SO SMALL AND HELPLESS. LOOK, IT'S TREMBLING!
OF COURSE! IT'S SCARED BEING GRABBED BY THOSE HUGE HANDS OF YOURS!!
MU MU
MU MU MU
HUH?
CHOMP
AAAAAAAAH!!!!
GET RID OF THAT MONSTER! THROW HIM OUT THE WINDOW! DO IT, NOW!!
THAT'S MEAN, BIG BROTHER.
OH.
KLANK
GRIND GRIT
GRIND GRIT
IT'S OKAY, LI'L FELLA.
IT DOESN'T HURT.
YOU'RE SAFE NOW.

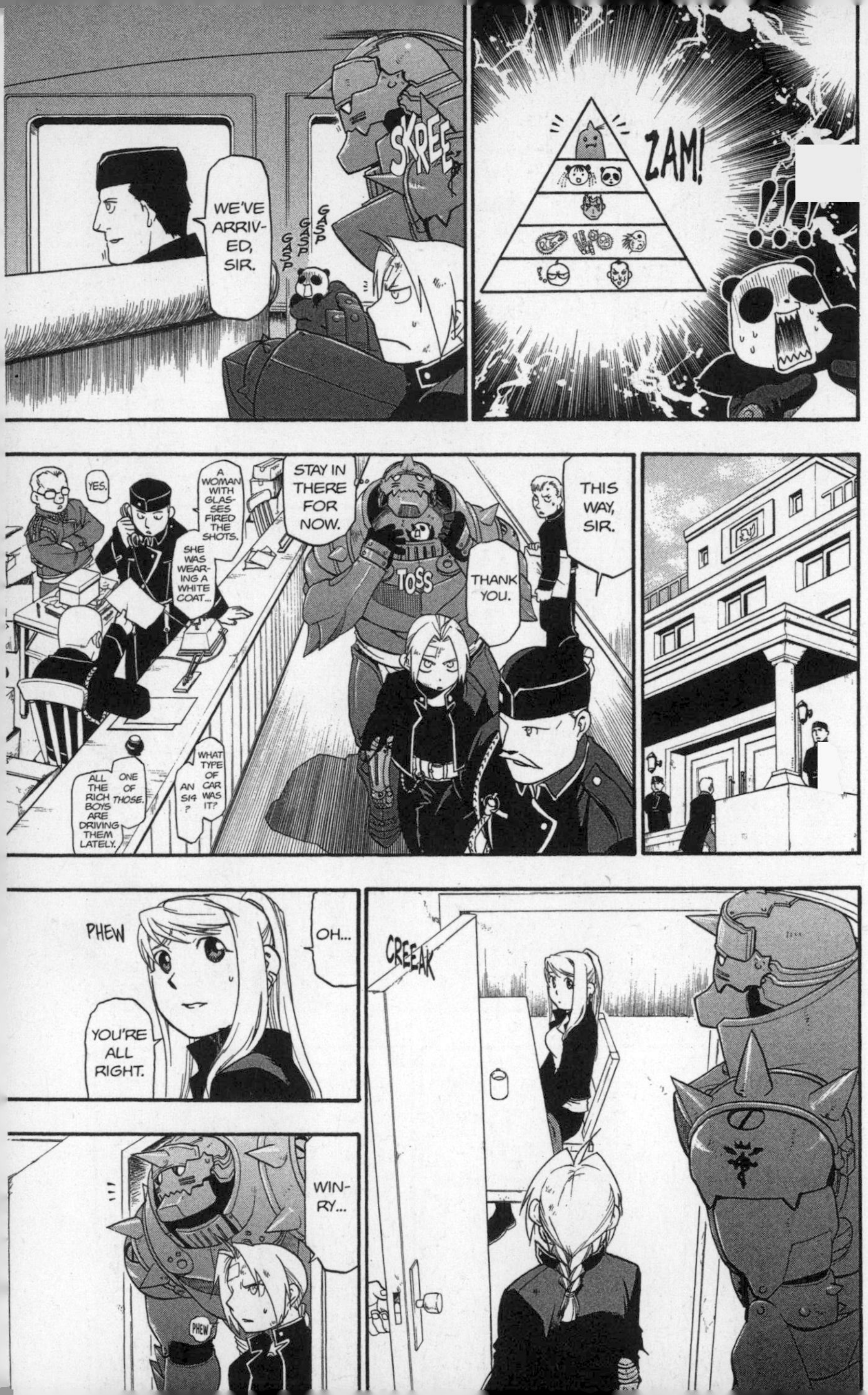
ZAM!
!!!
SKREE
WE'VE ARRIVED, SIR.
GASP GASP GASP
THIS WAY, SIR.
THANK YOU.
STAY IN THERE FOR NOW.
TOSS
A WOMAN WITH GLASSES FIRED THE SHOTS.
YES.
SHE WAS WEARING A WHITE COAT...
WHAT TYPE OF CAR WAS IT?
AN S14?
ONE OF THOSE.
ALL THE RICH BOYS ARE DRIVING THEM LATELY.
CREEAK
OH...
PHEW
YOU'RE ALL RIGHT.
WIN-RY...
PHEW

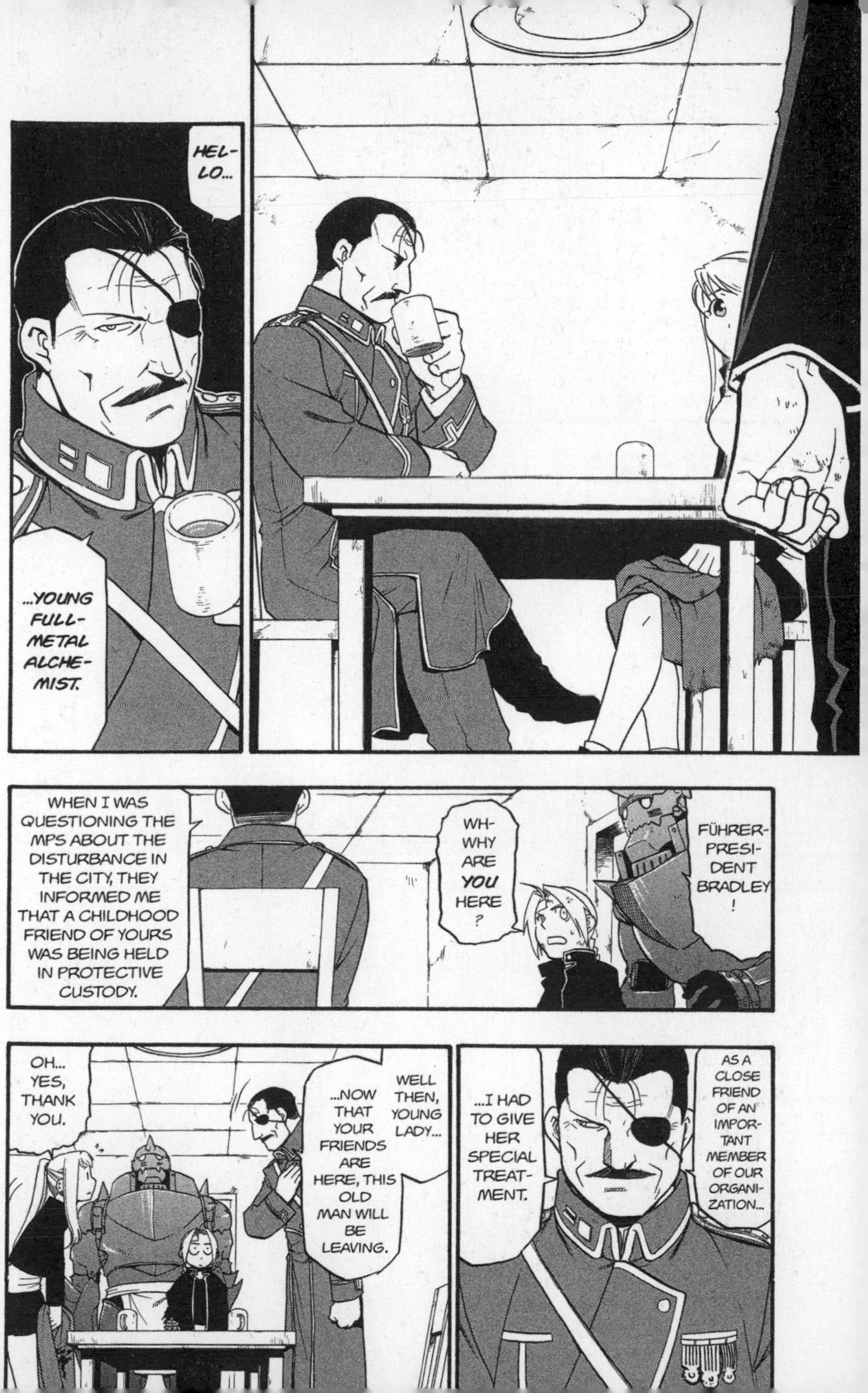
HELLO...
...YOUNG FULLMETAL ALCHEMIST.
FÜHRER-PRESIDENT BRADLEY!
WH-WHY ARE YOU HERE?
WHEN I WAS QUESTIONING THE MPS ABOUT THE DISTURBANCE IN THE CITY, THEY INFORMED ME THAT A CHILDHOOD FRIEND OF YOURS WAS BEING HELD IN PROTECTIVE CUSTODY.
AS A CLOSE FRIEND OF AN IMPORTANT MEMBER OF OUR ORGANIZATION...
...I HAD TO GIVE HER SPECIAL TREATMENT.
WELL THEN, YOUNG LADY...
...NOW THAT YOUR FRIENDS ARE HERE, THIS OLD MAN WILL BE LEAVING.
OH... YES, THANK YOU.

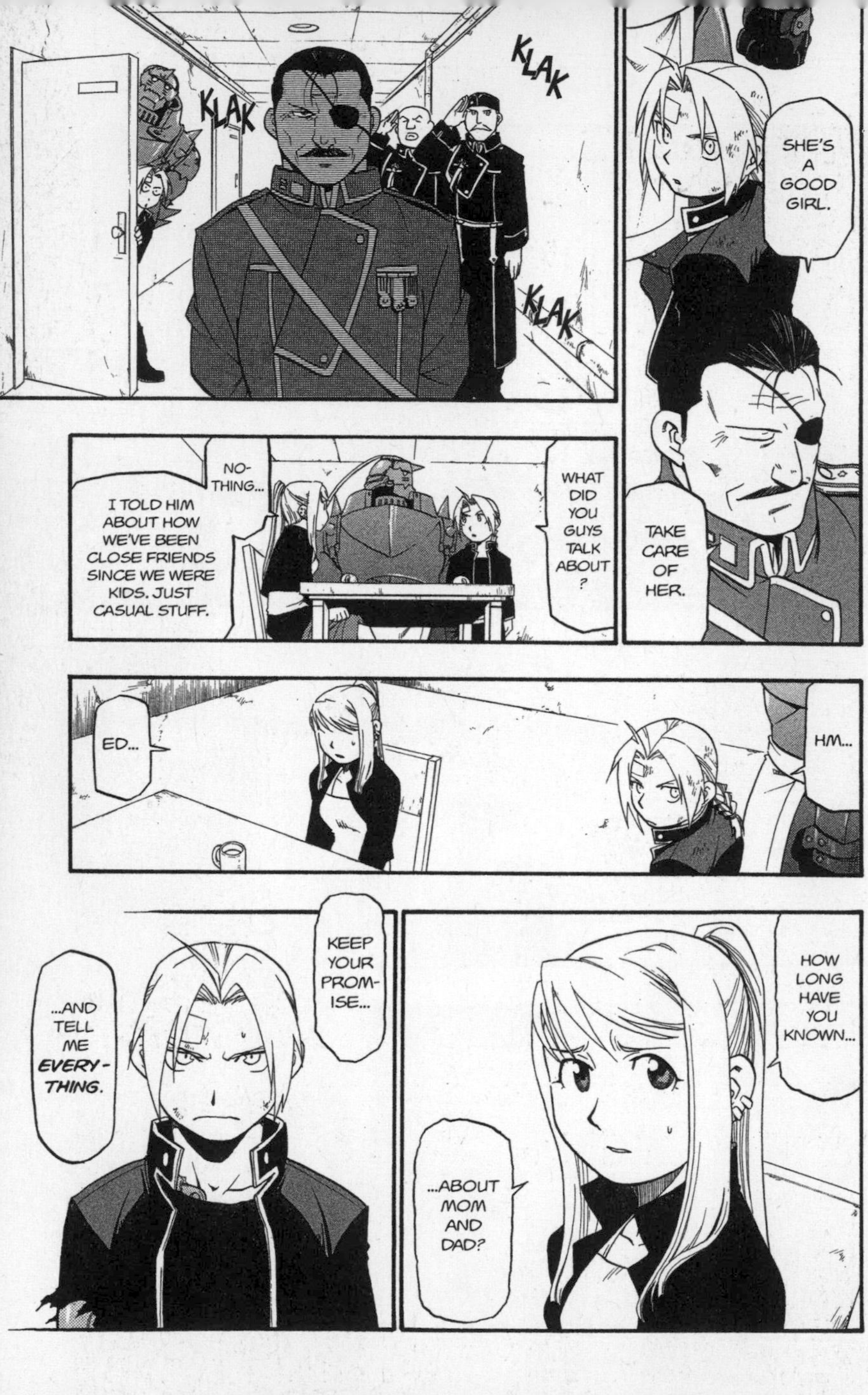
SHE'S A GOOD GIRL.
TAKE CARE OF HER.
KLAK
KLAK
KLAK
WHAT DID YOU GUYS TALK ABOUT?
NO-THING...
I TOLD HIM ABOUT HOW WE'VE BEEN CLOSE FRIENDS SINCE WE WERE KIDS. JUST CASUAL STUFF.
HM...
ED...
HOW LONG HAVE YOU KNOWN...
...ABOUT MOM AND DAD?
KEEP YOUR PROM-ISE...
...AND TELL ME *EVERY-THING*.

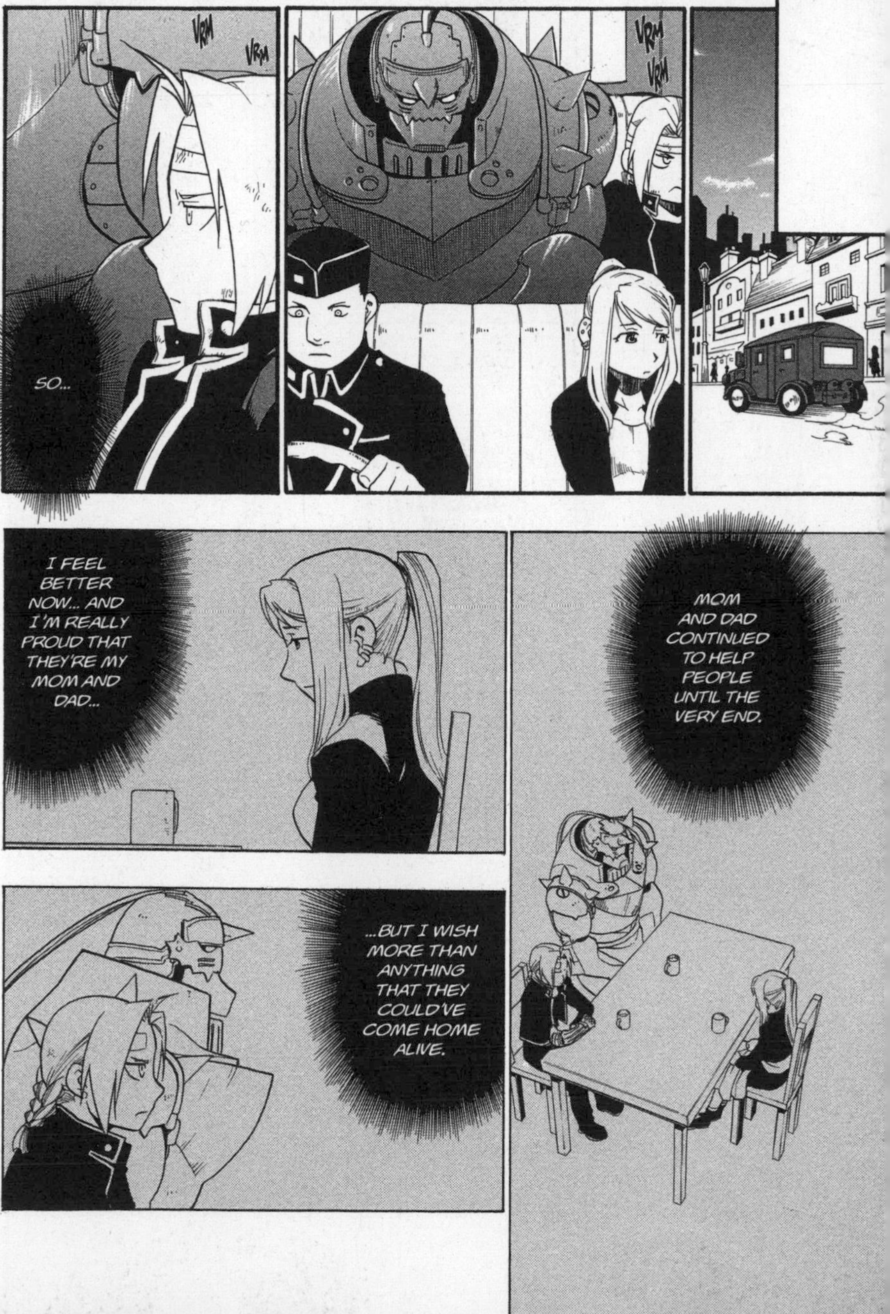
VRM
VRM
VRM
VRM
SO...
MOM AND DAD CONTINUED TO HELP PEOPLE UNTIL THE VERY END.
I FEEL BETTER NOW... AND I'M REALLY PROUD THAT THEY'RE MY MOM AND DAD...
...BUT I WISH MORE THAN ANYTHING THAT THEY COULD'VE COME HOME ALIVE.

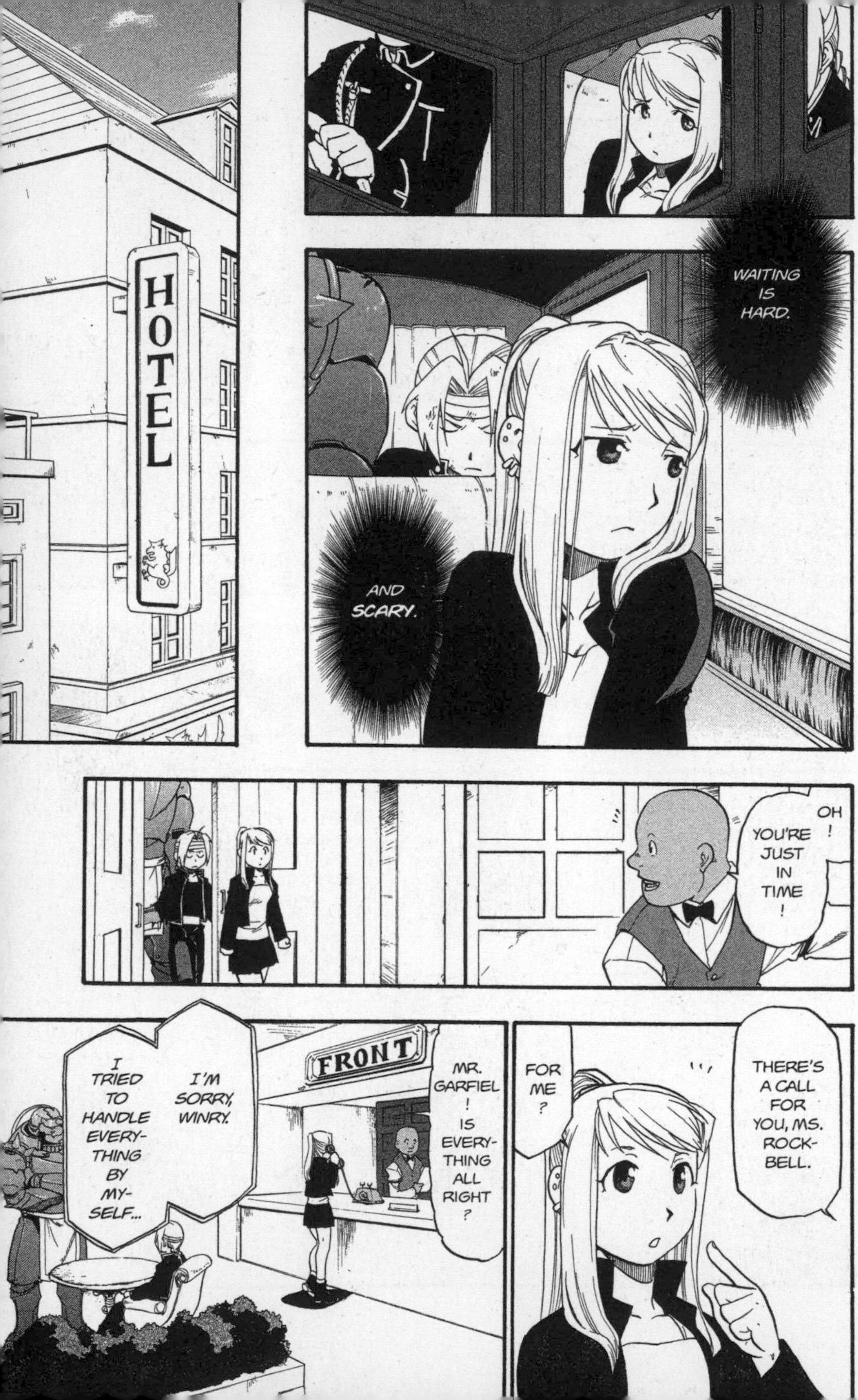
WAITING IS HARD.
AND SCARY.
HOTEL
OH! YOU'RE JUST IN TIME!
THERE'S A CALL FOR YOU, MS. ROCKBELL.
FOR ME?
MR. GARFIEL! IS EVERYTHING ALL RIGHT?
FRONT
I'M SORRY, WINRY.
I TRIED TO HANDLE EVERYTHING BY MYSELF...

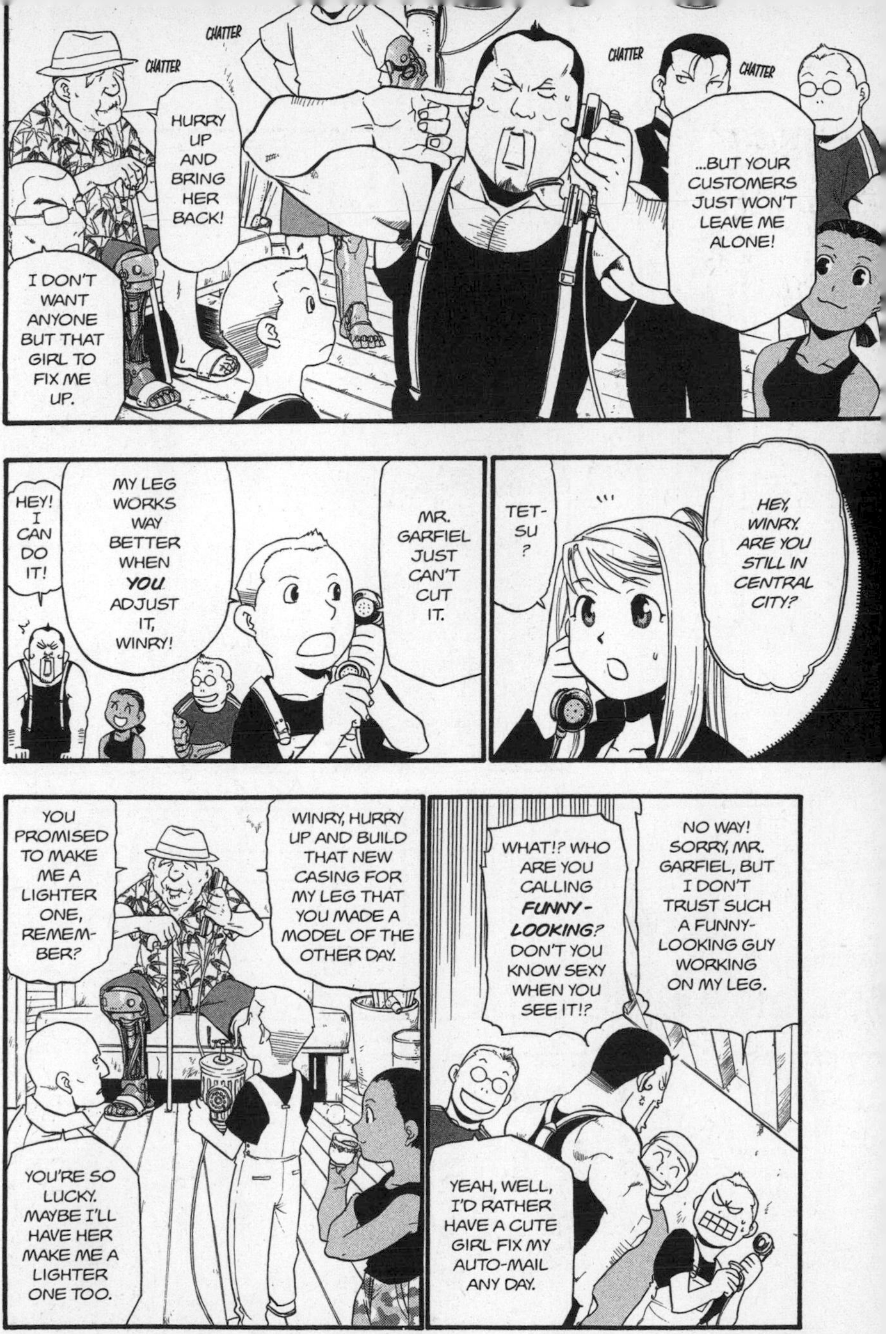
CHATTER
CHATTER
...BUT YOUR CUSTOMERS JUST WON'T LEAVE ME ALONE!
CHATTER
CHATTER
HURRY UP AND BRING HER BACK!
I DON'T WANT ANYONE BUT THAT GIRL TO FIX ME UP.
HEY, WINRY. ARE YOU STILL IN CENTRAL CITY?
TET- SU?
MR. GARFIEL JUST CAN'T CUT IT.
MY LEG WORKS WAY BETTER WHEN *YOU* ADJUST IT, WINRY!
HEY! I CAN DO IT!
NO WAY! SORRY, MR. GARFIEL, BUT I DON'T TRUST SUCH A FUNNY-LOOKING GUY WORKING ON MY LEG.
WHAT!? WHO ARE YOU CALLING ***FUNNY-LOOKING***? DON'T YOU KNOW SEXY WHEN YOU SEE IT!?
YEAH, WELL, I'D RATHER HAVE A CUTE GIRL FIX MY AUTO-MAIL ANY DAY.
WINRY, HURRY UP AND BUILD THAT NEW CASING FOR MY LEG THAT YOU MADE A MODEL OF THE OTHER DAY.
YOU PROMISED TO MAKE ME A LIGHTER ONE, REMEMBER?
YOU'RE SO LUCKY. MAYBE I'LL HAVE HER MAKE ME A LIGHTER ONE TOO.

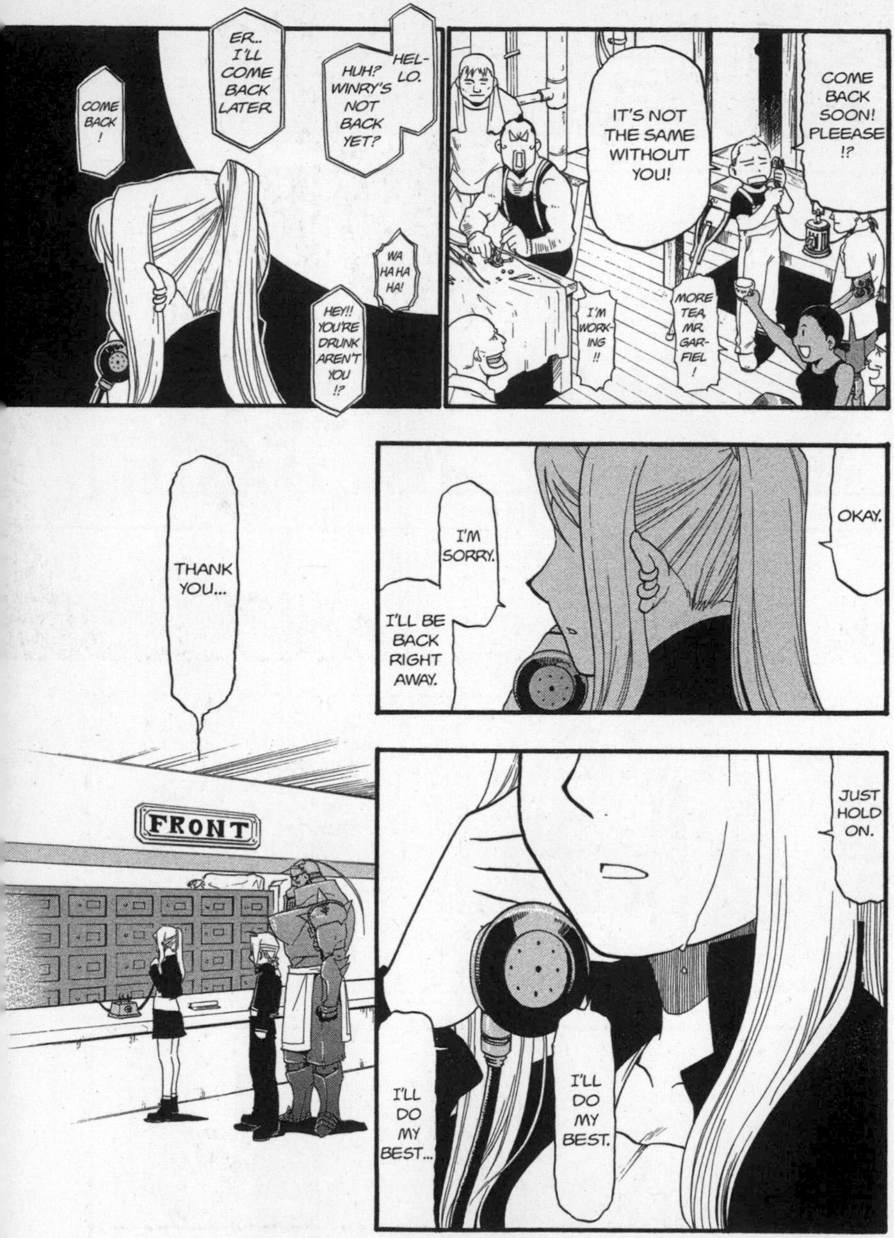
COME BACK SOON! PLEEASE!?
IT'S NOT THE SAME WITHOUT YOU!
MORE TEA, MR. GAR-FIEL!
I'M WORK-ING!!
HEL-LO.
HUH? WINRY'S NOT BACK YET?
ER.. I'LL COME BACK LATER
COME BACK!
WA HA HA HA!
HEY!! YOU'RE DRUNK AREN'T YOU!?
OKAY.
I'M SORRY.
I'LL BE BACK RIGHT AWAY.
JUST HOLD ON.
I'LL DO MY BEST.
I'LL DO MY BEST...
THANK YOU...
FRONT

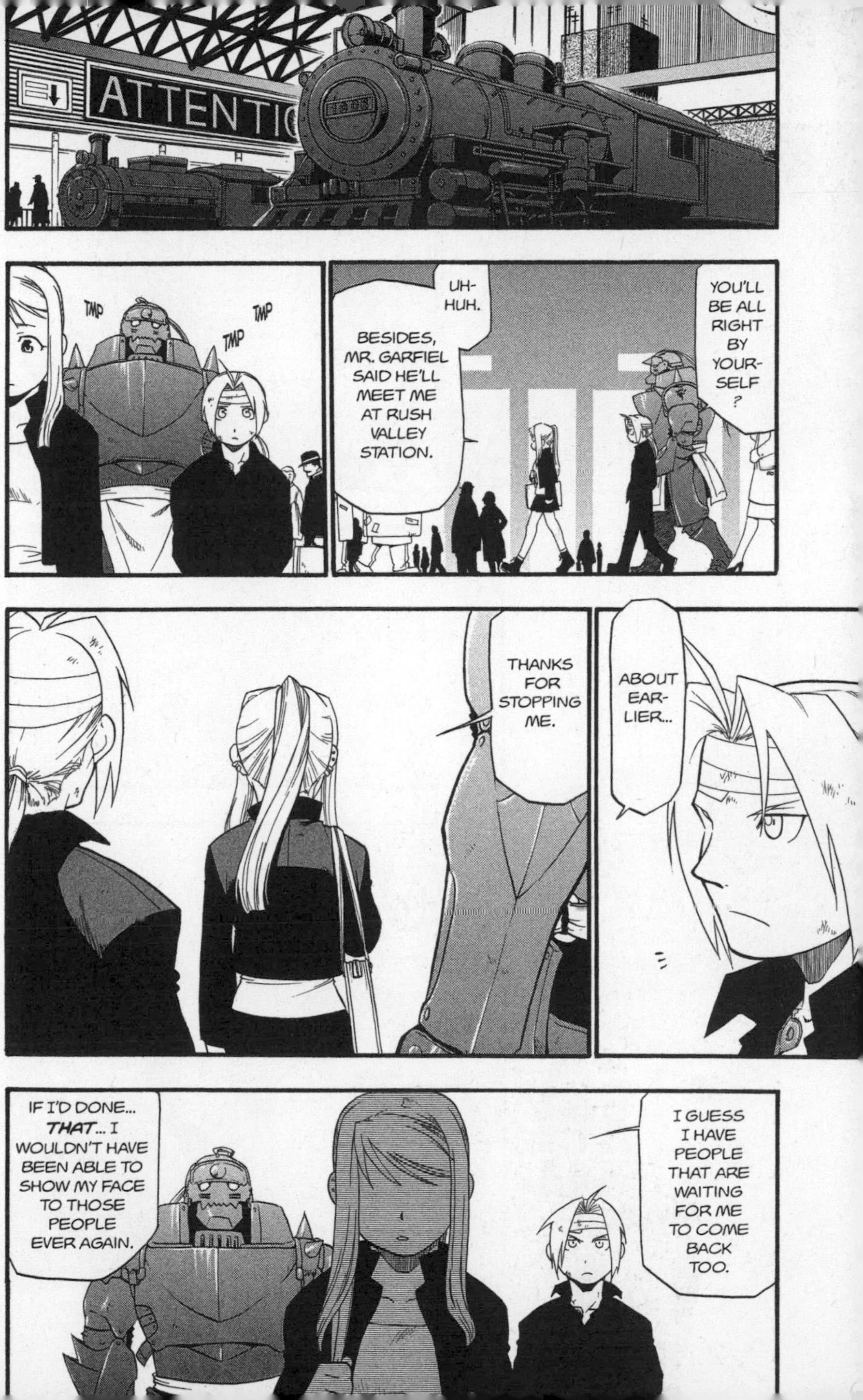
ATTENTIO
YOU'LL BE ALL RIGHT BY YOURSELF?
UH-HUH.
BESIDES, MR. GARFIEL SAID HE'LL MEET ME AT RUSH VALLEY STATION.
TMP
TMP
TMP
ABOUT EARLIER...
THANKS FOR STOPPING ME.
I GUESS I HAVE PEOPLE THAT ARE WAITING FOR ME TO COME BACK TOO.
IF I'D DONE... *THAT*... I WOULDN'T HAVE BEEN ABLE TO SHOW MY FACE TO THOSE PEOPLE EVER AGAIN.

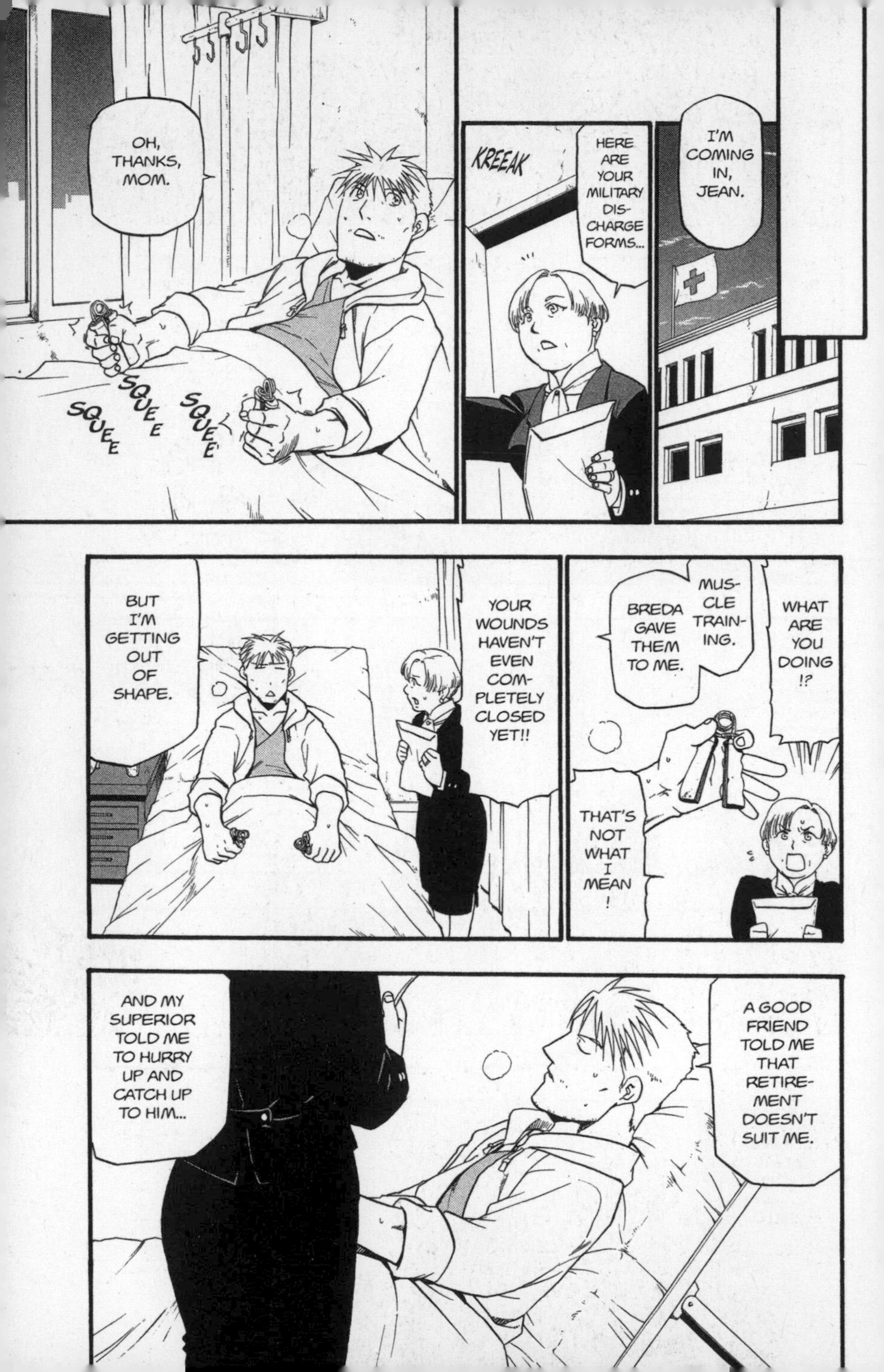
I'M COMING IN, JEAN.
KREEAK
HERE ARE YOUR MILITARY DISCHARGE FORMS...
OH, THANKS, MOM.
SQUEE
SQUEE
WHAT ARE YOU DOING!?
MUSCLE TRAINING.
BREDA GAVE THEM TO ME.
THAT'S NOT WHAT I MEAN!
YOUR WOUNDS HAVEN'T EVEN COMPLETELY CLOSED YET!!
BUT I'M GETTING OUT OF SHAPE.
A GOOD FRIEND TOLD ME THAT RETIREMENT DOESN'T SUIT ME.
AND MY SUPERIOR TOLD ME TO HURRY UP AND CATCH UP TO HIM...

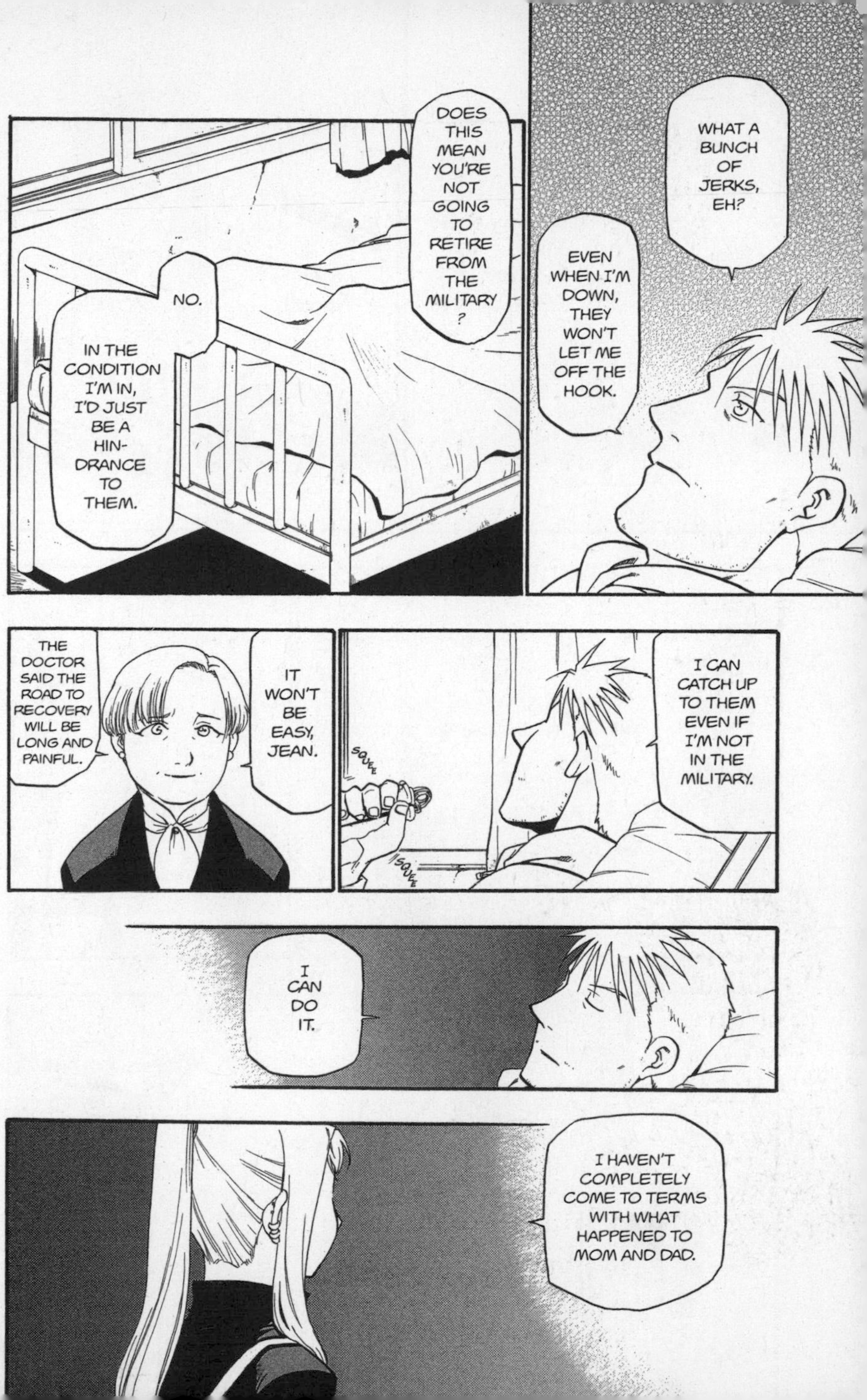
WHAT A BUNCH OF JERKS, EH?
EVEN WHEN I'M DOWN, THEY WON'T LET ME OFF THE HOOK.
DOES THIS MEAN YOU'RE NOT GOING TO RETIRE FROM THE MILITARY?
NO.
IN THE CONDITION I'M IN, I'D JUST BE A HINDRANCE TO THEM.
I CAN CATCH UP TO THEM EVEN IF I'M NOT IN THE MILITARY.
SQUEE
SQUEE
IT WON'T BE EASY, JEAN.
THE DOCTOR SAID THE ROAD TO RECOVERY WILL BE LONG AND PAINFUL.
I CAN DO IT.
I HAVEN'T COMPLETELY COME TO TERMS WITH WHAT HAPPENED TO MOM AND DAD.

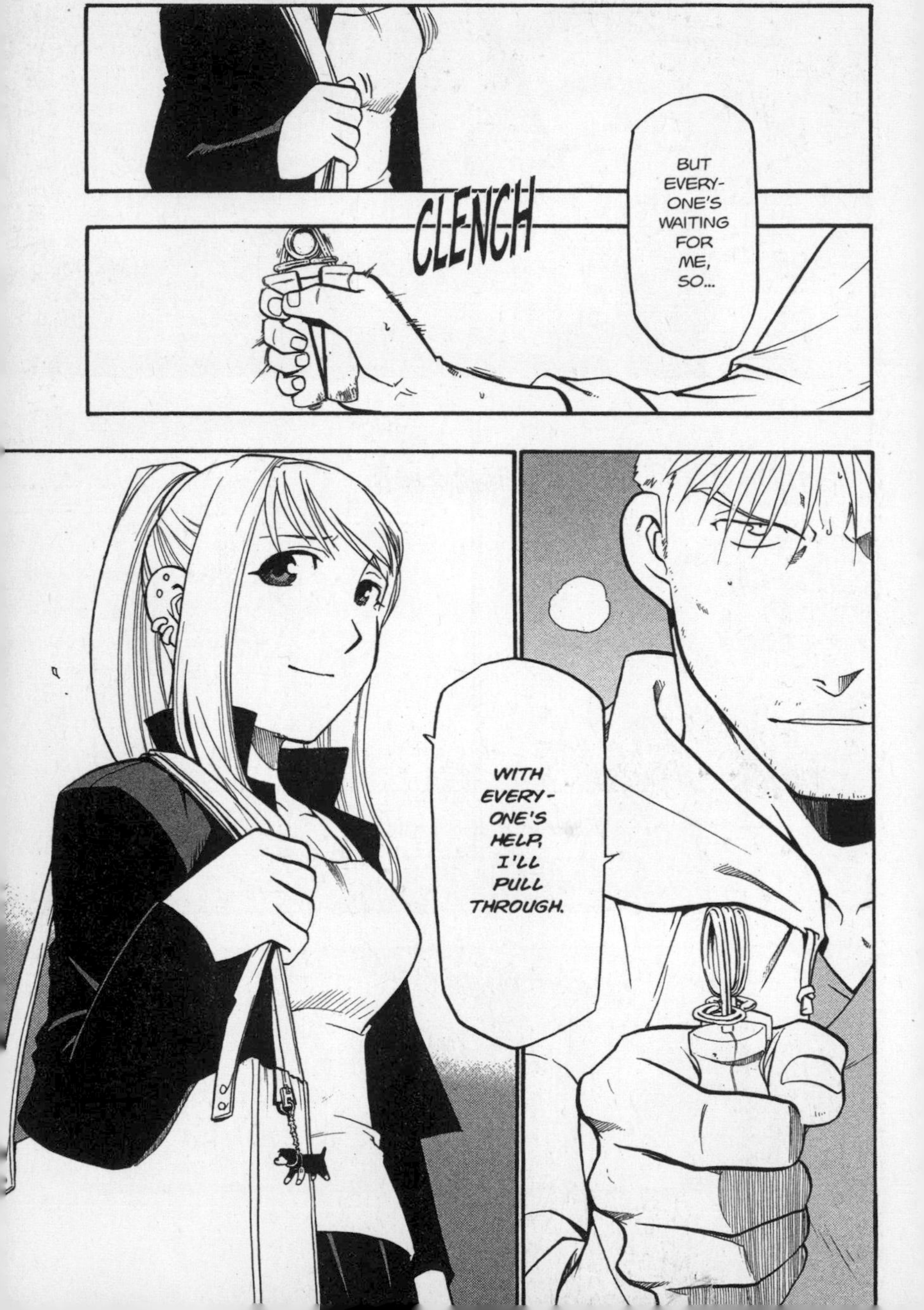
BUT EVERY-ONE'S WAITING FOR ME, SO...
CLENCH
WITH EVERY-ONE'S HELP, I'LL PULL THROUGH.

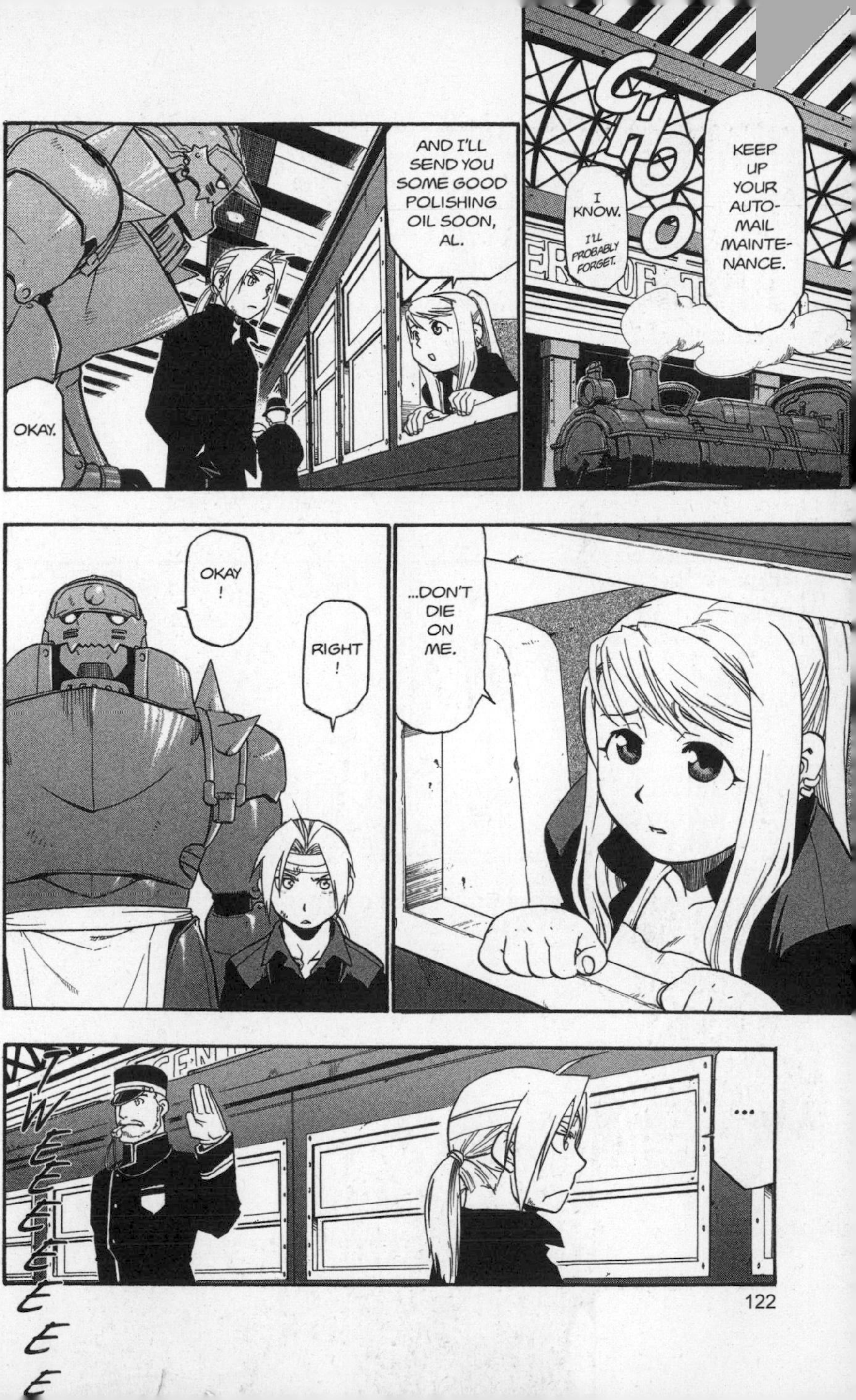
CHOO
KEEP UP YOUR AUTO-MAIL MAINTE-NANCE.
I KNOW.
I'LL PROBABLY FORGET.
AND I'LL SEND YOU SOME GOOD POLISHING OIL SOON, AL.
OKAY.
...DON'T DIE ON ME.
OKAY!
RIGHT!
TWEEEEEEEEE
...

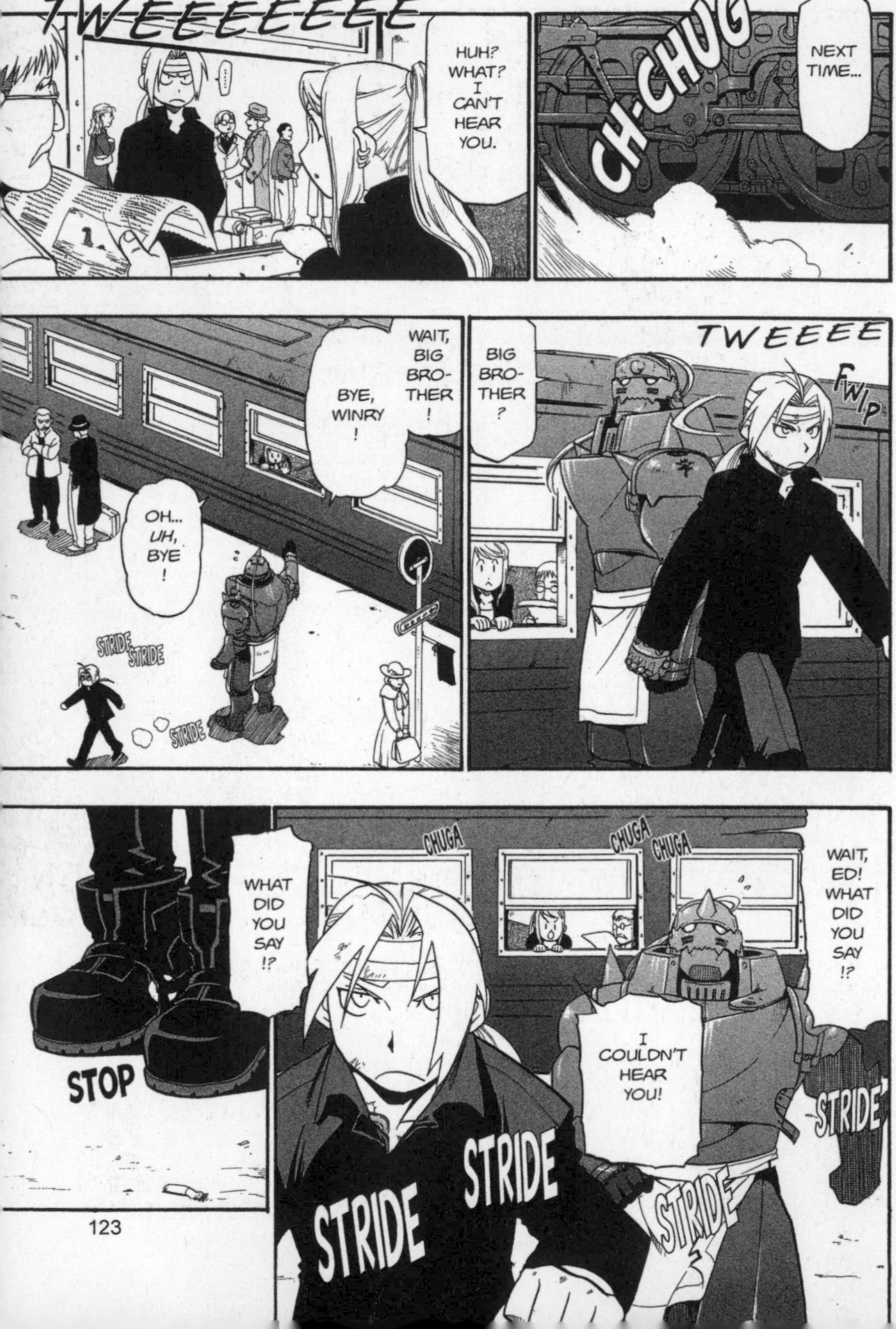
CH-CHUG
NEXT TIME...
TWEEEEEEEE
HUH? WHAT? I CAN'T HEAR YOU.
TWEEEE
FWIP
BIG BROTHER?
WAIT, BIG BROTHER!
BYE, WINRY!
OH... UH, BYE!
STRIDE STRIDE
STRIDE
WAIT, ED! WHAT DID YOU SAY!?
CHUGA CHUGA
CHUGA
WHAT DID YOU SAY!?
I COULDN'T HEAR YOU!
STRIDE
STRIDE
STRIDE
STRIDE
STOP

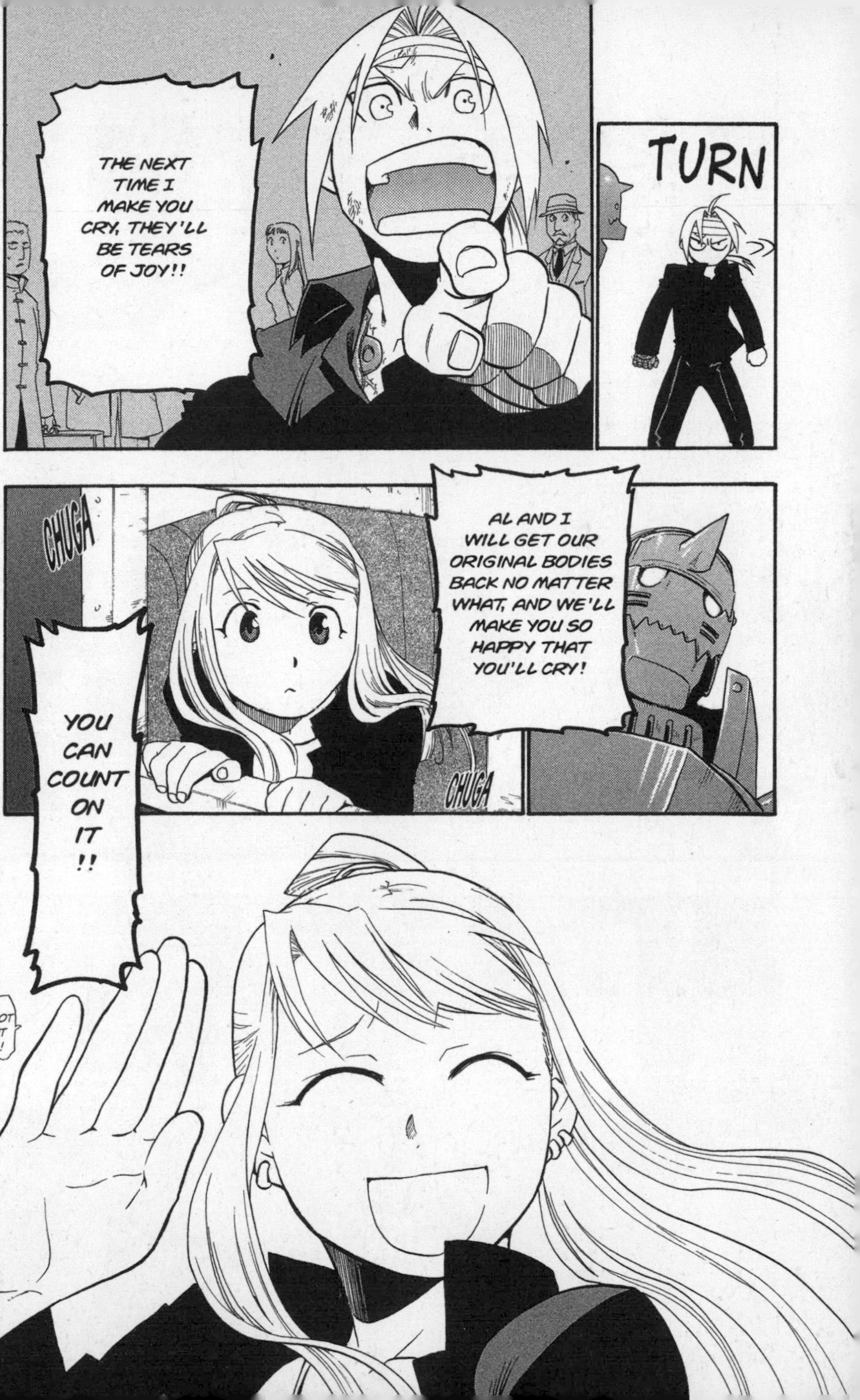
TURN
THE NEXT TIME I MAKE YOU CRY, THEY'LL BE TEARS OF JOY!!
AL AND I WILL GET OUR ORIGINAL BODIES BACK NO MATTER WHAT, AND WE'LL MAKE YOU SO HAPPY THAT YOU'LL CRY!
CHUGA
CHUGA
YOU CAN COUNT ON IT!!
GOT IT!

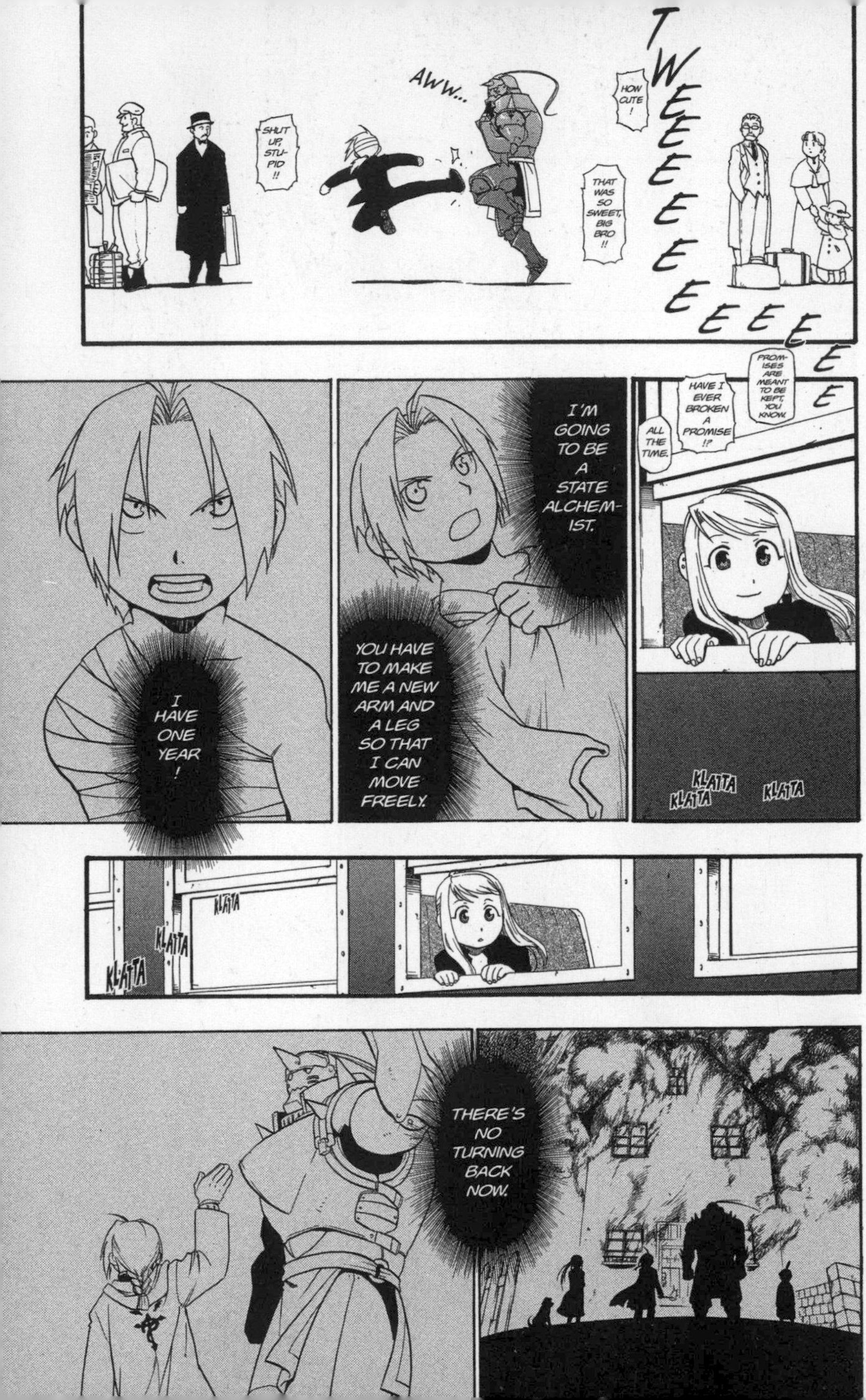
TWEEEEEEEEEEEE
HOW CUTE!
THAT WAS SO SWEET, BIG BRO!!
AWW...
SHUT UP, STUPID!!
PROMISES ARE MEANT TO BE KEPT, YOU KNOW.
HAVE I EVER BROKEN A PROMISE!?
ALL THE TIME.
KLATTA KLATTA KLATTA
I'M GOING TO BE A STATE ALCHEMIST.
YOU HAVE TO MAKE ME A NEW ARM AND A LEG SO THAT I CAN MOVE FREELY.
I HAVE ONE YEAR!
KLATTA KLATTA KLATTA
THERE'S NO TURNING BACK NOW.

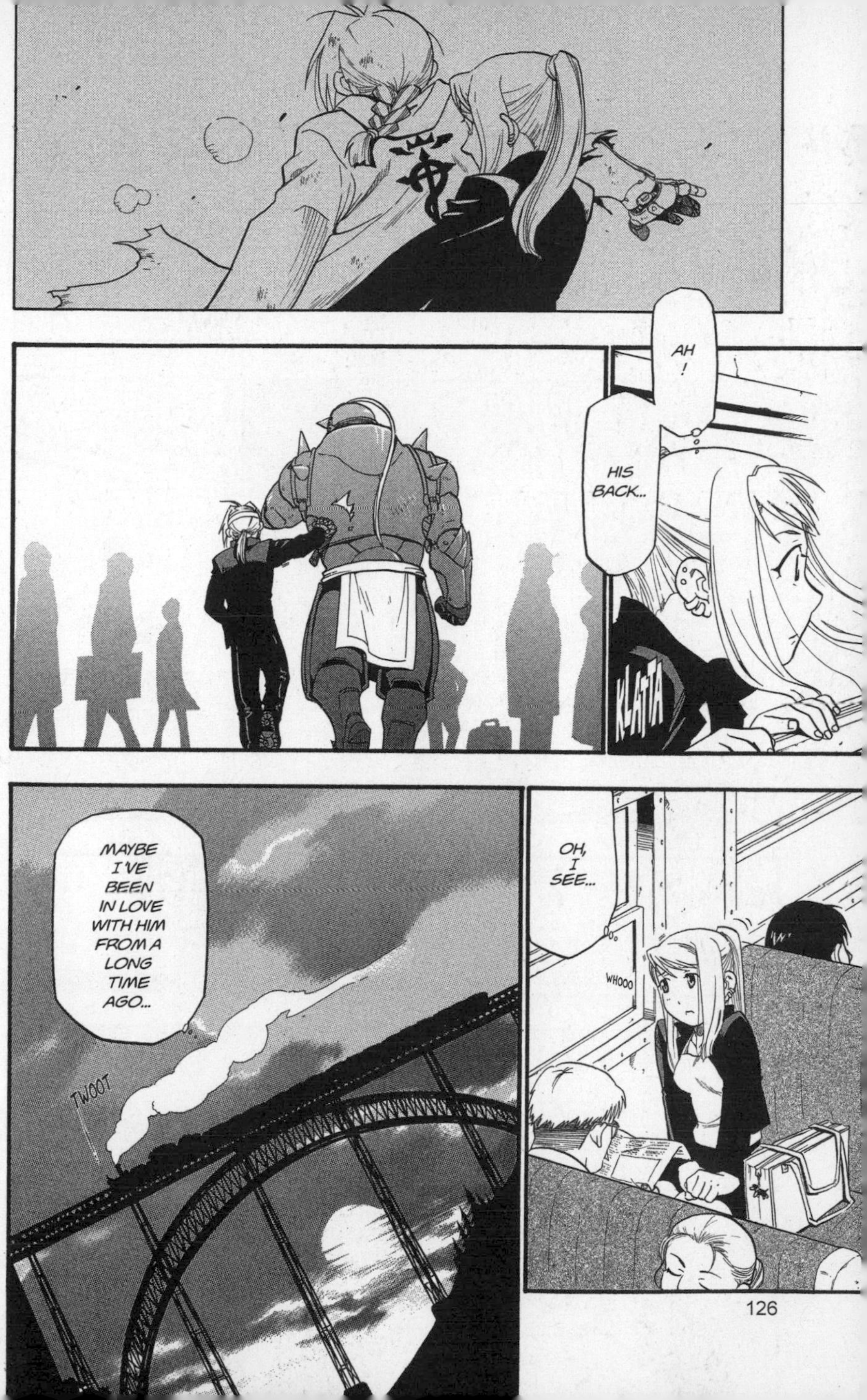
AH!
HIS BACK...
KLATTA
OH, I SEE...
WHOOO
MAYBE I'VE BEEN IN LOVE WITH HIM FROM A LONG TIME AGO...
TWOOT

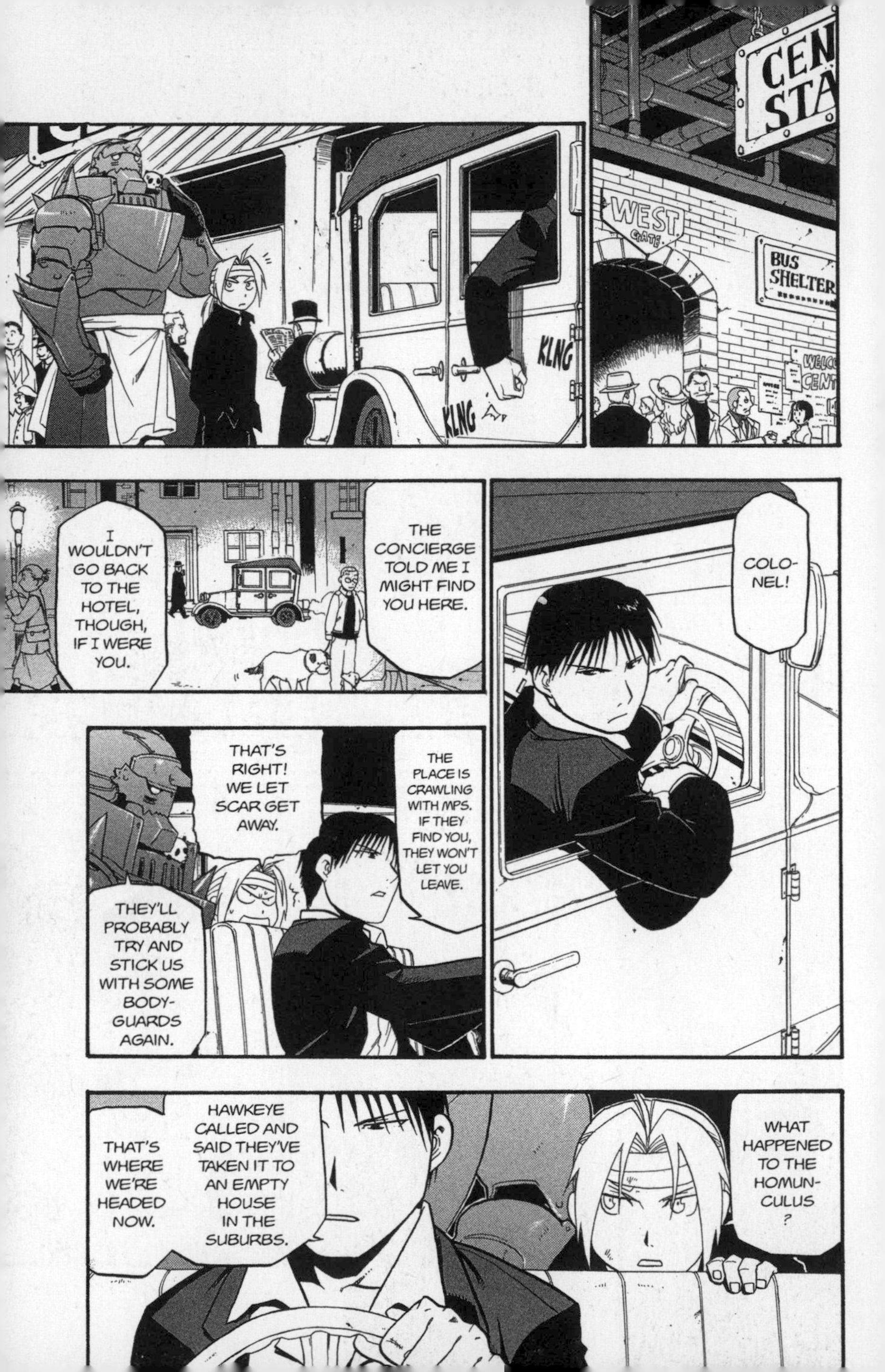
CEN STA
WEST GATE
BUS SHELTER
WELC CENT
KLNG
KLNG
COLONEL!
THE CONCIERGE TOLD ME I MIGHT FIND YOU HERE.
I WOULDN'T GO BACK TO THE HOTEL, THOUGH, IF I WERE YOU.
THE PLACE IS CRAWLING WITH MPS. IF THEY FIND YOU, THEY WON'T LET YOU LEAVE.
THAT'S RIGHT! WE LET SCAR GET AWAY.
THEY'LL PROBABLY TRY AND STICK US WITH SOME BODYGUARDS AGAIN.
WHAT HAPPENED TO THE HOMUNCULUS?
HAWKEYE CALLED AND SAID THEY'VE TAKEN IT TO AN EMPTY HOUSE IN THE SUBURBS.
THAT'S WHERE WE'RE HEADED NOW.

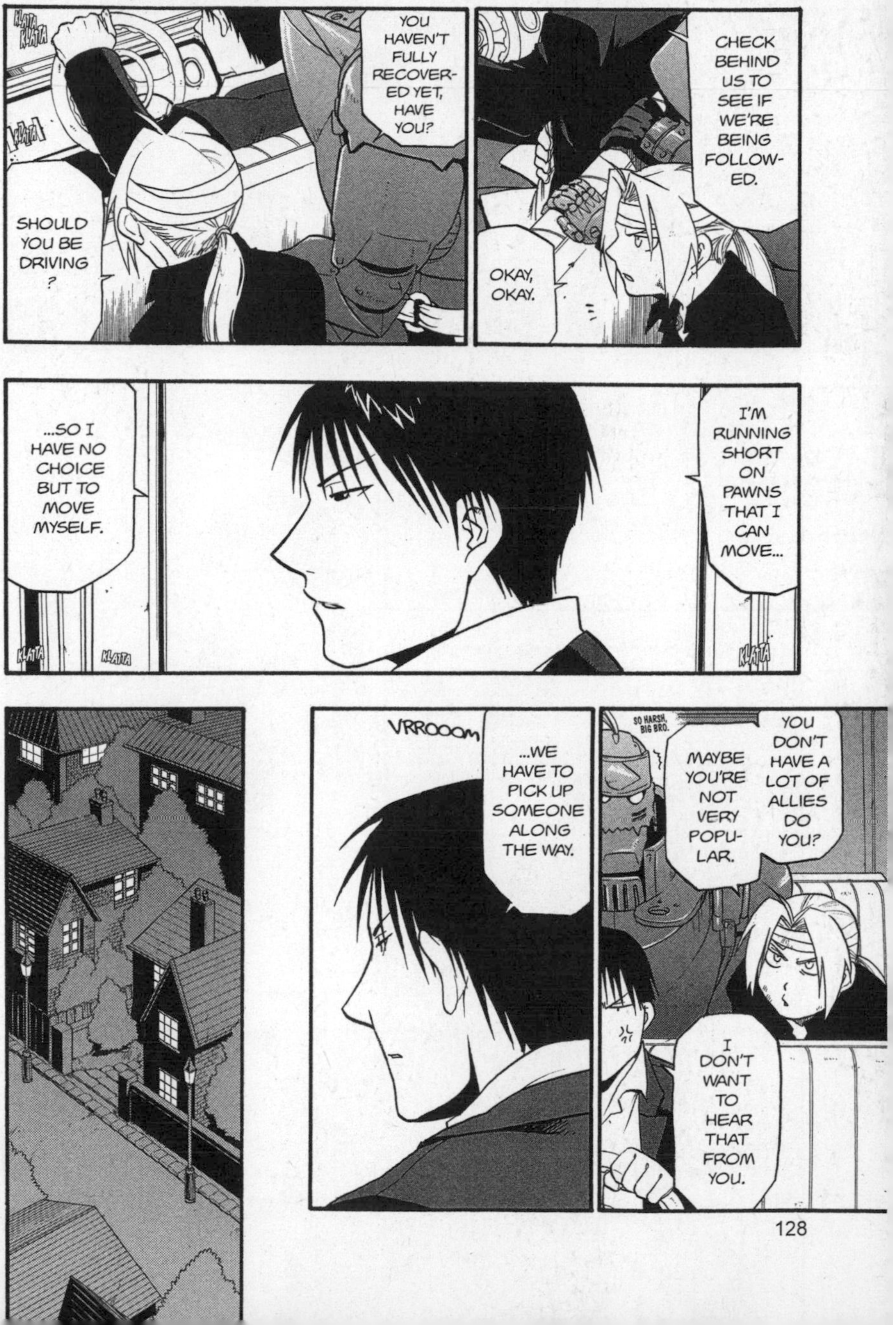
CHECK BEHIND US TO SEE IF WE'RE BEING FOLLOW-ED.
OKAY, OKAY.
YOU HAVEN'T FULLY RECOVER-ED YET, HAVE YOU?
KLATTA KLATTA
KLATTA
SHOULD YOU BE DRIVING?
KLATTA
I'M RUNNING SHORT ON PAWNS THAT I CAN MOVE...
...SO I HAVE NO CHOICE BUT TO MOVE MYSELF.
KLATTA
KLATTA
YOU DON'T HAVE A LOT OF ALLIES DO YOU?
SO HARSH, BIG BRO.
MAYBE YOU'RE NOT VERY POPU-LAR.
I DON'T WANT TO HEAR THAT FROM YOU.
VRROOOM
...WE HAVE TO PICK UP SOMEONE ALONG THE WAY.

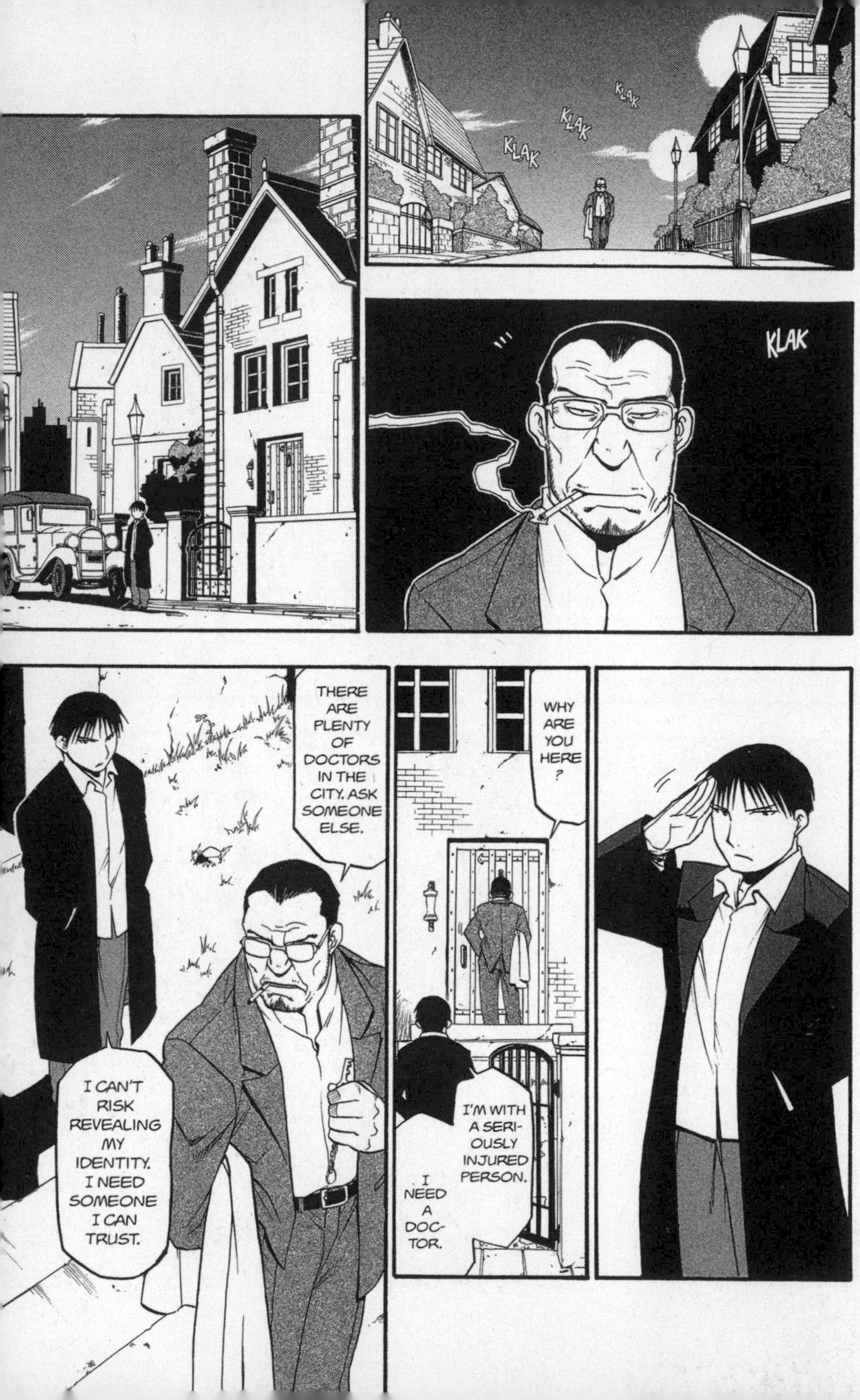
KLAK KLAK KLAK
KLAK
WHY ARE YOU HERE?
I'M WITH A SERIOUSLY INJURED PERSON.
I NEED A DOCTOR.
THERE ARE PLENTY OF DOCTORS IN THE CITY. ASK SOMEONE ELSE.
I CAN'T RISK REVEALING MY IDENTITY. I NEED SOMEONE I CAN TRUST.

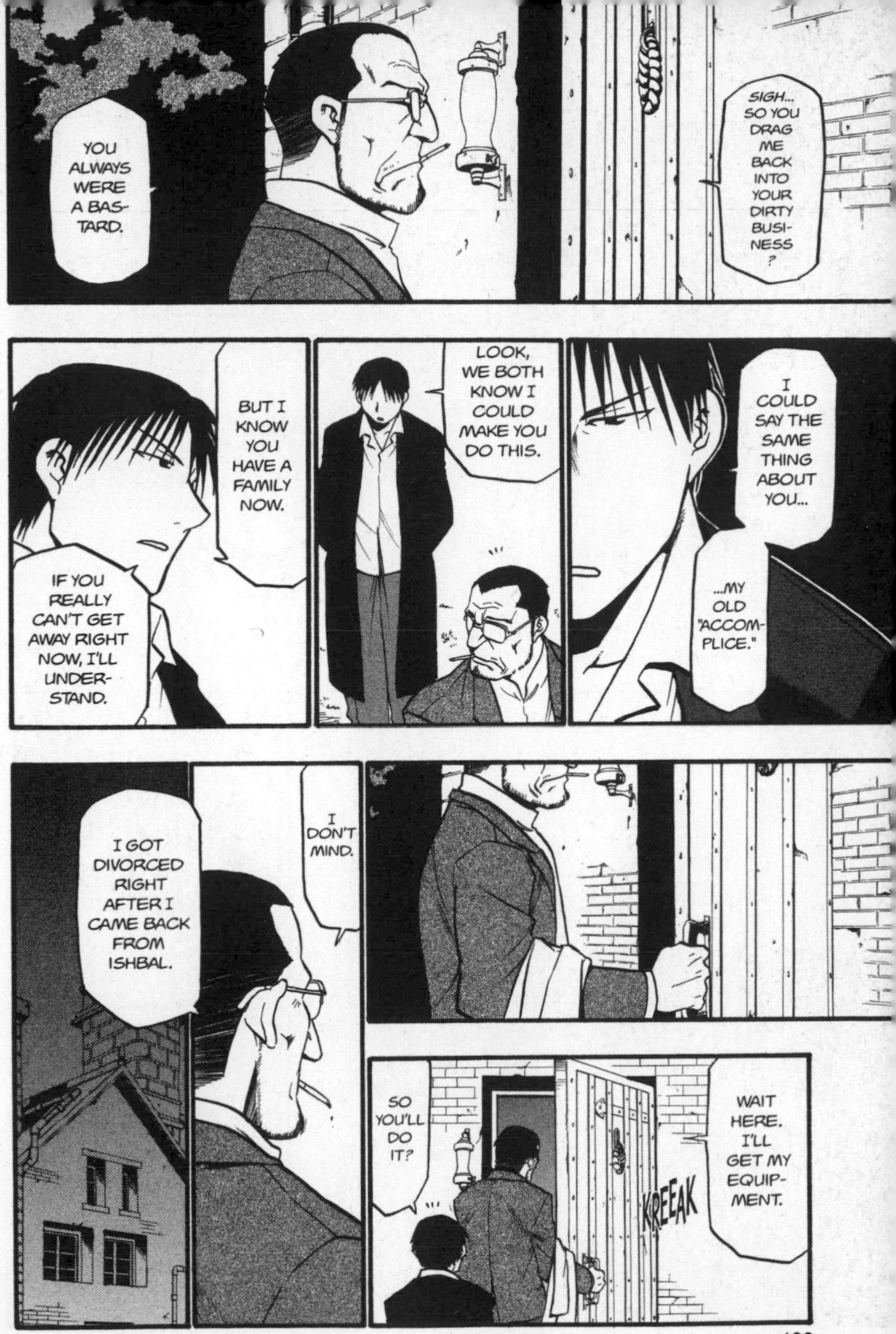
SIGH... SO YOU DRAG ME BACK INTO YOUR DIRTY BUSINESS?
YOU ALWAYS WERE A BASTARD.
I COULD SAY THE SAME THING ABOUT YOU...
...MY OLD "ACCOMPLICE."
LOOK, WE BOTH KNOW I COULD MAKE YOU DO THIS.
BUT I KNOW YOU HAVE A FAMILY NOW.
IF YOU REALLY CAN'T GET AWAY RIGHT NOW, I'LL UNDERSTAND.
WAIT HERE. I'LL GET MY EQUIPMENT.
KREEAK
SO YOU'LL DO IT?
I DON'T MIND.
I GOT DIVORCED RIGHT AFTER I CAME BACK FROM ISHBAL.

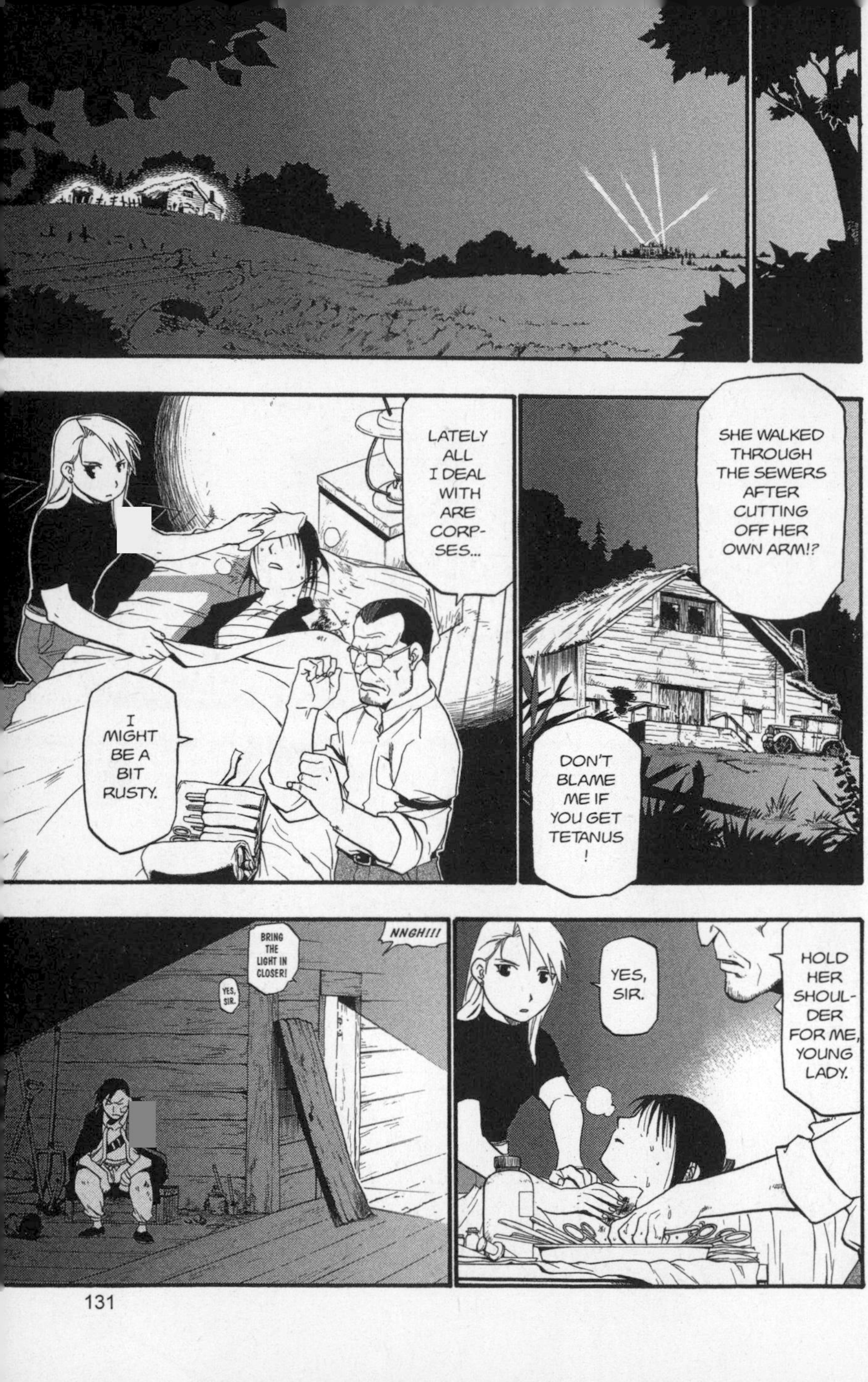
SHE WALKED THROUGH THE SEWERS AFTER CUTTING OFF HER OWN ARM!?
DON'T BLAME ME IF YOU GET TETANUS!
LATELY ALL I DEAL WITH ARE CORPSES...
I MIGHT BE A BIT RUSTY.
HOLD HER SHOULDER FOR ME, YOUNG LADY.
YES, SIR.
NNGH!!!
BRING THE LIGHT IN CLOSER!
YES, SIR.

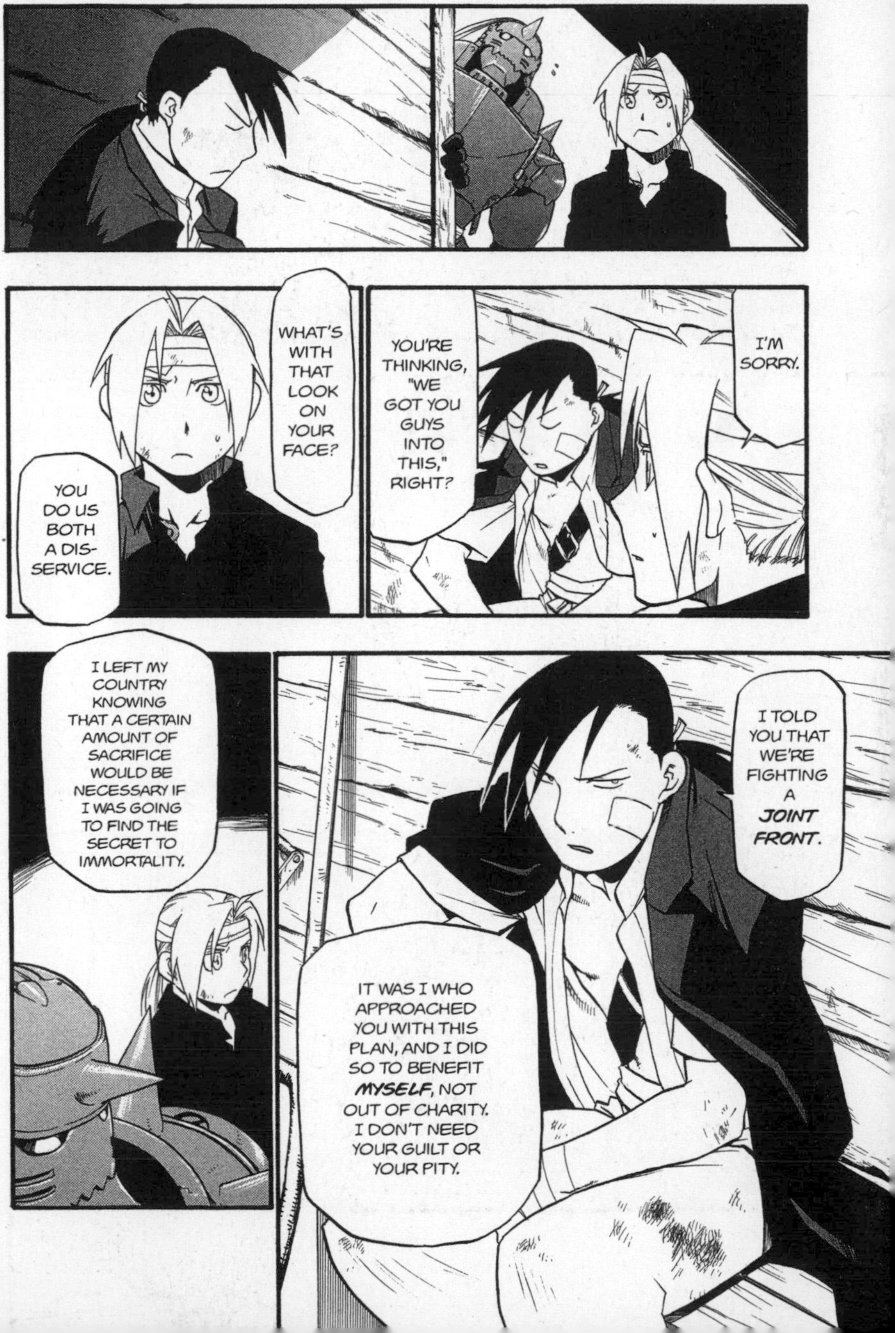
I'M SORRY.
YOU'RE THINKING, "WE GOT YOU GUYS INTO THIS," RIGHT?
WHAT'S WITH THAT LOOK ON YOUR FACE?
YOU DO US BOTH A DISSERVICE.
I TOLD YOU THAT WE'RE FIGHTING A ***JOINT FRONT***.
IT WAS I WHO APPROACHED YOU WITH THIS PLAN, AND I DID SO TO BENEFIT ***MYSELF***, NOT OUT OF CHARITY. I DON'T NEED YOUR GUILT OR YOUR PITY.
I LEFT MY COUNTRY KNOWING THAT A CERTAIN AMOUNT OF SACRIFICE WOULD BE NECESSARY IF I WAS GOING TO FIND THE SECRET TO IMMORTALITY.

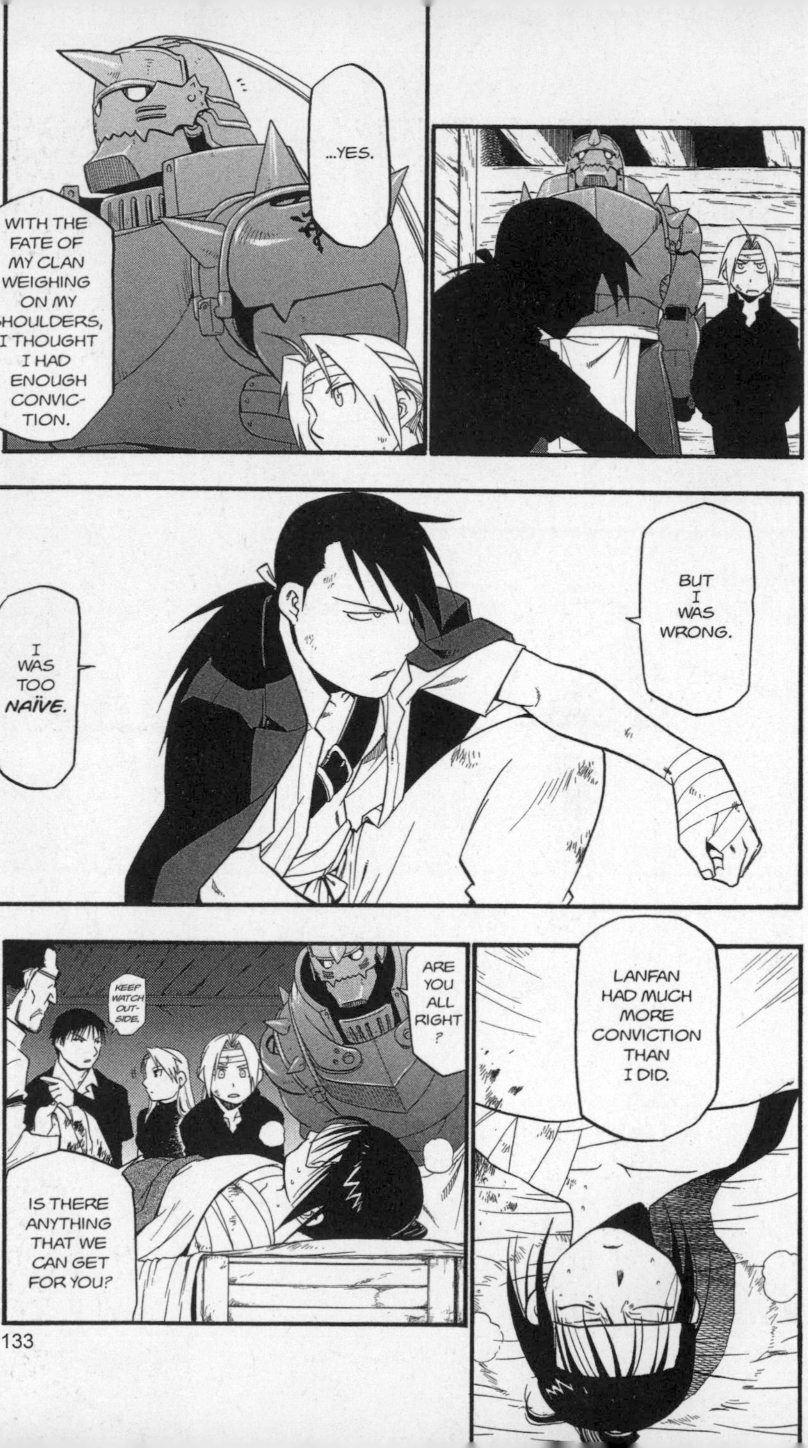
...YES.
WITH THE FATE OF MY CLAN WEIGHING ON MY SHOULDERS, I THOUGHT I HAD ENOUGH CONVICTION.
BUT I WAS WRONG.
I WAS TOO *NAÏVE*.
LANFAN HAD MUCH MORE CONVICTION THAN I DID.
ARE YOU ALL RIGHT?
KEEP WATCH OUTSIDE.
IS THERE ANYTHING THAT WE CAN GET FOR YOU?

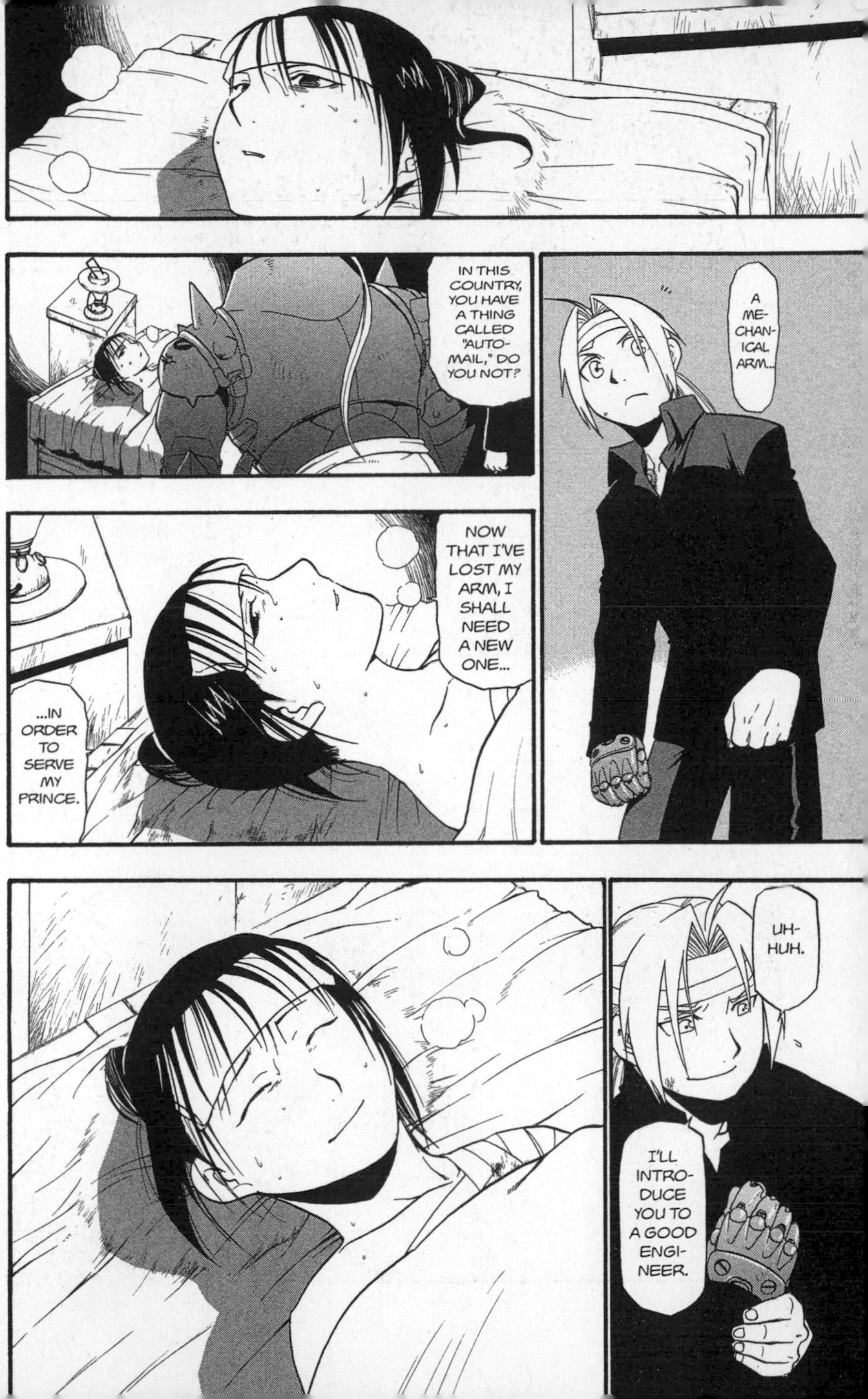
A MECHANICAL ARM...
IN THIS COUNTRY, YOU HAVE A THING CALLED "AUTO-MAIL," DO YOU NOT?
NOW THAT I'VE LOST MY ARM, I SHALL NEED A NEW ONE...
...IN ORDER TO SERVE MY PRINCE.
UH-HUH.
I'LL INTRODUCE YOU TO A GOOD ENGINEER.

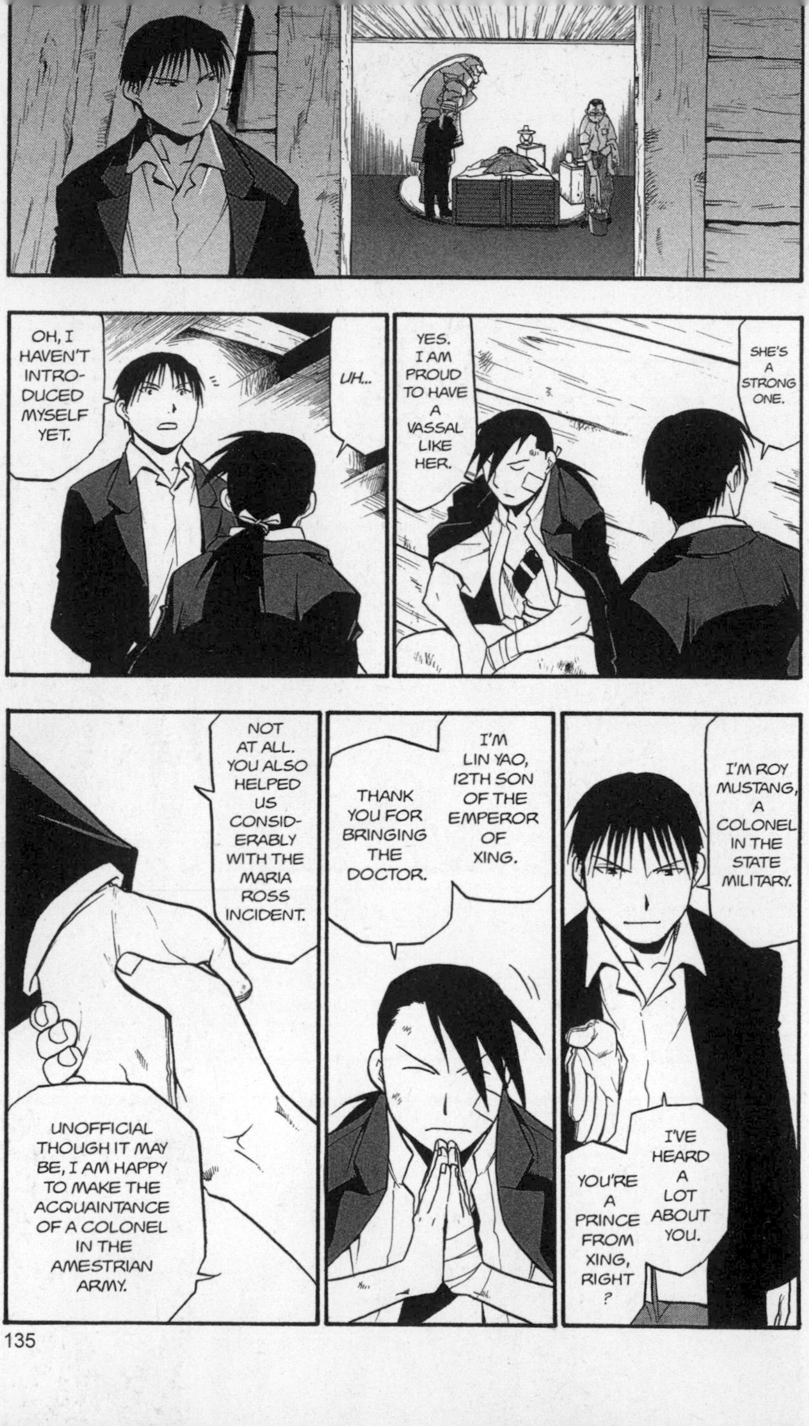
SHE'S A STRONG ONE.
YES. I AM PROUD TO HAVE A VASSAL LIKE HER.
UH...
OH, I HAVEN'T INTRODUCED MYSELF YET.
I'M ROY MUSTANG, A COLONEL IN THE STATE MILITARY.
I'VE HEARD A LOT ABOUT YOU.
YOU'RE A PRINCE FROM XING, RIGHT?
I'M LIN YAO, 12TH SON OF THE EMPEROR OF XING.
THANK YOU FOR BRINGING THE DOCTOR.
NOT AT ALL. YOU ALSO HELPED US CONSIDERABLY WITH THE MARIA ROSS INCIDENT.
UNOFFICIAL THOUGH IT MAY BE, I AM HAPPY TO MAKE THE ACQUAINTANCE OF A COLONEL IN THE AMESTRIAN ARMY.

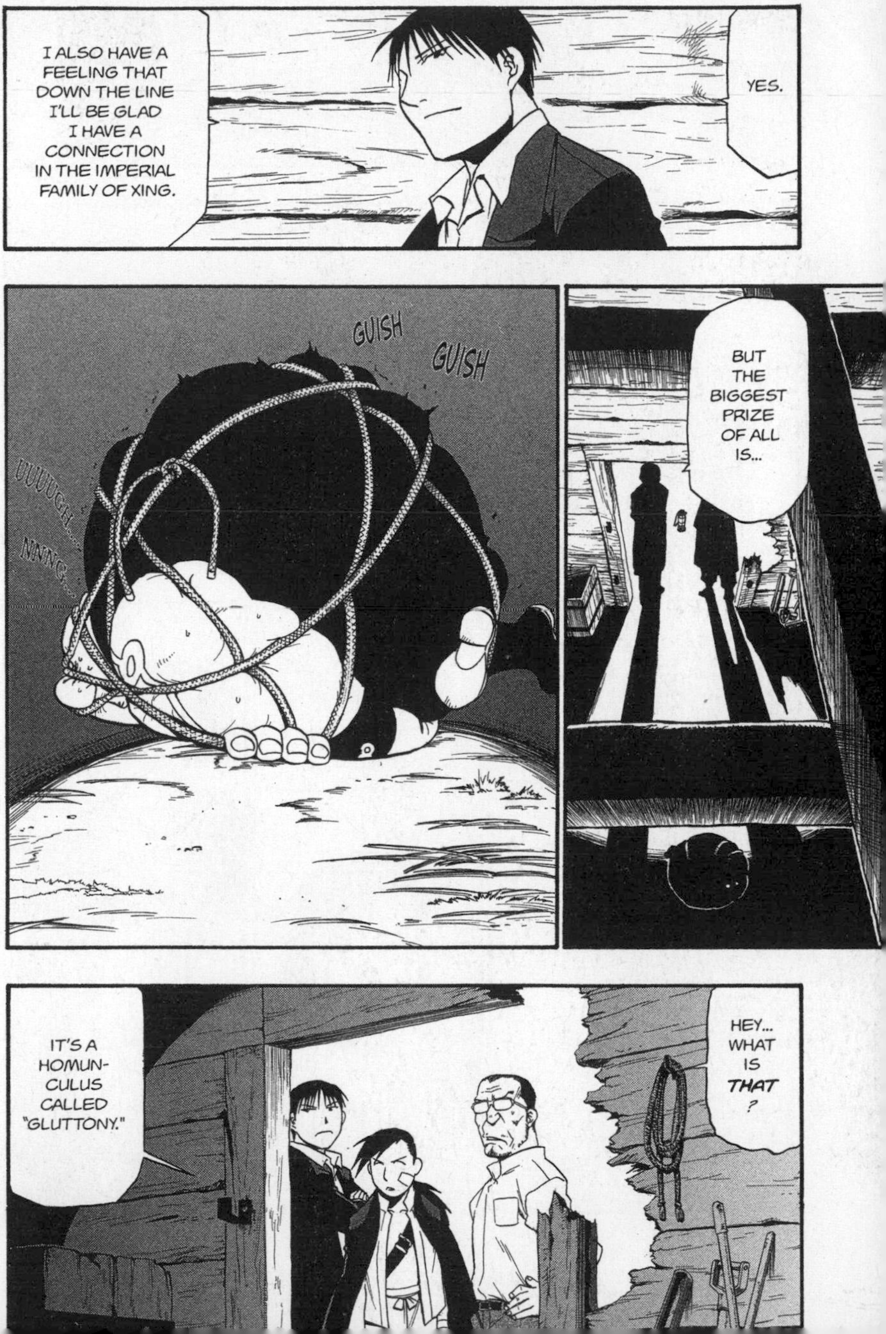
YES.
I ALSO HAVE A FEELING THAT DOWN THE LINE I'LL BE GLAD I HAVE A CONNECTION IN THE IMPERIAL FAMILY OF XING.
BUT THE BIGGEST PRIZE OF ALL IS...
GUISH
GUISH
UUUUGH...
NNNG...
HEY... WHAT IS THAT?
IT'S A HOMUNCULUS CALLED "GLUTTONY."

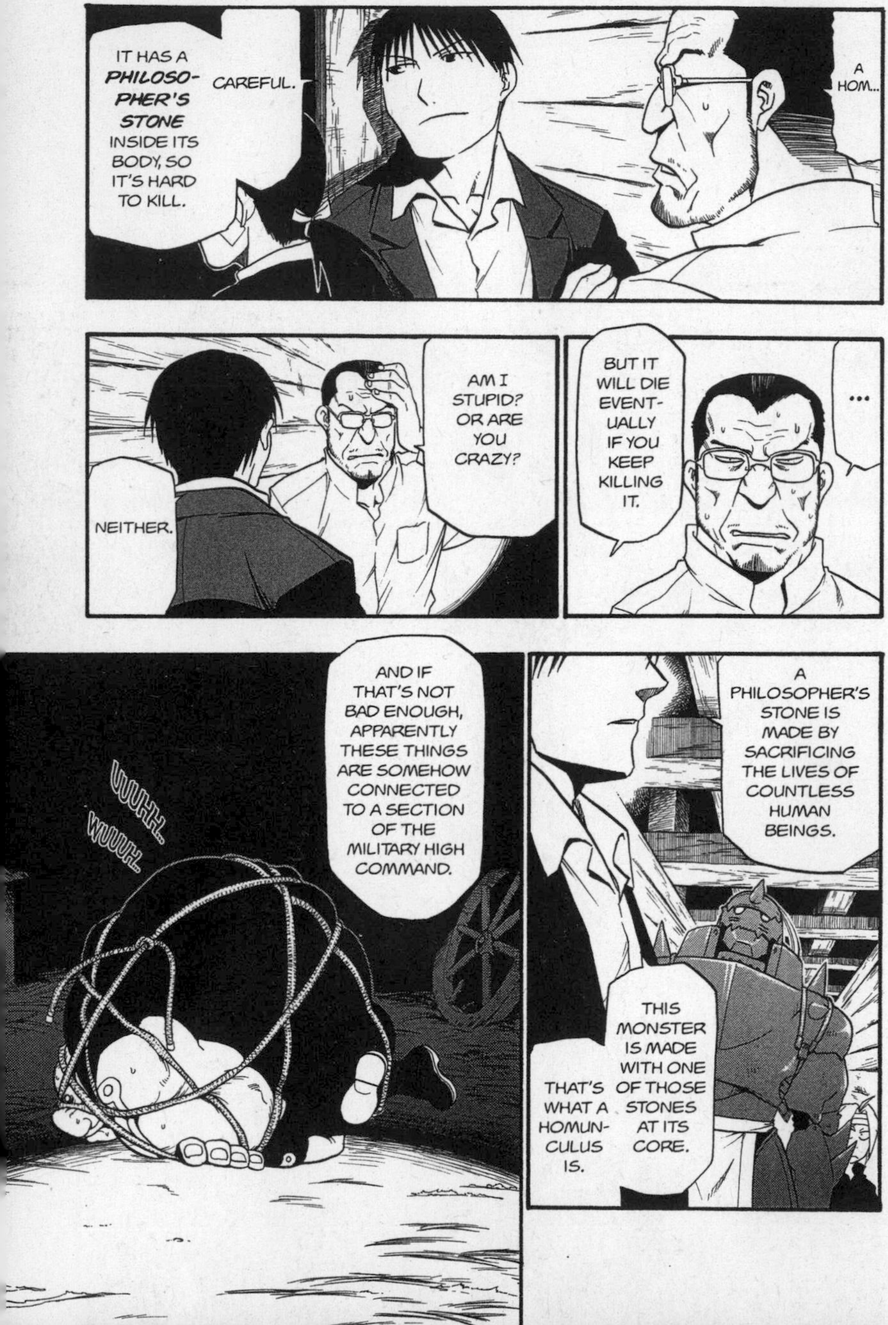
A HOM...
CAREFUL.
IT HAS A PHILOSOPHER'S STONE INSIDE ITS BODY, SO IT'S HARD TO KILL.
...
BUT IT WILL DIE EVENTUALLY IF YOU KEEP KILLING IT.
AM I STUPID? OR ARE YOU CRAZY?
NEITHER.
A PHILOSOPHER'S STONE IS MADE BY SACRIFICING THE LIVES OF COUNTLESS HUMAN BEINGS.
THIS MONSTER IS MADE WITH ONE OF THOSE STONES AT ITS CORE.
THAT'S WHAT A HOMUNCULUS IS.
AND IF THAT'S NOT BAD ENOUGH, APPARENTLY THESE THINGS ARE SOMEHOW CONNECTED TO A SECTION OF THE MILITARY HIGH COMMAND.
UUUHH...
WUUUH...

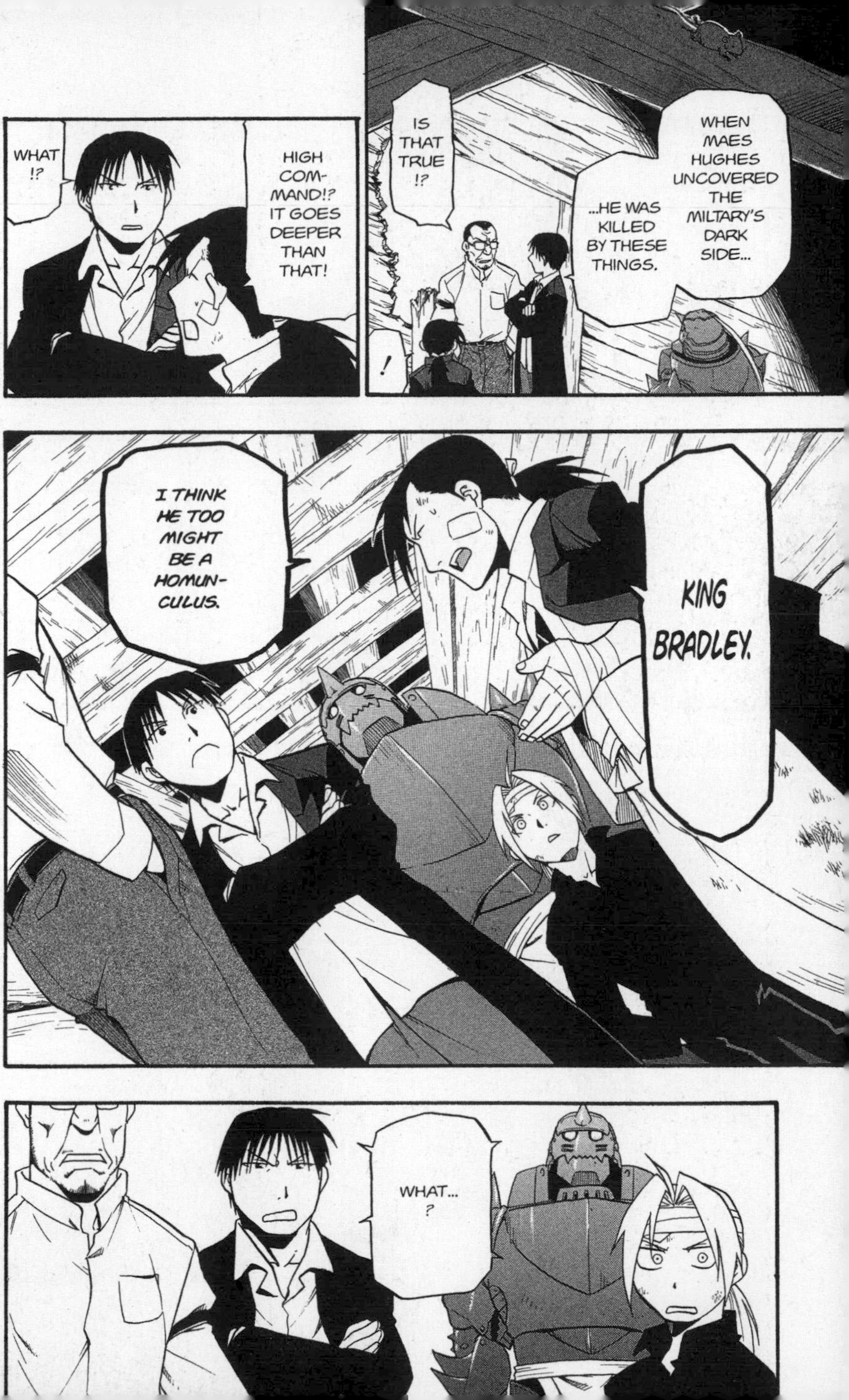
WHEN MAES HUGHES UNCOVERED THE MILTARY'S DARK SIDE...
...HE WAS KILLED BY THESE THINGS.
IS THAT TRUE!?
!
WHAT!?
HIGH COM-MAND!? IT GOES DEEPER THAN THAT!
KING BRADLEY.
I THINK HE TOO MIGHT BE A HOMUN-CULUS.
WHAT...?

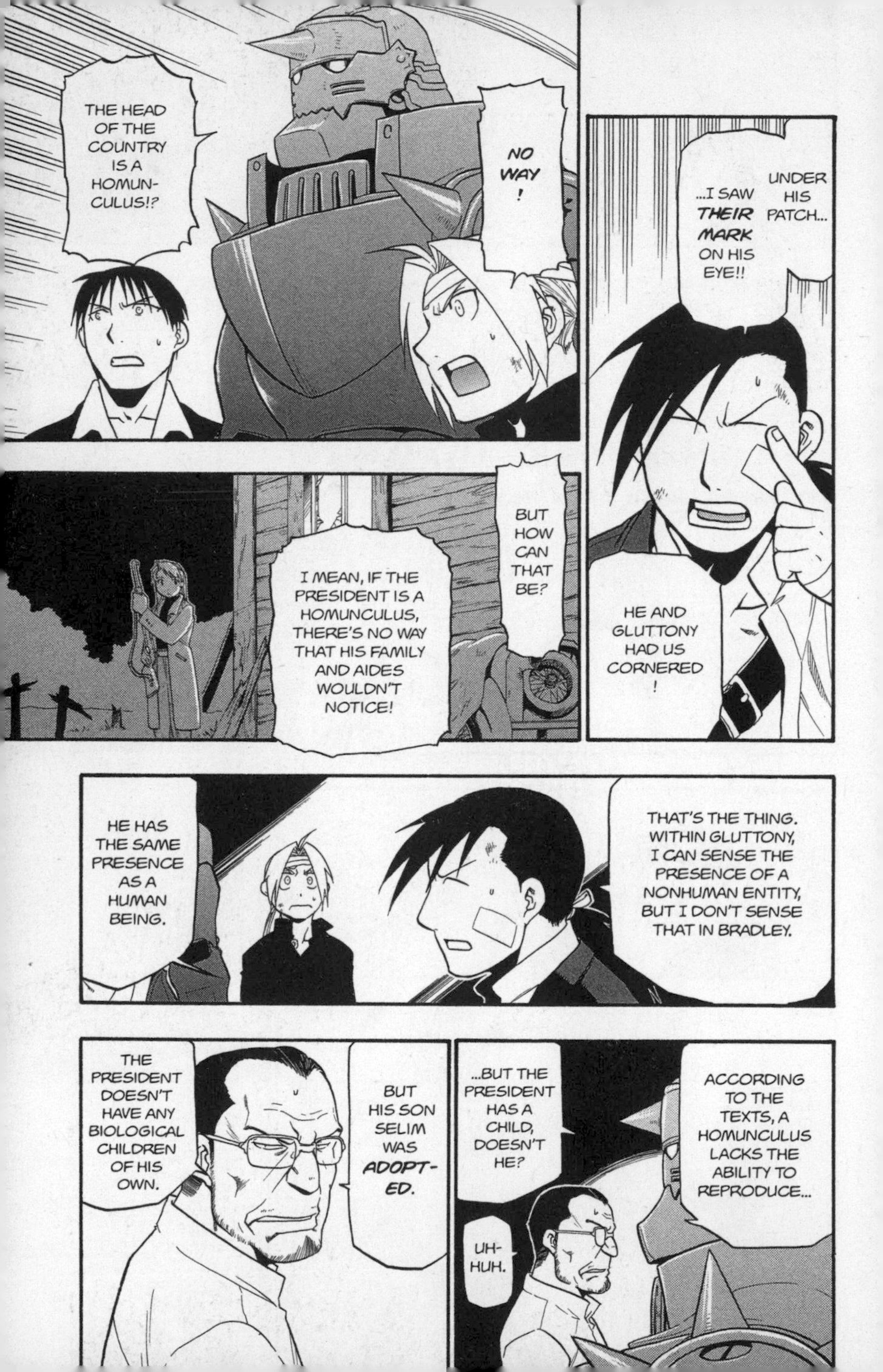
UNDER HIS PATCH...
...I SAW THEIR MARK ON HIS EYE!!
HE AND GLUTTONY HAD US CORNERED!
NO WAY!
THE HEAD OF THE COUNTRY IS A HOMUNCULUS!?
BUT HOW CAN THAT BE?
I MEAN, IF THE PRESIDENT IS A HOMUNCULUS, THERE'S NO WAY THAT HIS FAMILY AND AIDES WOULDN'T NOTICE!
THAT'S THE THING. WITHIN GLUTTONY, I CAN SENSE THE PRESENCE OF A NONHUMAN ENTITY, BUT I DON'T SENSE THAT IN BRADLEY.
HE HAS THE SAME PRESENCE AS A HUMAN BEING.
ACCORDING TO THE TEXTS, A HOMUNCULUS LACKS THE ABILITY TO REPRODUCE...
...BUT THE PRESIDENT HAS A CHILD, DOESN'T HE?
UH-HUH.
THE PRESIDENT DOESN'T HAVE ANY BIOLOGICAL CHILDREN OF HIS OWN.
BUT HIS SON SELIM WAS ADOPTED.

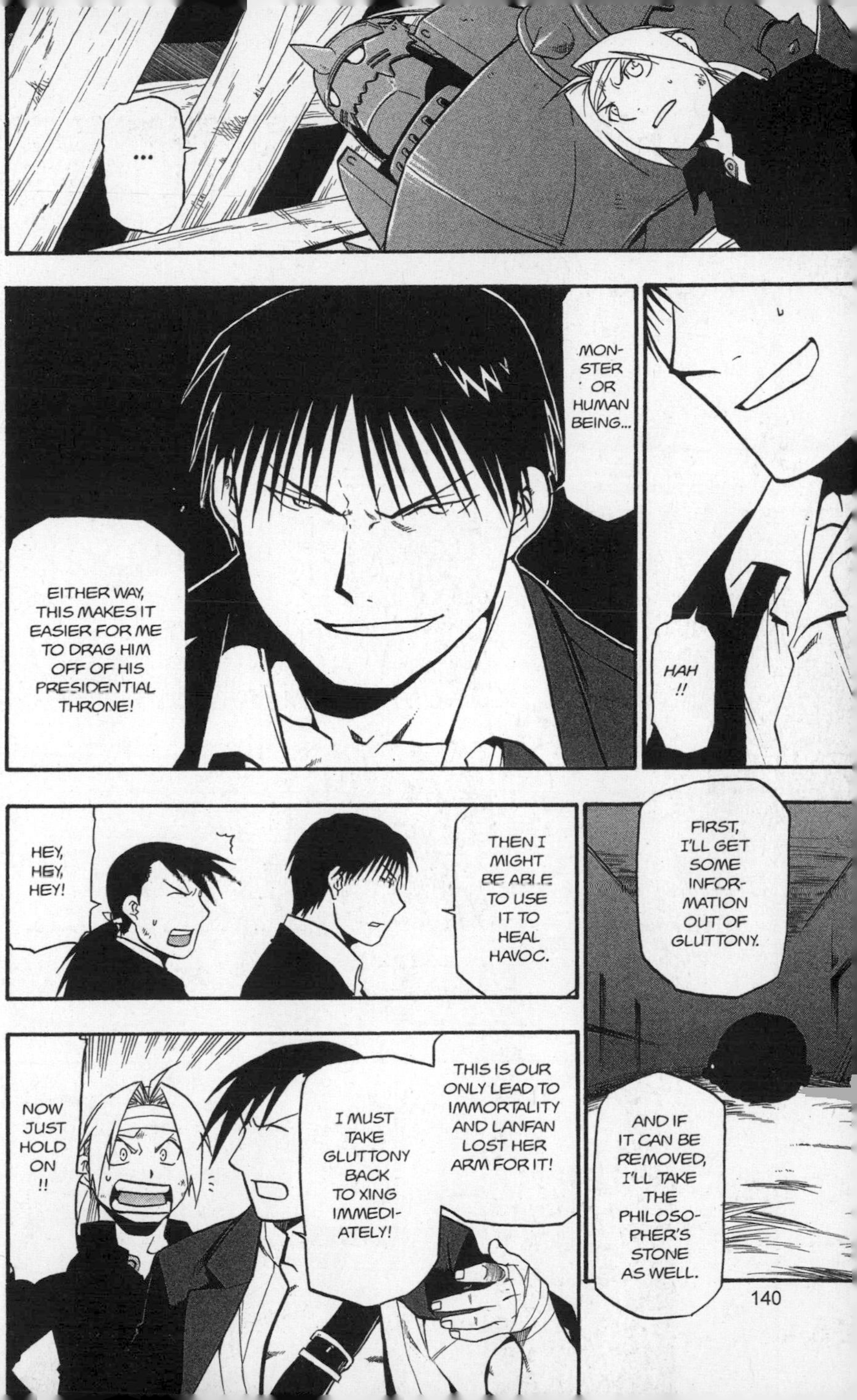
...
HAH !!
MON-STER OR HUMAN BEING...
EITHER WAY, THIS MAKES IT EASIER FOR ME TO DRAG HIM OFF OF HIS PRESIDENTIAL THRONE!
FIRST, I'LL GET SOME INFOR-MATION OUT OF GLUTTONY.
AND IF IT CAN BE REMOVED, I'LL TAKE THE PHILOSO-PHER'S STONE AS WELL.
THEN I MIGHT BE ABLE TO USE IT TO HEAL HAVOC.
HEY, HEY, HEY!
THIS IS OUR ONLY LEAD TO IMMORTALITY AND LANFAN LOST HER ARM FOR IT!
I MUST TAKE GLUTTONY BACK TO XING IMMEDI-ATELY!
NOW JUST HOLD ON !!

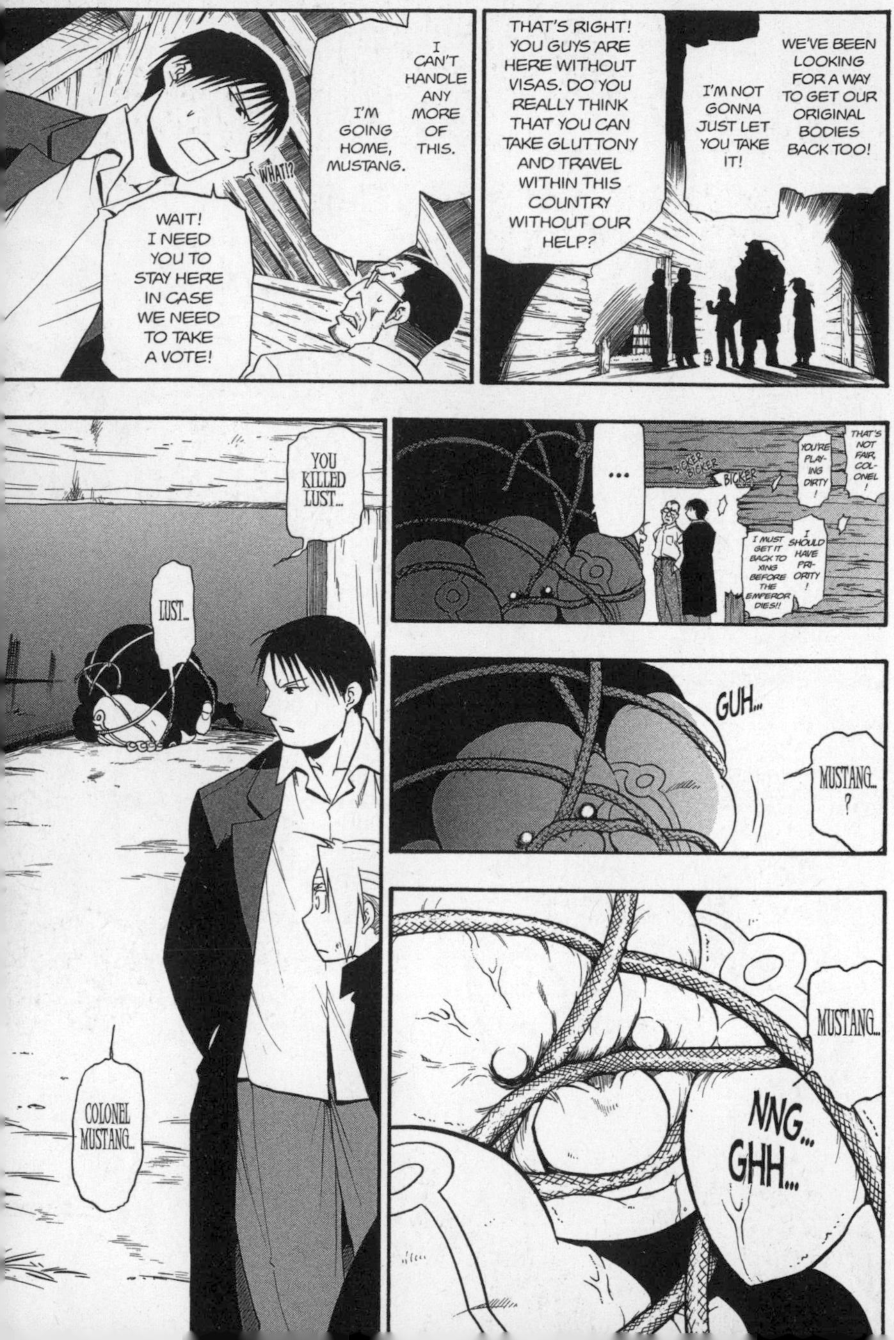
WE'VE BEEN LOOKING FOR A WAY TO GET OUR ORIGINAL BODIES BACK TOO!
I'M NOT GONNA JUST LET YOU TAKE IT!
THAT'S RIGHT! YOU GUYS ARE HERE WITHOUT VISAS. DO YOU REALLY THINK THAT YOU CAN TAKE GLUTTONY AND TRAVEL WITHIN THIS COUNTRY WITHOUT OUR HELP?
I CAN'T HANDLE ANY MORE OF THIS.
I'M GOING HOME, MUSTANG.
WHAT!?
WAIT! I NEED YOU TO STAY HERE IN CASE WE NEED TO TAKE A VOTE!
THAT'S NOT FAIR, COLONEL!
YOU'RE PLAYING DIRTY!
I SHOULD HAVE PRIORITY!
I MUST GET IT BACK TO XING BEFORE THE EMPEROR DIES!!
BICKER BICKER
BICKER
...
GUH...
MUSTANG...?
MUSTANG...
NNG... GHH...
YOU KILLED LUST...
LUST...
COLONEL MUSTANG...

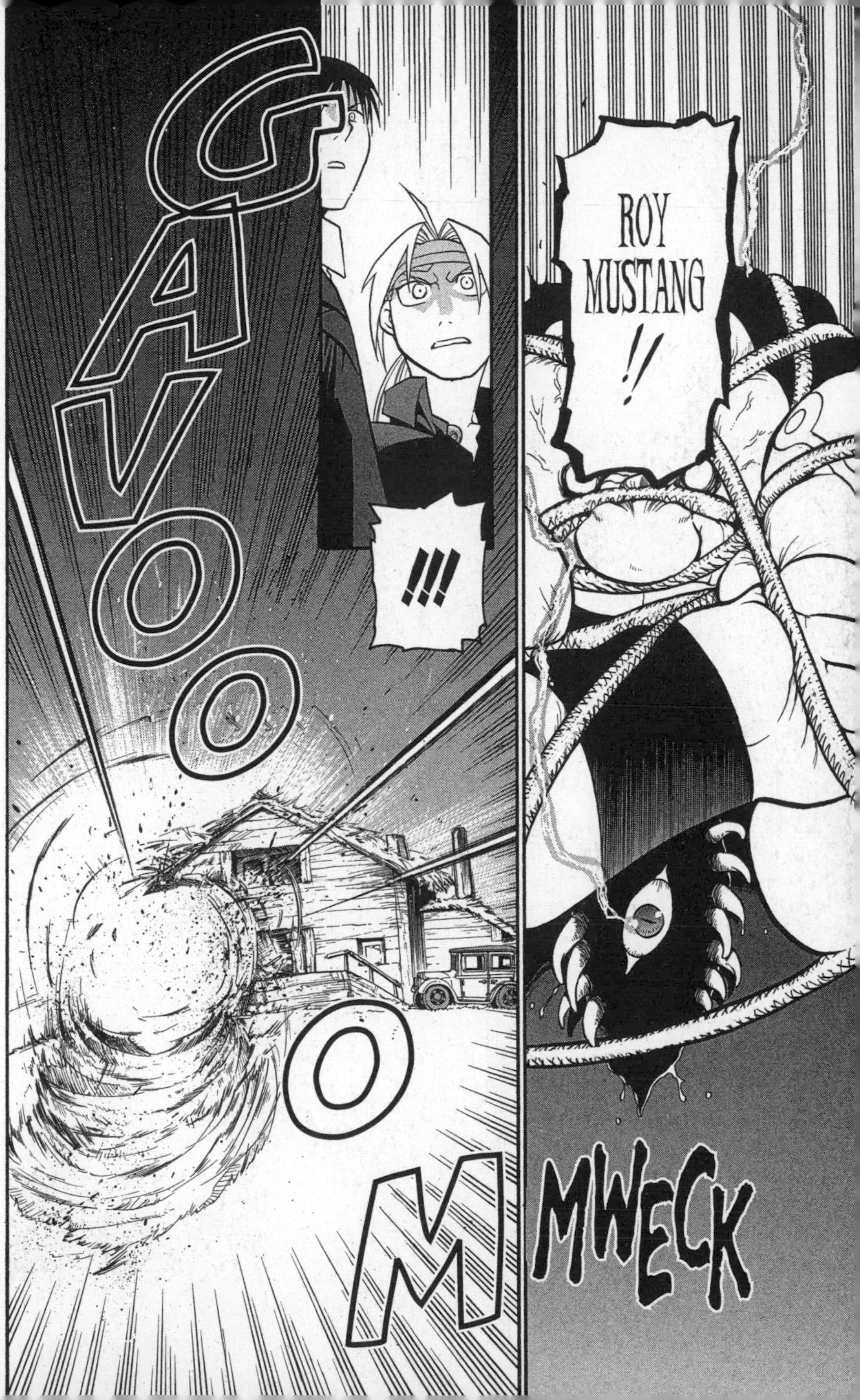
ROY MUSTANG !!
MWECK
!!!
GAVOOOM

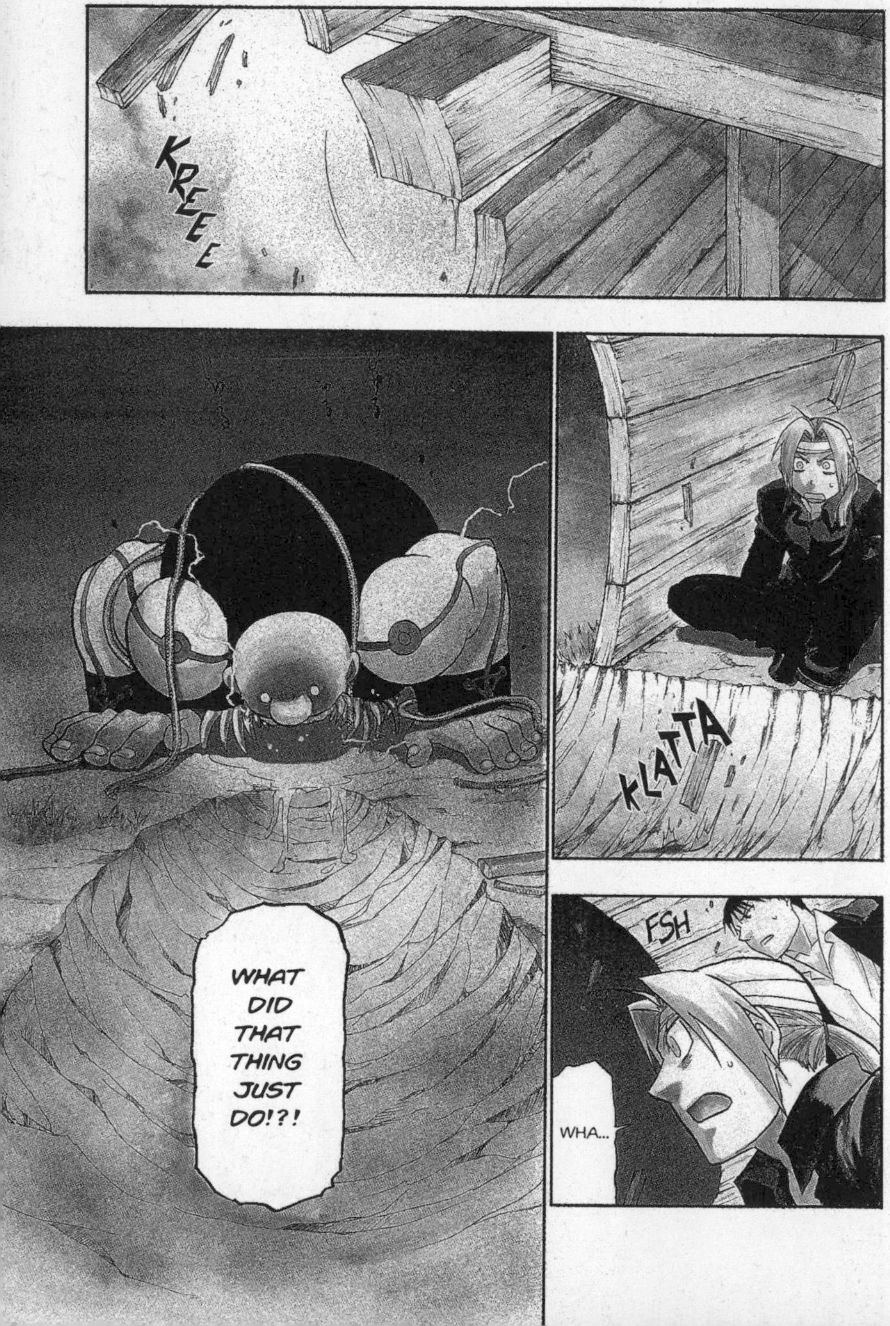
KREEEE
KLATTA
FSH
WHA...
WHAT DID THAT THING JUST DO!?!

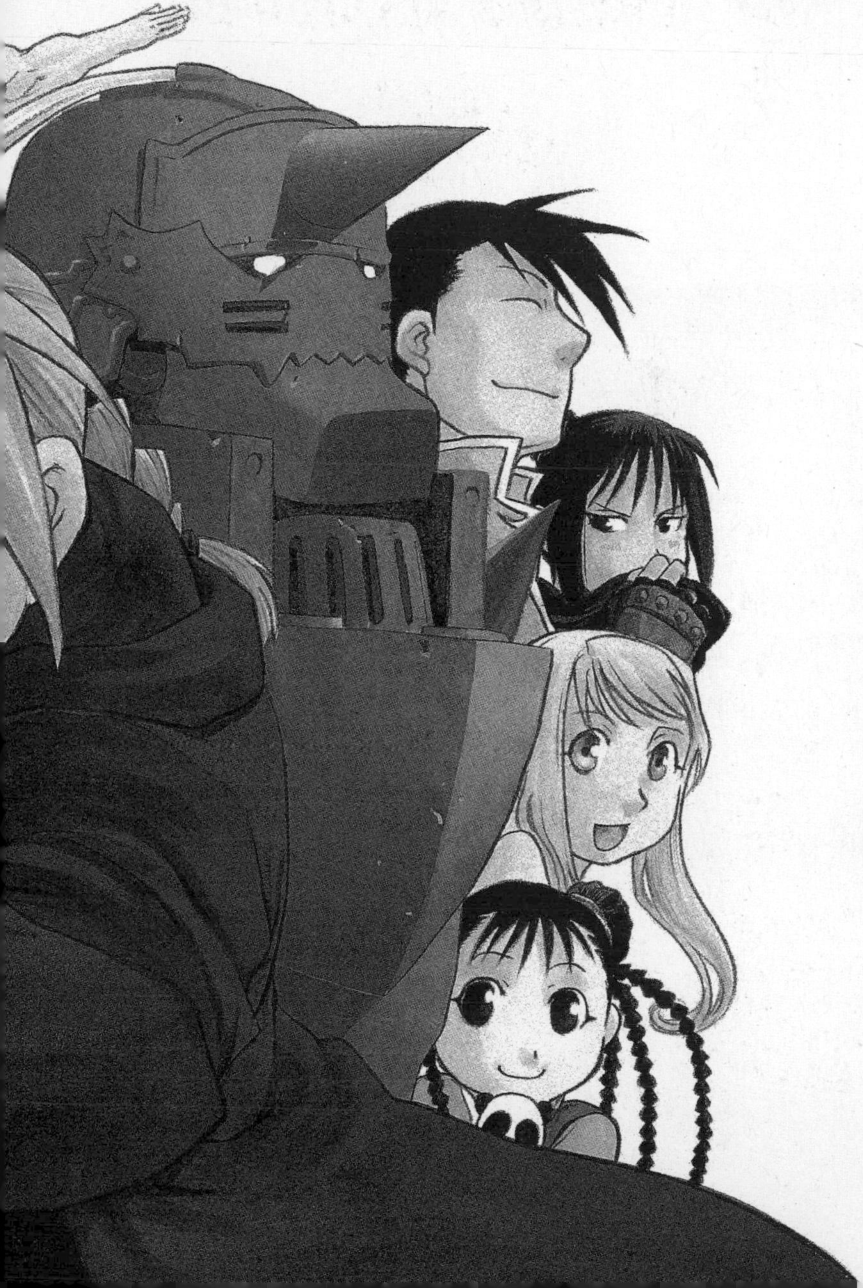

Chapter 49
A Monster Among Men

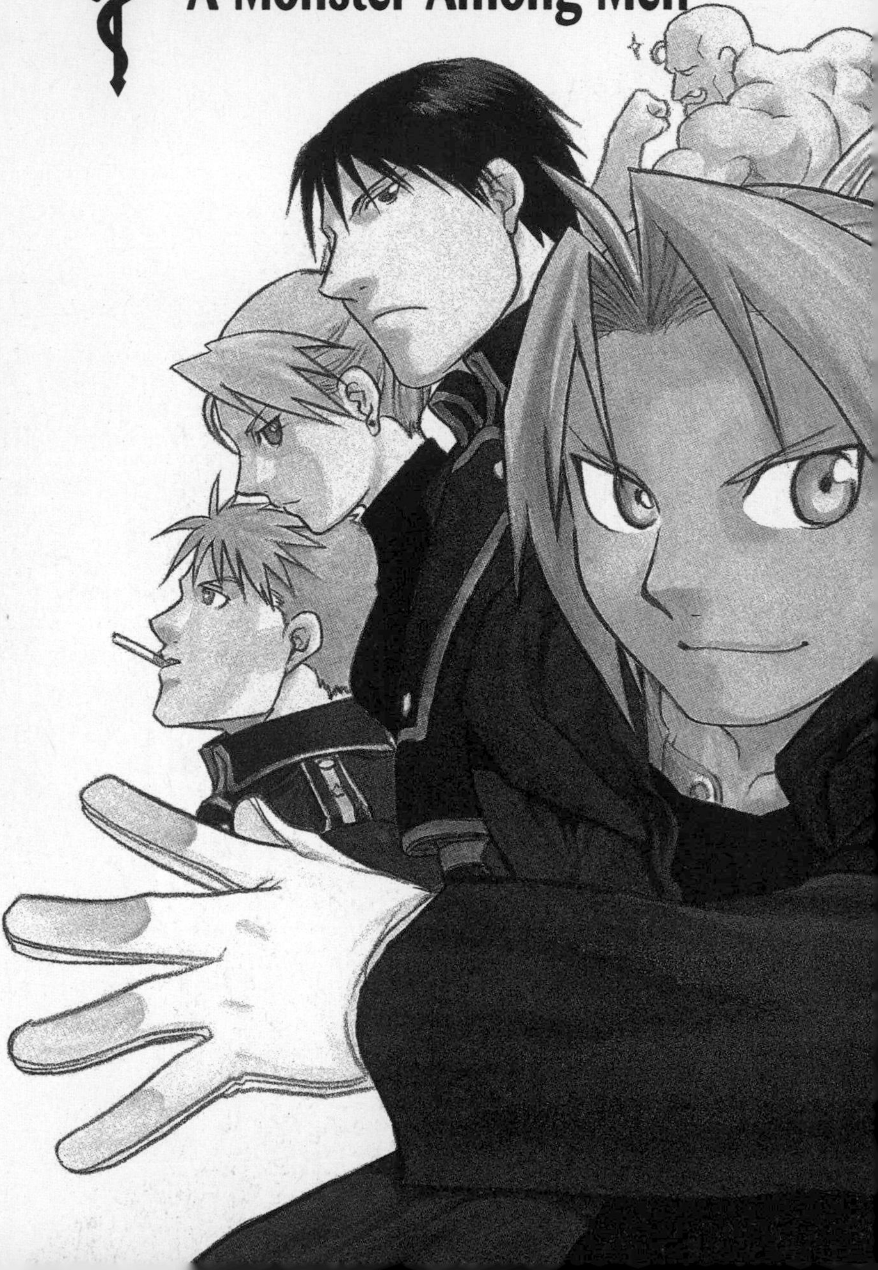

FULLMETAL
ALCHEMIST

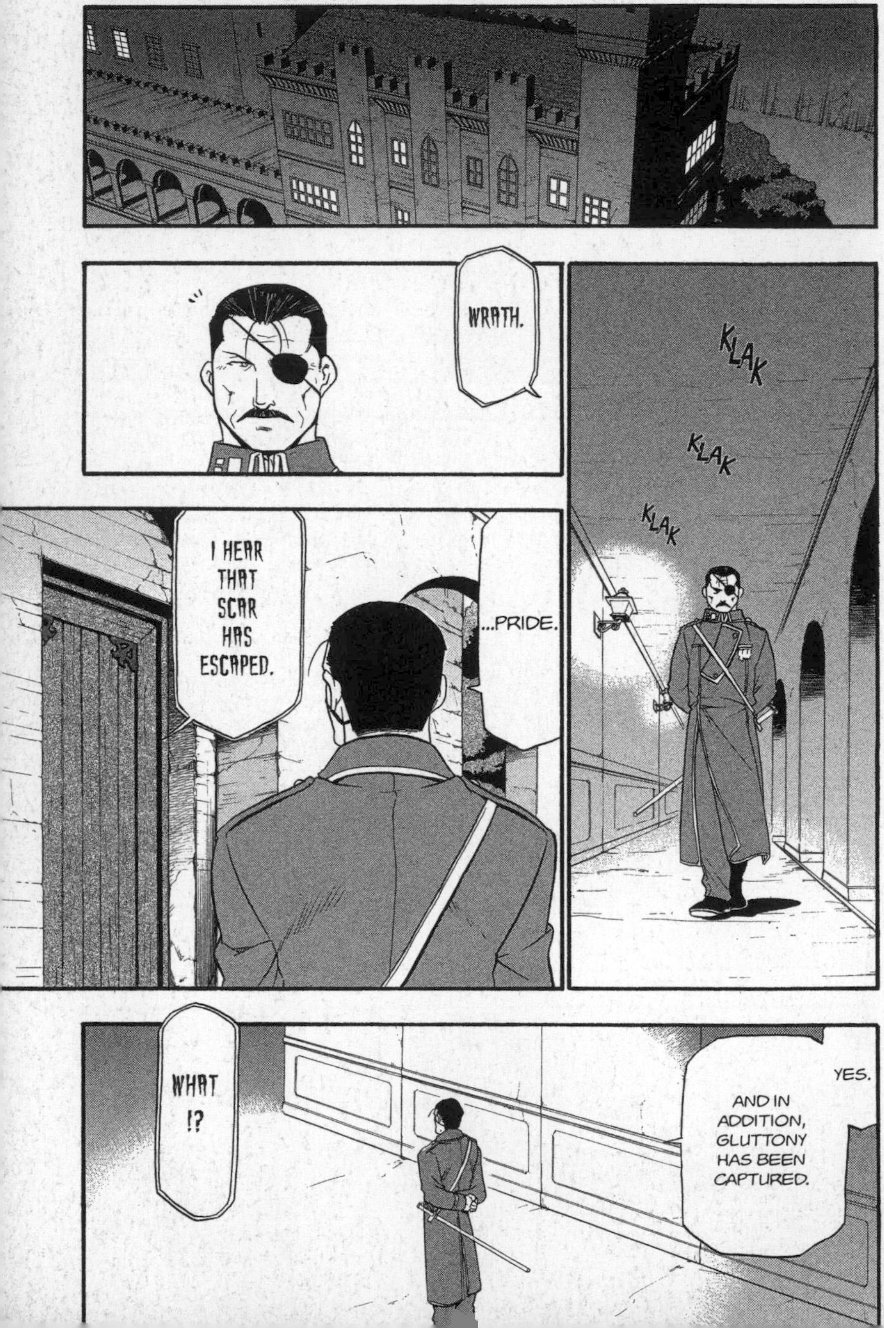
KLAK
KLAK
KLAK
WRATH.
...PRIDE.
I HEAR THAT SCAR HAS ESCAPED.
YES.
AND IN ADDITION, GLUTTONY HAS BEEN CAPTURED.
WHAT!?

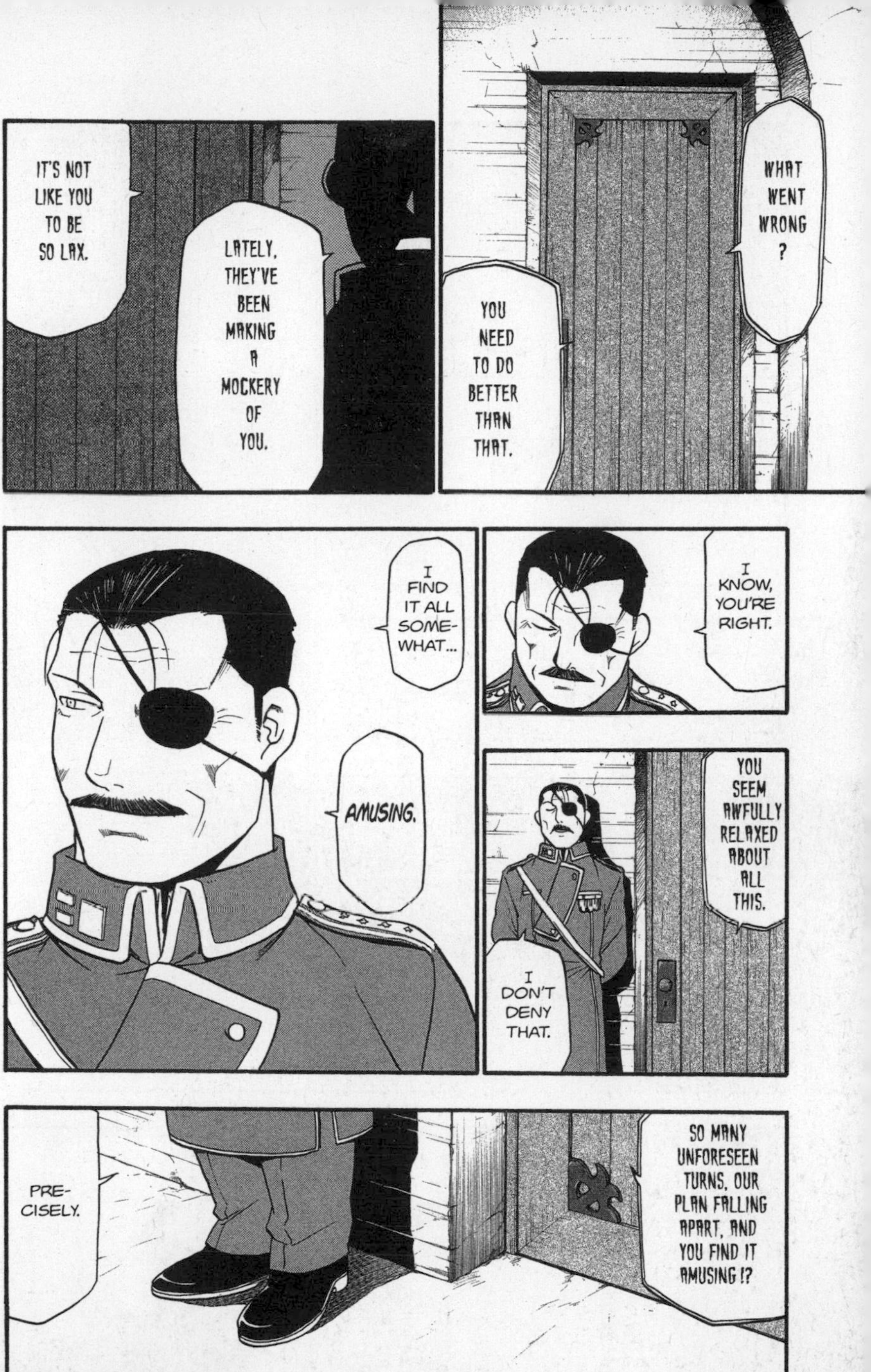
WHAT WENT WRONG?
YOU NEED TO DO BETTER THAN THAT.
LATELY, THEY'VE BEEN MAKING A MOCKERY OF YOU.
IT'S NOT LIKE YOU TO BE SO LAX.
I KNOW, YOU'RE RIGHT.
YOU SEEM AWFULLY RELAXED ABOUT ALL THIS.
I DON'T DENY THAT.
I FIND IT ALL SOME-WHAT...
AMUSING.
SO MANY UNFORESEEN TURNS, OUR PLAN FALLING APART, AND YOU FIND IT AMUSING!?
PRE-CISELY.

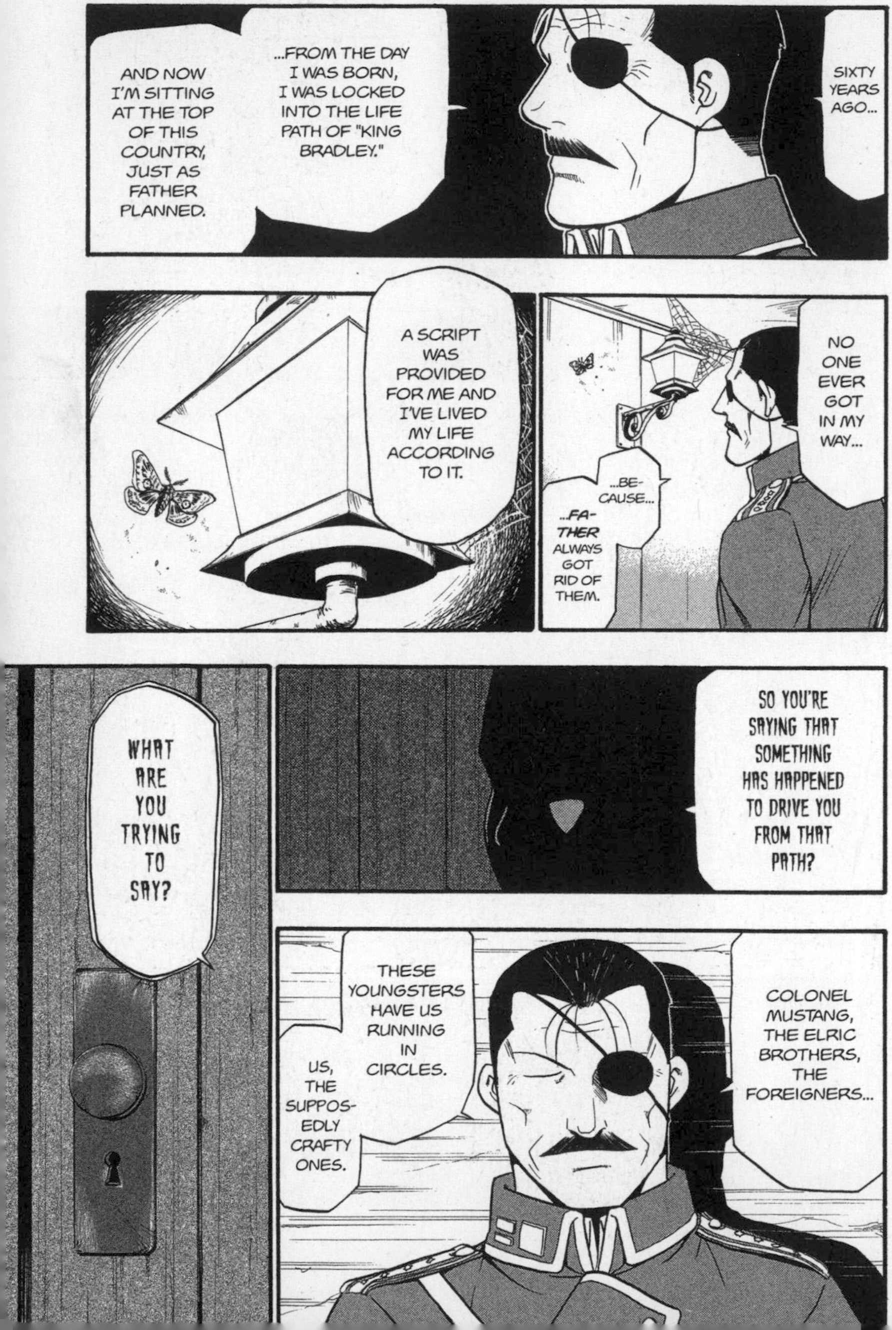
SIXTY YEARS AGO...
...FROM THE DAY I WAS BORN, I WAS LOCKED INTO THE LIFE PATH OF "KING BRADLEY."
AND NOW I'M SITTING AT THE TOP OF THIS COUNTRY, JUST AS FATHER PLANNED.
NO ONE EVER GOT IN MY WAY...
...BE-CAUSE...
...*FATHER* ALWAYS GOT RID OF THEM.
A SCRIPT WAS PROVIDED FOR ME AND I'VE LIVED MY LIFE ACCORDING TO IT.
SO YOU'RE SAYING THAT SOMETHING HAS HAPPENED TO DRIVE YOU FROM THAT PATH?
COLONEL MUSTANG, THE ELRIC BROTHERS, THE FOREIGNERS...
THESE YOUNGSTERS HAVE US RUNNING IN CIRCLES.
US, THE SUPPOS-EDLY CRAFTY ONES.
WHAT ARE YOU TRYING TO SAY?

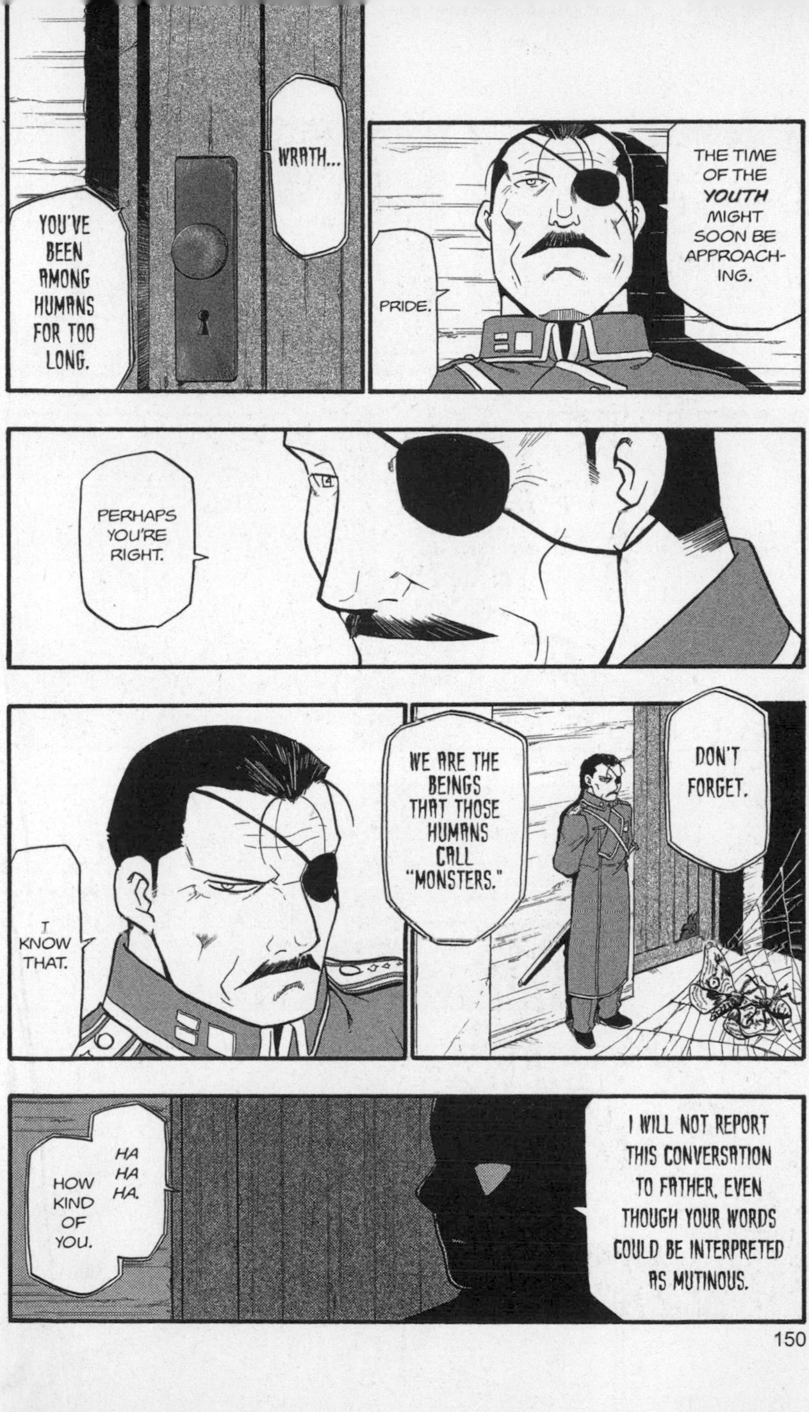
THE TIME OF THE YOUTH MIGHT SOON BE APPROACHING.
PRIDE.
WRATH...
YOU'VE BEEN AMONG HUMANS FOR TOO LONG.
PERHAPS YOU'RE RIGHT.
DON'T FORGET.
WE ARE THE BEINGS THAT THOSE HUMANS CALL "MONSTERS."
I KNOW THAT.
I WILL NOT REPORT THIS CONVERSATION TO FATHER, EVEN THOUGH YOUR WORDS COULD BE INTERPRETED AS MUTINOUS.
HA HA HA. HOW KIND OF YOU.

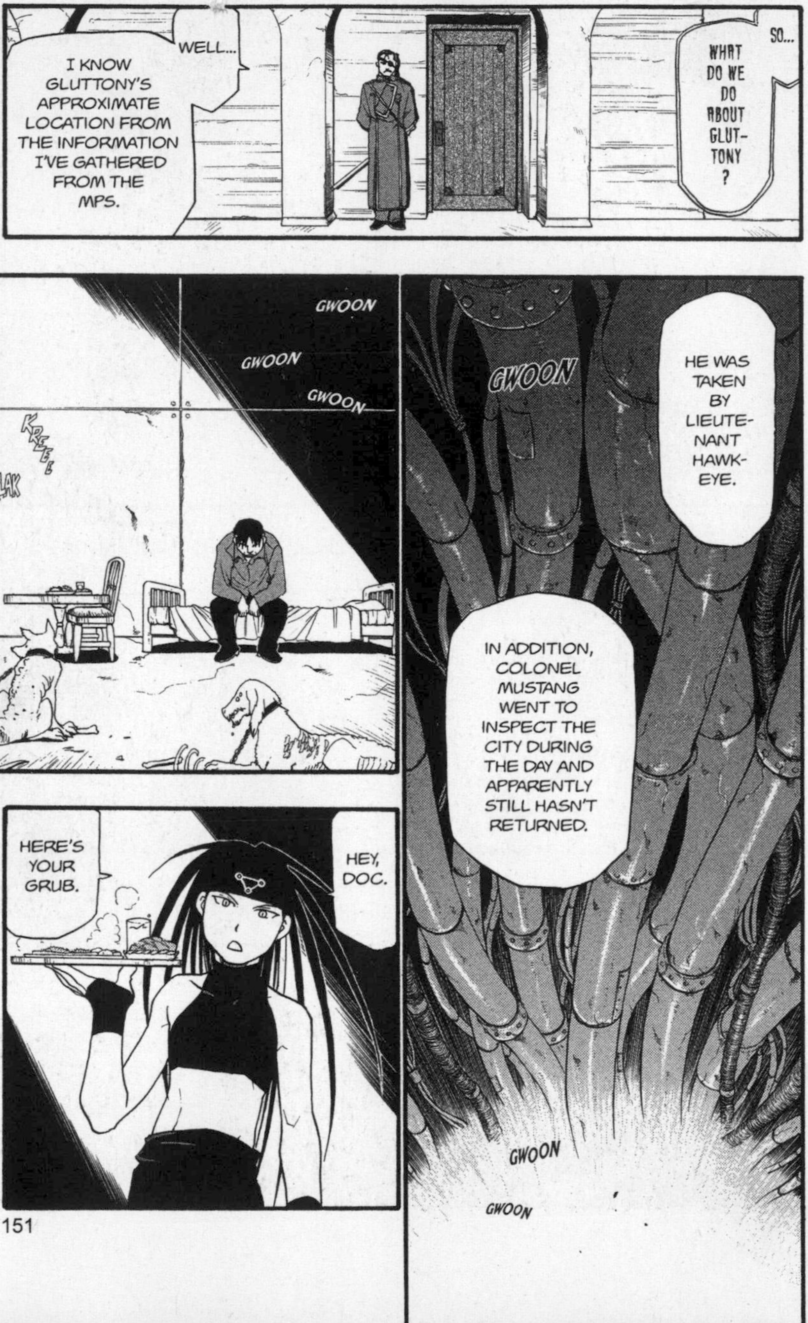

SO...
WHAT DO WE DO ABOUT GLUTTONY?
WELL...
I KNOW GLUTTONY'S APPROXIMATE LOCATION FROM THE INFORMATION I'VE GATHERED FROM THE MPS.
GWOON
HE WAS TAKEN BY LIEUTENANT HAWKEYE.
IN ADDITION, COLONEL MUSTANG WENT TO INSPECT THE CITY DURING THE DAY AND APPARENTLY STILL HASN'T RETURNED.
GWOON
GWOON
GWOON
GWOON
GWOON
KREEE
KLAK
HEY, DOC.
HERE'S YOUR GRUB.

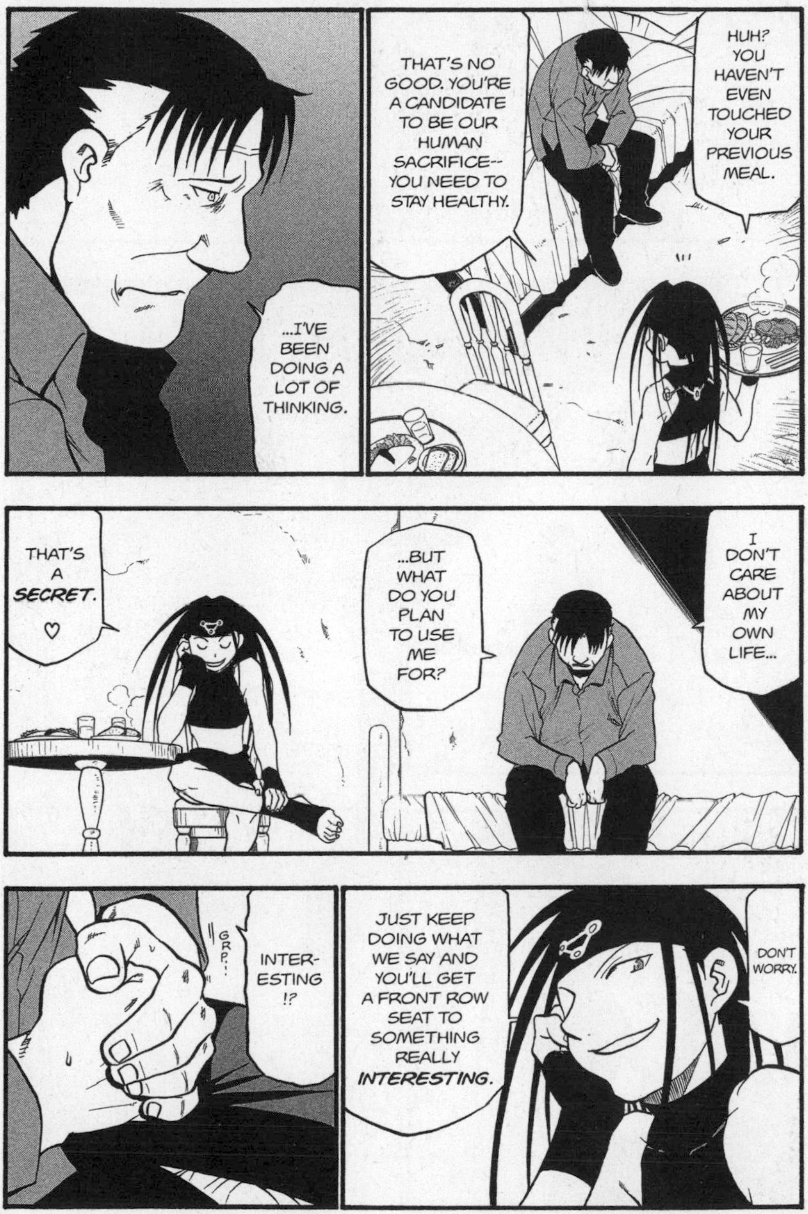
HUH? YOU HAVEN'T EVEN TOUCHED YOUR PREVIOUS MEAL.
THAT'S NO GOOD. YOU'RE A CANDIDATE TO BE OUR HUMAN SACRIFICE-- YOU NEED TO STAY HEALTHY.
...I'VE BEEN DOING A LOT OF THINKING.
I DON'T CARE ABOUT MY OWN LIFE...
...BUT WHAT DO YOU PLAN TO USE ME FOR?
THAT'S A ***SECRET***. ♡
DON'T WORRY.
JUST KEEP DOING WHAT WE SAY AND YOU'LL GET A FRONT ROW SEAT TO SOMETHING REALLY ***INTERESTING***.
GRP...
INTER-ESTING !?

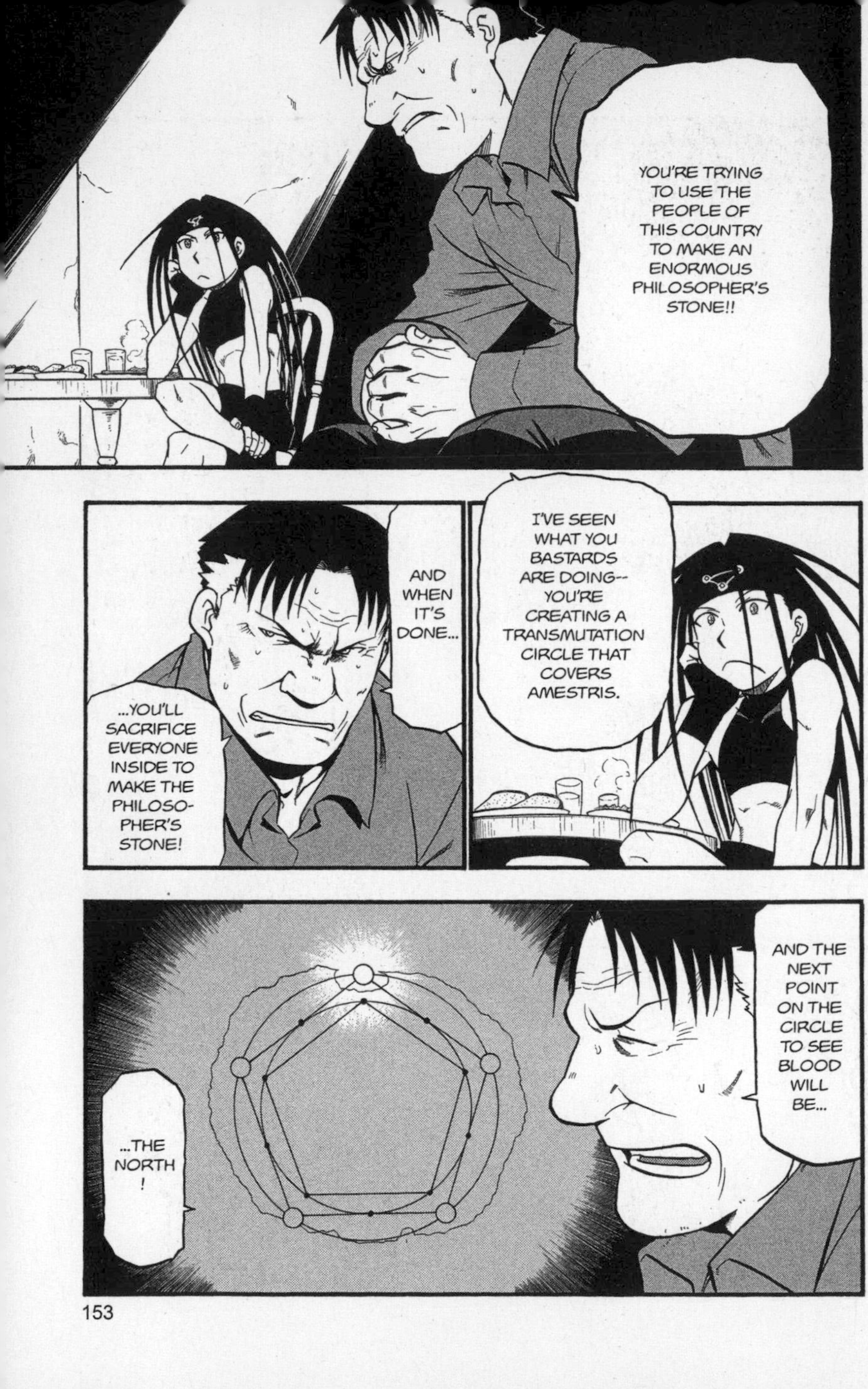
YOU'RE TRYING TO USE THE PEOPLE OF THIS COUNTRY TO MAKE AN ENORMOUS PHILOSOPHER'S STONE!!
I'VE SEEN WHAT YOU BASTARDS ARE DOING-- YOU'RE CREATING A TRANSMUTATION CIRCLE THAT COVERS AMESTRIS.
AND WHEN IT'S DONE...
...YOU'LL SACRIFICE EVERYONE INSIDE TO MAKE THE PHILOSO-PHER'S STONE!
AND THE NEXT POINT ON THE CIRCLE TO SEE BLOOD WILL BE...
...THE NORTH!

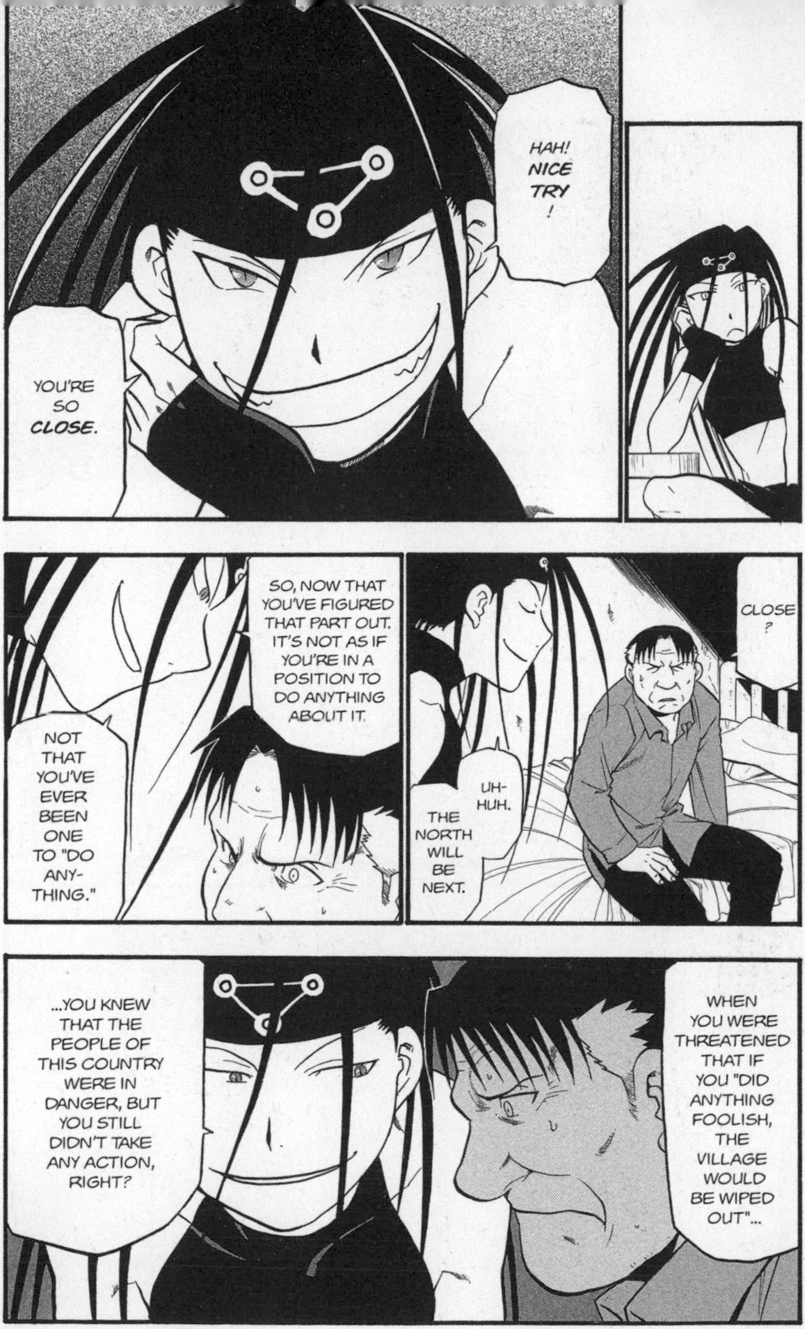
HAH! NICE TRY!
YOU'RE SO CLOSE.
CLOSE?
UH-HUH. THE NORTH WILL BE NEXT.
SO, NOW THAT YOU'VE FIGURED THAT PART OUT. IT'S NOT AS IF YOU'RE IN A POSITION TO DO ANYTHING ABOUT IT.
NOT THAT YOU'VE EVER BEEN ONE TO "DO ANY-THING."
WHEN YOU WERE THREATENED THAT IF YOU "DID ANYTHING FOOLISH, THE VILLAGE WOULD BE WIPED OUT"...
...YOU KNEW THAT THE PEOPLE OF THIS COUNTRY WERE IN DANGER, BUT YOU STILL DIDN'T TAKE ANY ACTION, RIGHT?

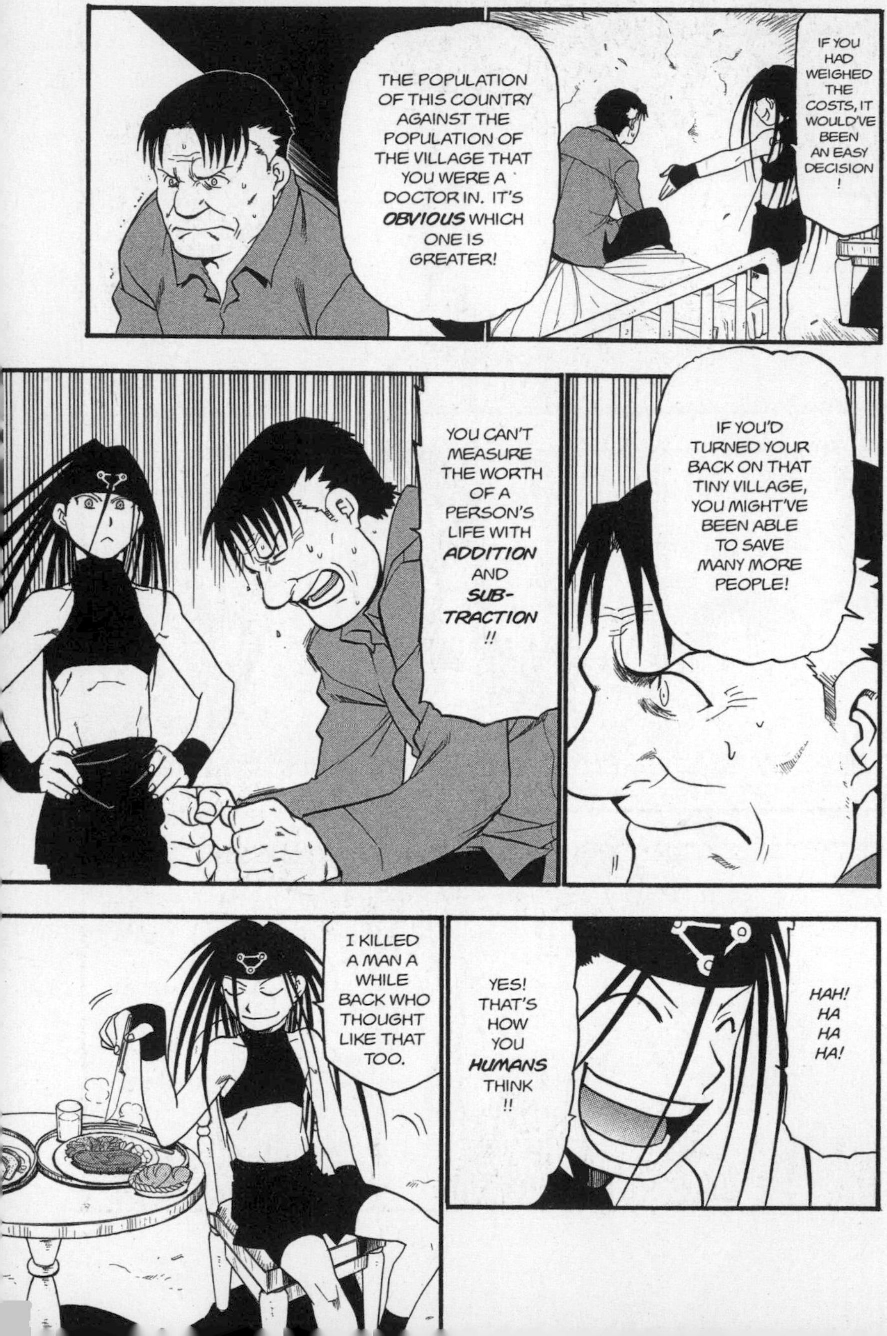
IF YOU HAD WEIGHED THE COSTS, IT WOULD'VE BEEN AN EASY DECISION!
THE POPULATION OF THIS COUNTRY AGAINST THE POPULATION OF THE VILLAGE THAT YOU WERE A DOCTOR IN. IT'S OBVIOUS WHICH ONE IS GREATER!
IF YOU'D TURNED YOUR BACK ON THAT TINY VILLAGE, YOU MIGHT'VE BEEN ABLE TO SAVE MANY MORE PEOPLE!
YOU CAN'T MEASURE THE WORTH OF A PERSON'S LIFE WITH ADDITION AND SUB-TRACTION!!
HAH! HA HA HA!
YES! THAT'S HOW YOU HUMANS THINK!!
I KILLED A MAN A WHILE BACK WHO THOUGHT LIKE THAT TOO.

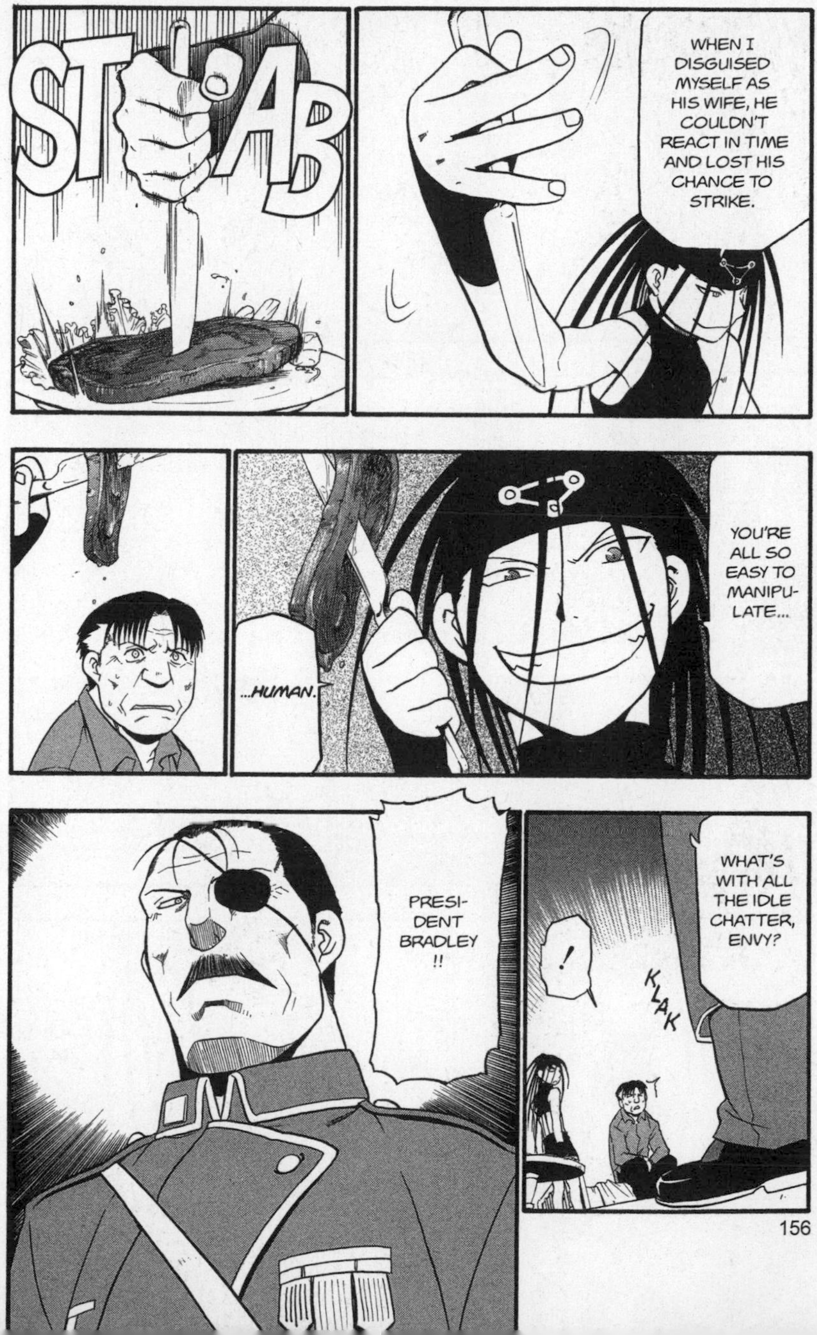
WHEN I DISGUISED MYSELF AS HIS WIFE, HE COULDN'T REACT IN TIME AND LOST HIS CHANCE TO STRIKE.
STAB
YOU'RE ALL SO EASY TO MANIPU-LATE...
...HUMAN.
WHAT'S WITH ALL THE IDLE CHATTER, ENVY?
!
KLAK
PRESI-DENT BRADLEY !!

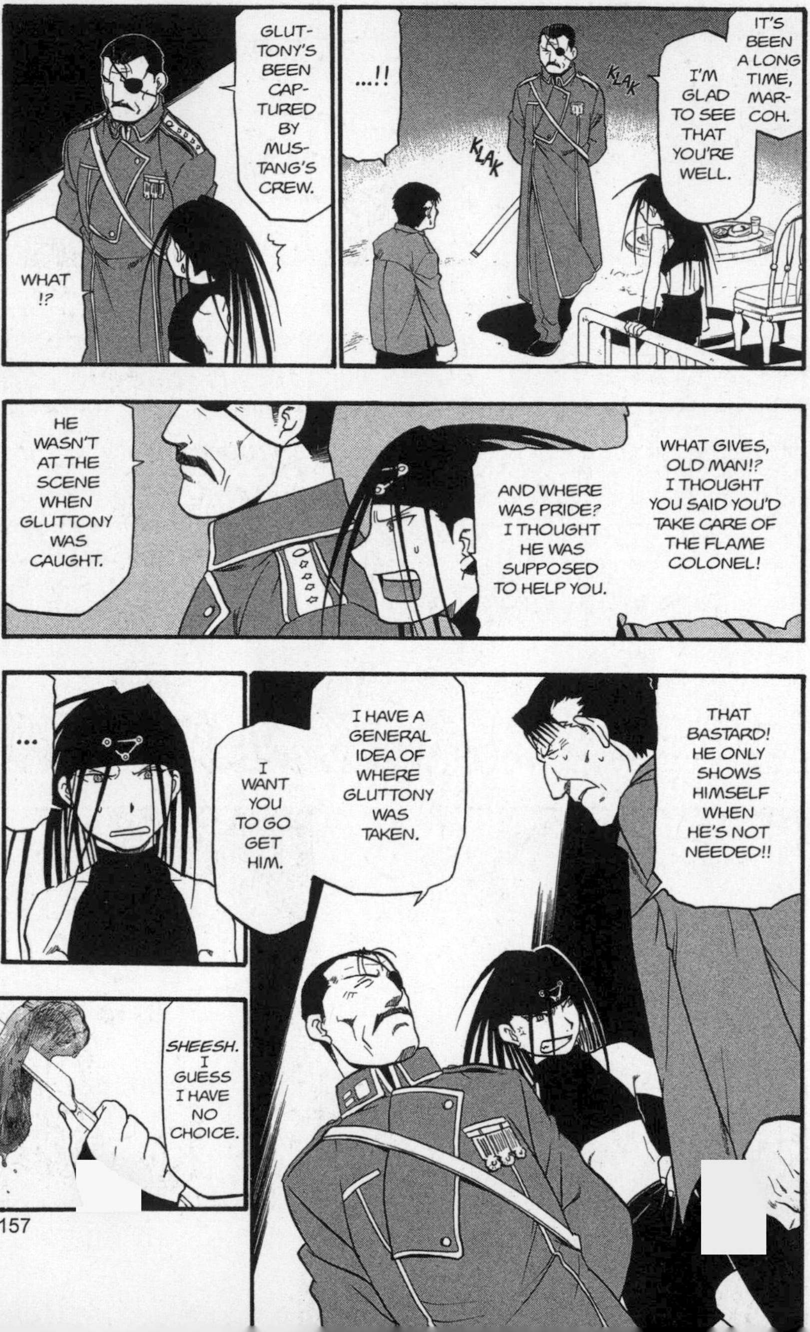
KLAK
KLAK
IT'S BEEN A LONG TIME, MARCOH.
I'M GLAD TO SEE THAT YOU'RE WELL.
...!!
GLUTTONY'S BEEN CAPTURED BY MUSTANG'S CREW.
WHAT!?
WHAT GIVES, OLD MAN!? I THOUGHT YOU SAID YOU'D TAKE CARE OF THE FLAME COLONEL!
AND WHERE WAS PRIDE? I THOUGHT HE WAS SUPPOSED TO HELP YOU.
HE WASN'T AT THE SCENE WHEN GLUTTONY WAS CAUGHT.
THAT BASTARD! HE ONLY SHOWS HIMSELF WHEN HE'S NOT NEEDED!!
I HAVE A GENERAL IDEA OF WHERE GLUTTONY WAS TAKEN.
I WANT YOU TO GO GET HIM.
...
SHEESH. I GUESS I HAVE NO CHOICE.

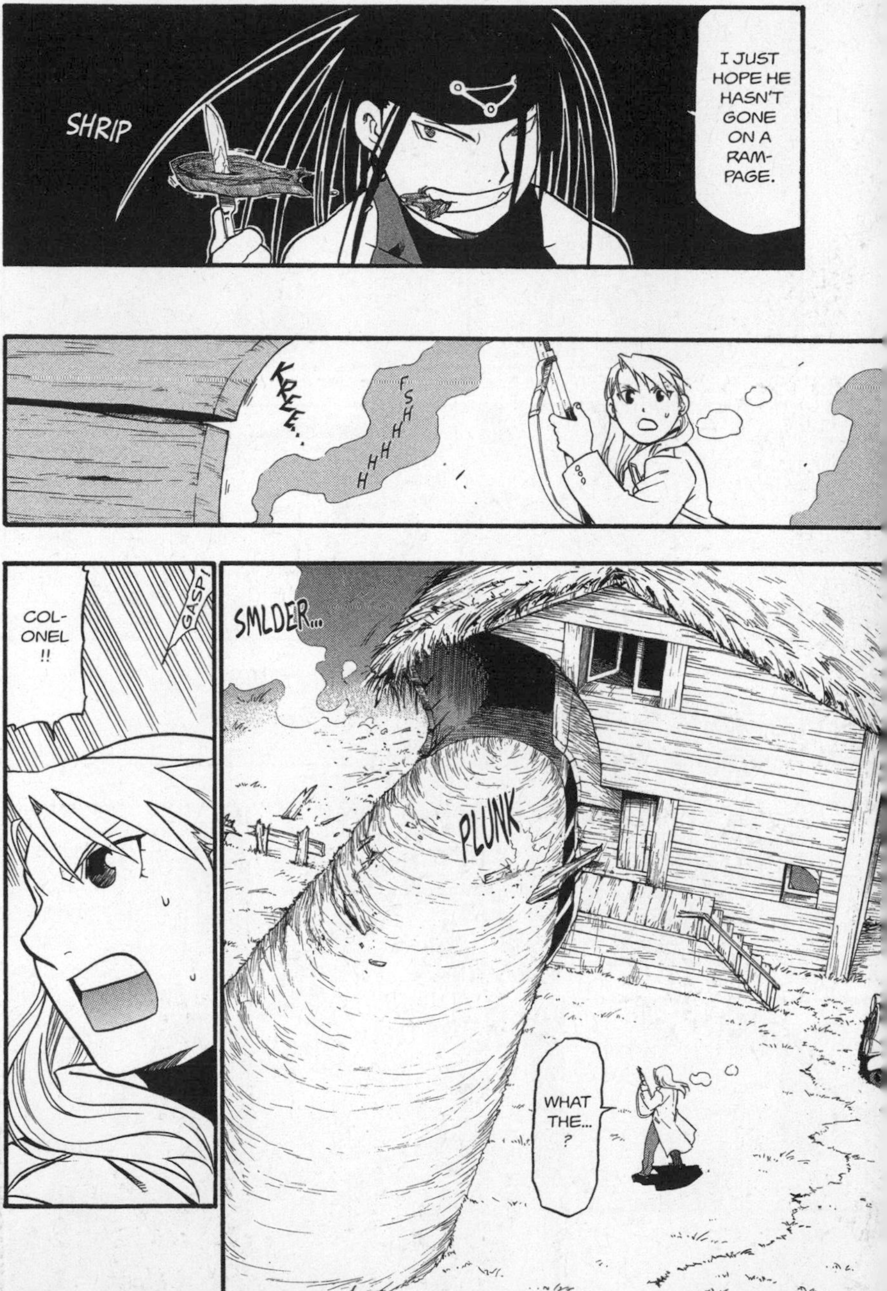

I JUST HOPE HE HASN'T GONE ON A RAM-PAGE.
SHRIP
KREEE...
FSHHHHH
SMLDER...
PLUNK
WHAT THE...?
GASP!
COL-ONEL!!

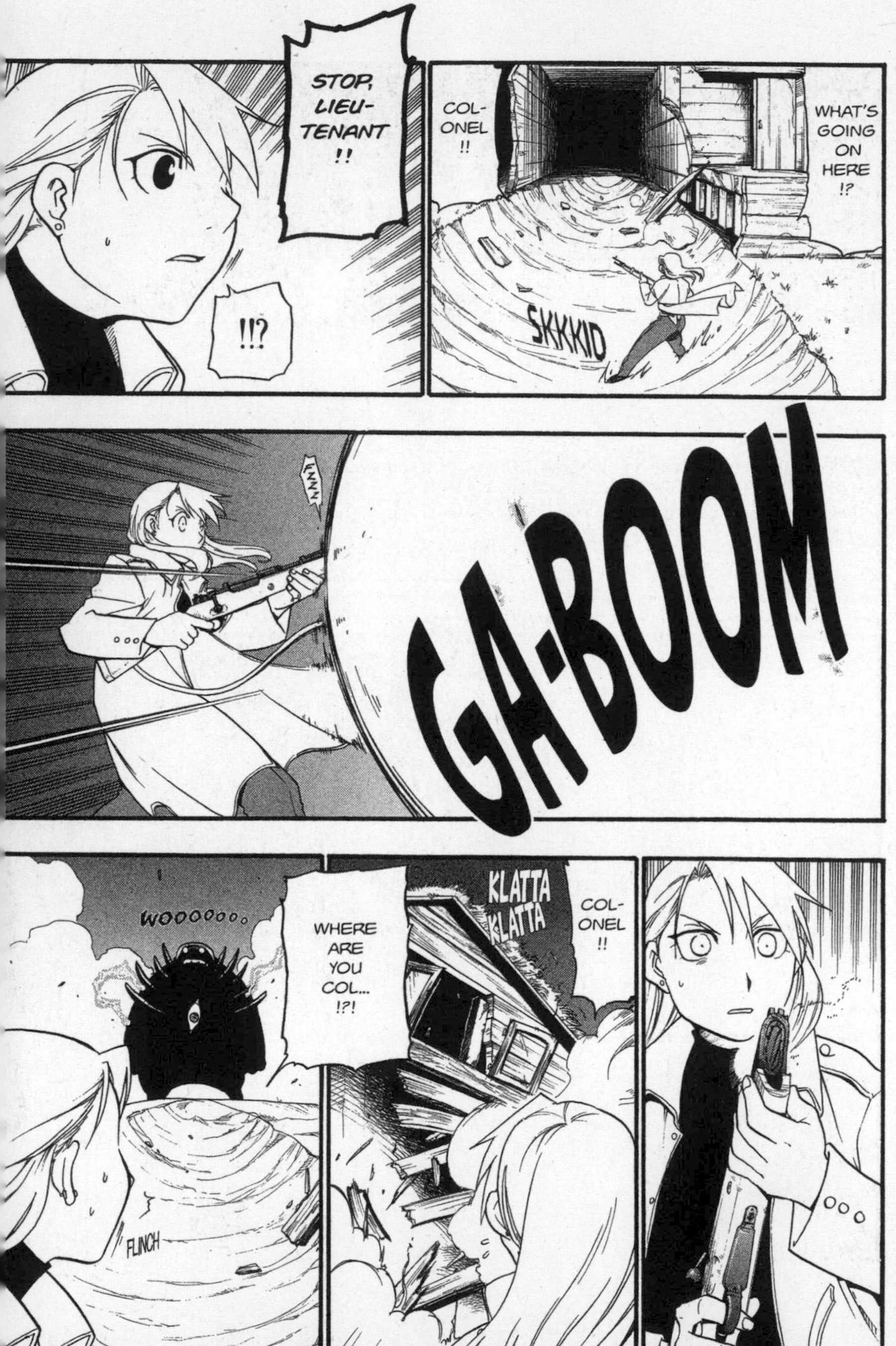
WHAT'S GOING ON HERE !?
COL-ONEL !!
SKKKID
STOP, LIEU-TENANT !!
!!?
GA-BOOM
FZZZ
COL-ONEL !!
KLATTA KLATTA
WHERE ARE YOU COL... !?!
WOOOOOOO
FLINCH

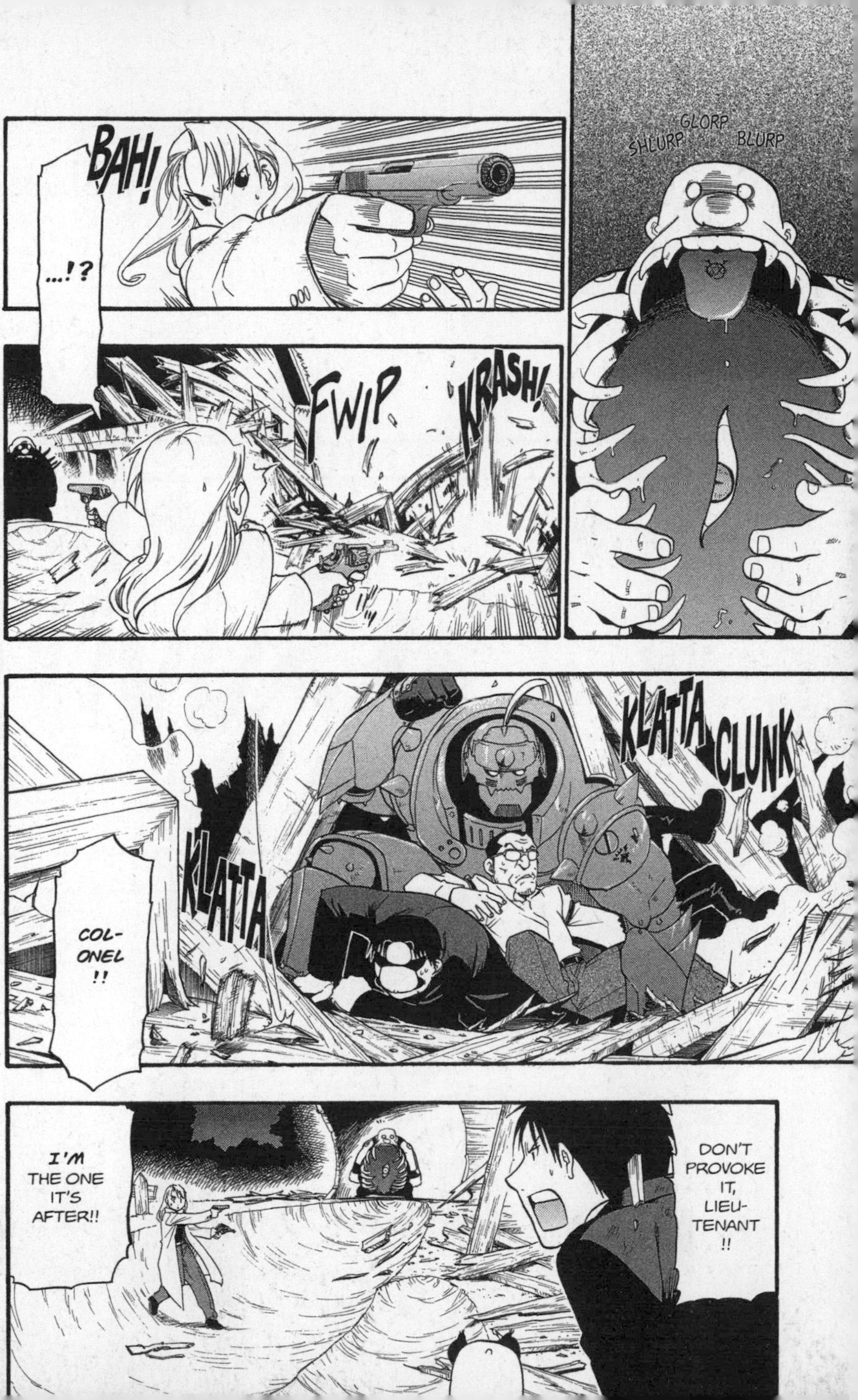
SHLURP
GLORP
BLURP
BAH!
...!?
FWIP
KRASH!
KLATTA
CLUNK
KLATTA
COL-ONEL!!
DON'T PROVOKE IT, LIEU-TENANT!!
I'M THE ONE IT'S AFTER!!

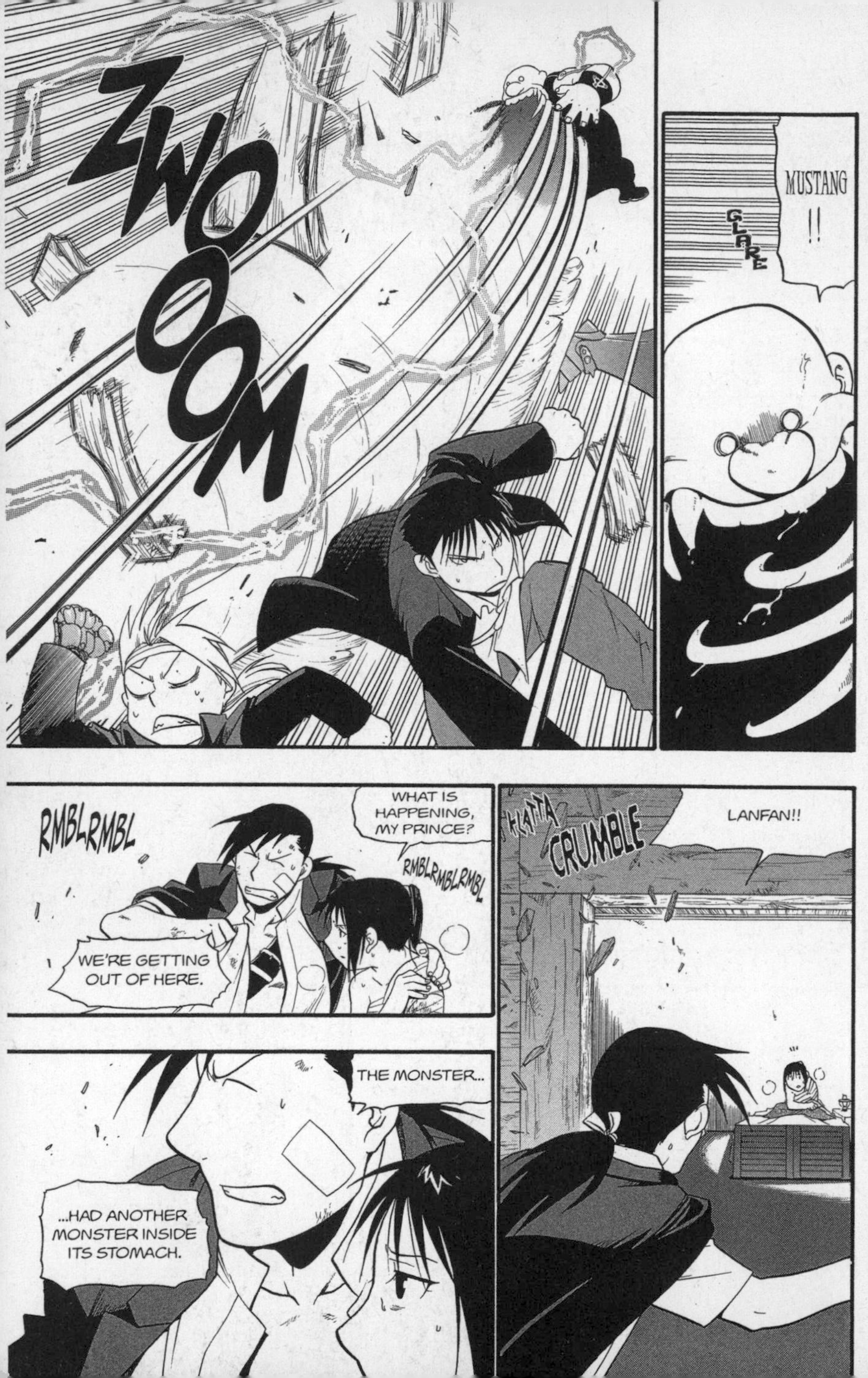
MUSTANG!!
GLARE
ZWOOOM
LANFAN!!
KLATTA
CRUMBLE
WHAT IS HAPPENING, MY PRINCE?
RMBLRMBLRMBL
RMBLRMBL
WE'RE GETTING OUT OF HERE.
THE MONSTER...
...HAD ANOTHER MONSTER INSIDE ITS STOMACH.

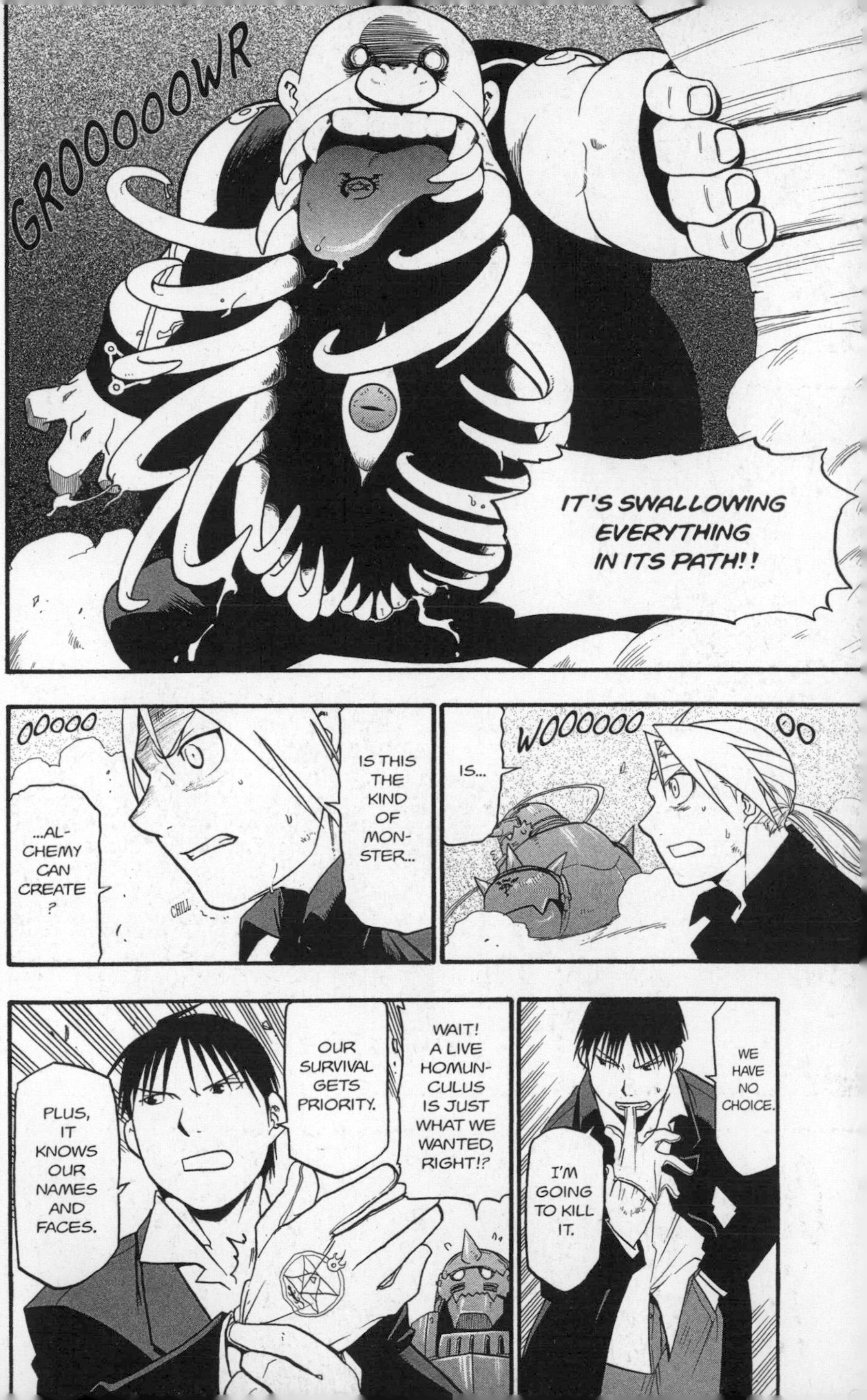
GROOOOOWR
IT'S SWALLOWING EVERYTHING IN ITS PATH!!
WOOOOOO
OO
IS...
OOOOO
IS THIS THE KIND OF MONSTER...
...ALCHEMY CAN CREATE?
CHILL
WE HAVE NO CHOICE.
I'M GOING TO KILL IT.
WAIT! A LIVE HOMUNCULUS IS JUST WHAT WE WANTED, RIGHT!?
OUR SURVIVAL GETS PRIORITY.
PLUS, IT KNOWS OUR NAMES AND FACES.

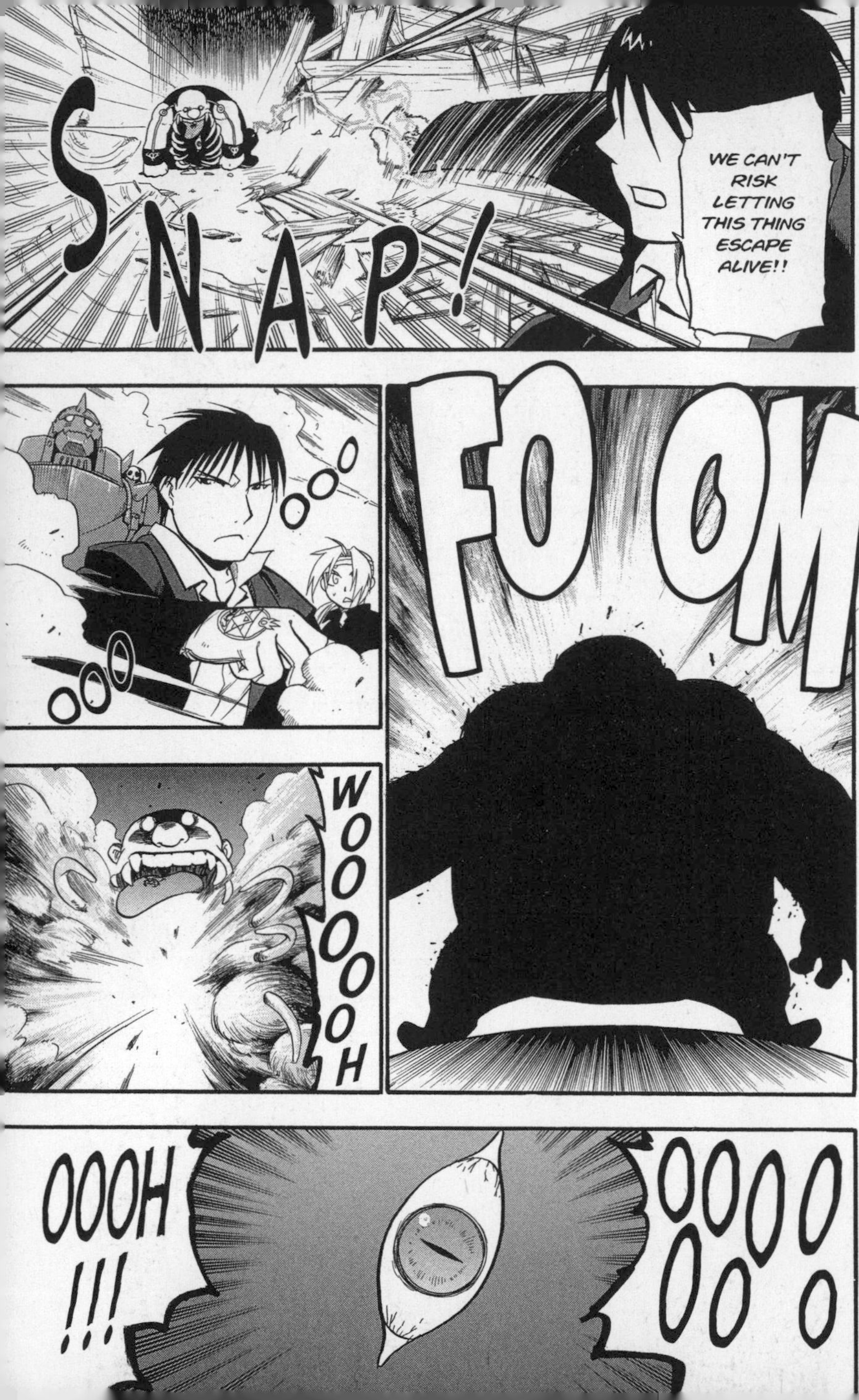
WE CAN'T RISK LETTING THIS THING ESCAPE ALIVE!!
SNAP!
FOOM
WOOOOOOH
OOOOOOOOOOO
OOOH!!!

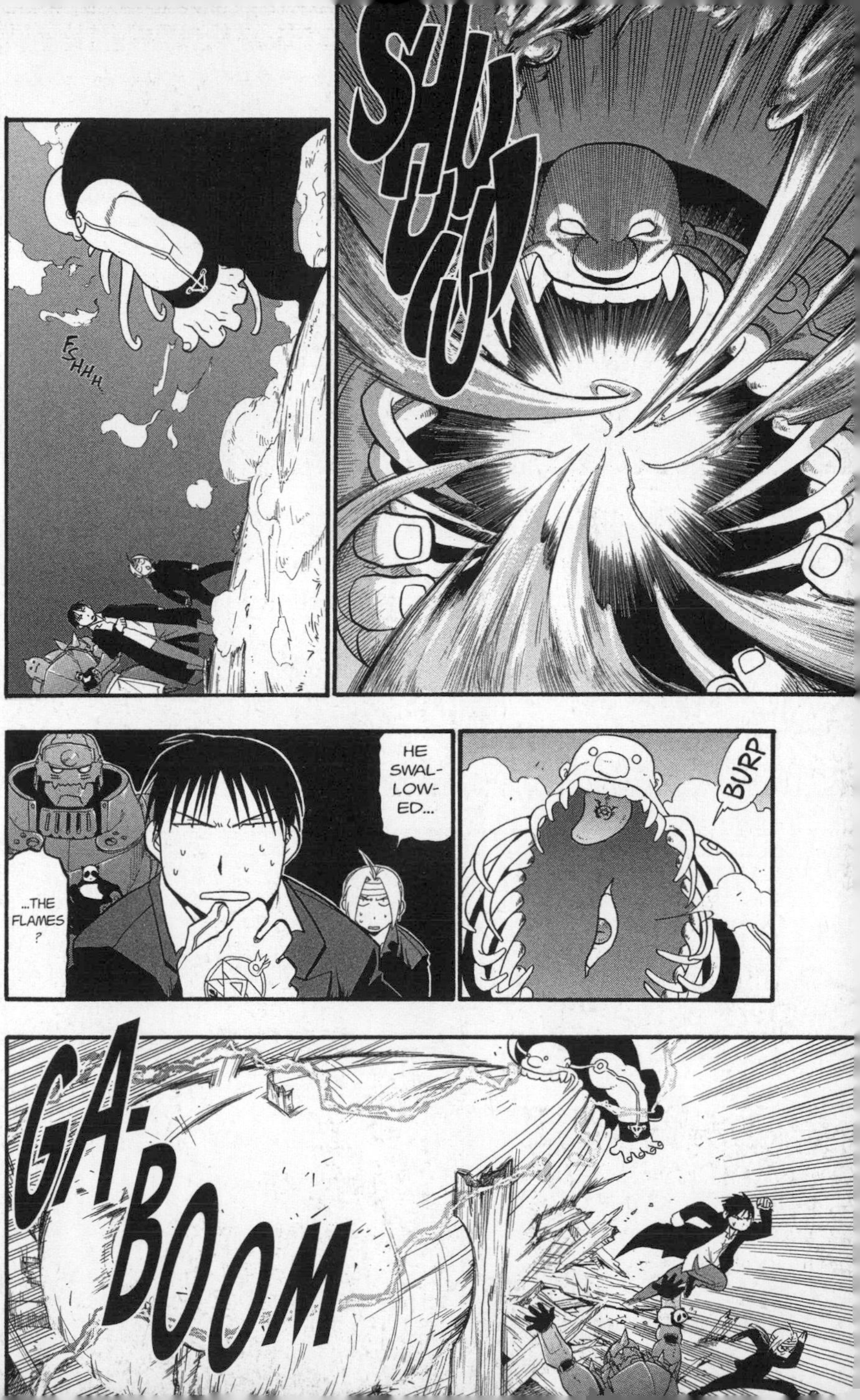
SHLUUUP
FSHHH
BURP
HE SWALLOWED...
...THE FLAMES?
GA-BOOM

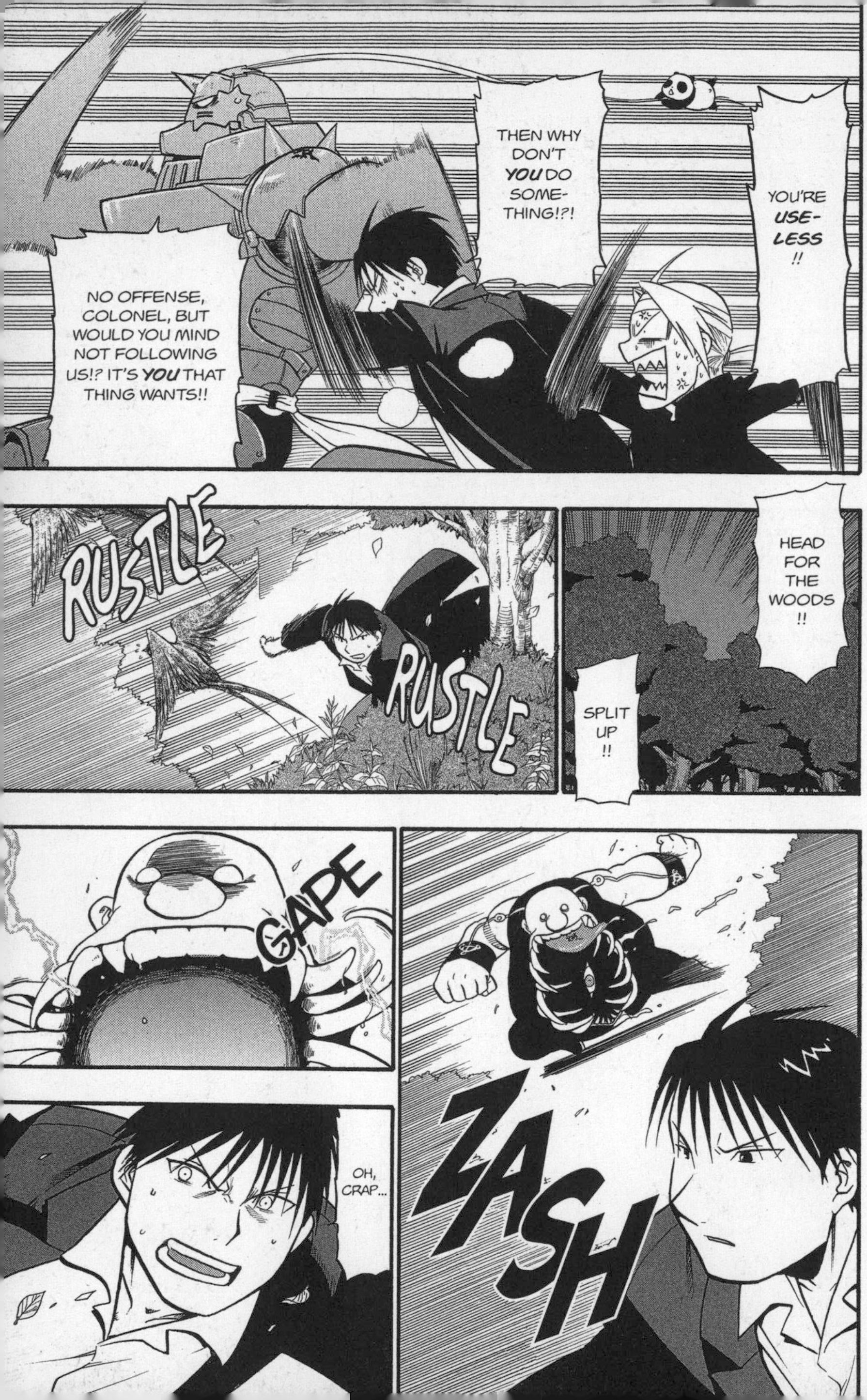
YOU'RE USE-LESS!!
THEN WHY DON'T YOU DO SOME-THING!?!
NO OFFENSE, COLONEL, BUT WOULD YOU MIND NOT FOLLOWING US!? IT'S YOU THAT THING WANTS!!
HEAD FOR THE WOODS!!
SPLIT UP!!
RUSTLE
RUSTLE
ZASH
GAPE
OH, CRAP...

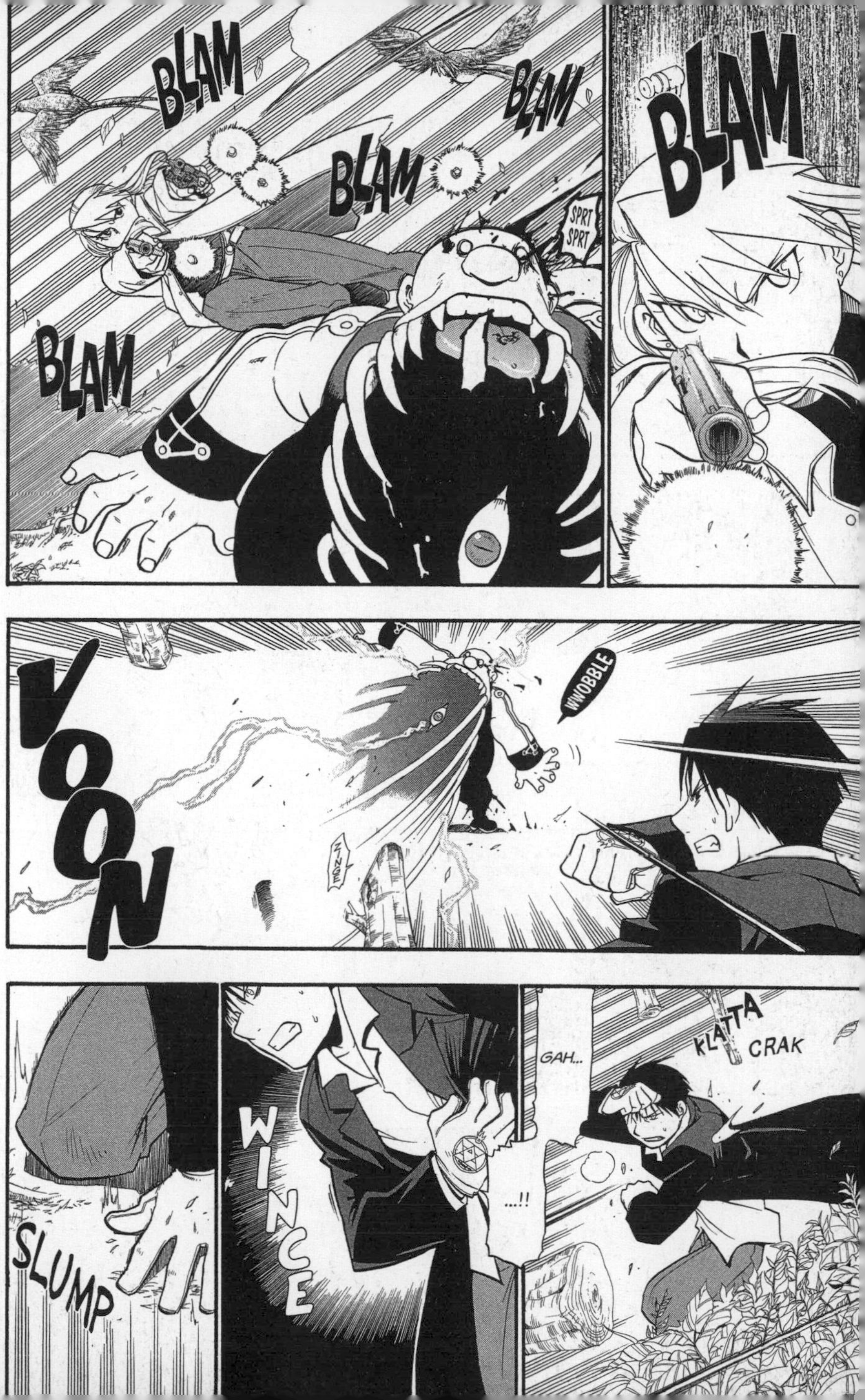
BLAM
BLAM
BLAM
BLAM
SPRT SPRT
BLAM
WWOBBLE
ZINGE
VOON
KLATTA
CRAK
GAH...
...!!
WINCE
SLUMP

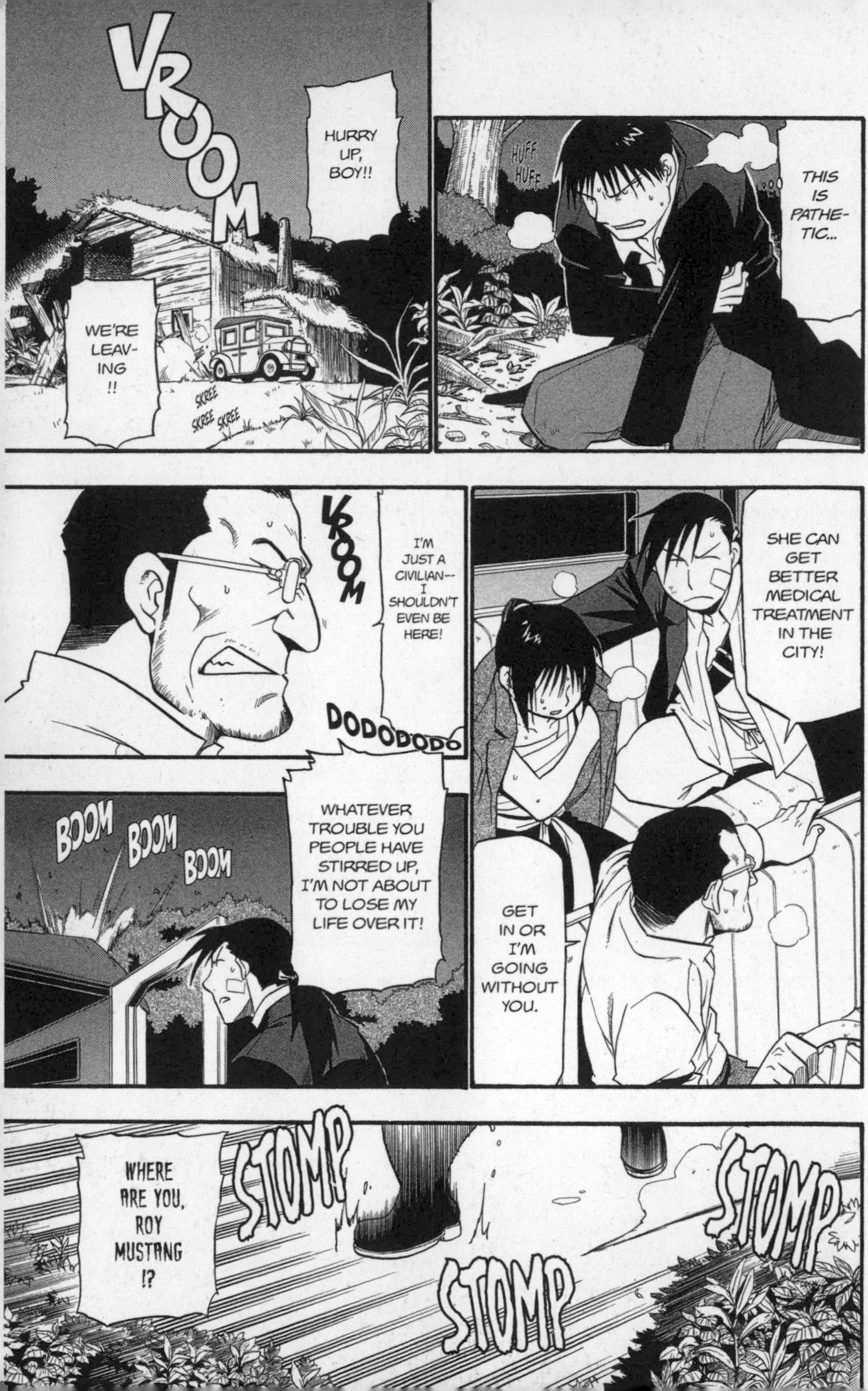
HUFF HUFF
THIS IS PATHETIC...
VROOM
HURRY UP, BOY!!
WE'RE LEAVING!!
SKREE SKREE SKREE
SHE CAN GET BETTER MEDICAL TREATMENT IN THE CITY!
GET IN OR I'M GOING WITHOUT YOU.
VROOM
I'M JUST A CIVILIAN-- I SHOULDN'T EVEN BE HERE!
DODODODO
WHATEVER TROUBLE YOU PEOPLE HAVE STIRRED UP, I'M NOT ABOUT TO LOSE MY LIFE OVER IT!
BOOM BOOM BOOM
STOMP
STOMP
STOMP
WHERE ARE YOU, ROY MUSTANG!?

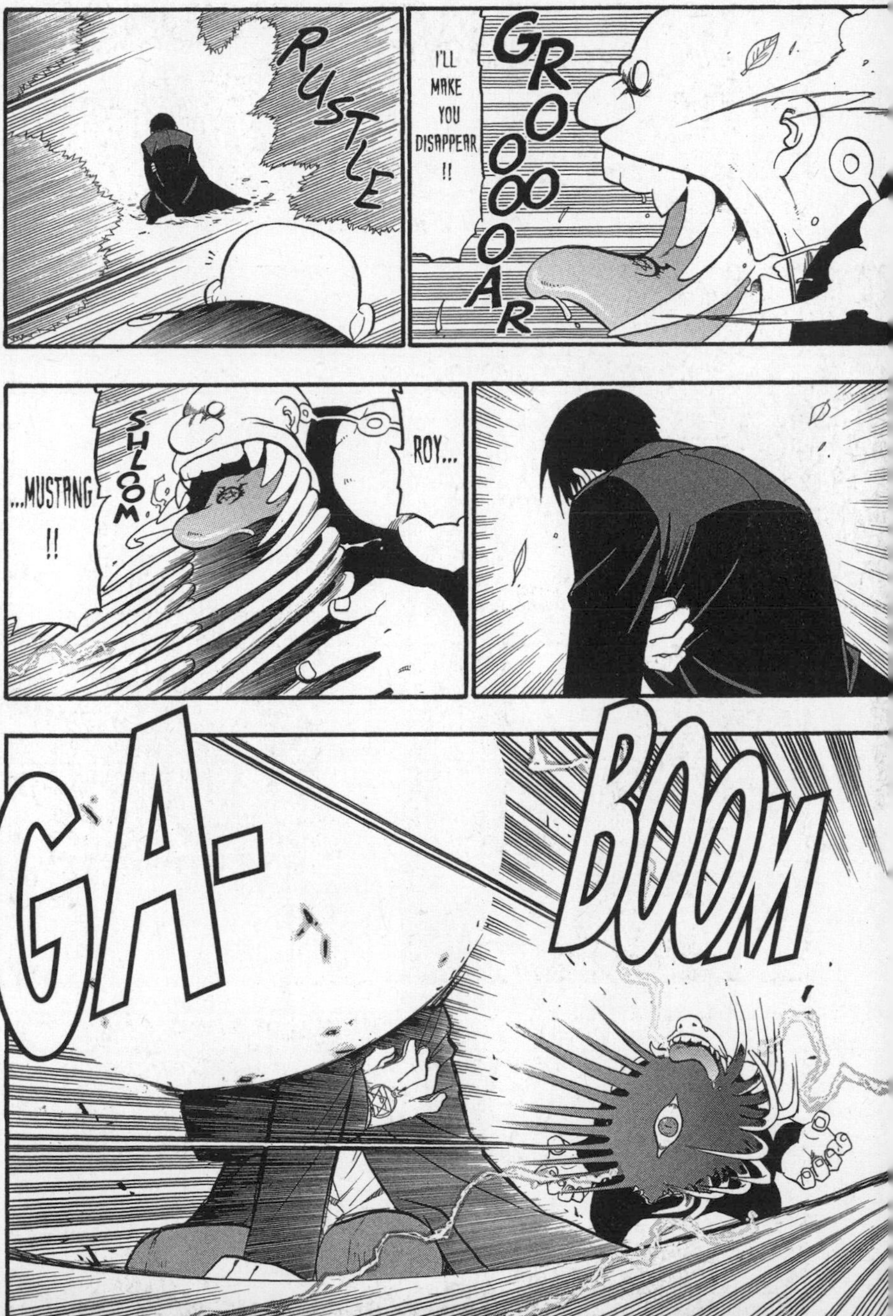
GROOOOOOAR
I'LL MAKE YOU DISAPPEAR !!
RUSTLE
ROY...
SHLOOM
...MUSTANG !!
GA-BOOM

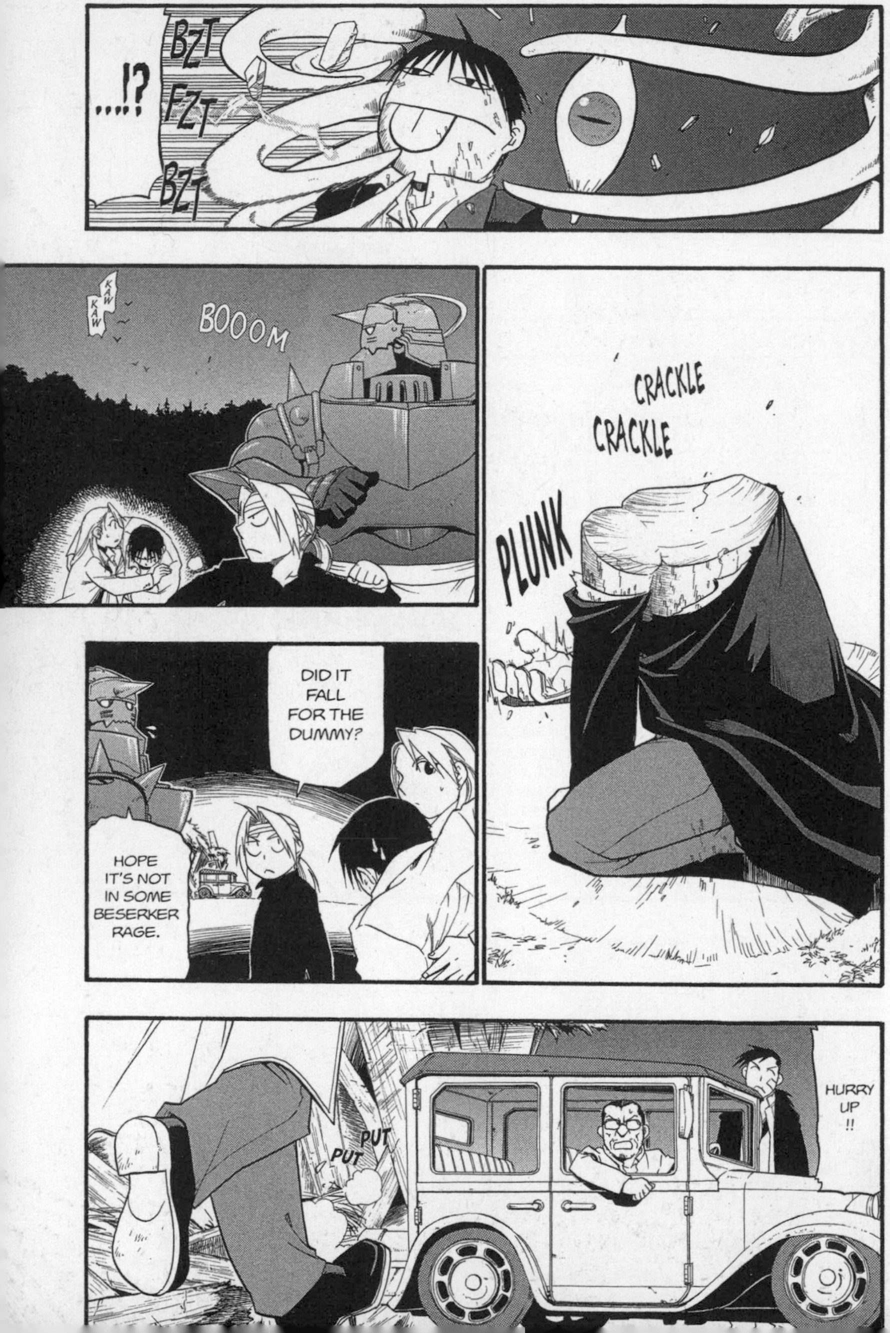
BZT
FZT
BZT
....!?
CRACKLE
CRACKLE
PLUNK
BOOOM
KAW KAW
DID IT FALL FOR THE DUMMY?
HOPE IT'S NOT IN SOME BESERKER RAGE.
HURRY UP !!
PUT PUT

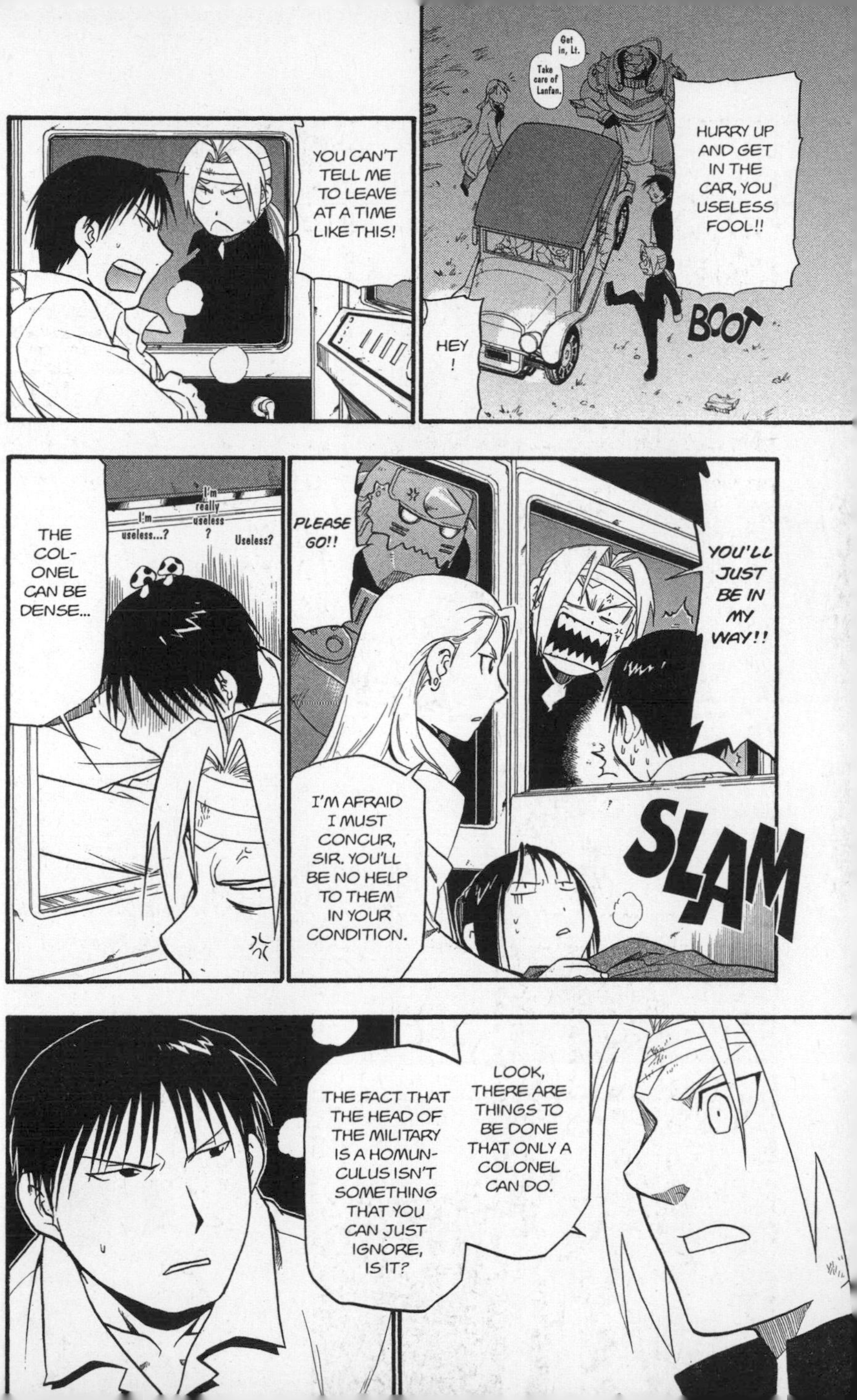
HURRY UP AND GET IN THE CAR, YOU USELESS FOOL!!
Get in, Lt.
Take care of Lanfan.
BOOT
HEY!
YOU CAN'T TELL ME TO LEAVE AT A TIME LIKE THIS!
YOU'LL JUST BE IN MY WAY!!
PLEASE GO!!
I'M AFRAID I MUST CONCUR, SIR. YOU'LL BE NO HELP TO THEM IN YOUR CONDITION.
SLAM
Useless?
I'm really useless?
I'm useless...?
THE COLONEL CAN BE DENSE...
LOOK, THERE ARE THINGS TO BE DONE THAT ONLY A COLONEL CAN DO.
THE FACT THAT THE HEAD OF THE MILITARY IS A HOMUNCULUS ISN'T SOMETHING THAT YOU CAN JUST IGNORE, IS IT?

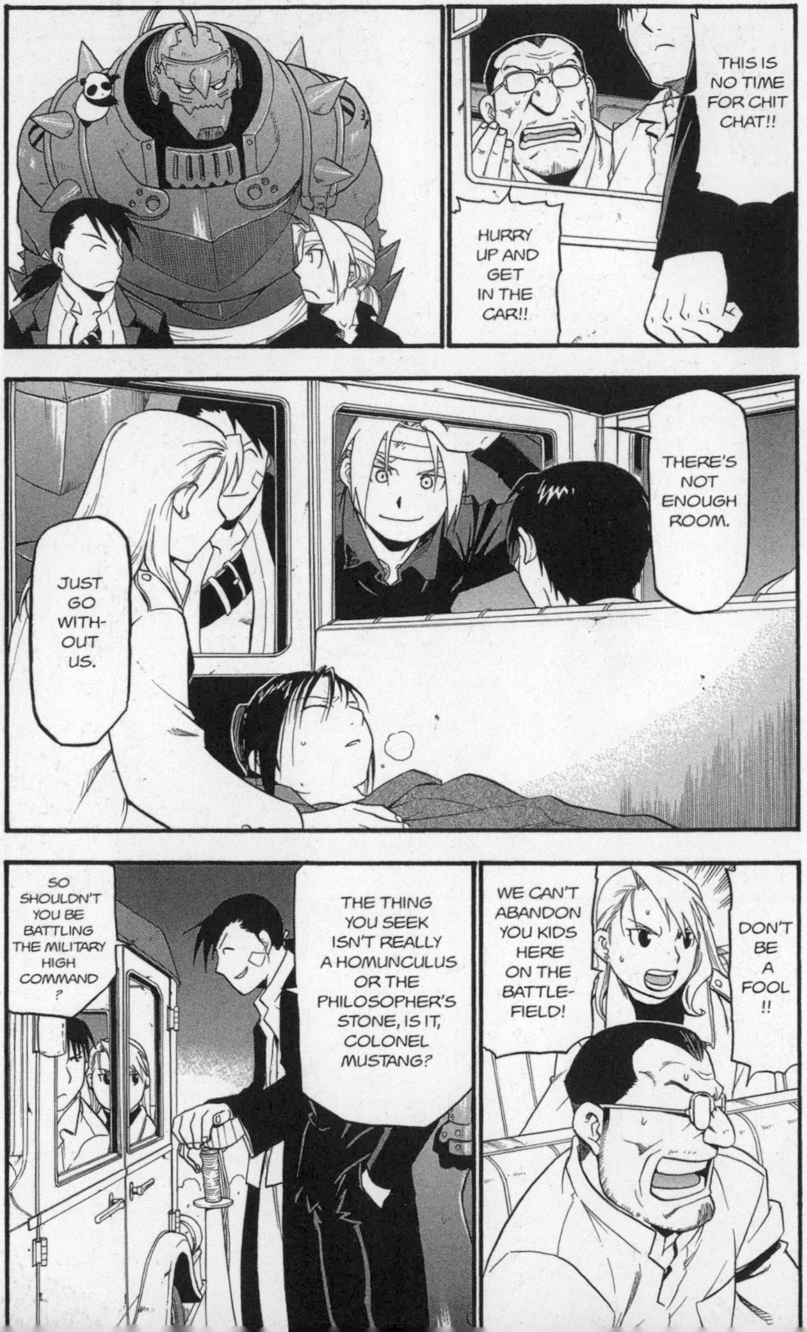
THIS IS NO TIME FOR CHIT CHAT!!
HURRY UP AND GET IN THE CAR!!
THERE'S NOT ENOUGH ROOM.
JUST GO WITH-OUT US.
DON'T BE A FOOL!!
WE CAN'T ABANDON YOU KIDS HERE ON THE BATTLE-FIELD!
THE THING YOU SEEK ISN'T REALLY A HOMUNCULUS OR THE PHILOSOPHER'S STONE, IS IT, COLONEL MUSTANG?
SO SHOULDN'T YOU BE BATTLING THE MILITARY HIGH COMMAND?

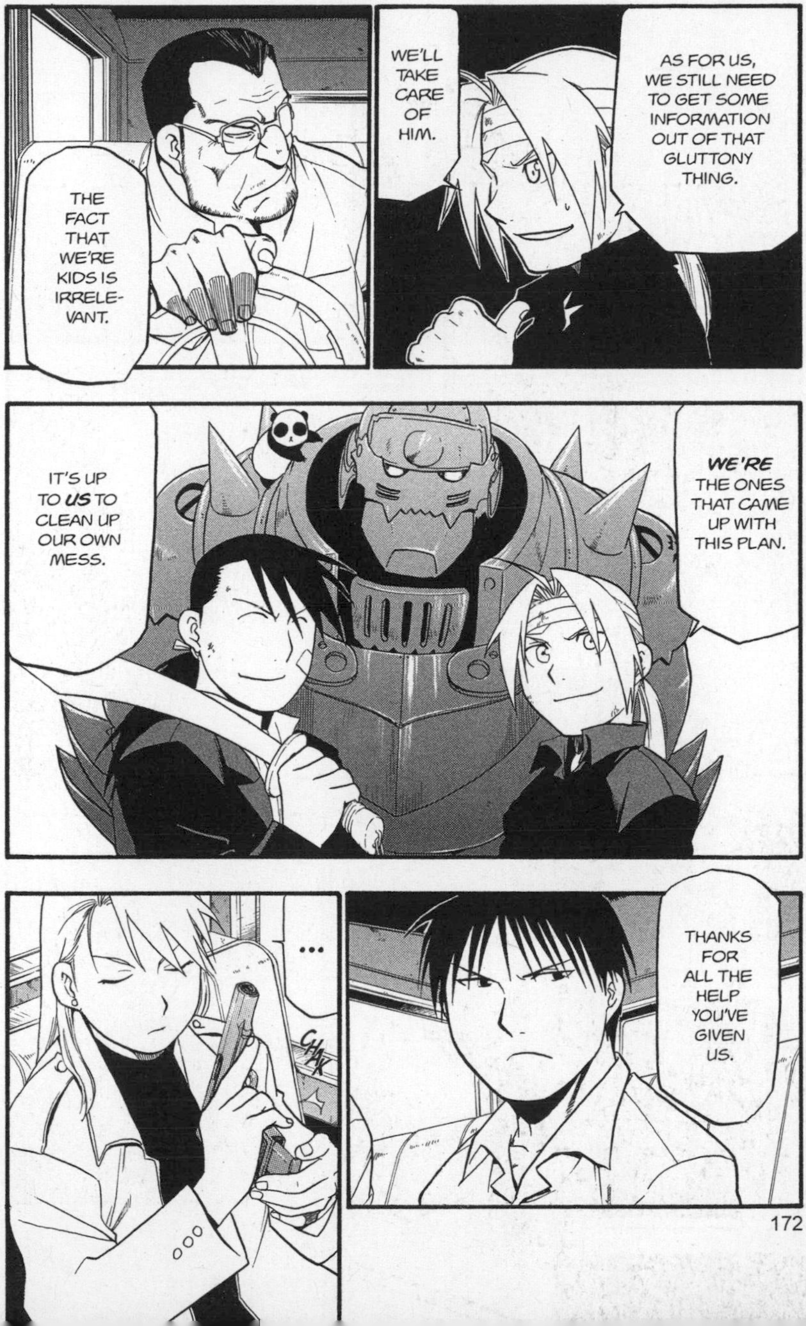
AS FOR US, WE STILL NEED TO GET SOME INFORMATION OUT OF THAT GLUTTONY THING.
WE'LL TAKE CARE OF HIM.
THE FACT THAT WE'RE KIDS IS IRRELE-VANT.
WE'RE THE ONES THAT CAME UP WITH THIS PLAN.
IT'S UP TO *US* TO CLEAN UP OUR OWN MESS.
THANKS FOR ALL THE HELP YOU'VE GIVEN US.
...
CHAK

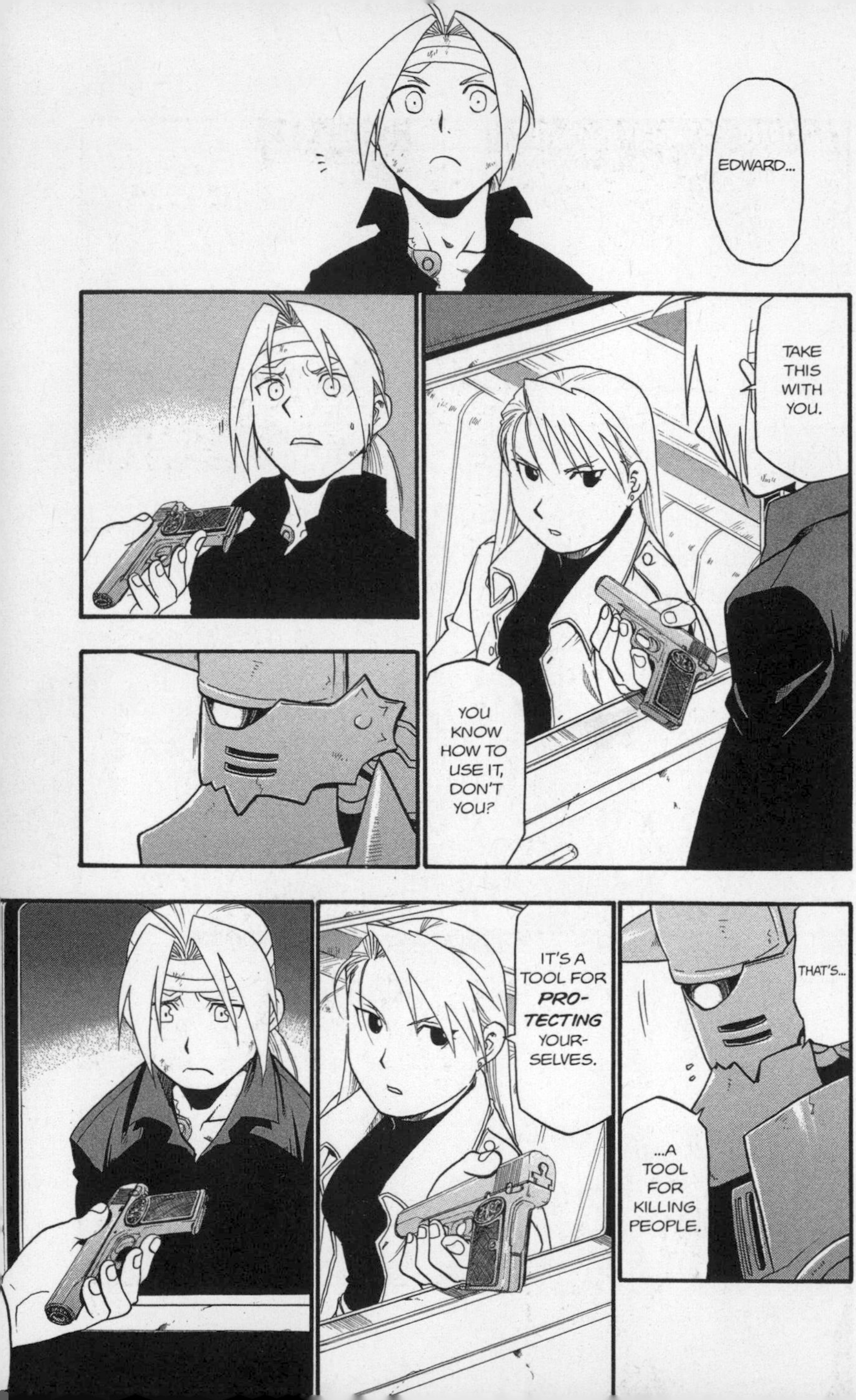
EDWARD...
TAKE THIS WITH YOU.
YOU KNOW HOW TO USE IT, DON'T YOU?
THAT'S...
...A TOOL FOR KILLING PEOPLE.
IT'S A TOOL FOR PROTECTING YOURSELVES.

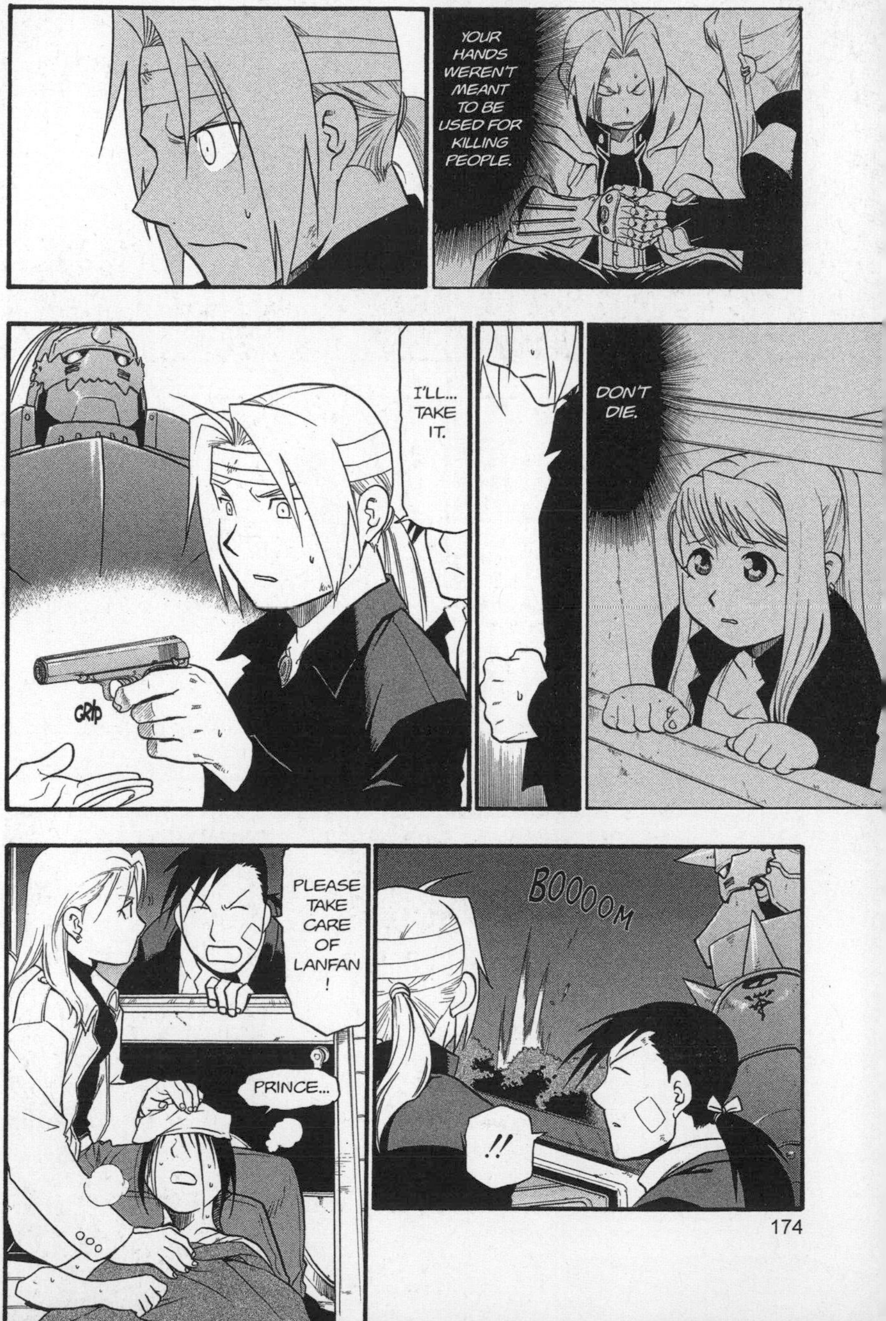
YOUR HANDS WEREN'T MEANT TO BE USED FOR KILLING PEOPLE.
DON'T DIE.
I'LL... TAKE IT.
GRIP
BOOOOM
!!
PLEASE TAKE CARE OF LANFAN!
PRINCE...

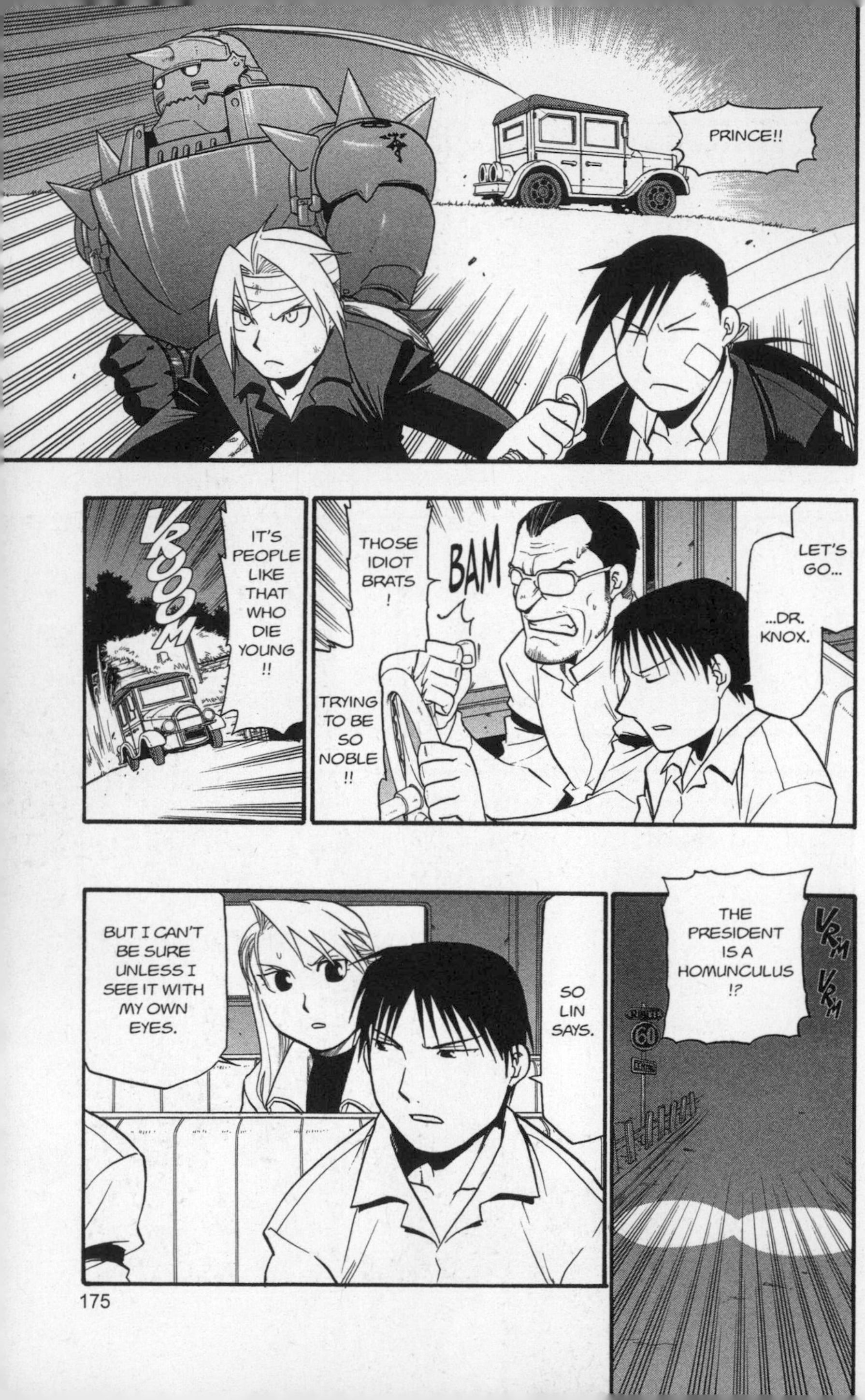
PRINCE!!
LET'S GO...
...DR. KNOX.
BAM
THOSE IDIOT BRATS!
TRYING TO BE SO NOBLE!!
VROOOM
IT'S PEOPLE LIKE THAT WHO DIE YOUNG!!
THE PRESIDENT IS A HOMUNCULUS!?
VRM VRM
SO LIN SAYS.
BUT I CAN'T BE SURE UNLESS I SEE IT WITH MY OWN EYES.

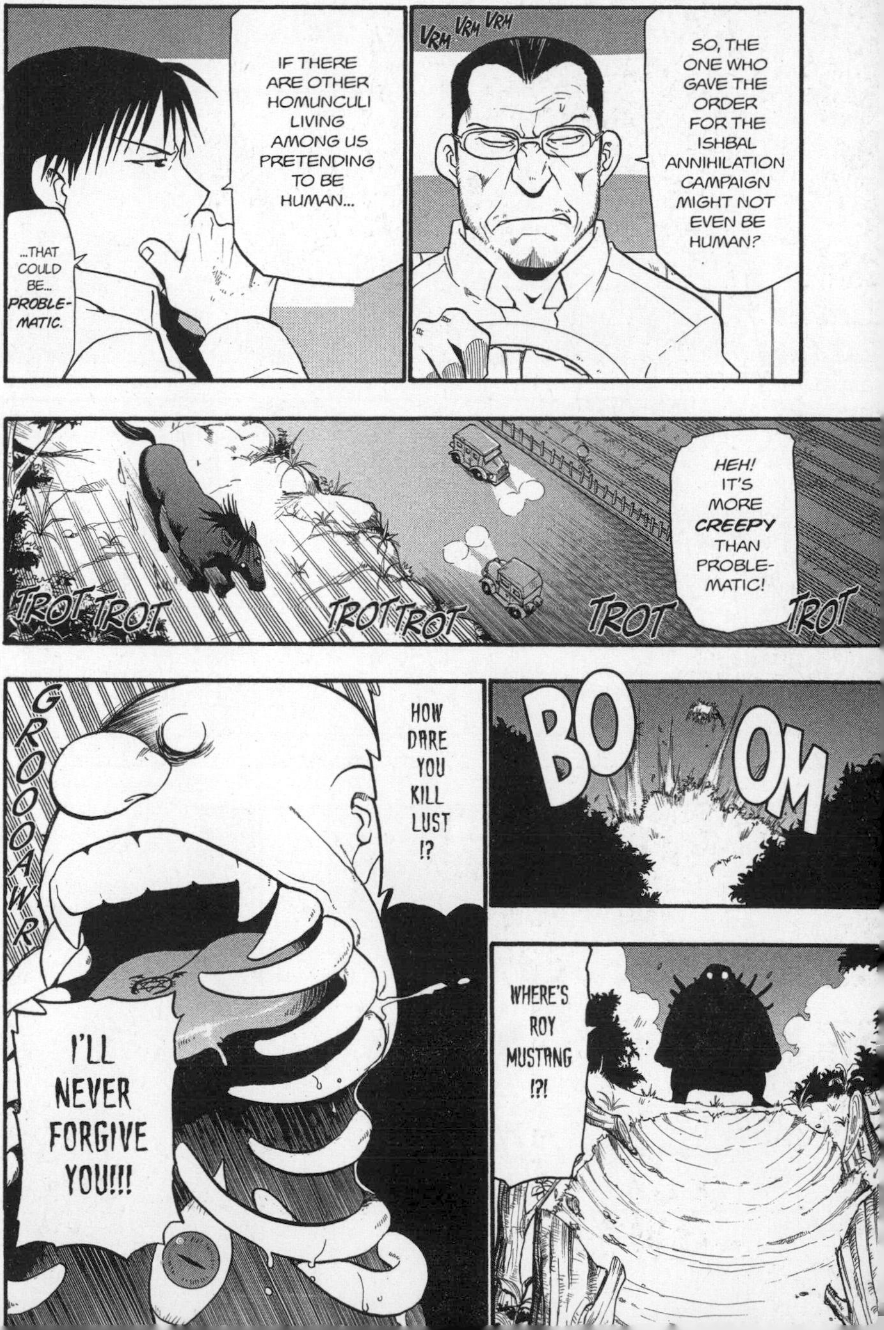
VRM VRM VRM
SO, THE ONE WHO GAVE THE ORDER FOR THE ISHBAL ANNIHILATION CAMPAIGN MIGHT NOT EVEN BE HUMAN?
IF THERE ARE OTHER HOMUNCULI LIVING AMONG US PRETENDING TO BE HUMAN...
...THAT COULD BE... PROBLEMATIC.
HEH! IT'S MORE CREEPY THAN PROBLEMATIC!
TROT TROT TROT TROT TROT TROT
BOOM
WHERE'S ROY MUSTANG !?!
HOW DARE YOU KILL LUST !?
GROOOAWR
I'LL NEVER FORGIVE YOU!!!

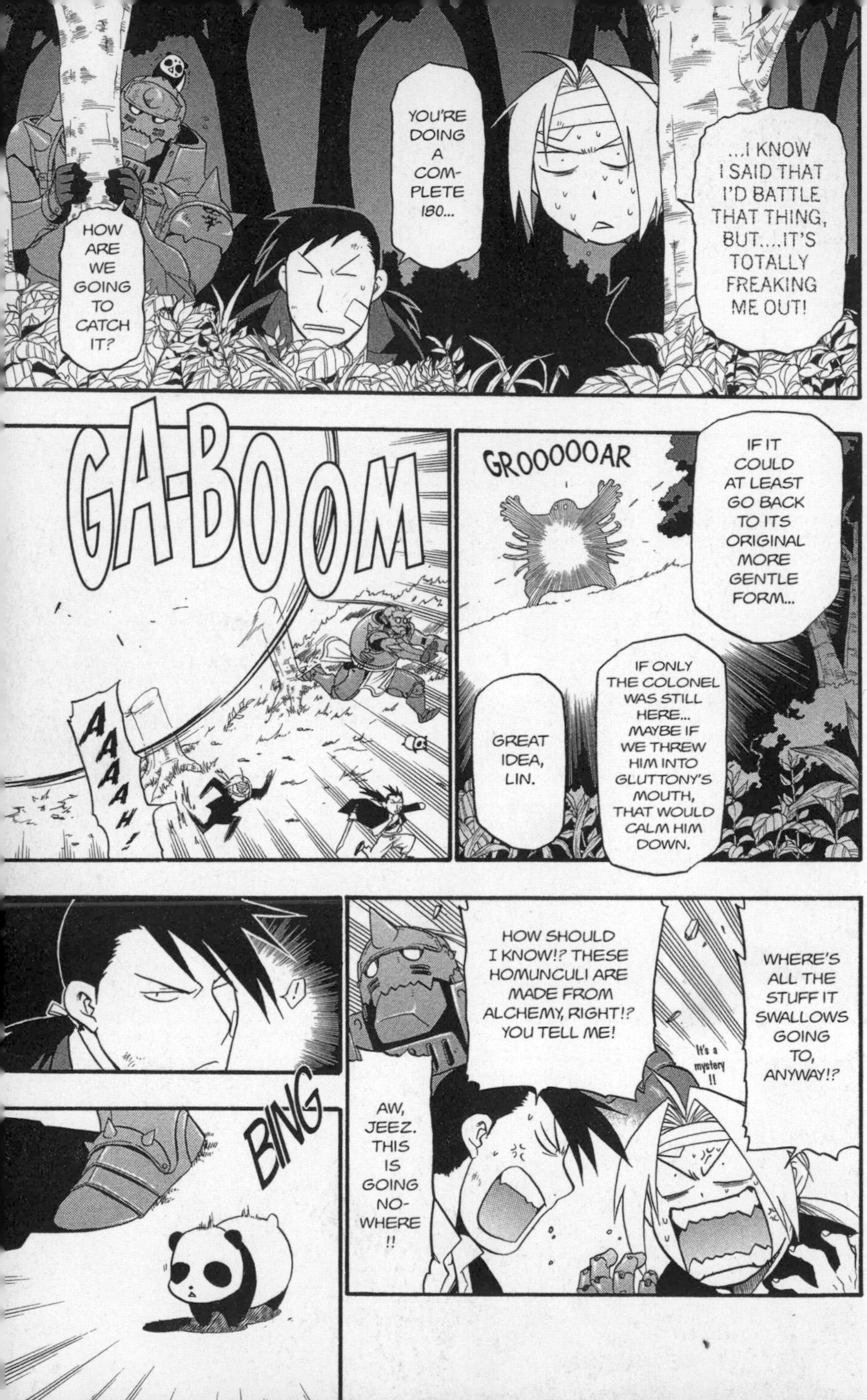
...I KNOW I SAID THAT I'D BATTLE THAT THING, BUT....IT'S TOTALLY FREAKING ME OUT!
YOU'RE DOING A COMPLETE 180...
HOW ARE WE GOING TO CATCH IT?
IF IT COULD AT LEAST GO BACK TO ITS ORIGINAL MORE GENTLE FORM...
GROOOOOAR
IF ONLY THE COLONEL WAS STILL HERE... MAYBE IF WE THREW HIM INTO GLUTTONY'S MOUTH, THAT WOULD CALM HIM DOWN.
GREAT IDEA, LIN.
GA-BOOM
AAAAAH!
WHERE'S ALL THE STUFF IT SWALLOWS GOING TO, ANYWAY!?
HOW SHOULD I KNOW!? THESE HOMUNCULI ARE MADE FROM ALCHEMY, RIGHT!? YOU TELL ME!
It's a mystery !!
AW, JEEZ. THIS IS GOING NOWHERE !!
!
BING

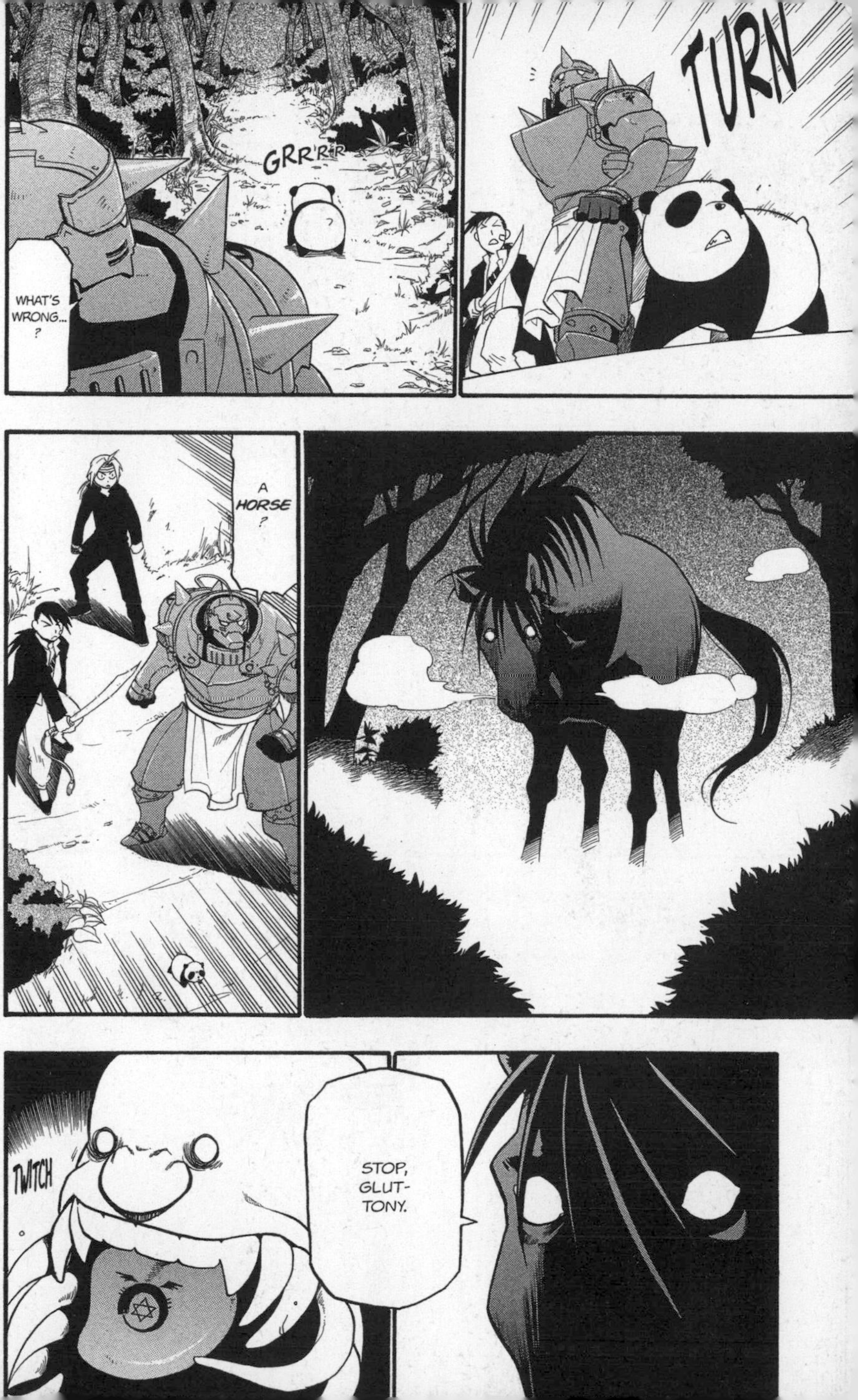
TURN
GRR'R'R
WHAT'S WRONG...?
A HORSE?
STOP, GLUT-TONY.
TWITCH

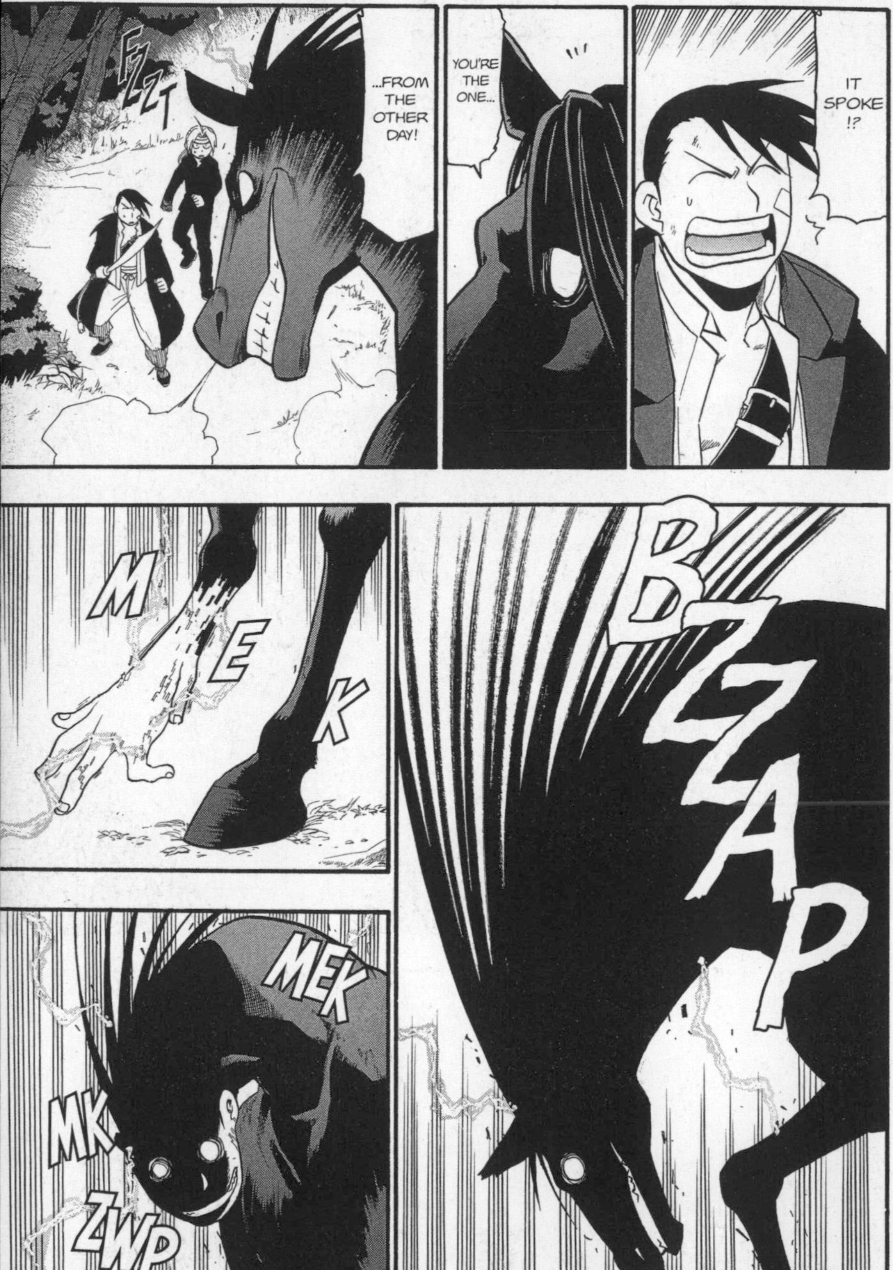
IT SPOKE !?
YOU'RE THE ONE...
...FROM THE OTHER DAY!
FZZT
BZZAP
MEEK
MEK
MK
ZWP

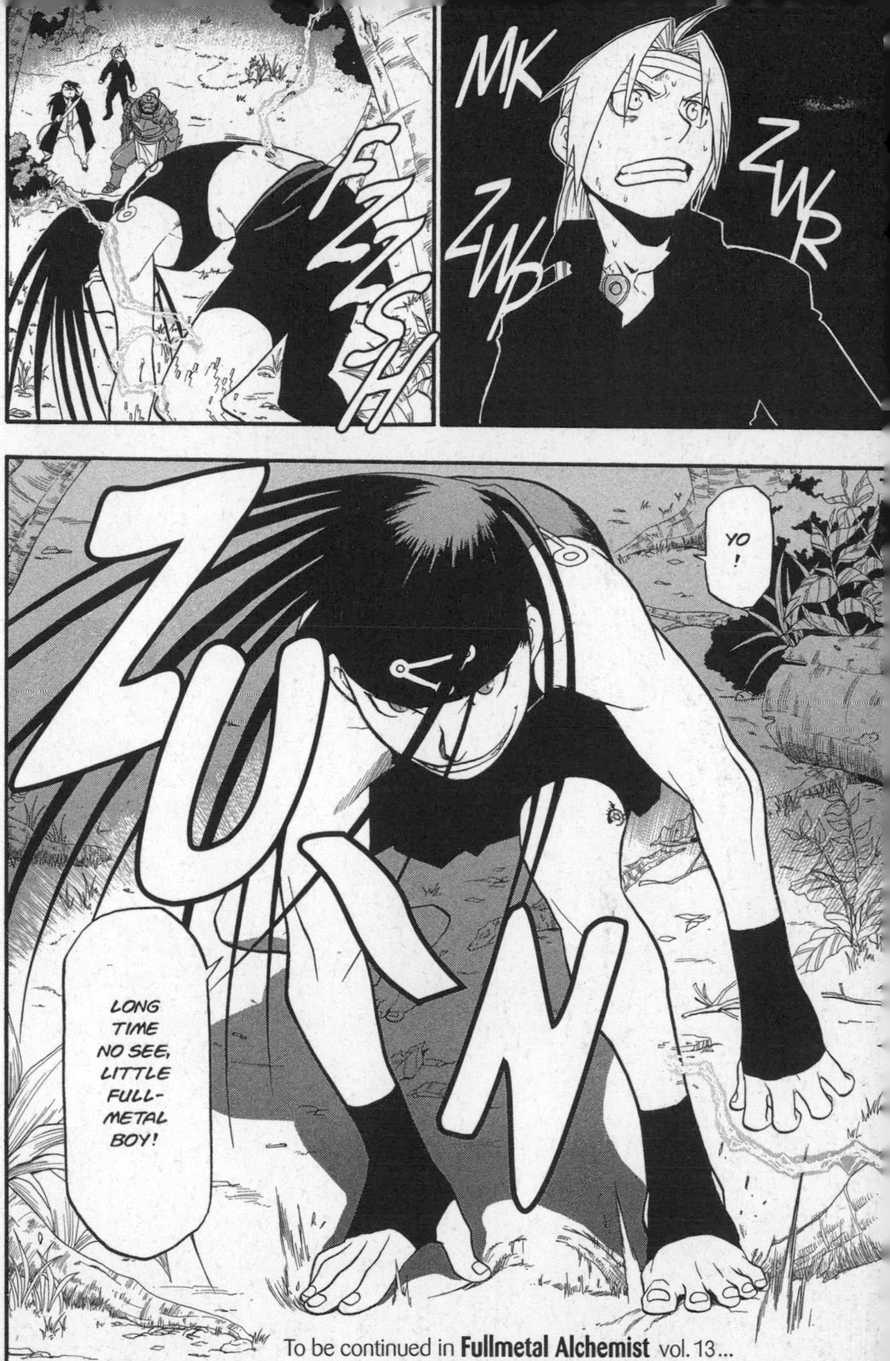
MK
ZWR
ZWP
FZZZSH
YO!
LONG TIME NO SEE, LITTLE FULL-METAL BOY!

To be continued in **Fullmetal Alchemist** vol. 13...

FULLMETAL
ALCHEMIST

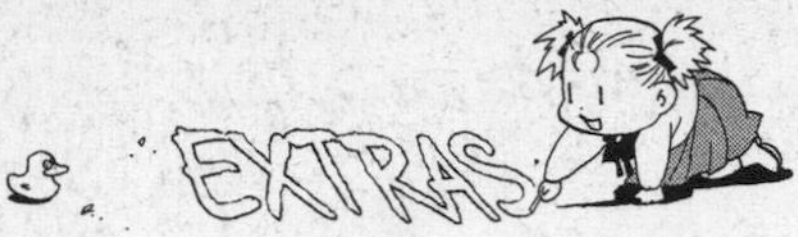
EXTRAS

Fake preview of next volume.

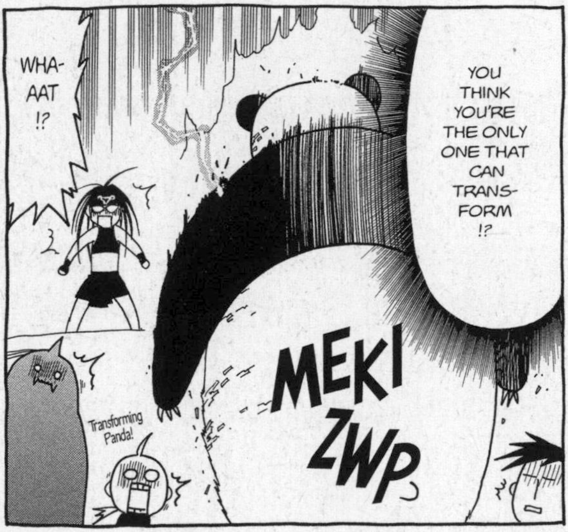
YOU THINK YOU'RE THE ONLY ONE THAT CAN TRANS-FORM !?
WHA-AAT !?
MEKI
ZWP
Transforming Panda!

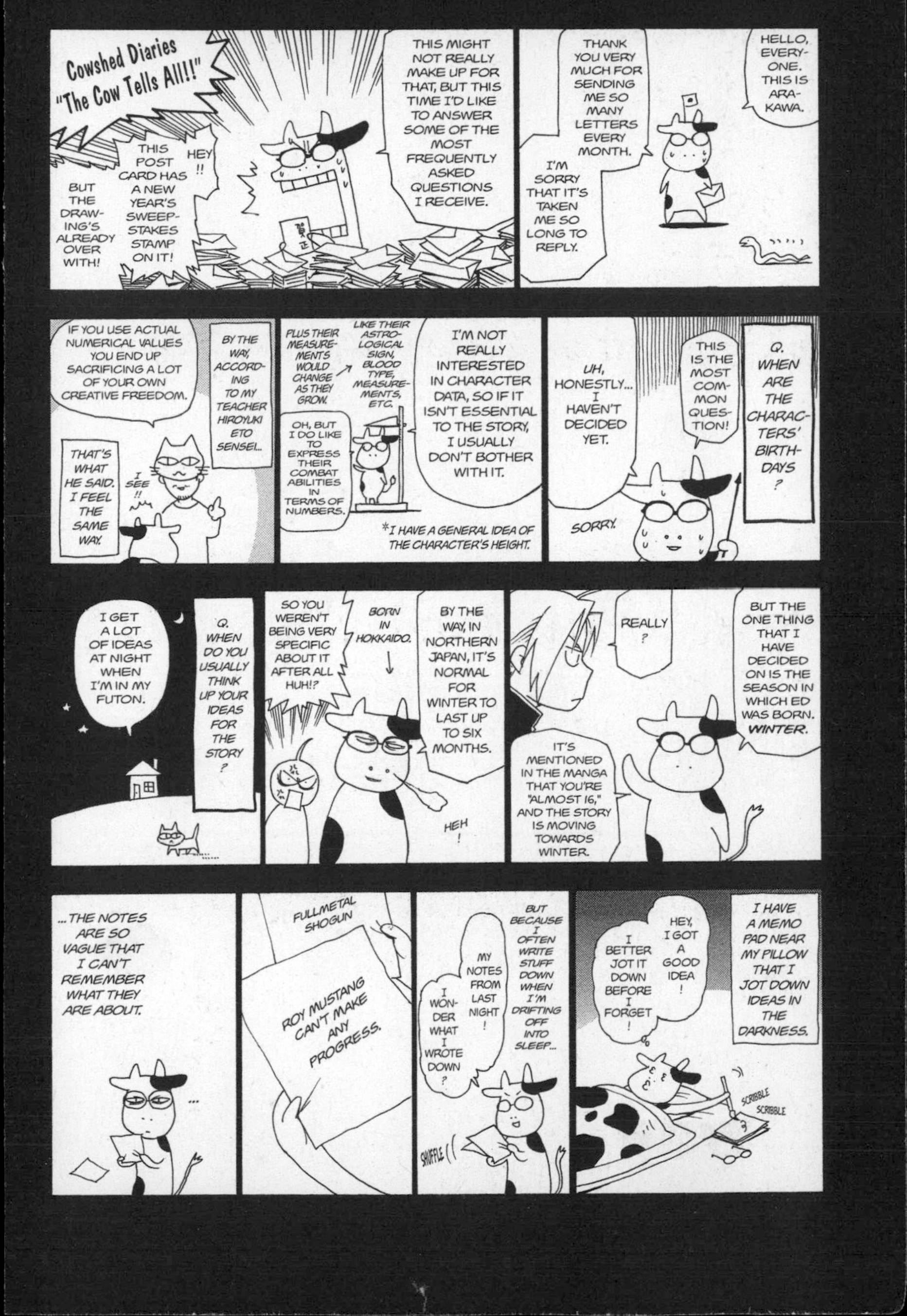
Cowshed Diaries "The Cow Tells All!!"
HELLO, EVERYONE. THIS IS ARAKAWA.
THANK YOU VERY MUCH FOR SENDING ME SO MANY LETTERS EVERY MONTH.
I'M SORRY THAT IT'S TAKEN ME SO LONG TO REPLY.
THIS MIGHT NOT REALLY MAKE UP FOR THAT, BUT THIS TIME I'D LIKE TO ANSWER SOME OF THE MOST FREQUENTLY ASKED QUESTIONS I RECEIVE.
HEY!!
THIS POST CARD HAS A NEW YEAR'S SWEEPSTAKES STAMP ON IT!
BUT THE DRAWING'S ALREADY OVER WITH!
Q. WHEN ARE THE CHARACTERS' BIRTHDAYS?
THIS IS THE MOST COMMON QUESTION!
UH, HONESTLY... I HAVEN'T DECIDED YET.
SORRY.
I'M NOT REALLY INTERESTED IN CHARACTER DATA, SO IF IT ISN'T ESSENTIAL TO THE STORY, I USUALLY DON'T BOTHER WITH IT.
LIKE THEIR ASTROLOGICAL SIGN, BLOOD TYPE, MEASUREMENTS, ETC.
PLUS THEIR MEASUREMENTS WOULD CHANGE AS THEY GROW.
OH, BUT I DO LIKE TO EXPRESS THEIR COMBAT ABILITIES IN TERMS OF NUMBERS.
*I HAVE A GENERAL IDEA OF THE CHARACTER'S HEIGHT.
BY THE WAY, ACCORDING TO MY TEACHER HIROYUKI ETO SENSEI...
IF YOU USE ACTUAL NUMERICAL VALUES YOU END UP SACRIFICING A LOT OF YOUR OWN CREATIVE FREEDOM.
THAT'S WHAT HE SAID. I FEEL THE SAME WAY.
I SEE!!
BUT THE ONE THING THAT I HAVE DECIDED ON IS THE SEASON IN WHICH ED WAS BORN. WINTER.
REALLY?
IT'S MENTIONED IN THE MANGA THAT YOU'RE "ALMOST 16," AND THE STORY IS MOVING TOWARDS WINTER.
BY THE WAY, IN NORTHERN JAPAN, IT'S NORMAL FOR WINTER TO LAST UP TO SIX MONTHS.
BORN IN HOKKAIDO.
SO YOU WEREN'T BEING VERY SPECIFIC ABOUT IT AFTER ALL HUH!?
HEH!
Q. WHEN DO YOU USUALLY THINK UP YOUR IDEAS FOR THE STORY?
I GET A LOT OF IDEAS AT NIGHT WHEN I'M IN MY FUTON.
I HAVE A MEMO PAD NEAR MY PILLOW THAT I JOT DOWN IDEAS IN THE DARKNESS.
HEY, I GOT A GOOD IDEA!
I BETTER JOT IT DOWN BEFORE I FORGET!
SCRIBBLE SCRIBBLE
BUT BECAUSE I OFTEN WRITE STUFF DOWN WHEN I'M DRIFTING OFF INTO SLEEP...
MY NOTES FROM LAST NIGHT!
I WONDER WHAT I WROTE DOWN?
SHUFFLE
FULLMETAL SHOGUN
ROY MUSTANG CAN'T MAKE ANY PROGRESS.
...THE NOTES ARE SO VAGUE THAT I CAN'T REMEMBER WHAT THEY ARE ABOUT.
...

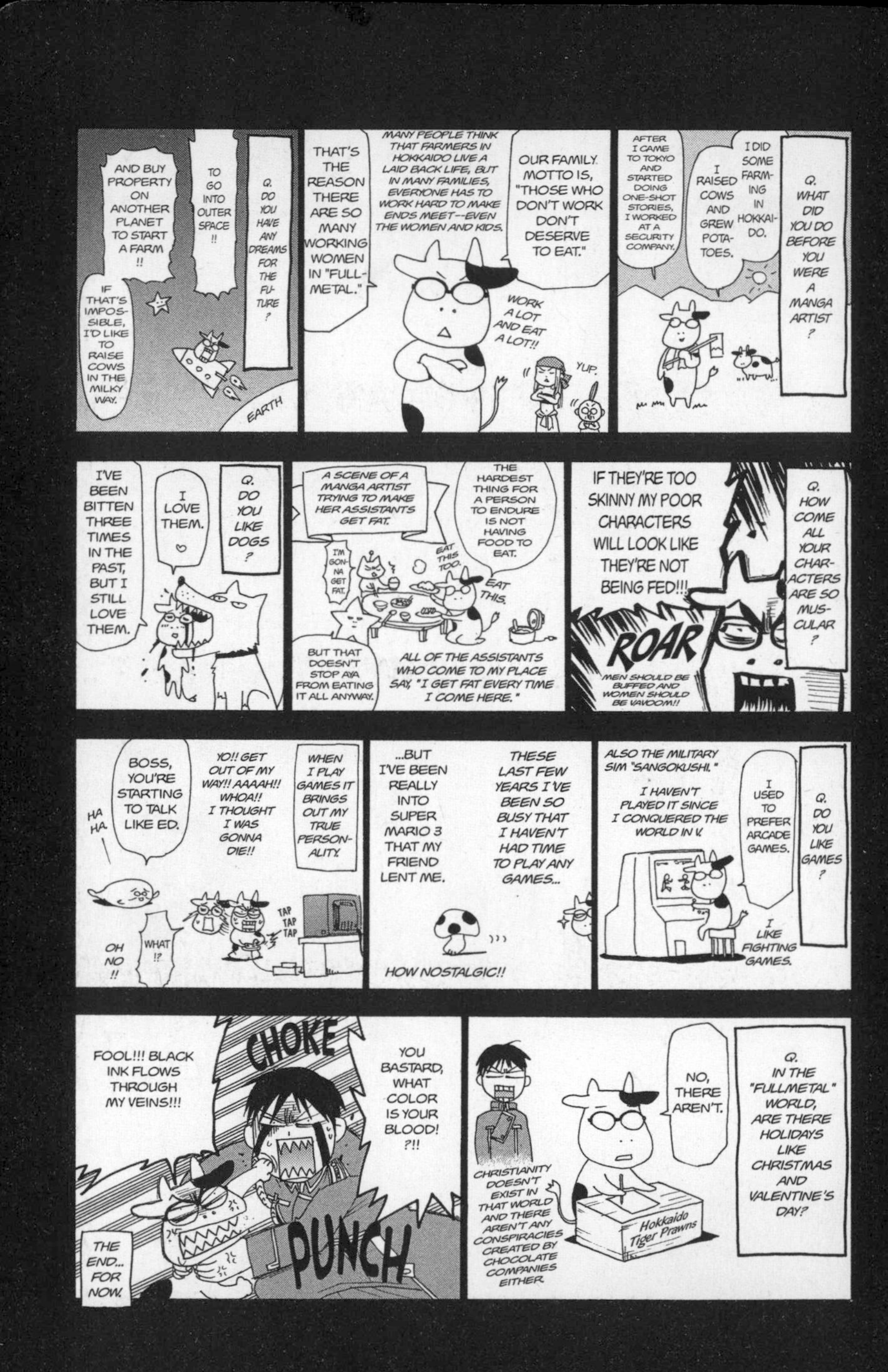
Q. WHAT DID YOU DO BEFORE YOU WERE A MANGA ARTIST?
I DID SOME FARMING IN HOKKAIDO.
I RAISED COWS AND GREW POTATOES.
AFTER I CAME TO TOKYO AND STARTED DOING ONE-SHOT STORIES, I WORKED AT A SECURITY COMPANY.
OUR FAMILY MOTTO IS, "THOSE WHO DON'T WORK DON'T DESERVE TO EAT."
MANY PEOPLE THINK THAT FARMERS IN HOKKAIDO LIVE A LAID BACK LIFE, BUT IN MANY FAMILIES, EVERYONE HAS TO WORK HARD TO MAKE ENDS MEET--EVEN THE WOMEN AND KIDS.
THAT'S THE REASON THERE ARE SO MANY WORKING WOMEN IN "FULLMETAL."
WORK A LOT AND EAT A LOT!!
YUP.
Q. DO YOU HAVE ANY DREAMS FOR THE FUTURE?
TO GO INTO OUTER SPACE!!
AND BUY PROPERTY ON ANOTHER PLANET TO START A FARM!!
IF THAT'S IMPOSSIBLE, I'D LIKE TO RAISE COWS IN THE MILKY WAY.
EARTH
Q. HOW COME ALL YOUR CHARACTERS ARE SO MUSCULAR?
IF THEY'RE TOO SKINNY MY POOR CHARACTERS WILL LOOK LIKE THEY'RE NOT BEING FED!!!
ROAR
MEN SHOULD BE BUFFED AND WOMEN SHOULD BE VAVOOM!!
THE HARDEST THING FOR A PERSON TO ENDURE IS NOT HAVING FOOD TO EAT.
A SCENE OF A MANGA ARTIST TRYING TO MAKE HER ASSISTANTS GET FAT.
EAT THIS TOO.
I'M GONNA GET FAT.
EAT THIS.
ALL OF THE ASSISTANTS WHO COME TO MY PLACE SAY, "I GET FAT EVERY TIME I COME HERE."
BUT THAT DOESN'T STOP AYA FROM EATING IT ALL ANYWAY.
Q. DO YOU LIKE DOGS?
I LOVE THEM.
I'VE BEEN BITTEN THREE TIMES IN THE PAST, BUT I STILL LOVE THEM.
Q. DO YOU LIKE GAMES?
I USED TO PREFER ARCADE GAMES.
ALSO THE MILITARY SIM "SANGOKUSHI."
I HAVEN'T PLAYED IT SINCE I CONQUERED THE WORLD IN V.
I LIKE FIGHTING GAMES.
THESE LAST FEW YEARS I'VE BEEN SO BUSY THAT I HAVEN'T HAD TIME TO PLAY ANY GAMES...
...BUT I'VE BEEN REALLY INTO SUPER MARIO 3 THAT MY FRIEND LENT ME.
HOW NOSTALGIC!!
WHEN I PLAY GAMES IT BRINGS OUT MY TRUE PERSONALITY.
YO!! GET OUT OF MY WAY!! AAAAH!! WHOA!! I THOUGHT I WAS GONNA DIE!!
BOSS, YOU'RE STARTING TO TALK LIKE ED.
HA HA
TAP TAP TAP
WHAT!?
OH NO!!
Q. IN THE "FULLMETAL" WORLD, ARE THERE HOLIDAYS LIKE CHRISTMAS AND VALENTINE'S DAY?
NO, THERE AREN'T.
CHRISTIANITY DOESN'T EXIST IN THAT WORLD AND THERE AREN'T ANY CONSPIRACIES CREATED BY CHOCOLATE COMPANIES EITHER.
Hokkaido Tiger Prawns
YOU BASTARD, WHAT COLOR IS YOUR BLOOD!?!!
CHOKE
FOOL!!! BLACK INK FLOWS THROUGH MY VEINS!!!
PUNCH
THE END... FOR NOW.

Anti-Homunculus Secret Weapon!

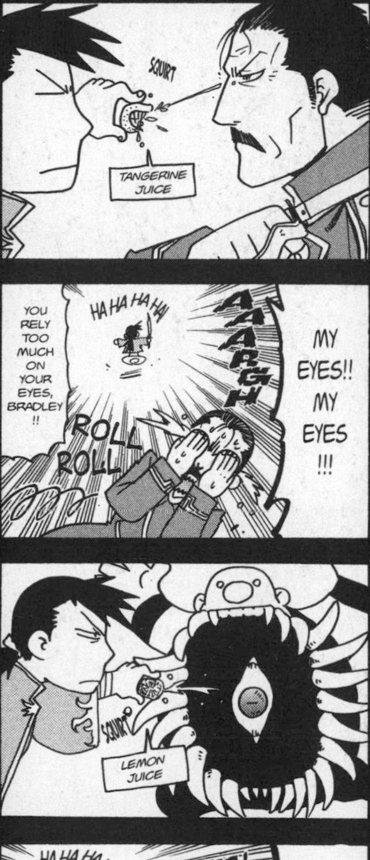
SQUIRT
TANGERINE JUICE
MY EYES!! MY EYES!!!
AAAARGH
HA HA HA HA!
YOU RELY TOO MUCH ON YOUR EYES, BRADLEY!!
ROLL ROLL
SQUIRT
LEMON JUICE
MY EYE!! MY EYE!!!
OWIEEE!
HA HA HA HA!
ROLL ROLL

STOP IT...

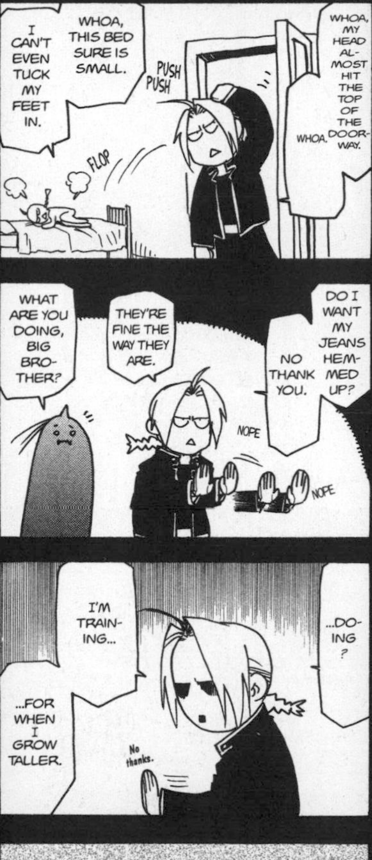
WHOA, MY HEAD ALMOST HIT THE TOP OF THE DOORWAY.
WHOA.
PUSH PUSH
WHOA, THIS BED SURE IS SMALL.
I CAN'T EVEN TUCK MY FEET IN.
FLOP
DO I WANT MY JEANS HEMMED UP?
NO THANK YOU.
THEY'RE FINE THE WAY THEY ARE.
WHAT ARE YOU DOING, BIG BROTHER?
NOPE
NOPE
...DOING?
I'M TRAINING...
...FOR WHEN I GROW TALLER.
No thanks.

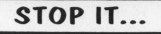

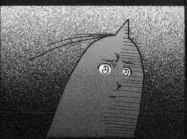

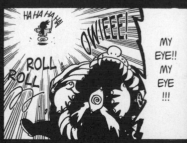

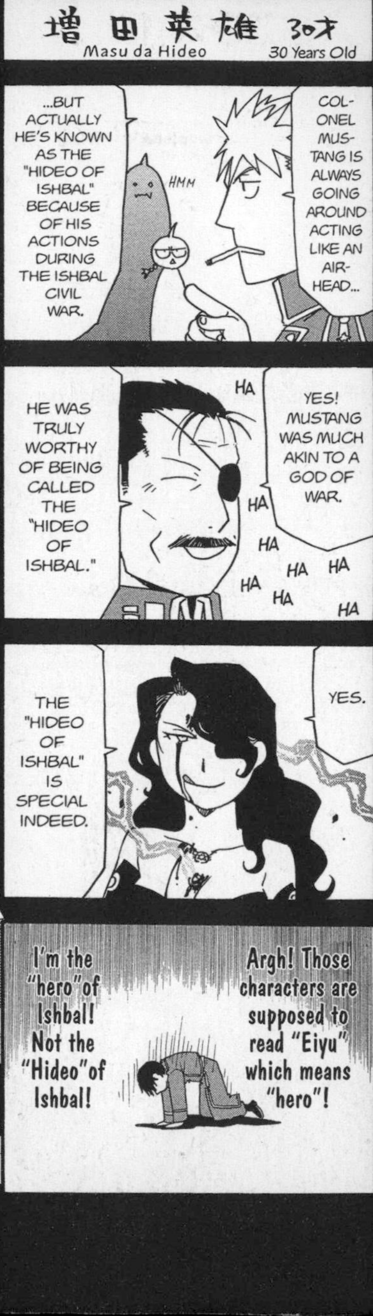
増田英雄 30才
Masu da Hideo
30 Years Old
COLONEL MUSTANG IS ALWAYS GOING AROUND ACTING LIKE AN AIR-HEAD...
...BUT ACTUALLY HE'S KNOWN AS THE "HIDEO OF ISHBAL" BECAUSE OF HIS ACTIONS DURING THE ISHBAL CIVIL WAR.
HMM
YES! MUSTANG WAS MUCH AKIN TO A GOD OF WAR.
HE WAS TRULY WORTHY OF BEING CALLED THE "HIDEO OF ISHBAL."
HA HA HA HA HA HA HA HA
YES.
THE "HIDEO OF ISHBAL" IS SPECIAL INDEED.
Argh! Those characters are supposed to read "Eiyu" which means "hero"!
I'm the "hero" of Ishbal! Not the "Hideo" of Ishbal!

FULLMETAL ALCHEMIST 12

SPECIAL THANKS

KEISUI TAKAEDA-SAN

SANKICHI HINODEYA-SAN

JUN TOKO-SAN

AIYABALL-SAN

NONO-SAN

BIG BROTHER YOICHI KAMITONO

JUNSHI BABA SENSEI

EDITOR YOICHI SHIMOMURA

AND YOU!!

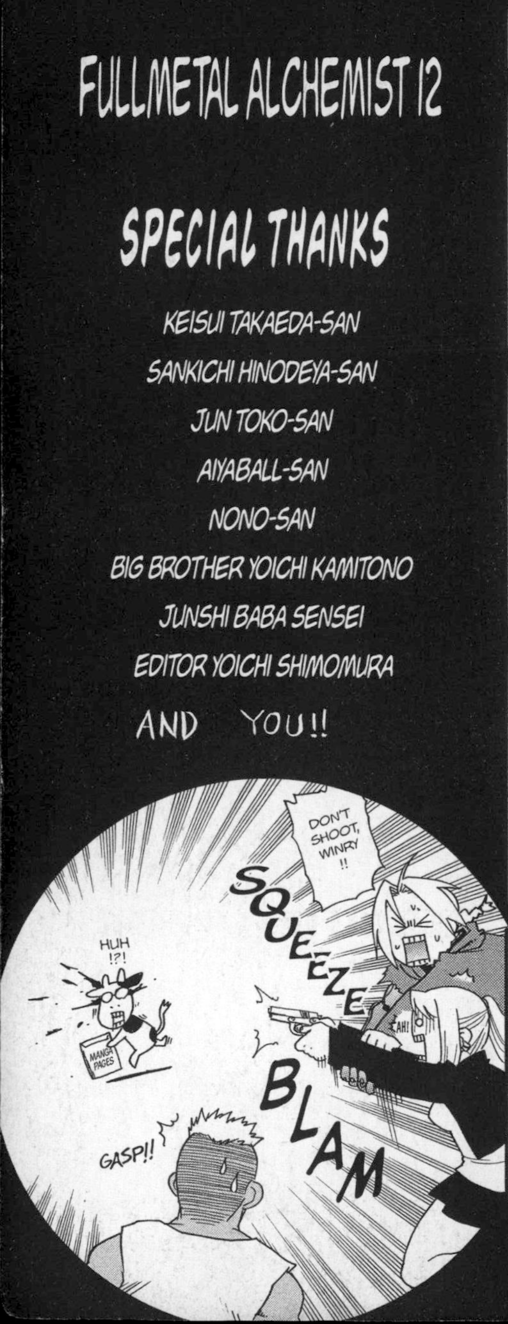
DON'T SHOOT, WINRY !!
SQUEEZE
AH!
HUH !?!
MANGA PAGES
BLAM
GASP!!

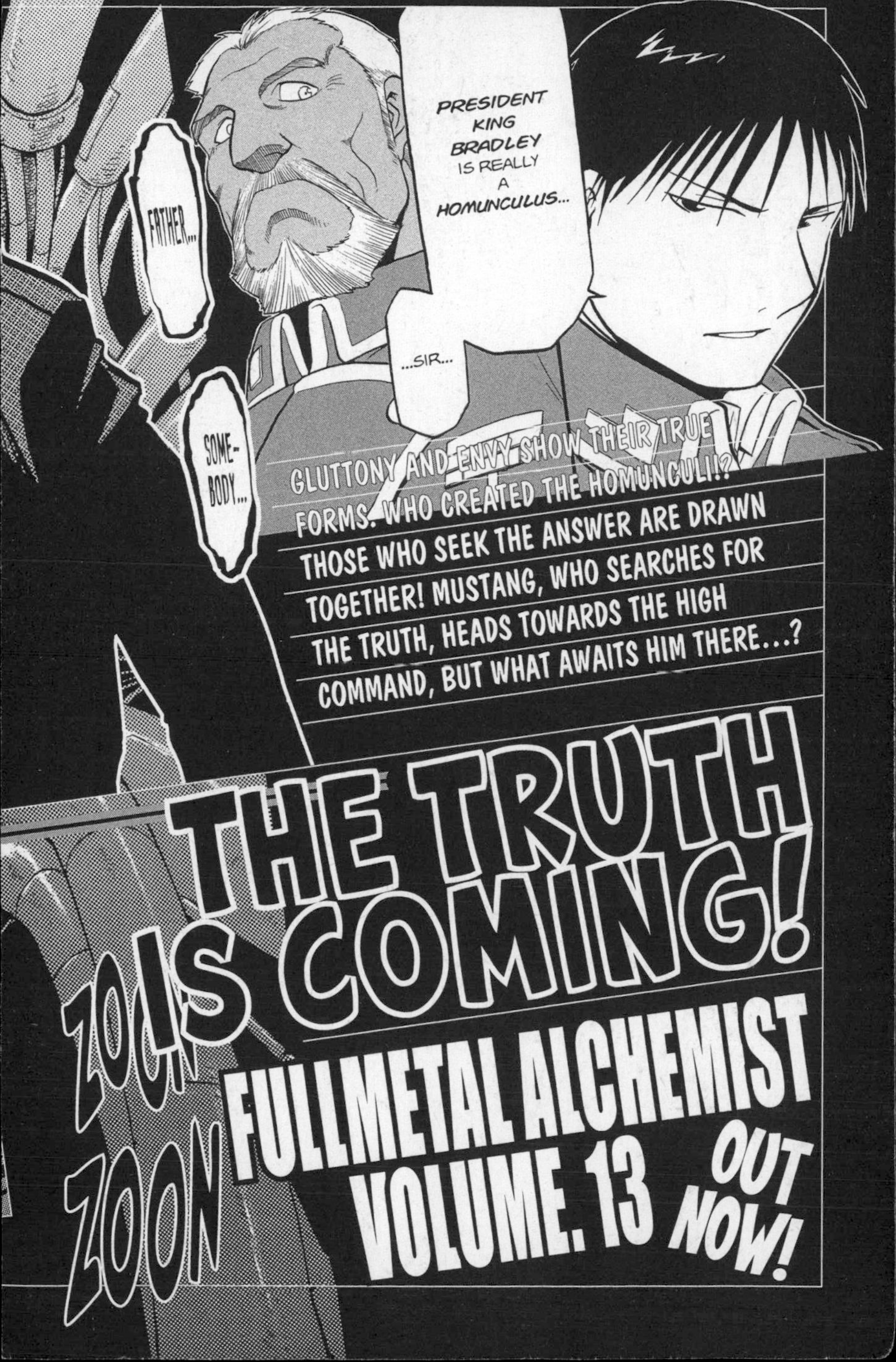
PRESIDENT KING BRADLEY IS REALLY A HOMUNCULUS...
...SIR...
FATHER...
SOME-BODY...
GLUTTONY AND ENVY SHOW THEIR TRUE FORMS. WHO CREATED THE HOMUNCULI!? THOSE WHO SEEK THE ANSWER ARE DRAWN TOGETHER! MUSTANG, WHO SEARCHES FOR THE TRUTH, HEADS TOWARDS THE HIGH COMMAND, BUT WHAT AWAITS HIM THERE...?
THE TRUTH IS COMING!
ZOON
ZOON
FULLMETAL ALCHEMIST VOLUME. 13
OUT NOW!

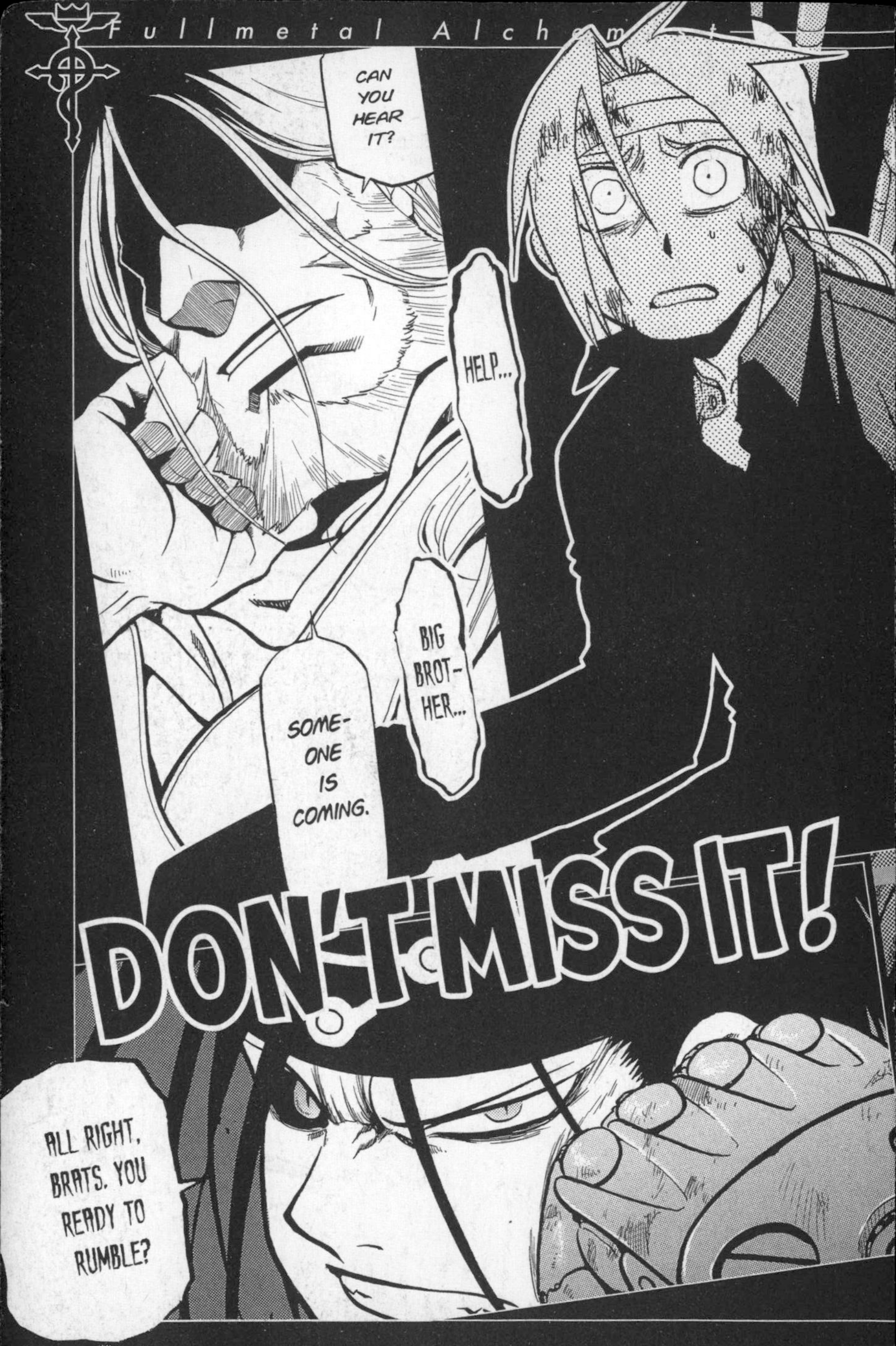
Fullmetal Alchemist
CAN YOU HEAR IT?
HELP...
BIG BROT-HER...
SOME-ONE IS COMING.
DON'T MISS IT!
ALL RIGHT, BRATS. YOU READY TO RUMBLE?

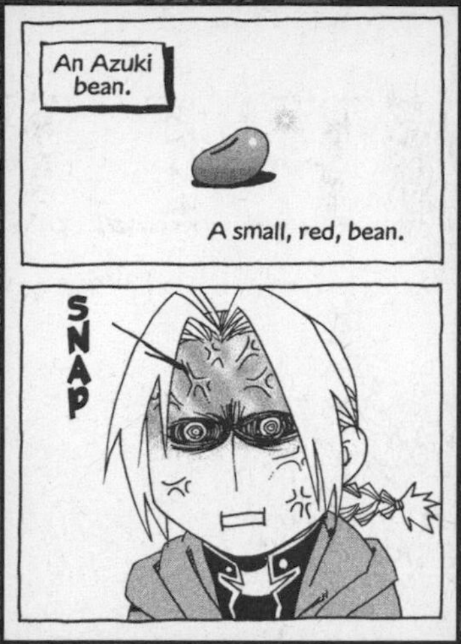
An Azuki bean.
A small, red, bean.
SNAP

"I'm the Flame Alchemist"

Lyrics by Roy Mustang

Snap snap snap snap my fingers
Snap snap snap snap my fingers

Who's the man that's gonna be president of all the land? The Flame Alchemist.
My dream is to have a miniskirt harem.
Who's that hot dude, standing in front of the mirror, snapping his fingers
striking a pose?
Uh-huh. That's me. The Flame Alchemist.

I'm going to light your heart on fire, baby. (Sizzle!)
My heart is a raging inferno, oh yeah. (Disco inferno!)
And tonight, baby, it's burning hotter than ever. (Like a flamethrower!)
Snap, crackle, pop, baby. It's my burning love. (Oh yeah!)
My love's gone and burned up all the oxygen in the room. (Thermodynamics!)
This one goes out to you, the girl in the mirage. (An illusion, baby!)

You know who I am. I'm Roy Mustang! (Then that's all right.)
I'm a colonel, baby. And this colonel's about to pop! (You mean "kernel"?)

(Line A) "You like breasts, huh? Well I'm a thigh man!"
(Line B) "Well, forget about it!"

(repeat)

Enter_the_world_of_

LOVELESS

story_+_art_by_YUN_KOUGA

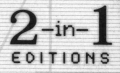

2-in-1
EDITIONS

Each 2-in-1
edition includes
6 color pages and
50 pages of
never-before-seen
BONUS comics,
artist commentary
and interviews!

Hey! You're Reading in the Wrong Direction!

This is the *end* of this graphic novel!

To properly enjoy this VIZ graphic novel, please turn it around and begin reading from **right to left.** Unlike English, Japanese is read right to left, so Japanese comics are read in reverse order from the way English comics are typically read.

Follow the action this way

This book has been printed in the original Japanese format in order to preserve the orientation of the original artwork. Have fun with it!